Global Logistics Management

For my wife Susan, who knows more about logistics now than she ever thought possible.

Global Logistics Management

A Competitive Advantage for the New Millennium

Kent N. Gourdin
School of Business and Economics
College of Charleston

First published 2001

Reprinted 2001

Blackwell Publishers Ltd
108 Cowley Road
Oxford OX4 1JF
UK

Blackwell Publishers Inc.
350 Main Street
Malden, Massachusetts 02148
USA

British Library Cataloguing in Publication Data

A CIP catalogue record for this book is available from the British Library.

Library of Congress Cataloging-in-Publication Data

Gourdin, Kent N.
Global logistics management : a competitive advantage for the new millennium / Kent N. Gourdin
p. cm.
Includes bibliographical references and index.
ISBN 1–55786–882–4 (hc : alk. paper) — ISBN 1–55786–883–2 (pb : alk. paper)
1. Business logistics—Management. I. Title.
HD38.5 .G68 2001
658.5—dc21

00-025858

Typeset in Photina 10 on 12 pt.
by Ace Filmsetting Ltd, Frome, Somerset
Printed in Great Britain by T. J. International Ltd, Padstow, Cornwall

This book is printed on acid-free paper.

Contents

Preface xiii

1 Introduction to Logistics 1

Logistics: The Historical Perspective 1
Logistics: The Modern Perspective 2
Components of a logistics system 3
The role of logistics in the organization 7
Logistics as a Source of Competitive Advantage 8
Why Is Management Interest in Logistics Growing? 10
Trends in global trade 10
Customers are demanding greater value 10
Transportation privatization and liberalization 11
Environmental concerns 12
Changing view of inventory 13
Continuing advances in information technology 13
Electronic commerce 14
Logistics in the Global Organization 14
Conceptual Model and Statement of Purpose 15
Chapter Summary 17
Study Questions 18

2 Logistics in the Organization 20

Introduction 20
The Marketing/Logistics Partnership 20
Marketing and Logistics Channels 21
Alternative channel structures 21
Why do channels develop? 23
Channel flows 23
Designing effective channels 24

Environmental Issues 24
Marketing Issues 25
Channel management issues 27
Formal and informal channel relationships 28
Domestic versus global channels 29
Future trends in channel structures 31
Managing the Logistics System 31
Trade-Off Analysis 32
Enhancing Corporate Profitability with Logistics 34
Chapter Summary 37
Study Questions 37

3 Customer Service 40

Introduction 40
What Is Customer Service? 40
Elements of Customer Service 41
Customer Service in a Global Setting 43
How Much Service Should Be Offered? 46
Barriers to Quality Customer Service 47
Controllable factors 47
Uncontrollable factors 48
Improving Customer Service Performance 50
The Consequences of Poor Customer Service 51
Improving Customer Service In Comparison to its Costs 56
Customer Service and the Internal Customer 56
Chapter Summary 57
Study Questions 57

4 Inventory Management 59

Introduction 59
Inventory and Customer Service 60
Purposes of Inventory 61
Types of Inventory 61
Objectives of Inventory Management 62
Inventory costs 62
Managing inventory costs 63
Classic Inventory Models 63
Economic order quantity (EOQ) model 63
Modifications to the basic EOQ model 64
Model limitations 64
Fixed order point/fixed order quantity model 65
Fixed order interval model 66
Safety stock requirements 66
Inventory Management: Signs of Trouble 70
Improving Inventory Management 72

Materials Requirements Planning (MRP) 74
Distribution Resource Planning (DRP) 75
Just-In-Time (JIT) Inventory Management 76
Basic tenets of JIT 76
Advantages of JIT 77
Disadvantages of JIT 78
JIT II/Vendor Managed Inventory (VMI) 79
The reality of JIT 79
Integrated Inventory Management: DRP, MRP, and JIT 80
Inventory Management in a Global Market 80
Chapter Summary 82
Study Questions 82

5 Global Transportation Systems 84

Introduction 84
The Five Modes of Transportation 85
Rail 85
Road transport 87
Pipelines 89
Air 90
Water carriage 90
Deregulation and Privatization of Transportation 91
Deregulation 91
Privatization 93
Future directions 93
Government's Role in Transportation 94
Direct control and regulation of transport firms 94
Provision of transport infrastructure 95
Promulgating and enforcing environmental and safety laws 95
Intermodal Transportation 96
Rail 97
Ocean transport 98
Air 98
Motor transport 100
Infrastructure issues 100
Concluding comments 100
Chapter Summary 101
Study Questions 101

6 Transportation Management Issues 103

Introduction 103
Developing Win/Win Shipper/Carrier Relationships 103
Transport Pricing 105
Market structure models 105
Relevant market area 106

Shipper demand 107
Carrier costs 108
Pricing in Practice 109
Price Negotiation: The Carrier's Perspective 110
Price Negotiation: The Shipper's Perspective 110
Private Transportation 111
Other Issues Affecting Transportation Cost and Service 111
Infrastructure availability and condition 112
Environmental and quality of life issues 116
Customs and cargo security 119
Carrier safety 120
Conclusions 120
Chapter Summary 121
Study Questions 121

7 Warehousing 123

Introduction 123
The Strategic Role of Warehousing in Logistics 124
Functions of Warehousing 125
Warehouse Roles 126
Warehouse Location Issues 128
Centralized versus decentralized warehouses 128
Selecting specific sites 130
Warehousing Alternatives 133
Private warehousing 133
Contract warehousing 133
Public warehouses 134
Warehousing Strategies 135
Warehousing Concerns in Overseas Markets 136
Chapter Summary 137
Study Questions 138

8 Materials Handling and Packaging 140

Introduction 140
Basic Warehouse Design 140
Manual Versus Automated Materials Handling Systems 141
Manual warehouses 141
Automated warehouses 142
Manual versus automated: making the choice 143
Trends in Material Handling 146
Reliability 146
Total integration 147
Flexibility and modularity 147
Upgradeability 147
Automated identification 147

Ease of use 148
Maintainability 148
Conclusions 148
Product Packaging 149
Types of packaging 150
Organizational influences on packaging 150
The role of packaging 151
Logistics packaging materials 151
Environmental issues 152
Packaging for global markets 153
Bar coding 154
Developments in packaging 155
Trade-offs with other components of the logistics system 155
Chapter Summary 155
Study Questions 157

9 Managing Logistics Information 159

Introduction 159
The Order Processing System 160
Logistics Information Systems 161
Environmental scanning 162
LIS and information management 162
Forecasting Methods 163
Qualitative forecasts 163
Time-series methods 163
Causal methods 164
Forecasting logistics needs 165
Selecting the right forecasting technique 165
Using Information to Link a Global Logistics System Together 165
Electronic data interchange (EDI) 165
Impediments to global implementation of EDI procedures 169
Developments in Logistics Information Systems 170
The Internet and electronic commerce 170
Open-systems computer networks 172
Wireless communication 172
Two-dimensional bar codes 172
Radio frequency identification (RFID) technology 174
Other advances in communications 174
Chapter Summary 175
Study Questions 175

10 Inbound Logistics and Purchasing 177

Introduction 177
The Growing Importance of Inbound Logistics 177
Inbound Logistics Activities 178

Customer service 179
Transportation 180
Inventory management 180
Warehousing and storage 180
Maintenance 181
Information management 181
Salvage and waste disposal 181
Production 182
Summary 182
Purchasing 182
Goals of purchasing 184
Purchasing tasks 184
Improving purchasing productivity 187
Management Techniques for Improving Materials Management 190
Chapter Summary 190
Study Questions 190

11 The Global Logistics Environment 193

Introduction 193
The Global Supply Chain 194
Changing Market Opportunities 194
Emerging nations 194
Multi-lateral trade organizations 196
Global sourcing 198
Cultural Issues in Logistics 198
Alternative Global Distribution Strategies 199
International Documentation 200
Customs Regulations 202
Foreign Trade Zones 203
Logistics Intermediaries and Facilitators 204
Controlling the Global Logistics System 206
Chapter Summary 207
Study Questions 209

12 Logistics Strategies 211

Introduction 211
Corporate Strategic Planning 211
Formulating Logistics Strategy 214
Integrating the Logistics Channel 216
Implementing Logistics Strategies 218
Centralization of logistics activities versus decentralization 220
Third-party service providers 220
Logistics strategy and improved corporate performance 223
Future Issues That Will Affect Logistics 223
Continued expansion of global business 224

Environmental and ecological issues 224
Transport infrastructure condition and capacity 224
Transportation deregulation 224
Government regulations 226
Consumerism 226
Technological advances 226
Implications for Logistics Managers 226
Chapter Summary 227
Study Questions 227

13 Developing High-Quality Logistics Systems 229

Introduction 229
Basic Quality Concepts: The Internal Perspective 230
Leadership 230
Cooperation 231
Learning 231
Process management 231
Employee outcomes 232
Organization performances 232
Basic Quality Concepts: The External View 232
The Service Quality Model 233
Total Quality Management (TQM) In Logistics 237
Developing a Formal Quality Process 238
Quality Process Success Factors for Logistics Management 240
ISO 9000: The International Quality Standard 241
The Cost of Quality 243
Chapter Summary 243
Study Questions 244

14 Improving Logistics Performance 246

Introduction 246
Improving Organizational Performance 246
Continuous and breakthrough improvements 248
Basic Tools for Improving Logistics Performance 249
Process analysis tools 249
Statistical analysis tools 251
Benchmarking 251
Activity-based costing 254
Effecting Meaningful Change 258
Logistics service quality 258
Productivity 259
Process effectiveness 260
Impediments to Improved Logistics Performance 260
Failure to adopt the customer's viewpoint 260
Lack of requisite cost data 262

Lack of broad-based management skills 263
Failure to think of logistics as a system 263
Need for cultural change within the organization 263
Creating a World-Class Logistics System 264
Chapter Summary 265
Study Questions 265

15 Organizing for Logistics Effectiveness 268

Introduction 268
Overview of Logistics Organizations 268
Building an Effective Logistics Organization 270
Centralization 270
Scope of responsibility/span of control 272
Formalization 272
Integration 273
The Role of Logistics in the Firm 273
Inter-organizational effectiveness 274
Variables Influencing Organizational Structure 275
Organization size 275
Corporate structure 276
Corporate strategy 276
The importance of logistics 276
Corporate information technology 277
Environmental uncertainty 277
Environmental heterogeneity 278
Summary 278
Reconciling Intra- and Inter-Organizational Issues 278
Moving Towards the "Best" Organizational Structure 281
Chapter Summary 281
Study Questions 282

Index 284

Preface

"While superior product quality and value remain critical factors for success in the marketplace, the ability to attract and keep customers increasingly depends upon outstanding service. At 3M . . . we've made large investments in more efficient ordering, warehousing, delivery and billing systems. We continue to make it even easier for customers to do business with us."

L. D. DeSimone
Chairman of the Board and Chief Executive Officer
3M Corporation, 1994

"I don't know what this logistics is, but I want some of it."

Admiral Ernest J. King
Chief of United States Naval Operations, 1942

Firms competing in the new millennium face a number of harsh competitive realities. First, manufacturing a quality product is no longer sufficient by itself to engender customer loyalty. Companies must consistently deliver that product when and where their customers demand it at a reasonable price. Second, the distinction between domestic markets (i.e. *within* an organization's home nation or economic alliance) and international ones (markets beyond those borders) is fading. Countries such as India and China are so vast and their citizens so culturally different that a firm's domestic logistics issues there may be virtually identical to those encountered when they sell internationally. Indeed, one could argue that *all* business is potentially global. Finally, logistics is becoming more important to companies as they strive to serve and satisfy customers in increasingly diverse markets wherever they may be.

Global Logistics Management is intended to accomplish three objectives: (1) to educate students and managers on the nature of individual logistics activities in general and how these tasks function in a global setting; (2) to show how these activities can be woven together to form an integrated logistics system; and (3) to provide present and future business leaders the knowledge and skills necessary to turn their corporate logistics activities into a source of sustainable competitive advantage in the global business arena.

To accomplish these objectives, *Global Logistics Management* is organized into three parts. Part I provides an overview of logistics and how it fits into the organization as a whole. Part II deals with managing specific logistics activities such as customer service, inventory management, transportation, warehousing, materials handling and packaging, information systems, and inbound logistics. Finally, Part III brings that functional discussion together into a cohesive examination of how to manage the total logistics process. Topics covered in this section include the global business environment, strategy formulation, quality, performance improvement, and organizational issues impacting logistics.

In order to keep students with little or no knowledge of logistics focused on the topic, the book is written in a straightforward and uncomplicated way. For those who, after reading this text, become believers in the power of logistics, there are several texts available that will provide a more in-depth look at the mathematical and analytical tools available to assist the more experienced logistician deal with specific problems. As often as possible, the concepts presented are illustrated with practical examples drawn from the real world of logistics. To that end, examples from the passenger transport industry are included where they reinforce a particular point because, after all, firms in that industry are very much involved in logistics as well. They simply move people rather than boxes. Furthermore, in an effort to retain a global view, no one country or region has been singled out for special attention. But regardless of what is being moved or where it is going, today is an exciting time to be in logistics. Hopefully, readers of *Global Logistics Management* will learn enough to appreciate all that integrated logistics management can offer as a source of competitive advantage.

chapter 1

Introduction to Logistics

Logistics: The Historical Perspective	1
Logistics: The Modern Perspective	2
Logistics as a Source of Competitive Advantage	8
Why Is Management Interest in Logistics Growing?	10
Logistics in the Global Organization	14
Conceptual Model and Statement of Purpose	15
Chapter Summary	17
Study Questions	18

Logistics: The Historical Perspective

Logistics is a term that many people have heard of but few can define. It is a word that is most often associated with the military, where it has come to stand for all of the activities associated with the wartime deployment and ongoing support of a nation's armed forces. In fact, the importance of logistics to the ultimate success of a military campaign has been well recognized and documented. As early as 500 BC, Sun Tzu Wu in *The Art of War* referred to logistical functions and their relationships with strategy and tactics. Alexander the Great was perhaps the first military leader to develop an actual logistics system to support his troops rather than relying on the more common practice of living off the land as the army progressed. The Romans carried a great deal of their equipment and supplies with them, relying on a baggage train incorporating hundreds of pack animals as well as the soldiers themselves for transport. They also utilized a system of fortified supply depots stationed throughout their empire at approximately 30 kilometer intervals (one day's march for the army) which contained food and fodder. Napoleon Bonaparte was also a logistician at heart; his preplanning and respect for support factors were instrumental in allowing him to move and maneuver more quickly than his enemies.[1]

However, ultimately Napoleon and, later, Hitler, learned a hard lesson about logistics:

the longer the supply line, the greater the chance it will be disrupted. Both men attempted invasions of Russia that failed at least partially because harsh winter weather disrupted resupply efforts. Certainly there are many more modern examples of logistics issues ultimately determining the success or failure of military endeavors. But it should be clear at this point that logistics is firmly rooted in the historical doctrine of war.

Logistics: The Modern Perspective

At its heart, logistics deals with satisfying the customer. This implies that management must first understand what those requirements are before a logistics strategy can be developed and implemented to meet them. As will be discussed in more detail later, customer service is the most important output of an organization's logistics system. This focus on customer satisfaction will be emphasized through the text just as it should be in the firm.

In a more practical sense, logistics refers to the systematic management of the various activities required to move benefits from their point of production to the customer. Often these benefits are in the form of a tangible product that must be manufactured and moved to the user; sometimes these benefits are intangible and are known as services. They too must be produced and made available to the final consumer. But logistics encompasses much more than just the transport of goods. The concept of benefits is a multifaceted one that goes beyond the product or service itself to include issues regarding timing, quantity, supporting services, location, and cost. So a basic definition of logistics is the continuous process of meeting customer needs by ensuring the availability of the right benefits for the right customer, in the quantity and condition desired by that customer, at the time and place the customer wants them, all for a price the buyer is willing to pay.[2] These concepts apply equally well to for-profit industries and non-profit organizations, as the earlier discussion on military requirements illustrated.

However, logistics can mean different things to different organizations. Some firms are more concerned with producing the benefits; that is, their management focus is on the flow of raw materials into the production process rather than on delivering the final goods to the user. The sourcing and managing of raw materials and component parts is often referred to as materials management and is illustrated in figure 1-1. For firms with very heavy flows into the production process, materials management and logistics may be synonymous. For example, Airbus Industrie produces an A-340 airliner in France for Singapore Airlines (SIA). Once the aircraft is finished, SIA sends a crew to Toulouse and flies the plane away. The logistics effort is not complete at this point, however. Rather, for firms like Airbus, post-production emphasis is on after-sales service and support as opposed to product delivery.

Alternatively, some companies experience greater management challenges once the product is finished. In other words, they are much more concerned with the flow of finished goods from the end of the production line to the customer. Depicted in figure 1-2, logistics in this situation is sometimes referred to as physical distribution and is a perspective in many consumer goods manufacturing firms.

Finally, some firms view logistics as embracing both materials management and

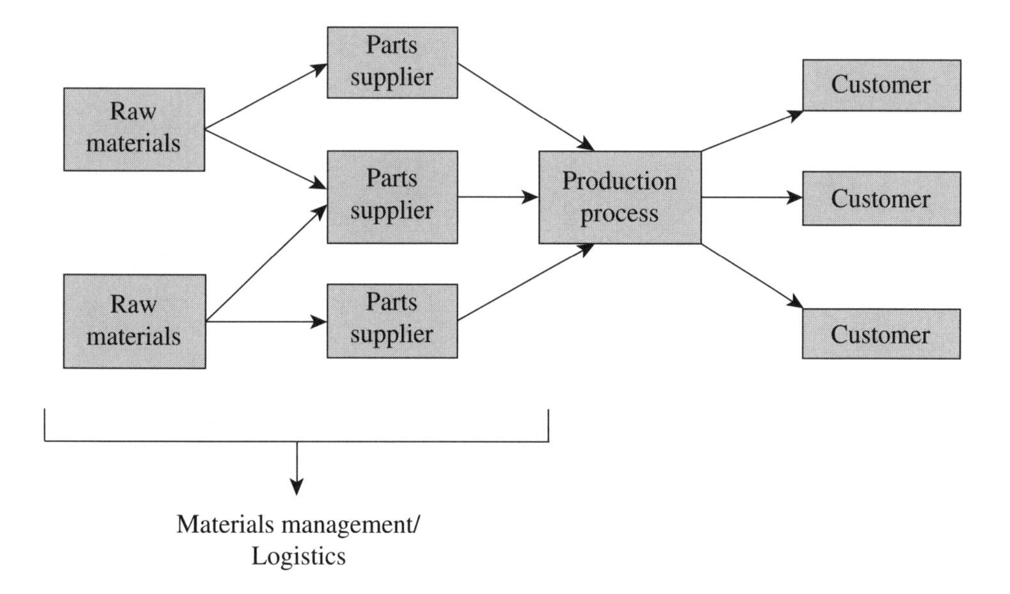

Figure 1-1 Logistics defined as materials management

physical distribution. These organizations look at logistics as a way to manage the entire process of customer satisfaction, from sourcing the necessary parts and material through production of the benefit to its delivery to the final user. Indeed, it is this approach that enables management to exploit the full potential of the logistics process. As shown in figure 1-3, this broader view of logistics integrates materials management and physical distribution tasks into a single supply chain that links the customer with all aspects of the firm. Viewing internal operations this way keeps seemingly disparate and historically separated activities focused on the common objective: to produce and deliver some benefit or benefits to the customer in a way that offers greater value than can be obtained from a competitor. In other words, this comprehensive view of logistics, sometimes referred to as supply chain management, can lead to lower costs and/or better service that enhance the value received by the buyer.

Logistics is a concept valuable to any firm regardless of size. Sometimes equated only with large organizations, logistics offers significant competitive advantages to small firms as well. NISA Today's is a United Kingdom buying consortium with 750 members including independent stores, small retail chains, and wholesalers. The group has its own private label, centralized distribution, and also supplies marketing services, all of which make NISA Today's members better able to compete with the giant chains.[3]

Components of a logistics system

A logistics system can be made up of many different functional activities, some of which are described briefly below:

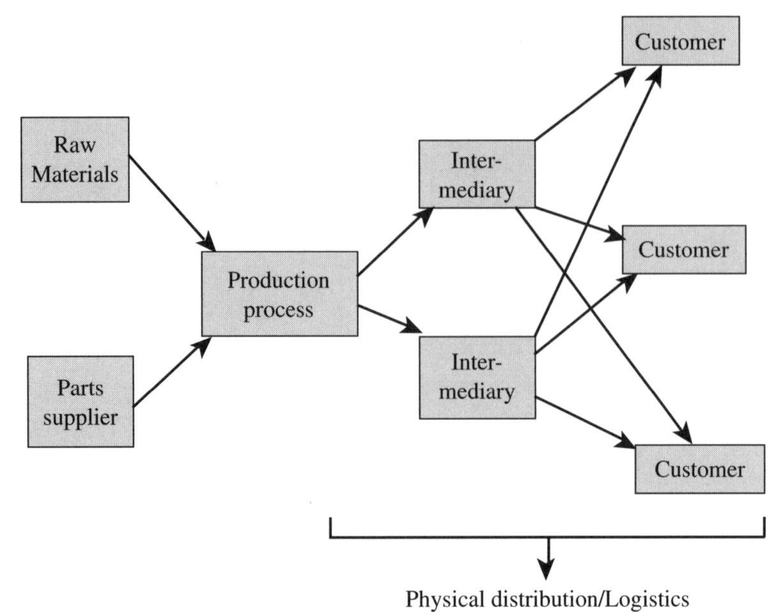

Figure 1-2 Logistics defined as physical distribution

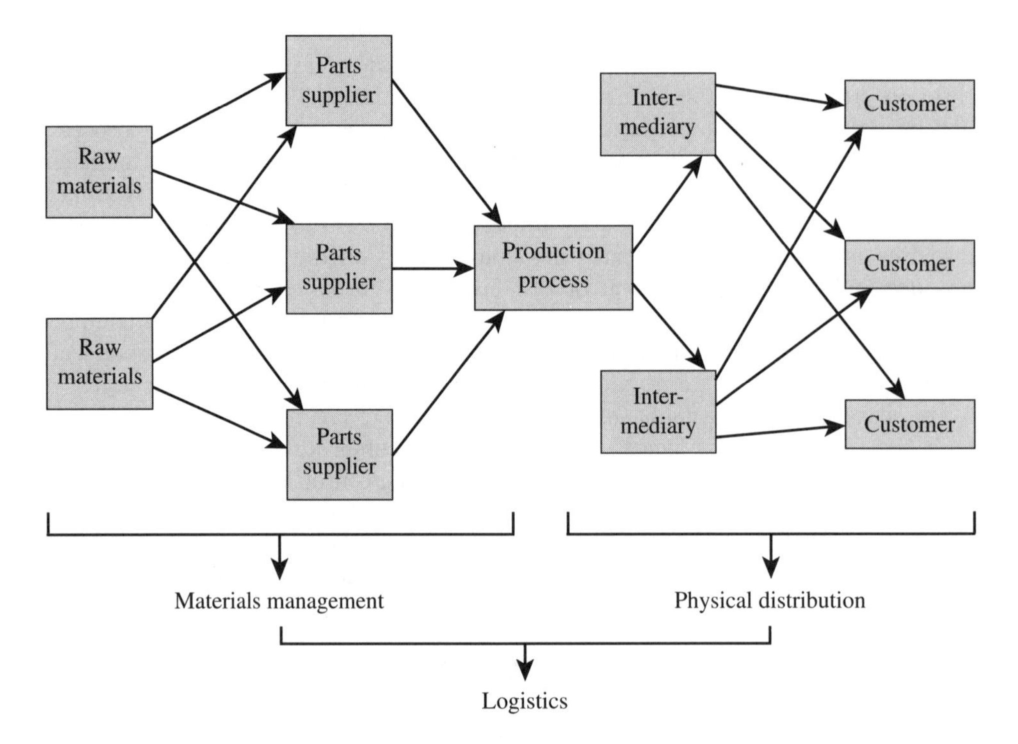

Figure 1-3 Comprehensive definition of logistics

- **Customer service** is a multi-dimensional and very important part of any organization's logistics effort. In a broad sense, it is the output of the entire logistics effort; that is, customer service and some resulting level of satisfaction are what the logistics system ultimately provides the buyer. However, many organizations do have a more narrow functional view of customer service as something they actually perform. For example, a firm may have a customer service department or customer service employees that handle complaints, special orders, damage claims, returns, billing problems, etc. For all intents and purposes, these employees *are* the organization as far as many buyers are concerned, so their role in the overall logistics system becomes crucial. Disappointment at this level can lead to dissatisfaction with the organization as a whole that effectively neutralizes the entire logistics effort.
- **Inventory management** deals with balancing the cost of maintaining additional products on hand against the risk of not having those items when the customer wants them (i.e. the cost of lost sales). This task has become more complex as firms have gradually lowered inventory levels. The challenge in this situation is to manage the rest of the logistics system to accommodate the lack of inventory so that customer service does not suffer. However, all of the interest in reducing inventories notwithstanding, the fact remains that they are still necessary for serving customers in many markets.

  So managers must decide whether they need additional products in a given market and, if so, how many of which items. It is also worth mentioning that for inventories of raw materials and component parts, the customer is the firm's own production line; for finished goods the customer is the final user of the product. Both "customers" have different needs which must be assessed in formulating an appropriate inventory policy that balances the cost of maintaining stocks on the one hand with the costs that could result from not having requisite items (i.e. production line stoppages, lost sales) on the other. For there is no doubt that holding inventory costs money, so firms don't want to have any more than is absolutely necessary to keep themselves and their customers satisfied.
- **Transportation** refers to the physical movement of goods from a point of origin to a point of consumption and can involve raw materials being brought into the production process and/or finished goods being shipped out to the customer. Transportation has assumed a greater role in many logistics systems for two reasons. First, the liberalization of transportation laws in many countries has provided opportunities for knowledgeable managers to obtain better service at lower prices then they could in the past. Second, as inventory levels have dropped in response to the popularity of just-in-time (JIT) strategies, transportation is frequently used to offset the potentially damaging impact on customer service levels that would otherwise result from those inventory reductions.
- **Storage and materials handling** address the physical requirements of holding inventory. Storage encompasses the tasks necessary to manage whatever space is needed; materials handling is concerned with the movement of goods within that space. Thus, the former would consider issues related to warehouse number, size, layout, and design; the latter would focus on the systems needed to move goods into, through, and out of each facility. Obviously, an organization's inventory

policies have a direct impact on their storage and handling needs. Thus, one result of the move to smaller inventories is the requirement for less storage space.

- **Packaging** focuses on protecting the product while it is being shipped and stored. Too much packaging increases costs while inadequate protection can result in merchandise damage and, ultimately, customer dissatisfaction. Furthermore, since every bit of packaging is ultimately discarded, logistics managers must also consider the societal costs associated with waste disposal. Increasingly, firms are working to develop materials that provide requisite levels of protection yet are recyclable or quickly biodegradable.
- **Information processing** is what links all areas of the logistics system together. The growth of reasonably priced computers and software has put sophisticated management information systems within the reach of even the smallest organization. Indeed, firms are now linking their internal logistics information systems with those of their vendors and customers as a means of adding more value to the entire channel. Such an open exchange of information can result in faster order placement, quicker benefit delivery, and greater accountability throughout the logistics process.
- **Demand forecasting** addresses the need for accurate information on future customer needs so that the logistics system can ensure the right products and/or services are available to meet those requirements. Logistics requirements necessitate going beyond market sales forecasting to obtain specific data on the timing, mix, and quantity of benefits desired by buyers. Without this information, the logistics system runs the risk of compromising customer satisfaction rather than enhancing it.
- **Production planning** can be included under logistics because manufacturing needs components and raw materials in order to make finished goods that are, in turn, demanded by a customer. Thus, production planning is arguably at the center of the entire logistics process, yet it is often viewed as a stand-alone entity with its own objectives and agenda. The risk here is that production rather than customer needs becomes the primary focus, a situation that can lead to customer dissatisfaction.
- **Purchasing** deals with the buying of goods and services that keep the organization functioning. Since these inputs can have a direct impact on both the cost and quality of the final product/service offered to the consumer, this activity is vital to the overall success of the logistics effort. In addition, the move away from local sourcing in favor of global buying has complicated this entire process dramatically in recent years.
- **Facility location** addresses the strategic placement of warehouses, plants, and transportation resources to achieve customer service objectives and minimize cost. Although not necessarily made often, these decisions can have very long-term and potentially costly implications for the organization.
- **Other activities** for a specific organization could include tasks such as after-sales parts and service support, maintenance functions, return goods handling, and recycling operations.

Clearly, any one organization is unlikely to require the accomplishment of all these specific tasks. For example, a service firm such as an airline might combine elements from the information processing, maintenance, demand forecasting, customer service, and purchasing functions discussed above into a logistics system designed to reach its customers. On the other hand, a manufacturer of consumer goods may draw from transportation, inventory management, storage, materials handling, and packaging in addition to customer service, purchasing, and demand forecasting for their logistics support. The point is that every organization, be it manufacturer or service provider, for-profit or non-profit, has customers that it wants to reach. By integrating the appropriate functions into a customer-focused logistics system, the enterprise can develop a sustainable advantage that is very difficult for a competitor to imitate.

Some of these activities have traditionally had a well-defined stand-alone role within a company (purchasing, production, information processing), while others have generally been more closely associated with logistics (transportation, warehousing, packaging). What ties all of these functions together is their ability to impact customer satisfaction. This is not to say that production, for example, should be subordinate to logistics. Rather, top management should utilize logistics as a way to integrate these corporate activities and keep them focused on the customer rather than on internal processes.

The role of logistics in the organization

Michael Porter's concept of the value chain provides an excellent way to better understand how logistics fits into an organization. Depicted in figure 1-4, Porter's model illustrates the activities that a firm must perform in order to provide benefits to its customers.

Primary activities (running vertically in the model) include those involved in the

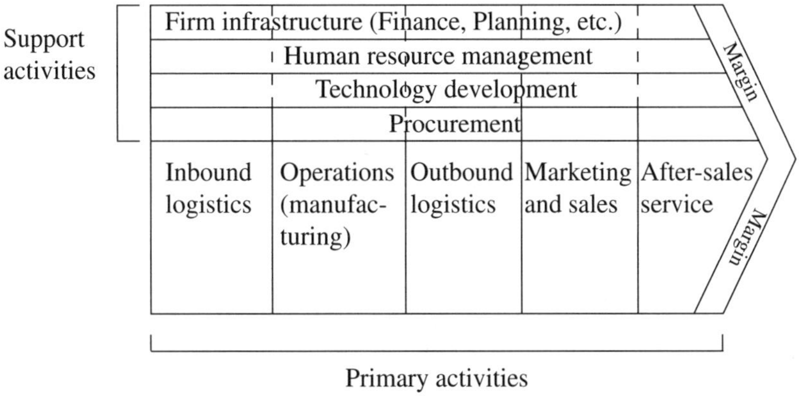

Figure 1-4 The value chain
Source: Porter, Michael E. *The Competitive Advantage of Nations* (New York: The Free Press, 1991), p. 41

ongoing production, marketing, delivery, and servicing of the product or service; support activities span those primary tasks and deal with the purchased inputs, technology, human resources, and overall infrastructure needed to support the primary activities.[4] It is important to note that two of the five primary activities focus on logistics: feeding raw materials, component parts, and related services into the production line (inbound logistics), and managing the flow of finished goods from the end of the production line to the customer (outbound logistics).

An organization's strategy guides the way the individual activities are performed and dictates the structure of the overall value chain.[5] In the long run, firms succeed relative to their rivals if they possess a sustainable competitive advantage. This advantage can come from an ability to provide comparable goods/services at lower costs or by differentiation (offering superior benefits to the buyer for the same cost).[6] Whether as a result of low costs or differentiation, the intent is to offer more value to customers than they can receive elsewhere. In other words, competitive advantage grows out of the way firms organize and perform the discrete activities that comprise their respective value chains.[7]

Organizations create value for their customers by performing those activities noted earlier. The ultimate value a firm creates is measured by the amount buyers are willing to pay for its product or service. A firm is profitable if this value exceeds the total cost of performing all the required activities. To gain competitive advantage over its rivals, a firm must either provide comparable buyer value by performing activities more efficiently than its competition (lower cost), or accomplish those tasks in a unique way that creates greater customer value and commands a premium price (differentiation).[8] (It is generally risky to attempt to do both since differentiation implies higher costs.) The key is to find sources of advantage that cannot be easily duplicated by the competition.[9]

For example, Wallenius Lines of Sweden, an ocean carrier of new automobiles, offers increased value to their customers by converting what had been treated as fixed costs into a variable cost per car. Specifically, the firm is able to compress the length of time the vehicles are in transit by moving them more quickly to and from each port, minimizing time spent at sea, and shortening the port waiting time at either end of the ocean transit. In fact, Wallenius believes lead time can be reduced by at least one-third, saving the manufacturer between $10 (on lower price models) and $20 (on more expensive cars) per car per day. If the average time an export car spends in the post-factory pipeline can be shortened from 30 days to 20, that comes to a saving of $200 to $400, which is about what the transportation costs.[10]

Logistics as a Source of Competitive Advantage

Managers are increasingly becoming aware that a well-run logistics system can provide the organization with a sustainable competitive advantage. However, this appreciation for logistics is a relatively recent phenomenon. Traditional sources of advantage centered around factors such as access to low labor costs, natural resources, large captive markets, or some unique technological expertise. Unfortunately, while still critically important to corporate success, these elements are declining in importance as sustainable advantages. New technologies are shrinking direct labor costs as a percentage of total costs; many nations with historically low labor costs are finding that emerging countries can undercut them; the rate of advancement in some industries seems to make technological developments obsolete almost as soon as new products reach the marketplace. Finally, the availability of natural resources and inexpensive components has become increasingly global, largely eliminating access to them as an advantage.[11]

Throughout the 1970s and early 1980s, some companies tried to achieve competitive advantage by improving productivity and reducing costs. As the 1980s unfolded, competitive advantage meant delivering flawless product quality, while in the 1990s, providing superior customer service became the objective of leading-edge firms.[12] However, this discussion highlights two points regarding competitive advantage. First, even the most successful advances lose their individual determinance over time so that yesterday's competitive advantage becomes today's minimum acceptable standard. Second, the window of opportunity for any given strategic innovation may be relatively narrow, so organizations must constantly be searching for new ways to meet their customers' needs better than the competition can. Though the topic will be discussed in some detail later, it is worth mentioning here that a competitive advantage built upon a well-planned and executed logistics strategy can be sustainable because it is very difficult for a competitor to copy.

What might be sources of competitive advantage in the next decade? Unfortunately, there is no easy answer to this question. Achieving meaningful competitive advantage requires that an organization have a thorough understanding of its customers and the additional value that they seek. In addition, the firm must have the internal skills (or competencies) necessary to exploit that knowledge in ways that no rival can duplicate. For example, there is a growing demand for time-based logistics management in developed markets where customers are relatively sophisticated and resultant competitive pressures are high. Speeding up the process means streamlining the flow of goods from the supplier to the customer by reducing or eliminating activities that add time but no value.[13] Customer demands for faster delivery, continuous shipment tracking, and electronic transfer of information reflect this desire to minimize wasted time. In response, Federal Express advertises that it can tell you where your package is at any time while it is in its care; United Parcel Service (UPS) is promoting its plan to speed up its early morning delivery time from 0830 to 0800 on domestic US shipments to ten large American markets.[14] (Remember that in the customer's mind this increased interest in speed is in addition to a desire for exceptional service, quality products, and low cost.) Alternatively, customers in less developed or emerging markets may not see rapid replenishment as a particular advantage given that it also implies higher costs. Indeed, a significant competitive advantage in this situation might be realized simply by having the ability to get the product to that customer on a regular basis at some reasonable cost. The challenge for any organization is to focus its skills on satisfying those customer needs that offer the greatest opportunities for obtaining a sustainable competitive advantage.

Why Is Management Interest in Logistics Growing?

Porter's theory of competitive advantage and the value chain is not new, yet, in general, logistics has remained a rather underappreciated part of many firms. However, dramatic changes in the international business environment in recent years have led to an increased role for logistics in firms operating globally. Several of these events and their impact on logistics will be discussed below.

Trends in global trade

Firms are searching for ways to capitalize on the growing demand for goods in markets such as Central and Eastern Europe, China, and the Commonwealth of Independent States (CIS). Indeed, with 1.2 billion consumers and increasing disposable income, China's retail industry alone has been growing at nearly 20 percent a year, reaching $300 billion in 1996 and $350 billion in 1997.[15] At the same time, new and cheaper sources for raw materials, manufacturing capability, and other inputs are encouraging firms to explore purchasing arrangements in countries they have never considered before. Exploiting these opportunities will inevitably require logistics systems that are different from those serving more developed markets.

Trade blocs are emerging as a way to give smaller countries economic power against their larger, more developed counterparts around the world. These arrangements have the added benefit of simplifying business transactions among the member states. At a more fundamental level, these economic unions are reshaping the entire perception of domestic versus international markets. For example, a British firm may realistically consider its "domestic" market to include all nations in the European Union (EU), while a Canadian firm may view other members of the North American Free Trade Association (NAFTA) in the same way. Of course, significant country-to-country differences continue to exist. But a well-run logistics system can provide the organization with a mechanism for dealing with those disparities so that customers' needs can be satisfied regardless of the market's geographic location.

Customers are demanding greater value

Customers prefer to buy from the firm that they perceive to offer the highest *customer delivered value*. As depicted in figure 1-5, *customer delivered value* is the difference between *total customer value* and *total customer cost* where *total customer value* is the bundle of benefits customers expect from a given product or service and *total customer cost* represents all direct and indirect costs associated with obtaining those benefits.[16]

As mentioned above, to increase the customer delivered value, the firm must either dispense more benefits (increase total customer value) for the same cost; give the same total customer value at a lower cost; or provide some combination of the two. The difficulty for global companies is that customers in different markets define value

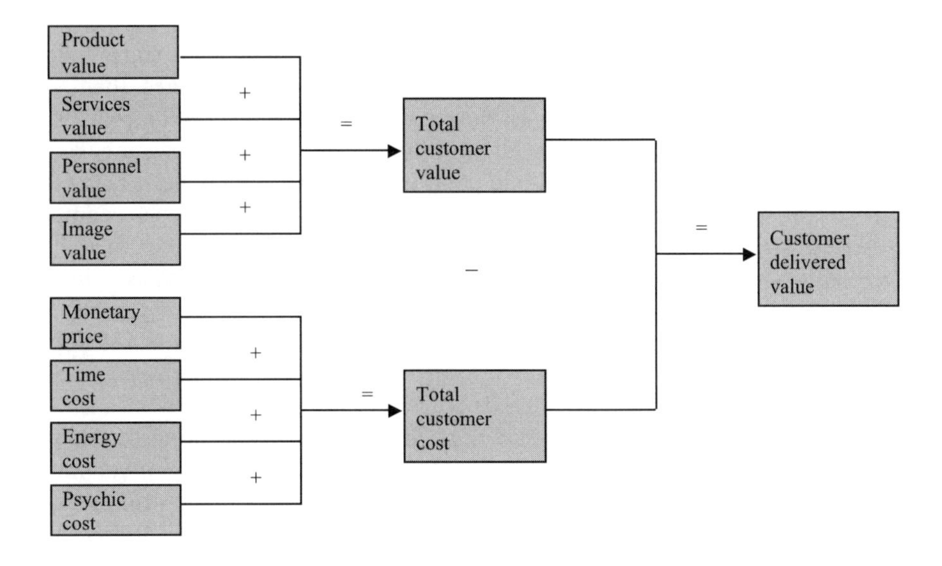

Figure 1-5 Determinants of customer delivered value
Source: Kotler, Philip. *Marketing Management*, 8th edn (Englewood Cliffs, NJ: Prentice Hall, 1994), p. 38

in dramatically different ways. Management, then, must have a clear idea of what is important to their various customer groups so that the appropriate benefits can be delivered to each one.

Unfortunately, people rarely lower their desired level of delivered value. Several years ago, Elcint, an Israeli maker of medical equipment, dealt with customers in Eastern Europe who had virtually no service expectations. Most were happy to see a field technician within six weeks of a problem arising. Now they expect a response within two weeks, which is still behind the US standard of 24 to 48 hours, but not by as much as it used to be.[17]

Transportation privatization and liberalization

Because of the key role played by transportation in a nation's economy, governments have historically taken a great interest in how it is accomplished. For some nations, this involvement has taken the form of outright national ownership of transport resources such as airlines, steamship lines, and railways; other countries have chosen to rely on the private sector to provide these services. However, regardless of location, transportation services have almost always taken place within a complex framework of laws and regulations seemingly intended to protect the industries themselves at the expense of efficient resource utilization and customer service.

In 1968, the United Kingdom was one of the first to reduce government's involvement in the provision of transportation services, specifically road freight movement. This reduction of government's role in the business affairs of transportation companies has come to be known as deregulation. The United States followed the British lead, starting with the all-cargo airlines in 1977. Since then, other countries have gradually moved to sell their government-owned or controlled transport companies to private interests while simultaneously reducing their involvement in the business of transportation. While great strides have already been made in air and road transport, more recent efforts have focused on rail. China, for example, is opening up its national railway to private operators. In early 1998, a privately run parcel express made history as it left Guangdong province in southern China for Liaoning province in the northeast. Now, a handful of private delivery services ply sections of rail across the country, while another operator leases carriages for special passenger services.[18] Similar interest in improving rail efficiency in Europe has led the EU to advocate splitting railway infrastructure and operational capacities into two separate entities so that private operators such as the European Rail Shuttle (ERS) can compete with state-owned railroads. ERS is a joint venture involving the Netherlands' railway system and approximately a dozen shipping lines that presently operates 18 dedicated container trains each week from the port of Rotterdam to points in Italy and southern Germany.[19]

Invariably such a reorientation towards more competitive transport systems provides opportunities for shippers to obtain better service and lower prices. However, the reality is that managing the transport function today has become more complex as logistics managers must now deal with an ever-changing array of cost/service options.

Environmental concerns

Well-to-do nations and their citizens are becoming more concerned with actions that adversely affect the environment and society's quality of life. Air, water, and noise pollution, solid waste disposal, energy conservation, and product-safety issues can all be viewed as public costs associated with meeting individual customer needs. For example, providing buyers with the goods they want requires the use of transport vehicles that pollute the air, create noise, add to traffic congestion, and consume scarce energy resources. Furthermore, these products must be packaged to protect them from damage while in transit, but very often the packing material that offers the most reasonably priced protection is the slowest to decompose once it is discarded. In response to customer concerns about packaging waste, logistics companies in the United Kingdom distributing to supermarkets are now collecting cardboard waste from their customers and selling it for pulping. The transport costs are minimal and a disposal cost to the retailer avoided.

On the other hand, developing nations where a competitive marketplace is still emerging tend to have a lower level of concern for these issues. They are more interested in raising their standard of living and acquiring the goods and services that their more advanced neighbors already possess. Customers in these markets are not willing to pay higher prices for environmentally friendly goods, despite the long-term benefits of doing so. Thus, the challenge for the logistics manager is to satisfy the customer while minimizing the adverse impact on the environment of doing so.

Changing view of inventory

The perception of inventory has changed dramatically over the years. Historically, inventory was used to compensate for internal problems that could ultimately result in a dissatisfied customer. In fact, from a purely functional point of view, everyone (other than the accountants) liked inventory. Manufacturing managers desired long production runs of similar products on lines that did not stop: work-in-process and finished goods inventories made that possible. The sales force relied on large inventories to back up promises of rapid goods delivery to the customer. Finally, customers liked inventory because it meant that items were always available on the shelf. Unfortunately, what became obvious to many managers in the early 1980s is that holding inventory costs money. As firms became more concerned with controlling costs, inventory levels fell as firms adopted some form of JIT system. But, over the longer term, many of these same firms found that while their overall costs fell, customer service deteriorated as stock-outs increased. Eventually, sales and profits declined as well, more than offsetting any cost savings.

Managing inventory becomes an especially crucial issue when selling globally because holding goods in non-domestic markets is virtually a necessity if customer service levels are to be maintained. So the issue of inventory management continues to be of great importance. Specifically, managers must decide how much (if any) to hold and how to administer the rest of the logistics system more creatively in order to ensure that customer service does not suffer as a result of lower inventory levels. Tesco, the giant British supermarket chain, adopted a just-in-time supply system that allowed it to add an extra 35,000 square feet (3,252 sq. m) of sales space to its stores simply by cutting out stockrooms.[20]

Continuing advances in information technology

Information systems are the glue that holds the logistics system together. Indeed, the dramatic improvement in computer technology over the past 20 years has made it possible to systematically manage logistics at all. As computing power has grown and prices have dropped, sophisticated computer resources are now within reach of even the smallest organization. Information transfer can occur instantaneously, not only within an organization, but between them as well. This capability means that data are captured and analyzed more quickly, leading to better decision making.

In fact, the capability to fully automate the logistics system is now available. A customer's order can be generated automatically as on-hand inventory drops to a certain level. The order is transmitted via electronic data interchange (EDI) to the supplier's computer, which then directs the required amount of the needed product be pulled automatically from the warehouse and shipped to the customer. Inventory levels are updated, billing initiated, and necessary documents generated at each appropriate step in the process. Theoretically, this entire process can occur without human intervention and with virtually no waiting time.

Other developments are taking place in the use of global positioning systems (GPS) which utilize satellites to monitor vehicles (and the shipments they are carrying) in real time. Sea-Land Service Company, the US-based international containership operator, utilizes GPS technology to track the exact location of each of its ships anywhere in the world. In addition, it can depict this information on large screens in its Tactical Planning Center (TPC) at its Charlotte, North Carolina, USA headquarters. Not only does this provide Sea-Land the ability to tell its customers where their goods are at any given moment, but it also allows ships to be rerouted immediately should the need arise.

Electronic commerce

Electronic commerce, or e-commerce, is rapidly taking hold as a retail selling venue. Customers can now shop and order virtually any merchandise online from the comfort of their own homes. Security issues regarding the transmission of credit card information are being resolved, so buyers are becoming more comfortable with the Internet as a shopping tool. However, if the full promise of e-commerce is to be realized, the goods must reach the buyer just as quickly. Thus, firms have had to reassess their logistics systems to ensure that their customers receive the goods that they have ordered in an expeditious manner. In other words, logistics is an essential element of a successful e-commerce venture.

Logistics in the Global Organization

As the world's markets become more open, managers are finding that new ways of doing business are necessary both to fully exploit the opportunities available as well as to guard against emerging threats to corporate success. The traditional international or multinational approach to business concentrates largely on geographic markets, developing a distinct marketing mix for each one.[21] This strategy, in turn, implies a primary focus on some domestic market, with international efforts a subordinate concern. Global organizations, on the other hand, look at the whole world as one potential market – sourcing, manufacturing, researching, raising capital, and selling wherever the job can be done best.[22] Ford's Taurus SHO model, for instance, utilizes an engine derived from pieces cast in Canada which are then shipped to Japan for final machining and assembly. The completed motor is ultimately returned to the United States for installation at the company's Atlanta final assembly plant.[23]

The challenge is how to manage this network of far-flung overseas activities as a single, effective unit. Firms are searching for ways to convert worldwide production, marketing, research and development, and financial presence into a competitive advantage.[24] There are two ways in which a firm can achieve that goal. The first is in the way a global organization can spread activities among nations to serve the world market. The second is via the ability of a global company to coordinate among those dispersed activities. In some instances these activities may be placed close to the buyer in the value chain. Outbound logistics, after-sales service, and marketing are usually tied to the buyer's location. In contrast, tasks such as sourcing, inbound logistics, and manufacturing can be performed anywhere. But geography is generally becoming less of a constraint. A firm with a global strategy locates such activities to optimize its cost position or differentiation from a worldwide perspective. For instance, each day California-based computer disk-drive maker Seagate Technology Inc. flies millions of dollars' worth of drives on a 6,000 mile, 12-hour trip from its Singapore plant to Amsterdam. Once there, the goods are reorganized at Seagate's Amsterdam distribution center and moved by road transport on set schedules to the production lines of 200 computer-making customers across Europe. With JIT delivery, the company can be as efficient delivering to Europe out of Singapore as out of somewhere physically closer to the customer.[25] As you can see, competitive advantage from an international presence comes from locating activities utilizing a global perspective and coordinating actively among them.[26]

Logistics is a particularly powerful management tool in a global organization because it is an approach to doing business that works anywhere. Clearly, fulfilling customer needs in North America or Europe requires different skills and resources than satisfying buyers in rural China or Azerbaijan. The objective, however, is the same: to meet those needs better than the competition. By understanding the basics of logistics management and how to put together a logistics system responsive to customer requirements, managers will be better able to deal with the unique challenges inherent in doing business outside the confines of their own country. Logistics profile 1-1 discusses Royal Caribbean Cruises Ltd and illustrates just how vital an asset logistics can be.

Conceptual Model and Statement of Purpose

This text is structured around the logistics system model shown in figure 1-6. The logistics system provides the means for moving goods from their point of origin to their point of consumption. The various activities discussed earlier must be performed together in order to meet customers' needs at the lowest total cost, a systems approach that involves weighing the impact of individual decisions on the logistics effort as a whole. The premise is that failing to adopt such a systematic view of logistics will impede the flow of value to customers either through poor service, increased costs, or both. Thus, while subsequent chapters will examine many of these activities in detail, their overall role as parts of a larger whole must not be forgotten.

As noted in the Preface, the purpose of this book is threefold. First, it will provide the reader with a concise description of individual logistics activities and how they function in a global setting. Second, the reader will be able to understand how those separate activities can be made to function as a cohesive system that adds great value to the firm's customers. Finally, this basic knowledge will enable managers to utilize logistics effectively as a competitive weapon in the continual fight for marketplace advantage.

Logistics Profile 1-1
ROYAL CARIBBEAN CRUISES LTD

One of the most daunting logistics jobs in the world is planning and implementing the replenishing of a cruise ship. Literally thousands of items, ranging from fresh bed linen to engine parts to perishable foodstuffs, must arrive at the vessel by a hard-and-fast deadline. "Every week brings a new crisis," said Jim Walton, director of materials and logistics for Royal Caribbean Cruises Ltd in Miami. "Recently, 1,500 pounds of lamb didn't make it to a vessel in time, so a chartered plane flew the lamb to the ship in Mexico." "Cruise ships are moving targets. You only have a short window to get what's critically needed to them. Otherwise, the captain doesn't wait around," he said.

As cruise ship designers have emphasized passenger amenities and cabin space over stowage space, the 90-day provisioning has been reduced to 14 days in all areas. This change transferred a huge responsibility to logistics to replenish ships in various outports. On this basis, logistics has one opportunity to ensure all goods arrive within a six-to-eight hour window. The itinerary for each Royal Caribbean vessel is planned two years in advance. With that data in hand, Walton's logistics department publishes a container load schedule, which specifies vendor delivery dates, by commodity for each vessel, over a six-month period. For each ship, there are delivery dates for chilled produce, frozen food, dry goods, bonded marine items, and gift shop and hotel items. The logistics department ships everything from blocks of ice to uniforms and tuxedoes; all manner of foodstuffs; radar domes, navigation equipment, floral arrangements, spare parts for machinery in a vessel's engineroom, even chemicals for each ship's photo-developing shop.

Royal Caribbean owns 17 vessels – 12 operated by Royal Caribbean International and five by Celebrity Cruises. Walton's 22-person staff handles logistics for all of the ships. "We work seven days a week, 24 hours a day. We load ships on weekends, working 10-to-12 hour days. We stagger our schedules so that some personnel are here all of the time, even on holidays. There are no days off for the logistics department." Walton's organization spends much of its time overseeing the physical handling of goods for the ships. A supplier may send a shipment covering eight different vessels. Walton's department segregates those goods by vessel and by service sector – beverage, hotel gift shop, marine (meaning the functioning of the ship), entertainment, cruise programs, aquatics, and hotel services. "We have to build specific pallets for each sector or department, and label them as such," he said. The reason is that goods are loaded on a cruise ship through different doors or hatches. When cargo arrives pierside, it must go aboard through the proper door. Royal Caribbean's cruise ships load at a rate of 40 pallets an hour, taking on a total of about 200 in five to six hours. At the same time, at least 2,000 passengers are boarding over other gangways.

Royal Caribbean regularly uses a core group of about 400 vendors. The company buys through distributors, especially on the hotel and food and beverage side, but negotiates many of its contracts directly with manufacturers. Distributors service the agreements, and maintain inventory stocks. "We try to keep as little inventory on hand as possible, and order on a just-in-time basis," Walton said. "If a vendor fails us, then they're chartering a plane at their expense.

If they ship the wrong product, or something that wasn't according to specification, they have to get the right product to the vessel at the next port of call. If that means arranging for an aircraft immediately, then they have to do it."

(**Source**: Mottley, Robert "Logistics for a floating city," *American Shipper*, December 1998, pp. 24–9)

Chapter Summary

Logistics is a concept familiar to students of military history. Long associated with the deployment and resupply of armed forces in wartime, logistics is proving to be a source of sustainable competitive advantage for firms competing in the global arena. Those firms view logistics as the process of moving benefits from their point of production to the customers whose needs they are intended to satisfy. Organizations tend to define logistics differently depending on whether they are for-profit or

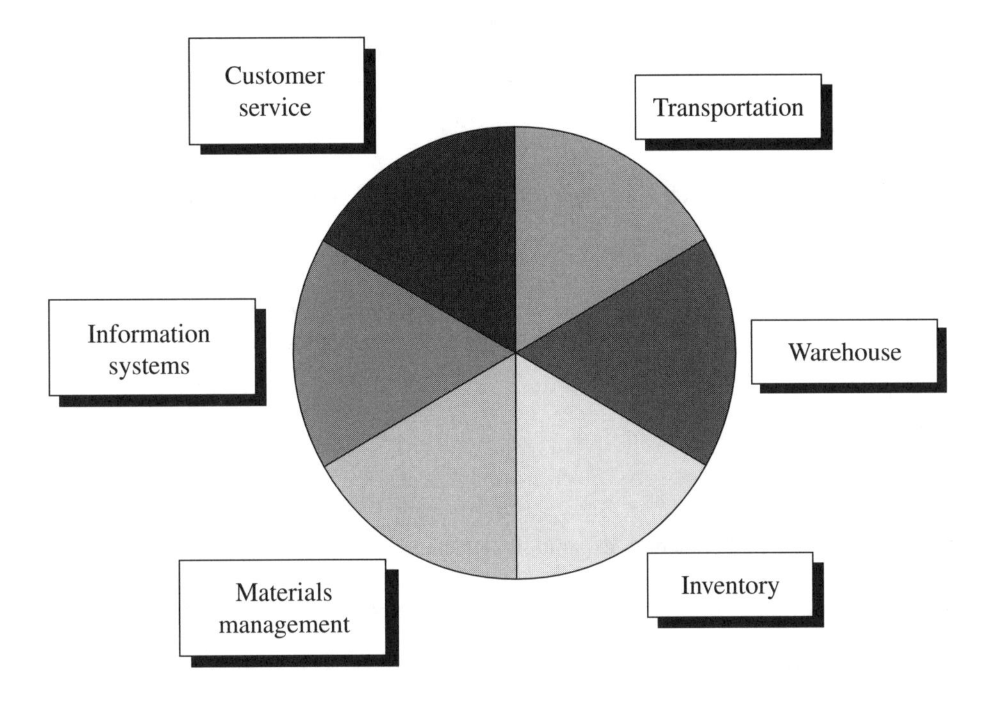

Figure 1-6 The logistics system

non-profit manufacturers of products or providers of services. But the overall objective remains the same: to satisfy the customer better than the competition. The remainder of the book will utilize the logistics system model to illustrate how logistics can be utilized to do just that.

Study Questions

1. Distinguish between logistics defined as materials management and logistics defined as physical distribution. What are the similarities in each situation? Differences?
2. Discuss the concept of customer benefits. What does logistics have to do with providing them?
3. How do customers define value? How does price affect that definition?
4. How has the nature of competitive advantage changed over the past 30 years?
5. What is the value chain and why is it relevant to a firm today?
6. How has the role of inventory in an organization changed over the years?
7. Should production be included as a logistics function? Defend your answer.
8. Why is it important for managers of global organizations to understand logistics?
9. How do environmental issues such as air pollution, fuel efficiency, and solid waste disposal influence logistics?
10. Refer to logistics profile 1-1 and figure 1-6. What logistics activities is Royal Caribbean performing? What benefit do these activities provide the company?

Notes

1. Rutenberg, David C. and Allen, Jane S. *The Logistics of Waging War* (Gunter Air Force Station, AL: Air Force Logistics Management Center, 1986), p. 2.
2. Adapted from Shapiro, Roy D. and Heskett, James L. *Logistics Strategy: Cases and Concepts*, (St. Paul, MN: West Publishing, 1985), p. 6.
3. "Buying groups to match the majors," *Grocer*, February 4, 1995, p. 79.
4. Porter, Michael E. *The Competitive Advantage of Nations* (New York: The Free Press, 1990), p. 40.
5. Ibid, p. 41.
6. Ibid, p. 37.
7. Ibid, p. 38.
8. Ibid, p. 40.
9. Ibid, p. 43.
10. Canna, Elizabeth. "Wallenius expands in logistics," *American Shipper*, February 1995, p. 56.
11. Porter, Michael E. *Competition in Global Industries* (Boston: Harvard Business School Press, 1986), p. 4.
12. Byrne, Patrick M. "Going beyond quality for competitive advantage," *Transportation and Distribution*, December 1991, vol. 32, no. 12, p. 5.
13. Murphy, David J. and Farris, Martin T. "Time-based strategy and carrier selection," *Journal*

of Business Logistics, vol. 15, no. 2, 1993, p. 27.
14. "Firm will speed up time of early morning delivery," *The Wall Street Journal*, June 14, 1995, p. B10.
15. Gui, Geng. "Is retailing in China coming of age?" *International Business*, July/August 1998, p. 18.
16. Kotler, Philip. *Marketing Management*, 8th edn, (Englewood Cliffs, NJ: Prentice Hall, 1994), p. 37.
17. Landau, Nilly. "Are you being served?" *International Business*, March 1995, p. 38.
18. Saywell, Trish. "High rollers," *Far Eastern Economic Review*, September 3, 1998, p. 42.
19. Banham, Russ. "Getting on track," *International Business*, March 1997, p. 17.
20. "New weapon in retail war?" *Management Today*, August 1995, p. 10.
21. Dahringer, Lee D. and Muhlbacher, Hans. *International Marketing: A Global Perspective* (Reading, MA: Addison-Wesley Publishing Company, 1991), p. 33.
22. Ibid, p. 32.
23. *Road and Track*, July 1995, p. 50.
24. Porter, 1986, p. 2.
25. Miles, Gregory L. "Virtual logistics," *International Business*, November 1994, p. 37.
26. Porter, 1990, pp. 54–5.

chapter 2

Logistics in the Organization

Introduction 20
The Marketing/Logistics Partnership 20
Marketing and Logistics Channels 21
Environmental Issues 24
Marketing Issues 25
Managing the Logistics System 31
Trade-Off Analysis 32
Enhancing Corporate Profitability with Logistics 34
Chapter Summary 37
Study Questions 37

Introduction

As a part of their marketing strategy, managers must develop what is known as a channel of distribution that links the organization with their customers. Based upon the channel design selected, the logistics system is then structured to support that channel. This chapter will examine that crucial relationship between marketing and logistics. First, channels and their role in the firm's marketing strategy will be explained. Next, issues related to channel design and management will be covered. Finally, the importance of systematically managing logistics to support channel objectives will be explored in detail.

The Marketing/Logistics Partnership

Logistics decisions cannot be made until management has decided upon an appropriate marketing strategy for the organization. Far-sighted managers realize that they must first determine what their customers need and want, then develop an integrated marketing strategy that will satisfy those desires better than their competition.

Their goal is to maintain a customer orientation; that is, conceiving of and then making the business do what suits the interests of the customer.

Once a marketing strategy has been developed, managers utilize a mix of four key variables to implement it. As shown in figure 2-1, these variables are referred to as the firm's marketing mix. The most fundamental of these elements is the **product** or service being offered to the customer. Based on the product, management must develop a **price**, communicate the value of their good or service to the market **(promotion)**, and deliver the product to the consumer **(place)**.

Each of these variables interacts with the others. For example, improving the quality of a product may necessitate raising the price, which could reduce demand. Initiating a large promotional campaign should cause sales to increase which means additional product will have to be manufactured and moved to the marketplace.

However, the component of the marketing mix of greatest concern in the marketing/logistics partnership is **place,** because it encompasses logistics decisions regarding how best to supply the product to the customer. Because the firm's logistics strategy must support its overall marketing plan, it cannot by definition be formulated until marketing objectives have been established. Upon the development of fundamental marketing goals, management can then address issues pertaining to logistics.

Marketing and Logistics Channels

Alternative channel structures

In a macro sense, one of the first decisions that must be made is how to get the goods to the customer. This process involves designing a channel of distribution or logistics

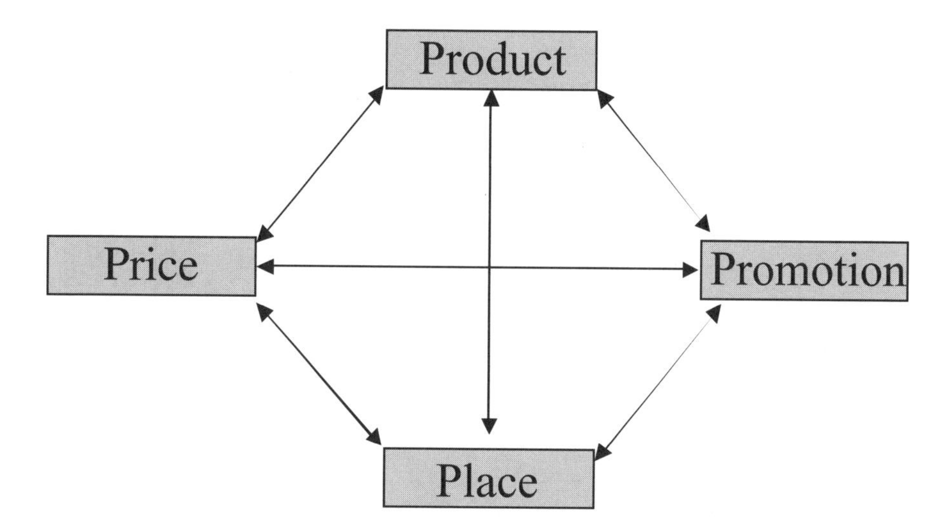

Figure 2-1 The marketing mix

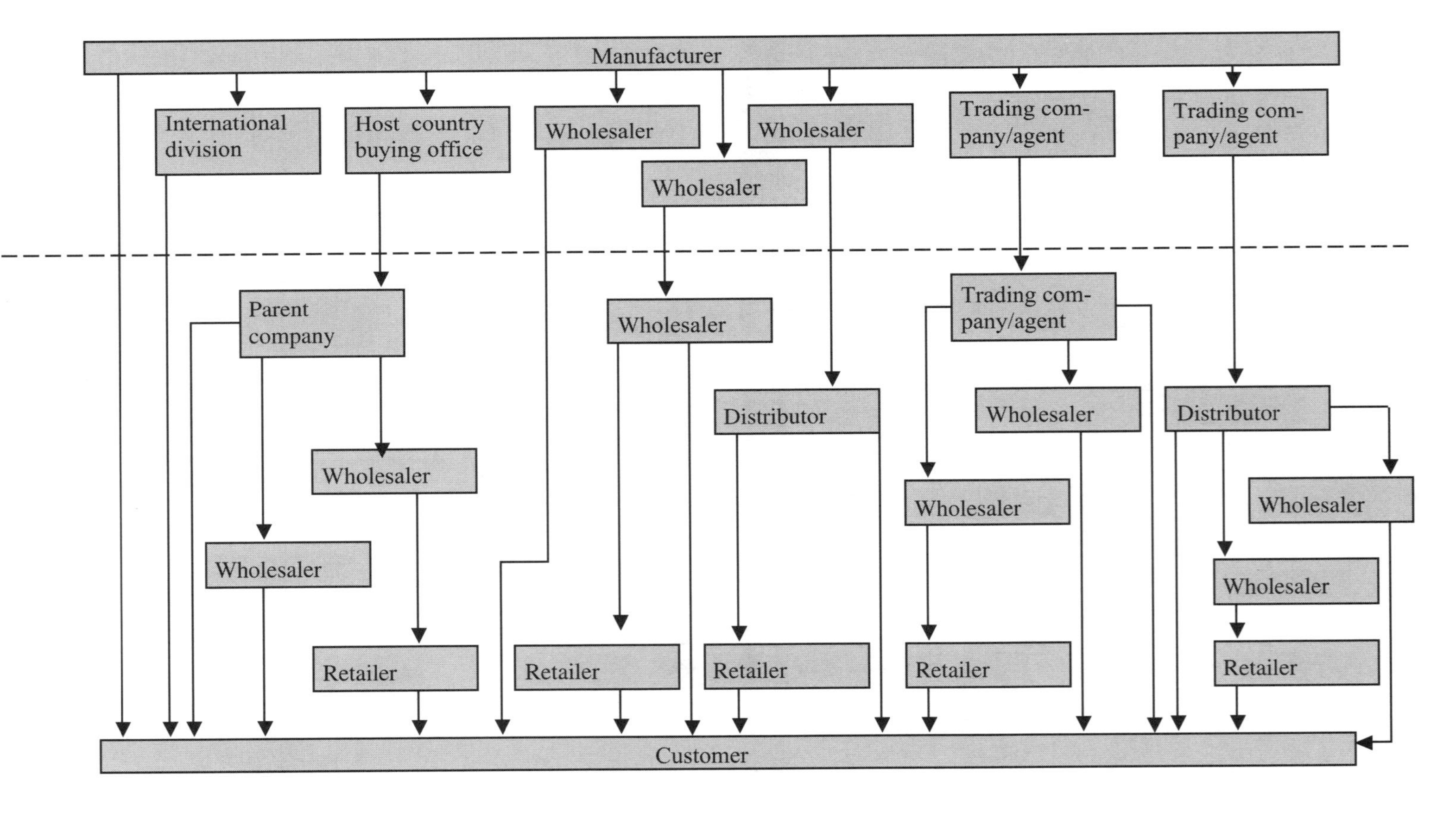

Figure 2-2 Alternative channel structures

Source: Jain, Subhash C. *International Marketing Management* (Belmont, CA: Wadsworth, Inc., 1993), p. 564.

Note: Above the dotted line are domestic channel members; below the dotted line are overseas middlemen.

channel to connect the manufacturer to the customer. Various channel structures are shown in figure 2-2.

Sometimes a channel can be very simple. For example, in some cases, the producer sells directly to the final user. At one time, a brewery in Iraq put bottles filled with beer into cases, placed the cases on pallets, and transported them from the end of the production line to the fence surrounding the company's property. Customers climbed to the top of the fence, where the cases were lifted up to them and the price was paid.[1] This structure is also known as a direct channel and frequently requires that buyers perform a number of logistics activities. In the previous example, customers must go to the plant, transport the product to the place of consumption, store it, and finance the purchase. Alternatively, a channel may be extremely complex involving numerous intermediaries or middlemen between the producer and the buyer. The more intermediaries there are, the longer the channel.

Why do channels develop?

Historically, barter was the way people satisfied needs that could not be met through their own efforts. Because trading quickly becomes untenable as needs increase, channels have evolved to facilitate the entire exchange process by performing all of the functions associated with product marketing: selling, storing, transporting, financing, risk-bearing, promotion, etc. More specifically, intermediaries work to present customers with the selection of goods they desire. For example, a wholesaler might gather different items together into an assortment that appeals to retailers. Alternatively, a middleman might break down large quantities into smaller lots. For instance, a wholesaler might buy in containerload lots that are then broken down into case lots that are sold to retailers. Retailers, in turn, break down cases into the individual units sold to consumers.

At least initially, the producer may accomplish most of these activities via a direct channel, relying on the customer to perform the rest. However, at some point it may become more efficient to rely on intermediaries to perform these tasks simply because they can do them better than either the manufacturer or the buyer.

Channel flows

The channel can be visualized as a pipeline connecting the manufacturer and the customer. Downward movement from the producer to the buyer includes the product itself, ownership, promotional information, and service. Upward flows from the market to the manufacturer can include money, market-research information, and even the product if it is being returned for some reason. Occasionally, firms might require different channels for the same product if, for example, they sell to both consumers and industrial customers.

Designing effective channels

Management must consider both environmental (external) and marketing (internal) factors in order to structure an effective channel.

Environmental Issues

The firm's **global presence** profoundly impacts the channel structure chosen. Indeed, very few companies today have the luxury of defining their missions as domestic corporations. Foreign suppliers, global communication technology, and foreign competition affect even companies that market their products solely within the borders of one country.[2] Today, firms are attempting to exploit opportunities in nations that have historically been closed to foreign goods. However, penetrating those emerging markets can prove extremely challenging. For example, many companies cite distribution-related problems among the top three difficulties facing their operations in China. The problems stem primarily from the chaotic, fragmented state of China's existing distribution system, in which remnants of the old State-planned networks co-exist with more market-oriented forces. In addition, government protectionism continues to limit foreign participation in many aspects of logistics, furthering hampering companies' efforts to reach Chinese consumers.[3]

The complexity of channel relations and the cost of logistics operations increase dramatically as the firm's global supplier/intermediary/customer networks expand. Attention must be paid to the fact that cultural preferences impact both the way customers in other countries shop and how channel members do business. In reality, cultural variations increase the probability of conflict between channel members and complicate the process of managing channel flows. Therefore, the more global the organization's operations, the more complex their channels become as distance and market diversity combine to increase the risk of failure. This evolution implies a greater need for cross-cultural channel management initiatives that can successfully deal with the formal and implied etiquette of each nation's business culture.

The **government regulatory environment** can be especially intimidating for a global organization operating in many countries. Deregulation of a number of industries in many nations has created an environment in which the rules of managing channel relationships are constantly changing. While US logistics managers have lived with the deregulation of their domestic transportation, financial, and communications industries for a number of years, they must now deal with growing international deregulation movements. In addition, such international initiatives as the European Union and NAFTA could have profound effects upon the international transportation and financial environments of channel management by radically altering long-standing operating practices and protocols.[4]

Managers must develop flexible channel systems that survive and thrive in a constantly changing regulatory environment. Developing relationships that emphasize adaptability while maintaining a value focus in the face of fundamental environmental changes is a challenge channel managers cannot ignore.[5]

Corporate reconfiguration, both domestically and internationally, is evidenced by the growth of vertical and horizontal channel mergers, acquisitions, leveraged buyouts, and spin-offs, all of which can complicate the structural decisions within many channels. A former competitor is suddenly a part of the same corporate umbrella, while a former supplier is now owned by a major competitor. While forecasting such structural changes can be virtually impossible, management must develop channel systems that can be molded to the changing corporate situation so that customer service is maintained.[6]

The rate of **technological innovation** shows no signs of decreasing. Comparing the technology of the 1990s to the 1970s reveals a number of innovations that influence channels today that did not exist 20 years ago: instantaneous satellite order transmission, precise satellite tracking of transport vehicles, immediate customer feedback on order status, robotic materials handling systems, personal computer-aided logistics systems analysis, bar coding, and electronic data interchange (EDI), just to name a few. The most significant impact of technology upon channels is the use of these innovations by one channel to establish a competitive advantage over its competitors.[7]

Total quality management is a critical component of the channel-design process since it implies that the pipeline is focused on providing a quality offering as defined by customers. As more channels adopt a TQM approach, quality will cease to be a basis for competitive advantage and evolve into a standard of performance. Channels that cannot identify and deliver the quality demanded by customers will lose them to channels that can.[8]

Marketing Issues

Primarily, managers must decide what **type of distribution** is most supportive of their marketing strategies. **Intensive distribution** involves selling through as many outlets as possible and is typically used with products like soft drinks, cigarettes, and candy. This approach generally leads to a very wide channel owing to the large number of intermediaries that must be dealt with. **Exclusive distribution**, on the other hand, results in a very narrow channel because only one, or a very limited number of outlets, is used. The automobile industry tends to utilize this channel approach, having only one dealer in all but the largest cities. **Selective distribution**, somewhere in between these two extremes, incorporates some but not all possible outlets and is the method by which most consumer goods are handled. In addition, managers must factor in the **characteristics of the product** itself. For example, high-value items imply a large inventory investment that may limit the number or availability of intermediaries. Also, technical products may require demonstration by knowledgeable salespeople as well as the provision of after-sales maintenance and spare parts support. Finally, **customer service objectives** must be considered. Issues with respect to product availability, return policy, and delivery times must be analyzed. Logistics profile 2-1 illustrates how thoroughly considering these issues can result in a strong and flexible channel structure handling a very delicate product.

Logistics Profile 2-1
Move Them or Wilt

All cargo is, in a sense, time sensitive. Ships, trains, planes, and trucks move on schedules dictated by customer needs. This is particularly true of one of the fastest growing – no pun intended – international commodities, cut flowers. According to the Society of American Florists, more than 60 percent of flowers sold in the US are imported. There are about 27,000 traditional florists' shops in the country, but the nature of the business is changing so rapidly that other players are having a direct impact on where and how flowers are being distributed and sold.

The new players in the equation are supermarkets, both chain and independently owned, which are finding that selling flowers has rapidly become the next best thing to sliced bread. Purchasing a bouquet while shopping has been a European tradition for generations. But now the practice is becoming an American habit at more supermarkets around the country – more than 23,000 now have their own floral departments.

Cut-flower distributors like Miami-based Atlantic Bouquet make it their point to get fresh flowers to supermarkets fast. "We supply supermarkets with large varieties of flowers from farms primarily located in Columbia," says general manager Mitchell Fortner. Since most of the company's product has to be consumer-ready, the flowers are shipped from Bogota to the company's packaging facility in Miami, where they are combined with other shipments, carefully packed, and moved to distributors across the country by air in rapid order.

"This is a highly competitive business and supermarkets that offer full-service floral operations have found that they can more easily generate traffic and goodwill among their customers than those that don't," says Terry Humfeld, vice president of division programs for the Produce Marketing Association (PMA). The combination of perishable products and impulse purchasing are the key driving elements in strong distribution channels that, for many varieties of flowers, start in the rich soil of South America.

Atlantic Bouquet purchases most of its flowers from its sister company, Continental Farms, a grower and importer of fresh-cut flowers also based in Miami. Continental air freights its flowers from company-owned farms and other farms in Latin America to its warehouse in Miami. From there they are shipped nationwide either by air carriers designated by clients or – for distances of less than 300 miles or so – by trucking companies with specially equipped refrigerated vehicles. To speed the process, Continental does its own Customs clearance and documentation. The company never hires the services of third-party freight forwarders, and purchases air carrier service on its own.

Most Continental growing operations are located in Columbia, Costa Rica, Ecuador, and Mexico. Among Continental Farms' top criteria in selecting an air carrier are speed and temperature control. Some carriers offer charters that haul nothing but flowers. "The business is so big that carriers have refrigeration areas dedicated to flowers in their cargo bins. Immediate refrigeration is critical to cut-flower shipments. Most cut flowers are shipped dry with no water source, although an increasing number of shipments contain ready-made bouquets of cut flowers that come in specialized containers holding an adequate amount of water to keep them healthy. Unlike their "dry" counterpart, these need to be shipped standing upright – which might seem a minor issue, but is one that requires special stowage techniques and equipment. Regardless of whether the flowers are shipped with water or no water, most are cut the same day they are shipped. They arrive at Continental Farms' warehouse 24 to 30 hours later, depending on the distance of the flower farm from the airport. Once the flowers arrive at Continental Farms' warehouse, they are cooled to prolong shelf life. They are then stored in sealed refrigeration units.

The supply chains have been so successful that they have created strong competition for flowers from the big flower auction houses in the Netherlands. Continental is branching out to ship flowers grown in Latin America to Asia and even Europe, a market dominated for centuries by growers with long-established roots in Amsterdam. Shipments bound for either Asia or Europe fly direct from Continental-operated farms in Latin America. The only exception is flowers purchased by floral brokers in Miami. Shipments for Russia, for example, are selected in the United States, and shipped from there.

(**Source**: Thuermer, Karen E. "Move'em or wilt," *World Trade*, March 1998, pp. 61–2)

For a truly global organization, designing appropriate channels can be an extremely complex process. The factors just presented must be evaluated within the context of specific markets, countries, cultures, and standards of living. Clearly, some issues will be more or less important depending upon the customer's level of sophistication. However, once all of these matters have been considered, several alternative channel structures may emerge as candidates for implementation. The most important task is to estimate the costs and sales resulting from each one so that the channel offering the greatest profit potential can be selected. Intermediaries can then be approached to participate in the channel, performance measures developed, and control mechanisms established to ensure that the channel functions properly.

Channel management issues

Usually some entity emerges as the dominant force in the channel by virtue of its market power or financial strength. Known as the channel leader or channel captain, this entity is able to control the behavior of every other channel member. A manufacturer can fulfill this role when it is producing an item highly desired by customers. Buyer interest, in turn, makes intermediaries eager to handle the item. Most franchisers (e.g. McDonald's) and automobile makers dominate their channels, directing retailers to conform to specific procedures, building designs, and inventory requirements. Alternatively, channel leadership may come from a retailer when that organization is so large that manufacturers and intermediaries want representation in its stores. Wal-Mart, for example, is able to direct vendors to manufacture and label products specifically for its use. In fact, French mass distribution is now experiencing deep changes as a result of successive takeovers of Docks de France and La Rinascente by Auchan, of Spar by Intermarch and of Franprix by Casino in 1996 and 1997.[9] These retail giants will exert tremendous power over their channel members, forcing cost concessions and service improvements that only the channel leader can demand. Occasionally, even a wholesaler can dominate their channel when retailers are ordering small amounts of a lot of different manufacturers' products, a situation common in the retail grocery industry.

Invariably it falls to the channel leader to maintain discipline among the other intermediaries. The goal should be to optimize the overall efficiency of the channel, which requires all participants to be oriented that way. Sometimes individual middlemen may seize an opportunity that benefits them but hurts the rest of the channel. It is up to the leader to keep everyone focused on the greater good, eliminating nonconformists when they are actively compromising the effectiveness of the channel in their own interests. Today, mutual benefit should be the objective; that is, the manufacturer, customers, and intermediaries should be better off in a given channel than in another. If one participant is disadvantaged, the channel is suboptimized and it needs to be redesigned.

Formal and informal channel relationships

Channel relationships may be formally structured around a contract, or informal, relying instead on economic incentives to keep channel members motivated. A contract creates a stable environment by clearly articulating each participant's rights and obligations. This structure promotes more certainty in the relationship by leaving less room for misunderstandings that often lead to conflict. The relationship is also taken more seriously because the contract will specify performance objectives and the penalties assessed for nonperformance. Finally, adherence to a written contract may be the motivation needed to keep a relationship active even when short-term problems arise.[10]

Karstadt, a major German department store chain, has found two basic points important for establishing a partnership: (1) a detailed written contract, and (2) a strong desire to make the arrangement work in daily practice. Karstadt stresses that the contract must specify priorities (such as delivery windows on a store-by-store basis) for both partners. But no document will substitute for a trusting relationship, which can grow only over time and only in the context of mutual interest. To reduce the risks of failure, Karstadt takes an approach that emphasizes:

- brief initial contracts with open options;
- separate handling of contract and fee agreements;
- clear knowledge of the price/performance ratio of other service providers;

- establishing conflict management procedures; and
- data security.[11]

Informal relationships are generally associated with simpler and/or shorter channels. These arrangements are not regulated by a formal contract, relying instead on the power of the channel leader and the rewards of channel participation. There are several advantages to an informal approach. First, there is increased flexibility to respond to changing conditions in the marketplace. Second, trust builds more readily among channel members because the relationship is voluntary and there is a greater incentive to solve problems. Finally, informal partnerships are an important first step toward more complex forms of business relationships. Partners may use an informal period to learn each other's cultures, build trust, and evaluate each partner's commitment to the relationship.[12] In fact, recent research has suggested that contracts generally do not play an important role in channel relationships.[13] The implication is that informality may be a good way to maintain flexibility, nurture trust in the channel, and evaluate the commitment and competence of a candidate for more complex business relationships that may extend well beyond logistics issues.[14]

Still another approach to channel management is that followed by the retailer Ikea, which has managed to integrate the channel to a considerable degree without extensive partnerships. For example, the company manages both a central warehouse in Sweden that delivers slow-moving products directly to retail stores, and national warehouses which ship pallet-loads of faster-moving items to stores in their region. Inventory management is critical to Ikea. The company has developed a fully integrated inventory management system with full visibility into stocking levels at each marketing region. Inventory is allocated to store replenishment orders automatically, which facilitates quick replenishment. In the future, Ikea expects to direct store orders to a fixed warehouse in the system, providing a stable lead-time across Europe.[15]

Domestic versus global channels

It can be argued that no crucial differences in the *functions* of distribution exist among the European nations, the United States, and Japan. However, the focal point of any channel is the customer. Because that customer is affected by social, cultural, and historical conditions peculiar to his or her nation, channels become essentially country-specific. In many developing nations, for example, people's incomes are low. They must shop daily for small amounts and are limited to whatever quantity can be taken home on foot or on a bicycle. Their homes also lack storage and refrigeration space to keep food fresh for several days. Because consumers in emerging markets may be particularly price sensitive, packaging costs are kept low in order to keep the charge down. In India, cigarettes are often bought singly. Breaking large quantities down into smaller units remains an important function of middlemen in these countries and helps perpetuate the long channels of distribution that are major obstacles to the expansion of large-scale retailing.[16] Thus, the customs and practices in the distribution of products can differ substantially from one country to another, yet basically fulfill the same functions of moving products from manufacturers to consumers.[17]

China is the largest emerging market, with 1.2 billion consumers and increasing disposable income. China's retail industry has been growing at nearly 20 percent a year, reaching $300 billion in 1996 and $350 billion in 1997.[18] But reaching those buyers can be a daunting task. Location is critical for retailing and more so in China. Coastal cities and major urban markets with wealthier consumers are feasible locales. Since only a small percentage of Chinese can afford imported goods, retailers should target young people and the *nouveau riche*. Local shopping districts where city residents shop are critical. Locating a big store in a downtown shopping district may be a good tourist showcase but does not attract the local shoppers.[19] Yaohan of Japan found out just how difficult the entire process can be. After investing over $300 million in two Shanghai locations, Yaohan's department stores are losing money. Most shoppers buy small items while being entertained by the extravagance of marble stairs, water fountains, and high prices.[20] In addition, distribution and logistics present additional problems. Poor warehouse and sanitary conditions require careful scrutiny and extra packaging, while transportation may be slow, inconsistent, and costly.[21]

The retailing sector in Japan was deregulated in 1990.[22] The effect has been to foster the emergence of new, more efficient retailing forms. However, Japanese channels are still characterized by multiple layers of wholesalers, agents, and distributors, all supporting a network of tiny retailers. Differing more in number than in function from their American counterparts, these myriad intermediaries lengthen the channel and add cost to the price of the final product.[23] Furthermore, Japan's distribution channels have traditionally been segregated by product type, with the consequent development of many specialized marketing routes.[24]

Channels in Europe vary widely in stages of development and business style from nation to nation and region to region. Generally speaking, for example, the Northern European retail industry is more sophisticated and highly concentrated than that in Southern Europe. For instance, in France, Germany, the UK, and the Benelux countries, the ten largest retailers account for more than 70 percent of the total market. Similarly, in Austria, the two biggest food retailing organizations, BILLA and SPAR, accounted for two-thirds of total food sales to households in 1996.[25] Even in Finland, the number of retail outlets has diminished by one-half during the past fifteen years.[26] Such a high level of concentration is in contrast to the relatively fragmented industry in Italy, Portugal, and Greece.[27] In Spain, for example, traditional small shops still account for 70 per cent of retail outlets.[28] Channels in Eastern Europe are still at a low level of development. "Consumers" in the western sense of the word are still evolving. Suppliers and retailers perceive little demand to provide much more than minimal product quality or service throughout the entire channel.[29]

For a global firm, however, decisions about sourcing, production, and distribution may involve dozens of alternatives. At one extreme, all operations could be strictly local; at the other, a firm might have a complex mix of local, regional, and international sourcing, production, and distribution operations.[30] Organizations in the latter category must somehow link disparate channels so that customer needs are met in the most cost-effective way possible.

Future trends in channel structures

Several trends that affect channel structure and the resultant relationships are supply chain management, quick response logistics, strategic alliances, and third-party arrangements.

- **Supply chain management** integrates both the inbound and outbound flows of an organization in a way that will create the greatest net benefit for the customer.
- **Quick response logistics** does much the same thing but emphasizes the flow of finished goods from manufacturers to retailers. Each of these strategies has the goal of offering more value to the customer. However, they both tend to reduce the number of channel participants (that is, shorten the channel), which has a profound effect upon those intermediaries that remain.
- **Strategic alliances** or **partnerships** are long-term cooperative arrangements that transcend organizational boundaries to achieve channel goals. Though similar in concept to those approaches mentioned earlier, strategic alliances do not necessarily focus on one side of the production line or the other. Rather, they seek to intermingle business functions to provide higher levels of customer satisfaction than each firm could by itself and can involve any or all parts of the channel operation.[31]
- **Third-party arrangements** refer to the use of outside firms to provide singular logistics competencies. Some logistics service companies, for example, position themselves as providing efficient and effective delivery of the final product from the manufacturing plant to the retailer. No attempt is made to delve into the materials supply, financial risk, or manufacturing operations areas – these functions are left to other channel members. In other words, companies specialize in performing specific tasks for the channel because they do those jobs better than anyone else.[32]

While these strategies will be addressed in more detail in a later chapter, suffice to say that all are firmly rooted in the idea of establishing mutually beneficial, cooperative relationships with channel members. The goal is to provide greater value to the customer that should lead to higher sales and greater profits for all channel participants.

Managing the Logistics System

Once channels have been designed, a logistics system can be developed to move the product through that pipeline. Figure 2-3 disaggregates the logistics process model presented in the previous chapter in order to illustrate how it interfaces with the marketing activity through the **place** component of the marketing mix. Recall that the four marketing variables (**product**, **price**, **promotion**, and **place**) interact with each other; that is, a change to one has ramifications for all the others. The same relationship exists among the logistics components. For example, managers implementing a just-in-time (JIT) inventory system will expect their inventory costs to drop dramatically. However, reducing on-hand stocks alone can lead to increased stock-outs and, ultimately, lost sales. To prevent customer dissatisfaction, more expensive

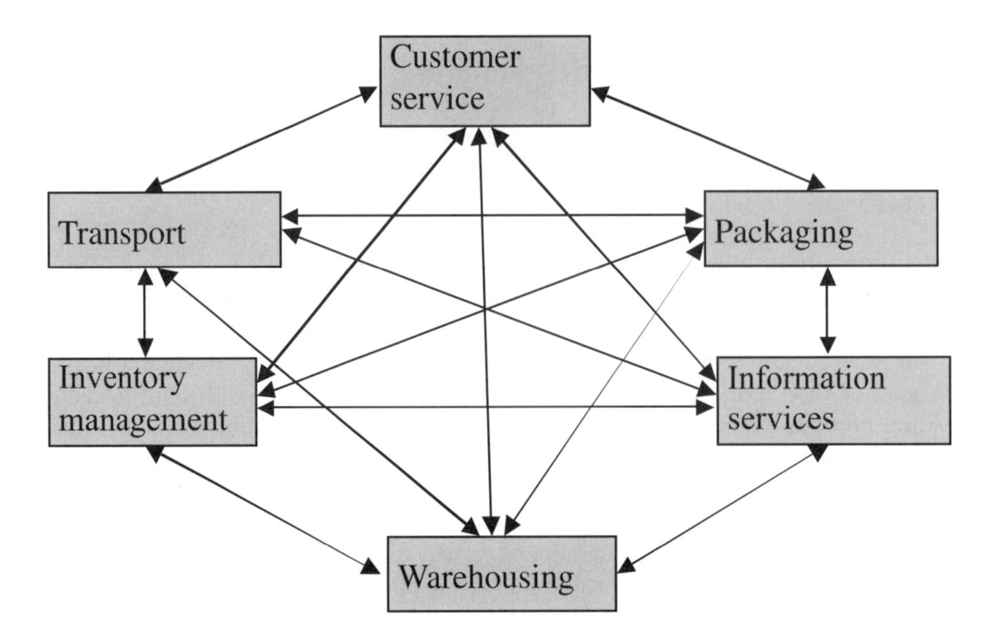

Figure 2-3 The logistics mix

(i.e. faster) forms of transportation are often used to offset lower inventories. To the extent that inventory savings more than compensate for the increase in transport costs, the organization benefits as a result of the change. Similarly, a decision to increase customer service by offering overnight delivery can impact transportation, inventory, warehousing, and order processing functions.

It is also possible for logistics decisions to impact the marketing mix. The use of low-cost transport may result in higher damage rates that, in turn, give the product a poor image with the customer. Similarly, offsetting inexpensive transportation with excessive protective packaging may give the impression that the firm is environmentally insensitive.

Trade-Off Analysis

All logistics activities must be managed in concert as an integrated system where individual decisions are made based upon how they impact the whole. The goal must be to minimize *total* cost while providing a given level of service to customers. Therefore, the costs of each individual area may *not* always be minimized because doing so could mean that other parts of the system experience higher costs, leading to higher total costs and a suboptimal system. Adopting a total cost view implies that senior management understands that costs in one area (i.e. transportation) may be up because expenses in another activity (for example, inventory) have been reduced.

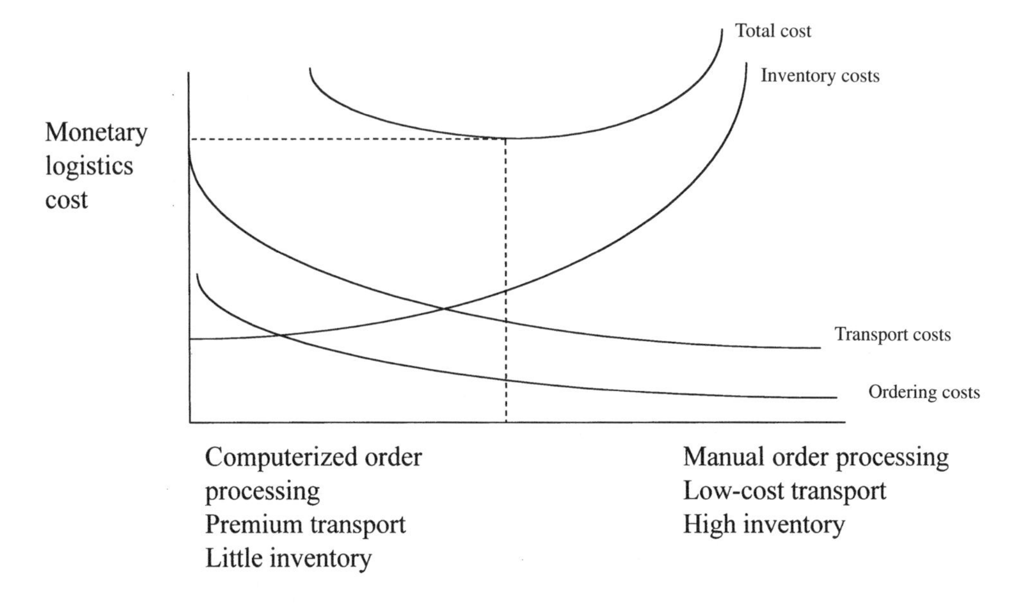

Figure 2-4 Logistics trade-offs

As long as *total* costs have fallen (i.e. inventory costs have fallen more than transport costs have risen), management should be satisfied.

The nature of these trade-offs is illustrated in figure 2-4. Two alternative logistics strategies are depicted, one relying on company-owned warehouses, little inventory, and premium (fast) transportation, and the other using public warehouses, high inventory levels, and inexpensive (slow) transport. Because the various costs behave differently from each other, it is virtually impossible to minimize one without adversely affecting another. On the other hand, minimizing total cost means that none of the individual activities are minimized, but the overall system is operating most efficiently.

The type of product being handled can dramatically impact the strategy chosen. In figure 2-5, those same strategies are being considered by a computer manufacturer. Owing to the high inventory costs that result any time high-value items must be stored and the susceptibility of computers to damage when handled, management would prefer to use a small number of company-owned warehouses and premium transportation. Contrast that with a company that produces automobile tires. As shown in figure 2-6, they would prefer exactly the opposite strategy: more warehouses and inexpensive transportation. Tires are relatively low-value items (especially compared to computers) that consume a great deal of space when being transported. (Items like tires and light bulbs are said to involve shipping a lot of air, since they are bulky and fill up a vehicle well before its weight limit is met.) Thus, it is cheaper to transport these commodities in bulk utilizing inexpensive transportation and incur the costs associated with storing them.

Trade-off analysis can also be viewed as a break-even problem in order to see how

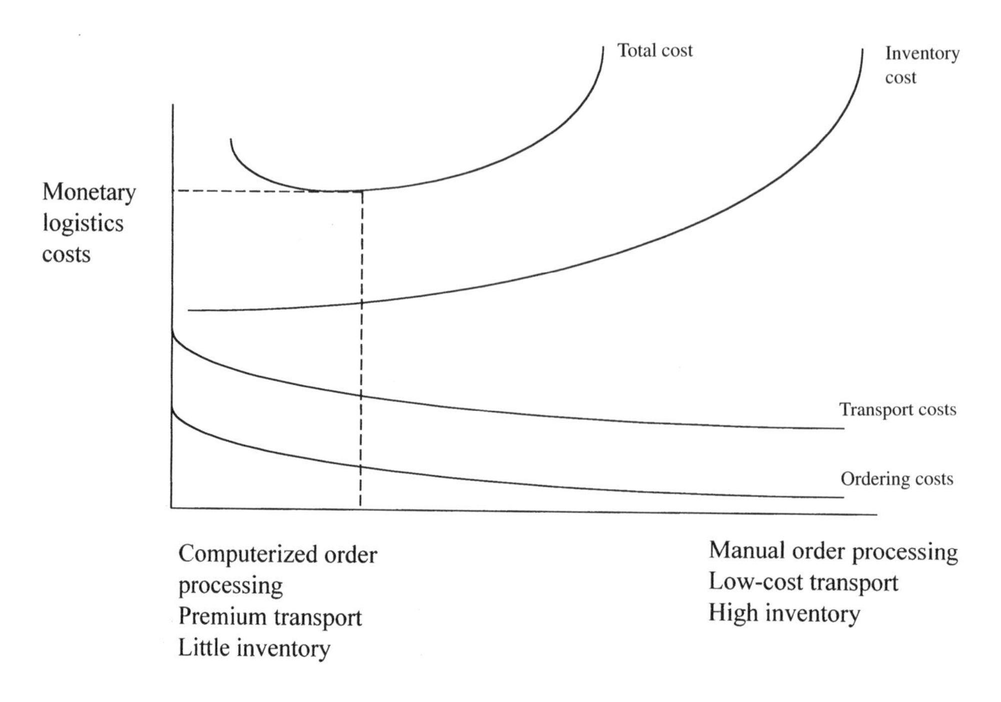

Figure 2-5 Logistics trade-offs for a computer manufacturer

logistics needs can change with volume. Figure 2-7 looks at two alternative strategies: strategy 1 incorporating a few warehouses and premium transport; strategy 2, multiple warehouses and low-cost transportation. Note that the total cost lines intersect at the break-even point, also known as the point of indifference. At that specific volume level, either strategy results in the same total cost, so management are (theoretically) unconcerned about which one to use. Management would want to know the exact break-even volume so that any needed changes in their logistics system could be anticipated well in advance of need. This calculation is relatively straightforward and is illustrated in figure 2-7. The example shows that at volume levels below 5,000 units, strategy 1 offers the lowest total cost; at volumes higher than that, strategy 2 is preferred. Note that changing from strategy 1 to strategy 2 involves major decisions for the firm (building warehouses, staffing them, changing transportation modes and carriers, etc.), so management would not want to act prematurely.

Enhancing Corporate Profitability with Logistics

Although managers are now realizing that logistics can improve profitability, basic mistakes still occur as a result of misguided attempts to minimize individual cost centers. For example, when a firm's profitability starts to deteriorate for some reason,

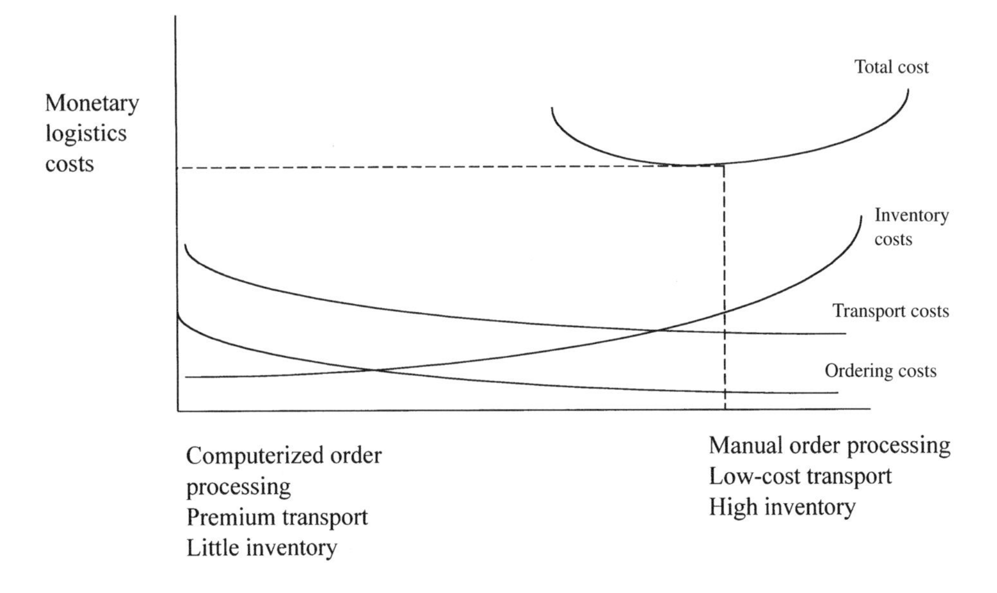

Figure 2-6 Logistics trade-offs for an automobile tire manufacturer

a common management reaction is to cut inventory levels and/or reduce the duration of accounts receivable. Both of these actions result in a reduction in the firm's total assets while a drop in inventory also lowers expenses. However, less inventory can also lead to a decline in customer service and, ultimately, lost sales. Similarly, reducing accounts receivable essentially requires that customers pay their bills faster which is virtually the same as raising the price. Clearly, such a move can lead to a drop in sales as well. Either way, the short-term improvement in the firm's profitability is quickly offset by a long-run decline in sales.

Unfortunately, many managers still have a functional view of these activities as tasks that should be accomplished at minimum cost. This shortsightedness breeds systemic inefficiency because forcing costs down in one area ultimately raises them in another. Appreciating the overall benefits that can result from reasoned analysis of trade-offs means that managers may choose to selectively *increase* some costs if that investment leads to profits that are greater than the higher expenses.

Sweden's Sandvik Coromant Company competes with three powerful domestic suppliers in the US market for industrial metal-cutting tools and parts. Sandvik ships everything from Sweden to America by air, paying up to ten times the cost of going by ocean. Management consider the faster transit of air essential to keeping customers happy, while also allowing the firm to reduce both inventories and the risk of product obsolescence. By comparing the cost of holding inventory in the US with the cost of air transportation, management determined that the former was far greater than the latter. Plus, the company is better able to react to customers' needs on a moment's notice, regardless of destination. In fact, Sandvik Coromant makes a point of keeping its inventories low worldwide, depending instead on the air cargo pipeline.[33]

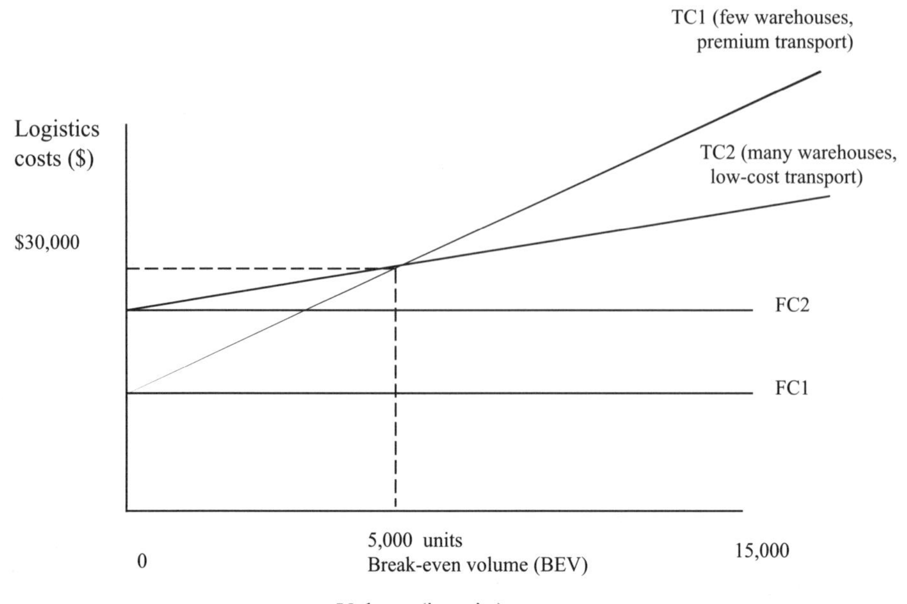

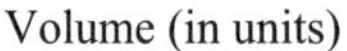

Example: Strategy 1 utilizes a small number of warehouses, but fast (expensive) transportation
Strategy 2 incoprorates more warehouses and slower (cheaper) transportation.
Fixed costs for strategy 1 (FC1) = \$10,000; variable costs for strategy 1 (VC1) = \$4/unit
Fixed costs for strategy 2 (FC2) = \$20,000; variable costs for strategy 2 (VC2) = \$2/unit.

Total cost for strategy 1 (TC1) = FC1 + VC1(BEV)
Total cost for strategy 2 (TC2) = FC2 + VC2(BEV)
TC1 = TC2 at the break-even volume, so, by substitution,
FC1 + VC1(BEV) = FC2 + VC2(BEV).
By combining terms, (VC1 – VC2)(BEV) = FC2 – FC1, and

$$\text{BEV} = \frac{\text{FC2} - \text{FC1}}{\text{VC1} - \text{VC2}}$$ so, substituting in the numbers shows that

$$\text{BEV} = \frac{\$20{,}000 - \$10{,}000}{\$4 - \$2}$$ or 5,000 units.

At volumes under 5,000 units, strategy 1 results in the lower costs; above 5,000 units, strategy 2 would be cheaper. At exactly 5,000 units, either choice results in the same total cost.

Figure 2-7 Break-even analysis

Similar sorts of trade-off analyses can be carried out at a more macro level as well. For example, the upgrading of distribution services at China's ports is prompting dramatic change in how retailers import their goods from China. Traditionally, American apparel importers almost exclusively used Hong Kong as the premier regional staging center for reorganizing their Chinese cargo for shipment to the US. Although shipping by road from China to Hong Kong was time consuming and expensive, it was the closest port that offered efficient consolidation and other distribution services. As China's leaders open the mainland's ports to Western transport companies, including consolidators, companies are finding that consolidating cargo and transporting it through mainland China's ports is cheaper and up to seven days faster than using Hong Kong. Even though consolidation fees are often much higher than in Hong Kong, this disadvantage can be offset by cheaper inland transport costs and the ability to offer faster service to US customers.[34]

Chapter Summary

Logistics decisions cannot be made until the firm has decided upon a marketing strategy and developed a marketing mix to implement that strategy. Since logistics supports that marketing effort through the **place** component of the marketing mix, management must decide on an appropriate channel structure for reaching the customer. For a global company this process can involve linking many country and region-specific channels together to form a coherent customer support system. Then a logistics strategy for supporting that distribution effort can be structured.

By viewing logistics as a set of interdependent activities rather than as individual stand-alone tasks, management can examine the cost/revenue implications of various functional decisions for the logistics effort as a whole. The goal is to maximize the efficiency of the system rather than any one component part. Managers able to adopt this systematic view are then able to use logistics as a profit-enhancing resource that can add tremendous value to their customers.

Study Questions

1. What is the relationship between logistics and marketing?
2. Why would a manufacturer utilize intermediaries in the distribution channel?
3. Briefly discuss some of the issues a global firm must address as they design their logistics channels.
4. What is a channel leader? What function(s) does the leader perform with respect to the channel as a whole?
5. Discuss the ways in which channels change as countries evolve from emerging to established markets.
6. What is the difference between a formal versus an informal channel structure?
7. How do channels in Japan differ from those found in Eastern Europe?

8. Distinguish between supply chain management and quick response logistics.
9. How might a decision to lower inventory levels impact the marketing mix?
10. How can product value affect the firm's choice of a logistics strategy?
11. Discuss trade-off analysis and its use as a tool to manage the logistics activity.
12. How does the Sandvik Coromant Company practice trade-off analysis?

Notes

1. Dahringer, Lee D. and Muhlbacher, Hans. *International Marketing* (Reading, MA: Addison-Wesley Publishing Co., Inc., 1991), p. 437.
2. Mentzer, John T. "Managing channel relations in the 21st century," *Journal of Business Logistics*, vol. 14, no. 1, 1993, p. 28.
3. Baldinger, Pamela. "Secrets of the supply chain," *The China Business Review*, September–October 1998, p. 8.
4. Ibid, p. 29.
5. Ibid.
6. Ibid, p. 30.
7. Ibid.
8. Ibid, pp. 30–1.
9. Packe, Gilles. "Retail logistics in France: the coming of vertical disintegration," *The International Journal of Logistics Management*, vol. 9, no. 1, 1998, p. 91.
10. Lassar, Walfried and Zinn, Walter. "Informal channel relationships in logistics," *Journal of Business Logistics*, vol. 16, no. 1, 1995, p. 84.
11. O'Laughlin, Kevin A., Cooper, James, and Cabocel, Eric. *Reconfiguring European Logistics Systems* (Oak Brook, IL: Council of Logistics Management, 1993), p. 141.
12. Lassar et al., ibid, p. 85.
13. Ibid, p. 103.
14. Ibid, pp. 103–4.
15. O'Laughlin et al., ibid, p. 141.
16. Kotler, Philip. *Marketing Management*, 8th edn (Englewood Cliffs, NJ: Prentice Hall, 1994), p. 425.
17. Jain, Subhash C. *International Marketing Management* (Belmont, CA: Wadsworth Publishing Co., 1993), p. 520.
18. Cui, Geng. "Is retailing in China coming of age?" *International Business*, July/August 1998, p. 18.
19. Ibid, p. 21.
20. Ibid,
21. Ibid, p. 18.
22. Miles, Gregory L. "Unmasking Japan's distributors," *International Business*, April 1994, p. 42.
23. Jain, ibid, p. 567.
24. Ibid.
25. Muhlbacher, Hans, Botschen, Martina, and Beutelmeyer, Werner. "The changing consumer in Austria," *International Journal of Research in Marketing*, vol. 14, 1997, p. 315.
26. Laaksonen, Pirjo, Laaksonen, Martii, and Moller, Kristian. "The changing consumer in Finland," *International Journal of Research in Marketing*, vol. 15, 1998, p. 175.
27. O'Laughlin et al., ibid, p. 133.
28. Nueno, Jose Luis and Bennett, Harvey. "The changing Spanish consumer," *International*

Journal of Research in Marketing, vol. 14, 1997, p. 25
29. Ibid, p. 145.
30. Ibid, p. 274.
31. Mentzer, ibid, p. 32.
32. Ibid.
33. Bownan, Robert J. "Weighty matters," *World Trade*, May 1995, p. 84.
34. Horowitz, Rose. "China's ports get with it," *International Business*, April 1994, p. 44.

chapter 3

Customer Service

Introduction	40
What Is Customer Service?	40
Elements of Customer Service	41
Customer Service in a Global Setting	43
How Much Service Should Be Offered?	46
Barriers to Quality Customer Service	47
Improving Customer Service Performance	50
The Consequences of Poor Customer Service	51
Improving Customer Service in Comparison to its Costs	56
Customer Service and the Internal Customer	56
Chapter Summary	57
Study Questions	57

Introduction

Customer service is the most important component of any logistics system. In fact, all other logistics activities must be structured to support the firm's customer service objectives. This chapter will first discuss the major elements that comprise customer service and how their implementation can vary from culture to culture. Impediments to good customer service will then be presented, as will several issues pertaining to service improvement. Finally, the concept of the internal customer will be presented.

What Is Customer Service?

Customer service is the way logistics interfaces with marketing and as such represents the output of the firm's entire logistics effort. Given that pivotal role, it is reasonable to assert that customer service is the most important logistics concern. The level of customer service provided has a direct impact on the company's market share, costs, and, by implication, its profitability. Yet despite the importance of customer service to the overall success of the organization's marketing strategy, managers often do not understand the crucial role that logistics plays in keeping customers happy.

Customer service can be viewed in one of several ways. Sometimes customer service is seen as an **activity**; that is, something that the organization provides. A customer service department that handles complaints, special orders, billing, etc. often evidences this aspect of customer service. Similarly, customer service can be viewed as a **measure of performance**. For example, if the firm can ship completed orders within 24 hours of receipt 95 percent of the time, it is providing good customer service. Unfortunately, both of these views are very narrow. In the former case, customer service activities seem to focus on resolving problems rather than proactively meeting customer needs. In many retail stores, for example, the customer service department is hidden away in a far corner of the building where it serves as a place for customers to take their grievances. In the latter instance, attaining some desired level of functional performance can lead management to focus on the tasks required to meet some standard rather than the needs of the customer.

Visionary firms view customer service as a **corporate philosophy** that defines the way the business is conducted. Certainly, this type of organization may also have a customer service department or utilize performance standards, but the focus in this case is on the customer, not the process. In other words, the logistics system is managed so as to provide customers the level of service they desire which, in turn, leads to customer satisfaction, repeat business, and profit.

Elements of Customer Service

A firm's customer service strategy is built around five key elements explained below.

- **Dependability** is perhaps the most important concern from the customer's point of view simply because it addresses very basic parts of the buying process. Dependability may be in the form of product availability; that is, the item is on the shelf when the customer wants to purchase it. It may also refer to such things as meeting promised delivery dates, filling orders correctly, and providing accurate billing statements. Indeed, dependability simply means that the firm can be relied upon to do what it claims it will do.
- **Time** relates to the order cycle; that is, how long it takes for the goods to be delivered after the order has been placed. The emphasis today in many developed markets is on speed, the faster the better. However, in emerging nations merely getting a product to the customer on a regular basis may be more important than how long it takes the item to make the journey. For example, the William Wrigley Jr. Company sells approximately 400 million sticks of chewing gum each year in China. The firm relies on a thousand-mile system of trucks, rusting freighters, tricycle carts, and bicycles to connect their factory in Guangzhou with the myriad of small shop owners and street vendors throughout the country that ultimately sell the product to customers. In short, though complex and risky, their distribution system routinely provides the buyer with a freshly soft and sugar-dusted product, but little else in the way of customer service.[1]

- **Convenience** deals with things like ordering accessibility, hours for pick-up and delivery, frequency of sales calls, technical assistance, and after-sales service. For instance, the British department store Marks & Spencer faces a unique set of problems as it continues its European expansion. Merely putting products on the shelf is not enough to satisfy customers in France, for example. When the company opened its second store in Paris, it offered carry-to-car service, a terminal for mobile phones, public telephones, and cash-dispensing machines. Furthermore, customers can utilize home computers to find out about the store through the French home shopping and information network Minitel.[2]
- **Communications** encompasses activities like cargo tracing, answering customer inquiries, billing, and information management. Federal Express and UPS both rely on extensive proprietary communications systems that allow carrier personnel to tell a shipper exactly where a given piece of cargo is in the transportation process. In addition, communication also implies that the firm listens to its customers, finds out what their needs are, and makes every effort to satisfy them. For example, Terrence A. Austin, an associate partner with Andersen Consulting LLP in San Francisco, suggests that personal computer (PC) manufacturers have traditionally been obsessed with technology features and price performance while ignoring customer needs. "PC manufacturers routinely announce 10 day order lead times ('but we wanted it in three days,' customers say), 90 percent order fill rates ('we think that should be at 95 percent or 99 percent'), and three days between request and commit ('we would like to see that drop to one day')," Austin says. "Yet when you ask PC customers what they actually got from the PC industry, you hear of order lead times of 20–30 days, 50 percent to 65 percent fill rates, and a 10-day to 30-day difference between request and commit."[3]
- **Honesty** implies that the company keeps the promises it makes to its customers. Pledging more than can be delivered virtually guarantees that customers will be dissatisfied, so managers must be careful not to overstate customer service levels when there may be considerable pressure to do so.

The way in which these elements are combined determines the firm's customer service strategy. Figure 3-1 shows how these specific elements relate to customer service as a component of the logistics process model. In addition, this mix of variables directly affects logistics costs, so managers must ensure that revenues justify these expenses. That is, the level of service offered must be consistent with customer needs. Providing too little service leaves customers dissatisfied and virtually guarantees that they will take their business elsewhere. Often, however, firms provide more service than their customers require. This practice raises costs because the company would have had many of these buyers anyway. It also elevates their expectations for the next encounter and, at times, can even be off-putting. The challenge, then, is to combine these variables in a way that meets customer needs at the lowest possible cost. Note that the firm may spend a significant amount on customer service when its buyers demand a great deal of attention. As long as the revenues generated justify those expenses, managers should be comfortable with those costs. Logistics profile 3-1 discusses the sophisticated logistics system Toyota has put into place in Australia to support its customers in that market.

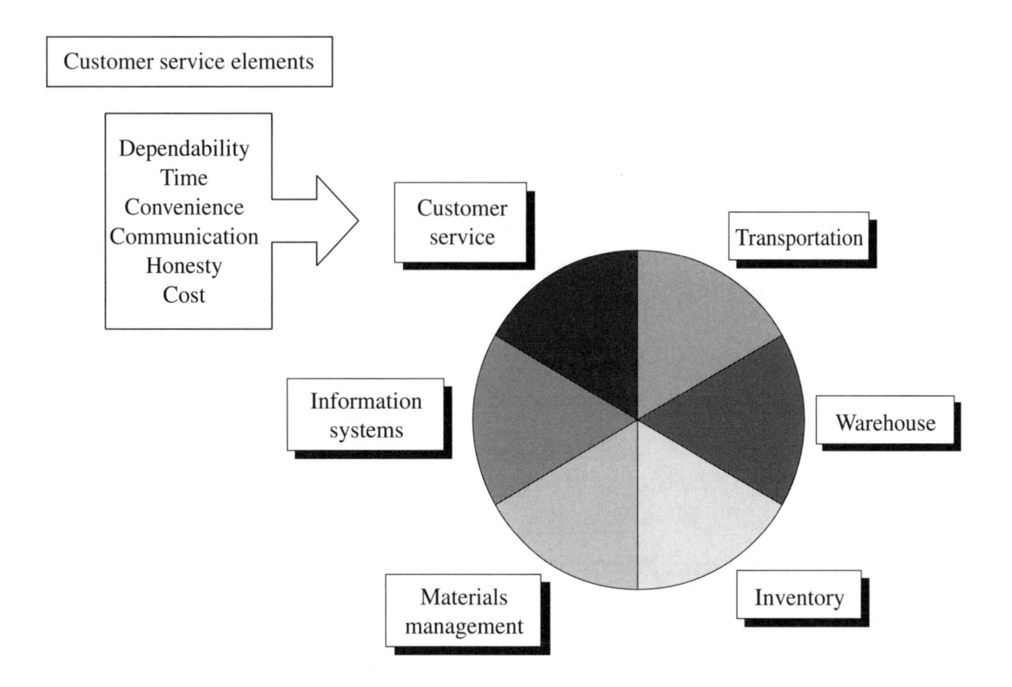

Figure 3-1 Customer service within the logistics system

Customer Service in a Global Setting

Cultural factors have a profound impact on how customer service is defined. As a result, customer service, especially at the retail level, is virtually country specific; that is, what appeals to people in one nation may not be appropriate in another. For example, European consumers want retailers that are situated in the heart of town because that is where people live. Convenience in this situation means a location close to mass transit or the customers' homes. Europeans still rely on individual shops handling one type of good, a situation that requires the customer to make multiple stops in order to acquire all of the goods needed. But generalizations about "European" customers are impossible, unification efforts notwithstanding. The French, for example, use credit less than those in other countries, while a British family wouldn't dream of driving out to breakfast on a Sunday morning. Spanish retailers generally have longer trading hours than many US merchants, but shops close for three hours in the middle of the day. German citizens are notoriously price-conscious and do much of their food shopping in no-frills discount stores not popular in other countries.[4] And, of course, customers in other parts of the world must still rely on government-owned retailers. Typically, these shops are dirty, offer indifferent service, charge extra for a plastic bag, and require that customers provide exact change.[5]

Logistics Profile 3-1
Toyota's Parts Logistics

When a Toyota breaks down in the dusty outback of Australia, chances are that the customer will not have to wait long for repairs to be done. Toyota Motor Corporation has developed a sophisticated system for distributing parts and accessories in Australia during the past five years, which has become a model for the rest of the Japanese automaker's worldwide operations. For Toyota, the parts and accessories business, known in the industry as the "after-sales" market, is just as important today as building and selling new cars. The company knows that nothing can ruin a customer's loyalty to a brand of car faster than being told a critical repair part is not available. "Profit margins on new cars are dropping and loyalty of customers is often as good as your last cost reduction," said Scott Grant, senior manager for national parts and accessories division for Toyota Australia. "The parts and accessories area – once the poor brother of the company – is now critical to an automobile manufacturer's long-term existence."

According to recent studies made by Toyota, customers are likely to continue buying the same brand of vehicles if they have experienced efficient after-sales service from the company. Toyota also found that during the first year of ownership 86 percent of customers return to dealerships for parts and service. After five years, however, the number of returning customers drops to about 20 percent. "Unfortunately, our customer retention is highest when demand for parts is lowest. As parts demand increases, particularly in years seven and eight, customers don't visit franchise dealers for maintenance as often," Grant said. "This is a huge sales opportunity for us and an area of focus at the moment." Nearly 75 percent of Toyota's parts are currently sold to wholesale body shops and mechanical parts businesses, which are outside the franchise network. But Toyota is also losing profits to this market, which faces intense competition from alternative parts sources.

Toyota started restructuring its Australian parts business about five years ago. With Australia's large size and diversity, Toyota has divided the country into regions to localize its understanding and support of end-users and dealers. The company operates six parts distribution centers throughout the country. The two largest parts centers – each with a capacity of more than 300,000 square feet – are located in Sydney and Melbourne. These facilities handle parts primarily for passenger vehicles on the country's populous East Coast. On the West Coast at Perth, Toyota has a smaller facility for carrying similar parts. Parts centers in the Queensland cities of Brisbane and Townsville and central Australia's Darwin handle parts mostly for commercial vehicles used in the country's mining and gas exploration industries. The distance between each parts center ranges from 700 to 3,000 miles. In Total, Toyota Australia's parts centers manage about 165,000 different parts and accessories at a value of about $70 million Australian.

So far, the improvements have exceeded Toyota's expectations. Stock reductions leveled off at 25 percent, while service rates to customers increased by 4 percent. Productivity at the warehouse rose by 20 percent and urgent order turnaround time dropped by 50 percent. Today Toyota's Sydney parts center fulfills 98 percent of dealer and wholesaler orders twice daily.

(**Source**: Adapted from Gillis, Chris. "Toyota's parts logistics," *American Shipper*, January 1998, pp. 31–4)

The situation is similar in China where the state system still predominates. Large government stores and supermarkets are used to distribute goods, supplemented by some free-market establishments and neighborhood shops offering convenience items. There are, in addition, some stores that specialize in specific kinds of merchandise such as bicycles or fruits and vegetables. Service is impersonal, no credit is extended, and prices are uniform across stores. There is no bargaining. The channel is short, since goods go directly from manufacturers to wholesalers to retailers.[6] Consumers in other parts of the Far East rely on many small retailers each handling a specific type of good. In addition, direct selling (selling to customers in their homes) is very popular in Japan, encompassing products as diverse as cosmetics and new automobiles. By and large, the car does not exert the influence on customer service in the Far East that it does in the United States, nor are shopping hours as important.

American consumers demand parking areas close to the retailers they patronize. They also want to be able to shop at any time, which has led more stores to remain open 12, 18, even 24 hours per day. This trend towards longer operating hours is even spreading to businesses such as auto dealerships, where it is not unusual to find service departments open daily until midnight or beyond and on Saturdays. Americans are also becoming increasingly intolerant of retail stock-outs and are more than willing to change stores when repeatedly faced with empty shelves. Perhaps the ultimate testament to the American demand for convenience is the "drive-thru" window that allows customers to conduct their business without leaving their cars (and is extremely productive for the firm as well). Long popular with fast-food establishments and banks, organizations as diverse as churches and grocery stores are utilizing the concept as well.

The point is that customer service must be tailored to each market. Customers in one country may define satisfactory service as being next-day delivery, while buyers in a different nation may think next-week service is excellent. Convenience can be defined in many different ways as well. Thus, McDonalds restaurants in Germany are situated in urban centers, convenient to mass transit and walk-in customers. In the United States, the stores are more often free-standing buildings with parking and a drive-through lane.

Because the firm's logistics system will be required to support the ultimate customer, management must first develop an appropriate customer service mix in each

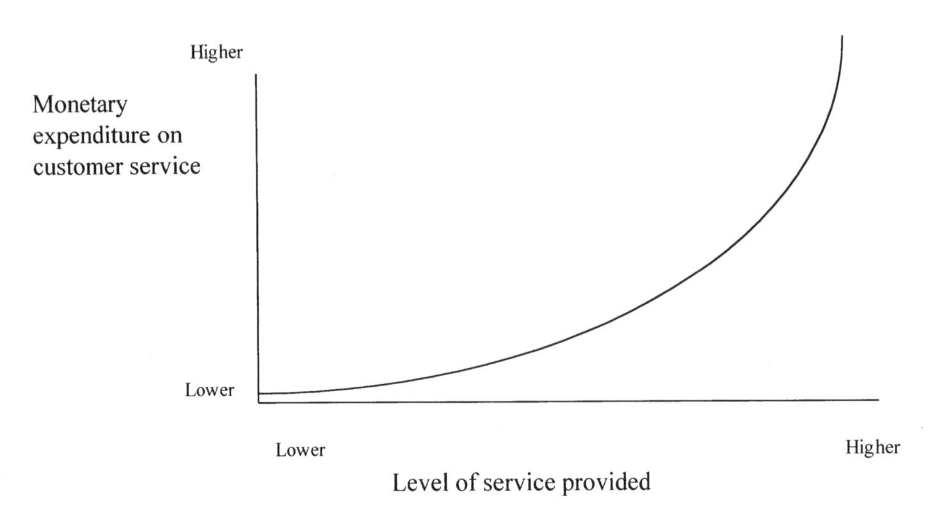

Figure 3-2 The relationship between customer service expenditures and level of service provided

market. Once those elements are specified, logistics resources can be marshaled to support them. As mentioned earlier, markets evolve differently with respect to "acceptable" service levels. Some view Western Europe, for example, as being three years behind the US on service, with emerging markets still further behind.[7] Failure to correctly identify customer service needs in each market will lead to the development of inefficient logistics systems, alienated customers, and, ultimately, loss of sales.

How Much Service Should Be Offered?

This question can be difficult to answer. Management wants to offer the service their customers demand. But, as illustrated in figure 3-2, the cost of providing increasing levels of service becomes prohibitive. In fact, at some point, customer service cannot be improved regardless of how much money is spent. Similarly, as shown in figure 3-3, demand will rise only so far, regardless of how much customer service is provided, given the limits of the available market.

In order to answer the question of how much customer service to offer, management must be able to somehow relate the cost of providing that service with the revenues that will result. This sort of analysis can be extremely difficult, because it is virtually impossible to isolate the impact of customer service variables on sales. For example, Wal-Mart stores in the United States employ a greeter at the front entrance. This person (often a senior citizen) welcomes customers to the store, offers them a shopping cart, and answers questions. It is virtually impossible to identify the impact this person has on sales. But the fact that customers view this bit of personal contact

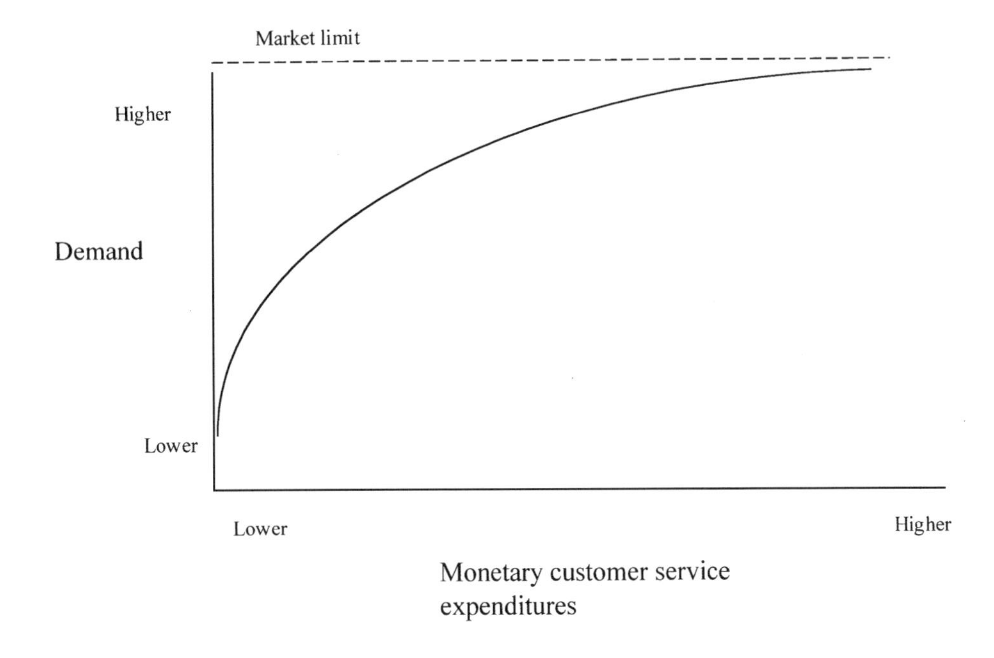

Figure 3-3 Relationship between customer service expenditures and demand stimulation

positively is enough to justify the cost. Thus, managers must have some idea of the benefits, tangible or otherwise, they are receiving for their expenditures on customer service.

Barriers to Quality Customer Service

There are a number of impediments to providing quality customer service on a continuous basis. Some of these variables are controllable by management, some are not.

Controllable factors

LACK OF CUSTOMER SEGMENTATION Some firms offer all customers the same level of service. This strategy could result from a conscious decision by management, but it may also reflect a lack of appreciation for customers' needs. The fact is that all customers should not necessarily receive the same service. Any organization has a small number of customers that generate a large share of corporate revenues. In fact, Pareto's Law (also known as the 80/20 rule) states that 80 percent of the firm's profits come from 20 percent of its customers. Management would probably do virtually anything to keep these people happy. Most buyers will not fall into this category; management want to satisfy this group as well, but they simply do not buy enough to warrant the higher service levels provided to the company's most important customers. When only one level of service is offered, it often tends to be high. Thus, managers find they are spending more on customer service than they need to and may, in fact, be alienating those premier buyers by making them feel less valued by the organization.

MISUSE AS A SELLING TOOL Occasionally, better customer service is promised as an incentive to close a sale. Faster delivery, liberal return policies, or other benefits may be offered even though they are not, in fact, a part of the firm's customer service strategy. This misuse of customer service virtually guarantees customer dissatisfaction since the firm may be unable or unwilling to keep those promises.

SHORT-TERM MANAGEMENT DECISIONS When an organization finds itself in financial difficulty, managers begin looking for ways to improve short-run profitability. Two options are immediately available. One is to cut inventories. This action not only lowers costs but reduces assets, thus benefiting the firm twice. A second action is to shorten the duration of accounts receivable, a move that makes customers pay sooner and improves the company's cash flow. However, both of these decisions can have long-term negative implications for customer service. Reducing inventories by itself can ultimately lead to more stock-outs and lost sales. As far as the buyer is concerned, reducing the grace period for accounts receivable is essentially the same as raising the price because interest income for those lost days disappears. Thus, sales can fall over time.

EMPLOYEES Hiring unqualified workers and insufficient employee training can both lead to poor customer service. Competent people must be employed and educated thoroughly in the firm's customer service philosophy. They must know what their responsibilities are and what actions they are empowered to take in order to satisfy the customer. Workers must thoroughly understand what management expects of them so that customers can be treated accordingly. If employees are afraid they will be disciplined because they offer a compensatory meal or a free airline ticket to a disgruntled customer, for example, they will never make that concession even if management expects them to do so.

Uncontrollable factors

Unfortunately, despite management's best procedures and intentions, customers may still be dissatisfied. Factors outside the control of the organization can also bear on the buyers' overall assessment of their experience. Figure 3-4 depicts some of the influences that can adversely impact the firm's customer service strategy and highlights the interactions that can develop between these forces.

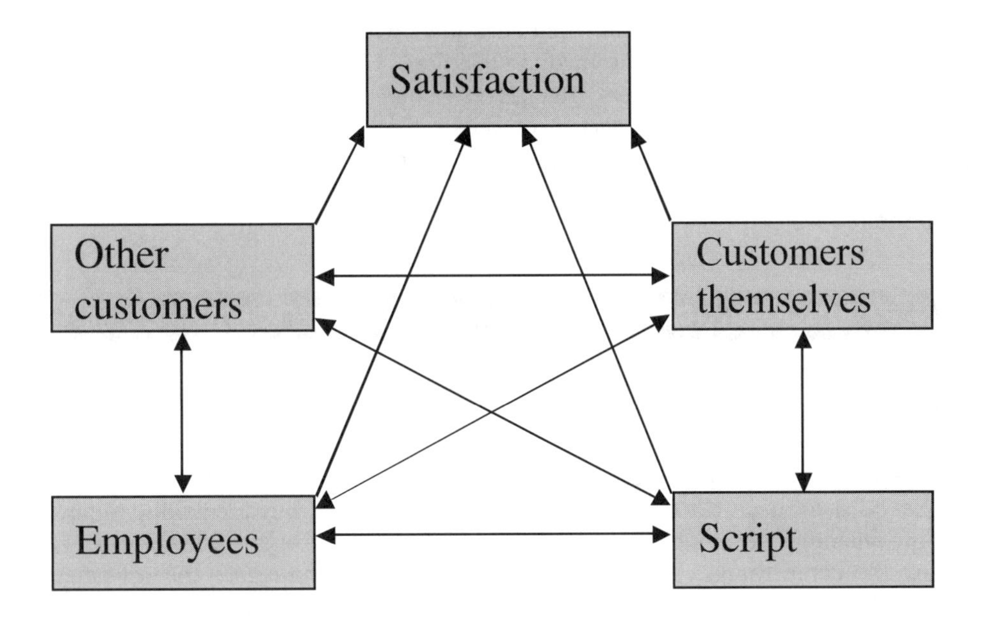

Figure 3-4 Uncontrollable variables impacting customer satisfaction

CUSTOMERS Sometimes customers can seem like their own worst enemies. They don't follow directions, comply with procedures, or generally do what they are supposed to do. In other words, individual traits, characteristics, and experiences can also influence the buyer's perception of satisfaction. Unfortunately, if the customer is having a bad day he or she may end up feeling dissatisfied regardless of the institution's intentions.

OTHER CUSTOMERS In instances where many customers are present, the number and behavior of others can impact one's level of satisfaction. If a restaurant is crowded with loud people, for example, customers seeking a quiet leisurely meal will probably be dissatisfied with their experience.

EMPLOYEES Workers can have bad days just like customers. Though indoctrinated to behave a certain way, they can occasionally let their emotions override their training with respect to customer treatment. An indifferent or rude employee can totally undo the firm's entire customer service effort.

SCRIPT A script describes a typical sequence of behaviors a customer must undertake to accomplish a task at a particular business. It is rarely written down; the customer is expected simply to know what to do based on experience or observing others. For example, when customers walk into a restaurant for the first time they must make some immediate decisions. Should they simply sit down or wait to be seated? If they seat themselves, where should they sit? How do they order their food? Are they served or do they serve themselves? After the first experience or two, people generally learn the script for that particular situation. If the script is too confusing or difficult to understand, however, customer dissatisfaction may result.

Improving Customer Service Performance

There are several things managers can do to improve the customer service offered by their firm.

UNDERSTAND CUSTOMER NEEDS It is absolutely essential that management learn what services their customers most value and how much they are willing to pay for those amenities. Invariably, this sort of research will show that all customers do not seek the same things. This effort will, in turn, give managers the information needed to conduct an ABC analysis whereby customers can be categorized based upon the profits they provide to the firm. Customer service strategies can then be developed to meet these specific needs. For example, the company's most important buyers (i.e. the top 20 percent in terms of revenue generation) would be included in the "A" group and could be offered very high service levels, while the "B" group might encompass the bulk of the firm's customers (the middle 60 percent) who buy less than the "A" group and would be satisfied with somewhat less attention. Finally, the least important users (the bottom 20 percent) would be placed in the "C" category and should receive a lower level still. Management should provide their customers the service they desire without spending more on customer service than necessary.

MONITOR SERVICE DELIVERY Because the uncontrollable variables discussed earlier can upset the best laid plans, managers must seek constant customer feedback in order to ensure that service deficiencies are quickly identified and corrected. Customer surveys and interviews can provide useful insights, as can personal experience. For example, managers may choose to put themselves into their customer's place by acting as a patron within their own organization. They might purchase items in one of their own stores, trace a shipment through the firm's logistics system, lodge a complaint, or eat in a corporate restaurant, and then evaluate their customer service strategies based upon that personal experience. Placing employees in the role of customers in order to evaluate service performance is sometimes referred to as "shopping," and is a technique that can provide some extremely powerful insights into how well or poorly management's customer service efforts are being received by buyers.

TRAIN EMPLOYEES Employees must understand what the firm's customer service strategies are so that they know what their role is in implementing those plans. Very often, the only interaction the customer has is with the front-line worker: the vehicle operator, order taker, or clerk. Therefore, for many customers, the company is represented by the lowest-ranking people in the entire organization. It is crucial that these employees understand the critical role they play in providing customer satisfaction and receive the training necessary to carry out their tasks. Top management must also give these customer contact workers the freedom and authority to take whatever action they deem necessary to keep the customer happy. The implication is not that unreasonable demands will be routinely satisfied. However, employees often know the best solution for a given situation and should be empowered to handle unforeseen events as they see fit.

Management must always keep in mind that the optimum service level may not be the alternative with the lowest cost; it *is* the one that advances the long-term profitability of the firm.

The Consequences of Poor Customer Service

STOCK-OUTS Product availability tends to be the most important customer service consideration because buyers are faced with a number of choices when confronted with an empty shelf. First, they can simply leave the store and either go somewhere else or return to the store another time. Alternatively, they can remain in the store and buy a substitute product, or perhaps the product they desire in a different form. In some instances, they may be able to special-order the item they want. But all of these options have one of two results: either buyers are given the opportunity to try a competitor's product or they are forced to make multiple trips to purchase the item(s) they want. Ultimately, perpetually stocking out by the retailer costs the manufacturer sales because customers may find a competing product they like just as well or they may simply get tired of seeing an empty shelf. For the retailer, the consequences may not be so direct because, in theory, customers may purchase a more expensive item than they originally intended. Over the long term, however, the same results ensue: customers start patronizing a store that can meet their needs the first time.

It is also worth pointing out that stock-outs can occur in service businesses as well. Restaurants run out of popular foods, airlines run out of seats, and auto repair shops fail to have necessary parts on hand. Arguably, customers find these shortages even more annoying then failing to find a product because they have fewer options. In other words, it is difficult for a customer to take his or her car to another shop when it is already in pieces in this one. Because customer dissatisfaction tends to be quicker to develop and more intense in a service encounter, providers must take particular care to ensure that stock-outs do not occur.

VARIABLE LEAD TIMES Order-cycle time is almost as important a customer service issue as product/service availability. Recall that order-cycle time is the elapsed time between order placement and product delivery. Figure 3-5 shows a hypothetical order-cycle time for a channel from Taiwan to the Netherlands.

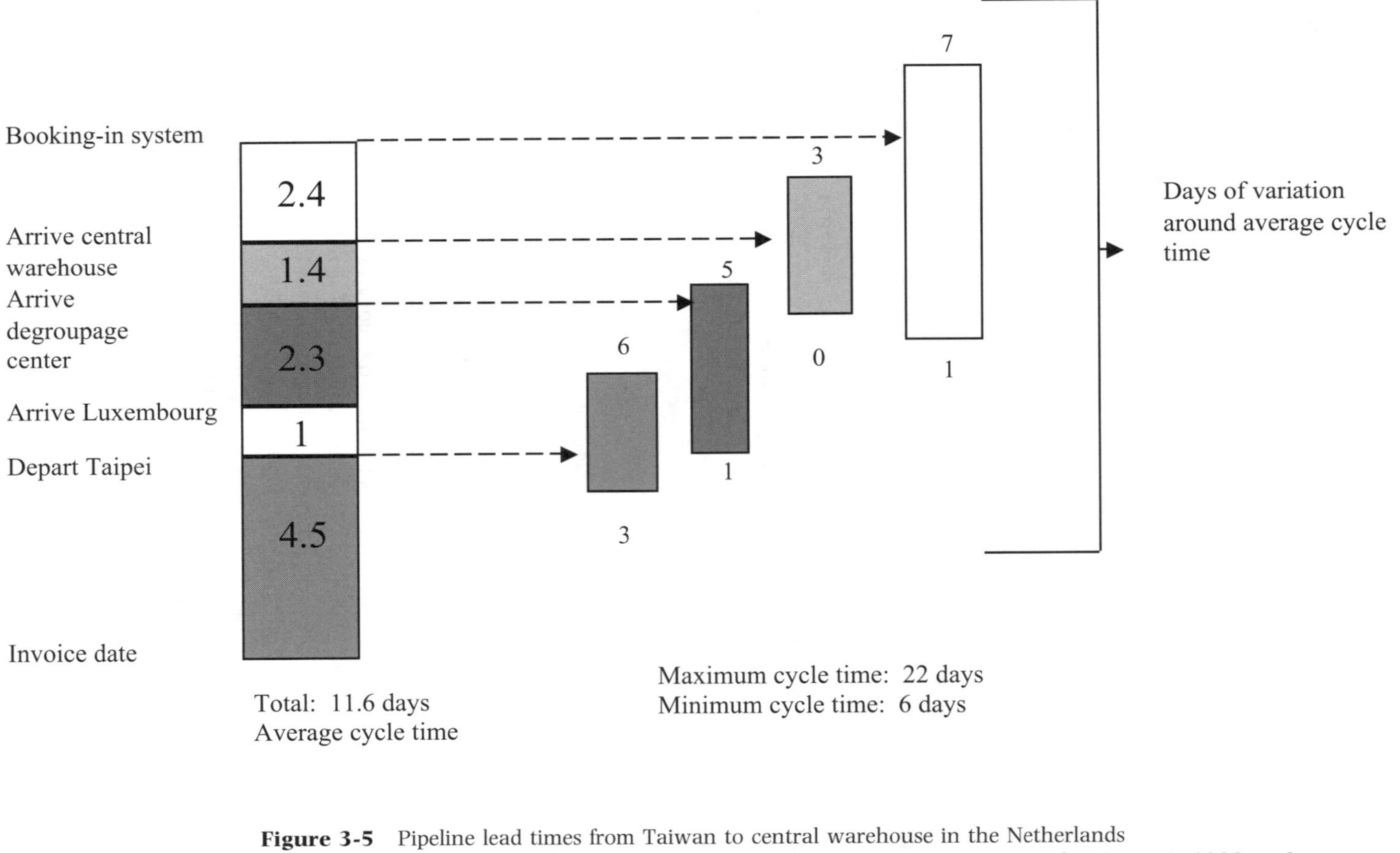

Figure 3-5 Pipeline lead times from Taiwan to central warehouse in the Netherlands
Source: Ploos van Amstel, M. J. "Managing the pipeline efficiently," *Journal of Business Logistics*, Vol. 11, No. 1, 1990, p. 9

The goods are manufactured and then moved to the airport at Taipei for air shipment to Luxembourg. Once in Luxembourg, the goods are moved to a degroupage, or breakdown, center where they are sorted and prepared for onward ground movement. From there they are transported by road to a central warehouse in Amsterdam and booked into the customer's system. Note that the fastest, slowest, and average times for each activity are shown. The average order-cycle time for goods transit, 12 days, is simply the sum of the average time needed to complete each individual part of the movement. Is 12 days good or bad? The answer is that "it depends." For some customers it may be perfectly satisfactory; for others it may be too slow. The real issue, from the customer's point of view, is the variability in that order cycle. In the example above, the goods may arrive in as few as six days or they may take as long as 22. This means that customers must always keep 22 days' worth of inventory on hand to minimize the risk of stocking out. Suppose, however, that the manufacturer is able to eliminate much of that variability through automation, for example, or improved information systems, so that the modified lead times are as shown in figure 3-6. Not only has the average time been reduced to seven days, variability has dropped from 16 days to eight. Hamilton Standard's efforts to improve order cycle time as a means of enhancing customer service are illustrated in logistics profile 3-2.

Management then faces the issue of what to do with the extra time. One possibility is simply to offer all customers the faster service. Remember, however, that some customers are happy with 12 days; they may not want to receive goods faster. Another alternative would be to retain the 12-day average order cycle, but provide it with much less variability. Finally, the firm could offer faster service to those customers that need it, but retain the 12–day cycle (or something in between seven and 12 days) for everyone else. In any case, the reduced variability will benefit all buyers since lower inventory levels can now be held. Consistency is what management should be seeking in their order-cycle time; that is, adhering to the average time as closely and as often as possible.

CUSTOMER ALIENATION For global companies, managing customer service is especially challenging. Strategies useful in one culture may be ineffective (or worse) in another. A firm simply cannot adopt a one-strategy-fits-all approach to customer service. In Japan, especially, negative perceptions of a company or product, often resulting from lack of attention to customer service, are very hard to overcome. In some instances, a company may never rebound from such serious mistakes or oversights. For example, in the auto-parts industry, US companies selling to Japanese automobile manufacturers are expected to provide the same level of customer support and service as Japanese auto parts manufacturers. Meeting this demand requires that US companies place engineers and technicians in Japan to work with automakers during the product design and development stages and establish a distribution network to provide just-in-time delivery of auto parts to the manufacturer. It is also critical to make frequent courtesy visits to Japanese business partners to strengthen business relations and to display commitment to making the business arrangement work.[8]

Losing a customer can cost as much as eight times more than retaining one. The

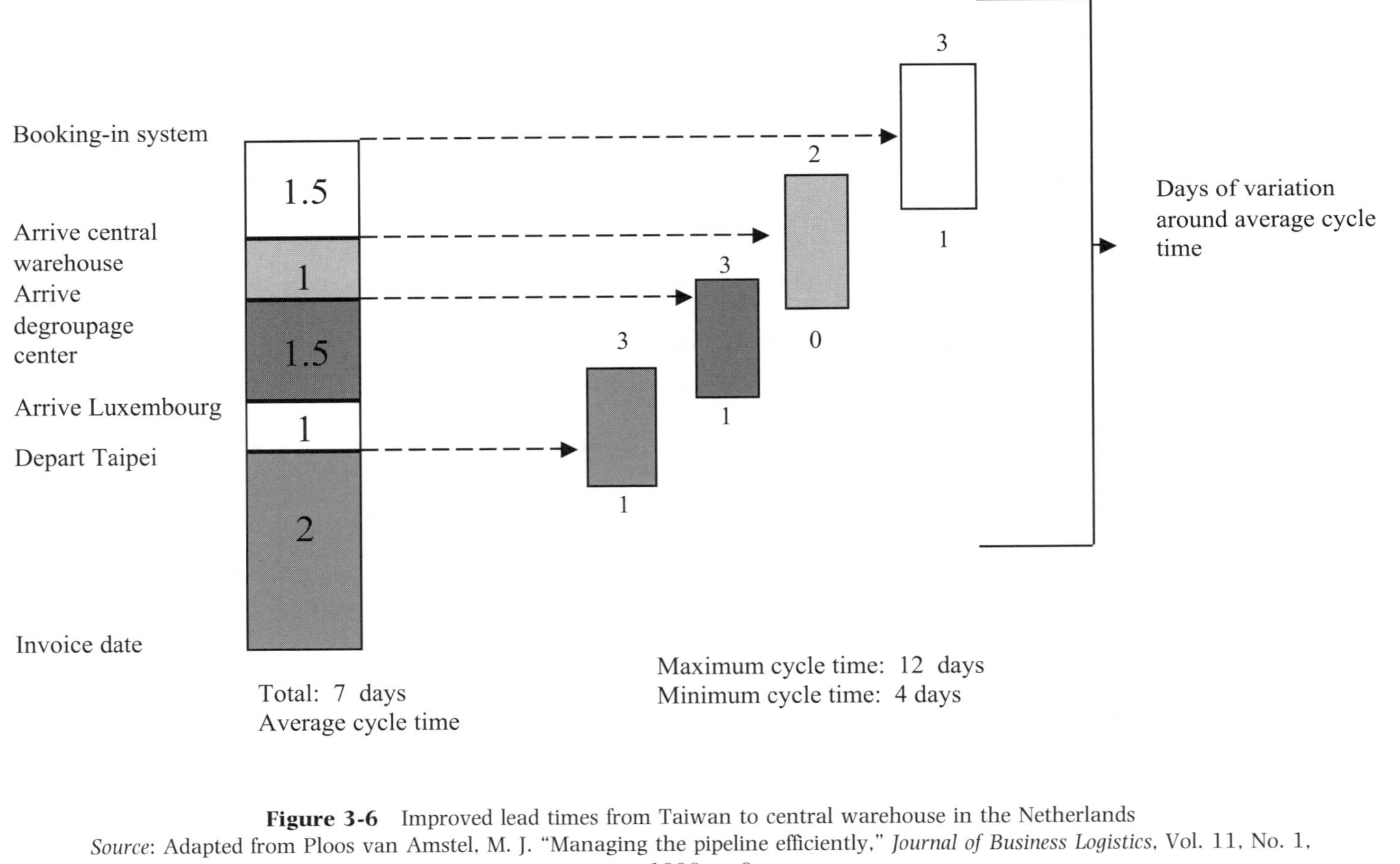

Figure 3-6 Improved lead times from Taiwan to central warehouse in the Netherlands
Source: Adapted from Ploos van Amstel, M. J. "Managing the pipeline efficiently," *Journal of Business Logistics*, Vol. 11, No. 1, 1990, p. 9

Logistics Profile 3-2
GETTING CLOSER TO THE CUSTOMER

The opening of Hamilton Standard's Asia/Pacific Distribution Center in Singapore underscores at least two core supply-chain imperatives at work: 1) strive to reduce order-cycle time and use that as a market differentiator and 2) to be become successful yourself, work to make your customers more successful.

The new distribution facility was established by Hamilton Standard's Worldwide Customer Support business unit to speed delivery of parts to airline customers in the Asia/Pacific region. Opened in late 1997 and operated by UPS Worldwide Logistics, the center currently serves more than 20 airlines from China, Japan, and Korea in the north to Australia and New Zealand in the south. Hamilton Standard, a division of United Technologies, designs and manufactures a range of components and parts for both commercial and military aircraft. The center currently stocks approximately 2,000 different kinds of parts, although 6,000 items will eventually be handled there. Ultimately, the facility will fulfill 85 to 90 percent of spare-parts requests in the Asia/Pacific region and serve more than 30 airline customers.

Before the distribution center was in place, parts were shipped from the United States to the airline customer in Asia. The extensive distance involved, coupled with customs procedures and other administrative requirements, often prolonged the shipping process. Typical cycle time from order placement to customer receipt was 10 to 12 days. Creation of the Singapore parts distribution center has cut that time sharply. "Airlines in the region now generally receive their parts within one or two days after placing the order," reports Greg DeSantis, vice president of Hamilton Standard's Worldwide Customer Support unit. And because the facility is located in a free-trade zone, he adds, delays associated with paperwork and customs issues have been eliminated or gratly reduced. Further expediting the process is the nature of the customers themselves. Every major air carrier supported by the center has at least one non-stop flight into or out of Singapore every day. This means that the needed parts can go directly from the distribution center to the customer's aircraft.

The reduced order-cycle time not only allows customers to work on their aircraft more quickly, but it also lets them manage their inventory more effectively. "Quicker deliveries will enable the airlines to cut costs by reducing their own parts inventories," notes Dave Galuska, Hamilton Standard's director of materials management. "Our in-region distribution strategy is part of a comprehensive in-region approach to customer service." In line with that philosophy, the company is considering establishing a similar parts distribution center in Europe to upgrade customer service in that market.

Hamilton Standard believes that getting closer to the customer – in this case, both literally and figuratively – makes good business sense. And by cutting order-cycle time for customers and helping them run their operations more efficiently, it is realizing the promised potential of supply-chain management.

(*Source*: Quinn, Francis J. "Getting closer to the customer," *Logistics*, May 1998, p. 69)

longer the customer remains, the more valuable the relationship. Loyal customers buy more and cost less with each subsequent sale. So losing a seven-year-old relationship is much more painful than parting after just one year.[9] Giving customers the service they demand is absolutely essential to sustaining that type of long-term sales relationship.

Improving Customer Service in Comparison to its Costs

Managers must constantly wrestle with cost/benefit trade-offs regarding customer service. In other words, management must decide whether a given customer service improvement is worth the investment. In a profit-making organization, this decision can be made once the cost of implementing the improvement is weighed against the expected increase in revenue that should result from the new strategy. If the former is larger than the latter, the change should not be made. As was mentioned earlier, however, it can be extremely difficult to equate an improvement in service directly to a positive change in sales or revenues. This need to measure benefit growth attributable to customer service is particularly hard in a non-profit organization where the benefit may not be readily quantifiable. The danger in this situation is the mind-set that any slight improvement is worth whatever it costs to attain it. However, the expected improvement in benefit (be it profit, enrollment, defense readiness, or whatever) resulting from an investment in customer service must somehow be determined so that management will know whether or not to expend the funds in order to make the change.

Customer Service and the Internal Customer

Many organizations are adopting the view that customer service precepts are just as relevant within the firm. That is, managers view workers at each stage in the benefit production process as "customers" of the task that must be completed before theirs. For example, an order-entry clerk receives order data from a sales representative; a warehouse operator receives a pick list from the order-entry department; a warehouse loading clerk receives cases of goods to be loaded on a truck from an order picker.[10] In other words, certain tasks must be satisfactorily completed before the next person can do his or her job. Management wants to minimize the opportunities for internal service failures because these mistakes can increase the likelihood of external customer dissatisfaction. By satisfying the needs and wants of internal customers, the firm upgrades its capability for satisfying the needs and wants of its final buyers. Certainly the nature of a firm's internal customer service mix will differ from that offered to the final consumer. But the intent is the same: to advance the objectives of the organization by satisfying customer requirements better than the competition.

Chapter Summary

Customer service is the most important component of the logistics system. Not only do customer service decisions have a direct impact on the firm's customers and employees, but they also determine how the rest of the logistics mix will be structured. Though it can be defined in different ways, an organization's customer service mix generally addresses issues related to dependability, time, convenience, communication, and honesty. The challenge for a global organization is to tailor that mix of variables to the needs of each market. Their objective is to offer customers the service they demand at the lowest cost to the organization. Invariably, misidentifying important customer service variables leads to dissatisfied buyers and, ultimately, lost sales.

Study Questions

1. Contrast the "activity" view of customer service with the "corporate philosophy" approach.
2. Briefly discuss the five key elements of customer service. Give examples of each from your own experience.
3. Can an organization offer too much service? Defend your answer.
4. How do cultural factors influence customer service?
5. Should management ever consider lowering the amount of customer service provided? Defend your answer.
6. What is a "script" and why is it important to customer satisfaction?
7. How do the firm's front-line workers affect the customer's level of satisfaction?
8. Discuss the concept of customer segmentation. What criteria could be used to separate buyers into groups?
9. When customers cannot find the product they want on the shelf, what actions might they take?
10. How do managers decide which customer service improvements, if any, to adopt?
11. What is the difference between an internal and an external customer? Why should management care about internal customer satisfaction?

Notes

1. Smith, Craig S. "Doublemint in China: distribution isn't double the fun," *The Wall Street Journal*, December 5, 1995, p. B1.
2. "Full Marks for France?" *SuperMarketing*, July 22, 1994, p. 22.
3. Mottley, Robert. "Dead in nine months," *American Shipper*, December 1998, pp. 30–2.
4. Waddell, Ian. "Global challenges set the scene for 1992," *Chain Store Age Executive*, May 1990, p. 190.
5. Engelberg, Stephen, "A treat for night owls in Poland," *New York Times*, August 21, 1990, p. D1.
6. Vernon-Wortzel, Heidi and Wortzel, Lawrence H. "The emergence of free market retailing in the People's Republic of China," *California Management Review*, Spring 1987, p. 62.
7. Landau, Nilly. "Are you being served?" *International Business*, March 1995, p. 40.
8. Christian, Allen. "Connecting with the Japanese customer," *Business America*, October 4, 1993, p. 23.
9. Landau, ibid, p. 39.
10. Byrne, Patrick M. and Markham, William J. *Improving Quality and Productivity in the Logistics Process* (Oak Brook, IL: Council of Logistics Management, 1991), p. 165.

chapter 4

Inventory Management

Introduction	59
Inventory and Customer Service	60
Purposes of Inventory	61
Types of Inventory	61
Objectives of Inventory Management	62
Classic Inventory Models	63
Inventory Management: Signs of Trouble	70
Improving Inventory Management	72
Materials Requirements Planning (MRP)	74
Distribution Resource Planning (DRP)	75
Just-In-Time (JIT) Inventory Management	76
Integrated Inventory Management: DRP, MRP, and JIT	80
Inventory Management in a Global Market	80
Chapter Summary	82
Study Questions	82

Introduction

Inventory management has received much attention in recent years, primarily from the point of view of eliminating as much inventory as possible. This chapter will explore the role of inventory in the logistics system, then explain some of the classic approaches to inventory management. Next, indicators of inventory management problems will be highlighted, as will ways to rectify those difficulties. Finally, the chapter will conclude by detailing several techniques available to minimize excess inventory levels throughout the pipeline while continuing to satisfy customer needs.

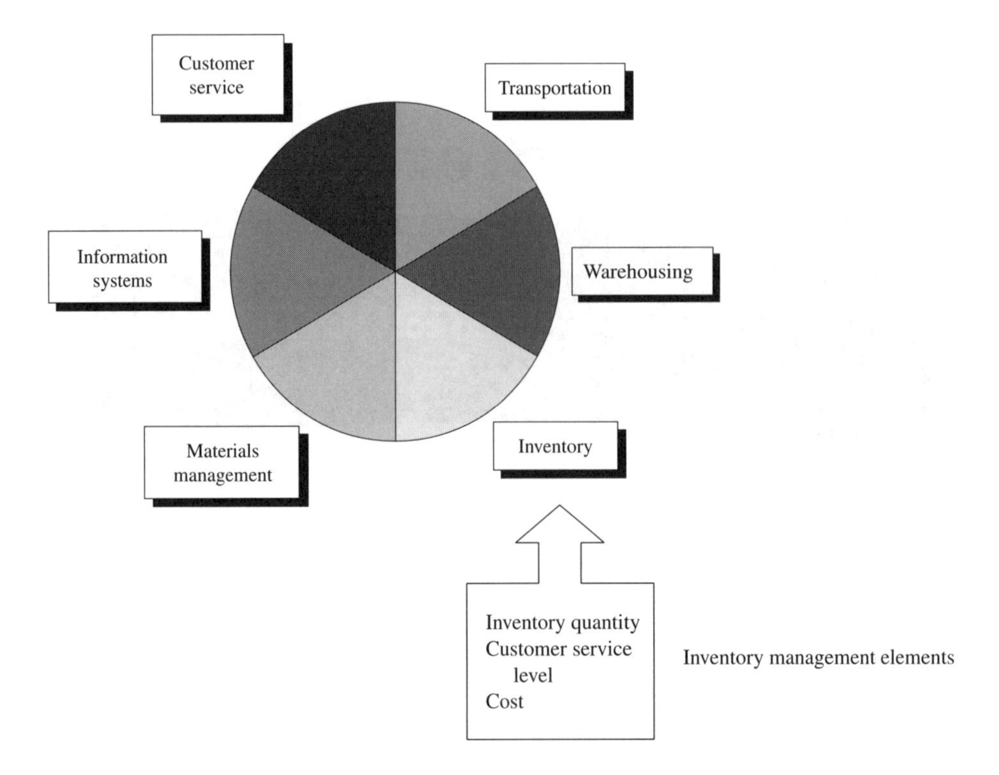

Figure 4-1 Inventory management in the logistics system

Inventory and Customer Service

Inventory issues are closely related to those of customer service. Customers expect to find the desired item available when they need it. If the internal customer is faced with an empty shelf, the benefit production process stops; the external customer unable to complete a purchase will most likely take his or her business to a competitor.

As depicted in figure 4-1, inventory management essentially encompasses balancing the cost of holding inventory on one hand with the cost of not holding it on the other. In the former case, the organization incurs direct expenses related to insurance, taxes, storage, and obsolescence as well as the funds tied up in the items on hand. As an example, in 1995, the cost of various computer components fell so quickly that Compaq Computer Corporation found itself holding more than $2 billion worth of inventory that it may not be able to sell for as much as the original cost.[1] Furthermore, total assets are increased by the amount of the inventory which, in turn, results in a lower return on investment. Alternatively, eliminating inventory can lead to other, even higher, costs in the form of poor customer service, lost sales or production stoppages. So managers must carefully weigh all the relevant logistics costs in deciding how much, if any, inventory to maintain.

Purposes of Inventory

Many firms in developed markets have embraced the concept of just-in-time (JIT) inventory. This term is a bit of a misnomer since, in its purest sense, it implies a complete lack of inventory. Rather, items arrive on the shelf exactly at the time they are needed by the customer. JIT will be discussed in more detail below. However, it is important to realize that inventory can serve a variety of useful purposes within an organization. Several of these uses are discussed below.

- **Facilitates economies of scale.** Management may decide, for example, to purchase large quantities of an item in order to qualify for a discount. Or lower transportation costs may be realized by shipping larger quantities at one time. Similarly, a long production run may significantly reduce manufacturing costs. In every case, inventory is being utilized as a way to obtain savings in other parts of the logistics system.
- **Offers a means of balancing supply and demand.** Some firms can only sell their products at certain times of the year. In order to utilize their fixed investment in buildings and equipment and maintain a skilled labor force, management may decided to produce all year and store the finished goods until the selling season arrives.
- **Provides protection from uncertain demand.** Despite management's best forecasting efforts, demand can never be known with absolutely certainty. Similarly, transport vehicles break down, raw materials may suddenly be unavailable, and manufacturing lines may stop. For all of these reasons, inventory is utilized to ensure that customer needs are met even when the production process itself is interrupted.

Managers must carefully weigh these benefits against the cost of holding inventory to achieve them. For example, is the quantity purchase discount greater than the expense of holding the extra items bought? Is it less expensive to produce all required seasonal goods in the six months preceding the demand period rather than accumulating inventory over the course of a year? Could uncertainty be better addressed with new forecasting software or the services of a more responsive transport firm? Often inventory is used as a means of coping with other issues in the benefit production process when in fact it would be much more advantageous to deal with those problems directly.

Types of Inventory

- **Normal** inventory is required to support the replenishment process under conditions of certainty. In other words, if demand and order-cycle (or lead) time never change, normal stocks are all the organization would require to meet their customers' needs.
- **Safety** stock is held in addition to normal inventory to cover uncertainty in

demand and lead time. Its purpose is to protect the firm and the customer against stock-outs.

- **In-transit** inventory is en route from one location to another. It may belong to the shipper or the customer depending upon the terms of sale.
- **Speculative** stock is held for reasons other than meeting current demand needs. Management may fear the price of a needed raw material will rise in the future or that availability may be limited for some reason and elects to buy a large quantity in anticipation of either eventuality. Alternatively, a vendor may offer an especially low price if a large quantity is purchased at one time.
- **Seasonal** inventory is accumulated in advance of a selling season. It provides management the ability to stabilize production and maintain a long-term labor force even when the majority of sales occur during a relatively small part of the year.
- **Dead** stock is inventory that no one wants, at least immediately. The astute student will wonder why any organization would incur the costs associated with holding these items rather than simply disposing of them. One reason might be that management expects demand to resume at some point in the future. Alternatively, it may cost more to get rid of an item than it does to keep it. But the most compelling reason for maintaining these goods is customer service. Perhaps an important buyer has an occasional need for some of these items, so management keeps them on hand as a goodwill gesture.

Objectives of Inventory Management

Inventory must be viewed as a positive contributor to corporate profitability. To that end, management must determine when various items should be ordered, how much to order each time, and how often to order to meet customer needs while minimizing associated costs.

Inventory costs

There are three types of costs that must be considered in setting inventory levels.

- **Holding (or carrying) costs** are expenses such as storage, handling, insurance, taxes, obsolescence, theft, and interest on funds financing the goods. These charges increase as inventory levels rise. In order to minimize carrying costs, management makes frequent orders of small quantities. Holding costs are commonly assessed as a percentage of unit value, i.e. 15 percent, 20 percent, etc. rather than attempting to derive a monetary value for each of these costs individually. This practice is a reflection of the difficulty inherent in deriving a specific per-unit cost for, for example, obsolescence or theft.
- **Ordering costs** are those fees associated with placing an order, including expenses related to personnel in a purchasing department, communications, and the handling of related paperwork. Lowering these costs would be accomplished

by placing a small number of orders, each for a large quantity. Unlike carrying costs, ordering expenses are generally expressed as a monetary value per order.

- **Stock-out costs** include sales that are lost, both short and long term, when a desired item is not available; the costs associated with back-ordering the missing item; or expenses related to stopping the production line because a component part has not arrived. These charges are probably the most difficult to compute, but arguably the most important because they represent the costs incurred by customers (internal or external) when inventory policies falter. Failing to understand these expenses can lead management to maintain higher (or lower) inventory levels than customer requirements may justify.

Managing inventory costs

The challenge from management's point of view is that holding and ordering costs must be dealt with simultaneously. Lowering carrying costs can lead to higher ordering and stock-out costs; attempting to reduce stock-out costs can cause carrying and ordering costs to rise; limiting ordering costs can lead to higher carrying costs but lower stock-out expenses. In other words, managers must develop an inventory management philosophy that strikes a balance between these three cost categories and is consistent with overall customer service objectives.

Classic Inventory Models

Economic order quantity (EOQ) model

Shown in figure 4-2, the basic EOQ model provides an order size in units that minimizes the total inventory costs (carrying and ordering) in a situation where demand and lead time are known with certainty.

The EOQ can be calculated using the formula:

$$EOQ = \sqrt{\frac{2CD}{IV}}$$

where: EOQ = number of units to be ordered

C = monetary ordering cost for placing one order

D = annual demand in number of units

I = annual inventory carrying cost as a percentage of unit value

V = average monetary value of one unit of inventory.

For example, if ordering costs (C) = \$100, annual demand (D)=10,000, annual carrying cost (I) = 20 percent, and unit value (V) = \$200, then

$$EOQ = \sqrt{\frac{2(100)(10000)}{(.2)(200)}} = \sqrt{\frac{2000000}{4}} = \sqrt{50000} = 223.61 \approx 224 \text{ units}$$

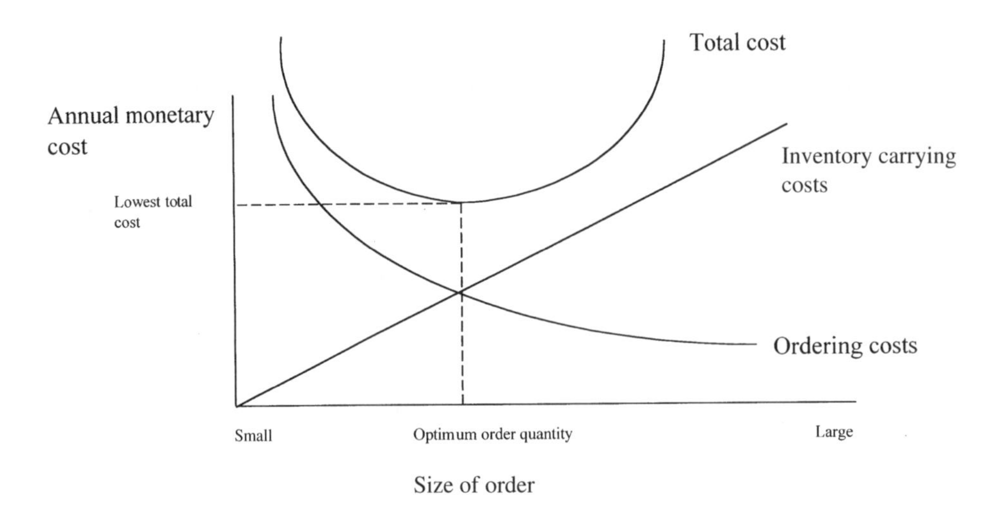

Figure 4-2 The economic order quantity

By dividing this number back into the annual demand, management will note that they should reorder approximately 45 times per year. Table 4-1 depicts different ordering scenarios utilizing the above figures in order to illustrate that the EOQ is in fact the lowest cost quantity.

Modifications to the basic EOQ model[a]

It is also possible to extend the basic model to account for volume transportation rates, transportation rate discounts, inventory in transit, and private carriage. For example, volume transportation rates are lower charges that are applied when a specified minimum quantity (weight) or more is being moved. Therefore, in inventory situations, the decision maker responsible for transporting goods should consider how the lower-volume rate affects total cost. Thus, in addition to considering storage (holding) cost and order or setup cost, the manager should consider how lower transportation costs affect total cost and order accordingly[2].

Model limitations

The simple EOQ is based upon several assumptions. First, demand and lead time are constant and known. Second, price is constant and does not change with order size.

[a] For an excellent discussion of special EOQ applications, see Coyle, John J., Bardi, Edward J. and Langley, C. John Jr. *The Management of Business Logistics*, 6th edn (St. Paul, MN: West Publishing Company, 1996), pp. 234–45.

Table 4-1 Economic order quantity trade-offs

Order qty (Q)	*Number of orders (D/Q)*	*Ordering cost ($) (Q × C)*	*Carrying cost (1/2Q × V × I) ($)*	*Total cost ($)*
50	200	20,000	1,000	21,000
100	100	10,000	2,000	12,000
200	50	5,000	4,000	9,000
250	40	4,000	5,000	9,000
300	34	3,400	6,000	9,400
400	25	2,500	8,000	10,500
500	20	2,000	10,000	12,000
1,000	10	1,000	21,000	21,000

Third, no stock-outs exist. Fourth, there is no inventory in-transit. Finally, there is only one item in inventory, or at least no interaction with other goods (i.e. demand for one product does not affect demand for another). These assumptions may seem too restrictive to make the model useful. However, there are situations where, for all practical purposes, these parameters are met. When purchasing common things like nuts and bolts, for example, the EOQ can work very well because these items are inexpensive and the assumption of certainty is not of major importance. It is also possible to alter the basic model slightly to account for discounts obtained for volume purchases or transportation movements. Since discounts effectively lower the price of each unit, thus changing the EOQ, these modifications serve to make the model more useful in real-world situations.

Fixed order point/fixed order quantity model

With the fixed order point/fixed order quantity technique, an order is placed whenever inventory on hand drops to a level where the remaining quantity available is just enough to satisfy demand during the order cycle. At this reorder point the economic order quantity will be purchased. As illustrated in figure 4-3, the limitations of this model become obvious. Assuming an EOQ of 1,000 units, average usage of 50 units per day, and a five-day order cycle, the reorder point is established at 250 units. In the first period, inventory dropped to 250 units on day 15 so another 1,000 units were ordered. These arrived on day 20 just as on-hand inventory fell to zero. In period 2, however, demand was higher than expected. The same 1,000 units were ordered on day 27 when goods available fell to 250, but because demand was up, a two-day stock-out occurred before the new shipment arrived on day 32. In period 3, demand slowed, so reordering on day 60 resulted in the new shipment arriving on day 65 before existing inventories were consumed.

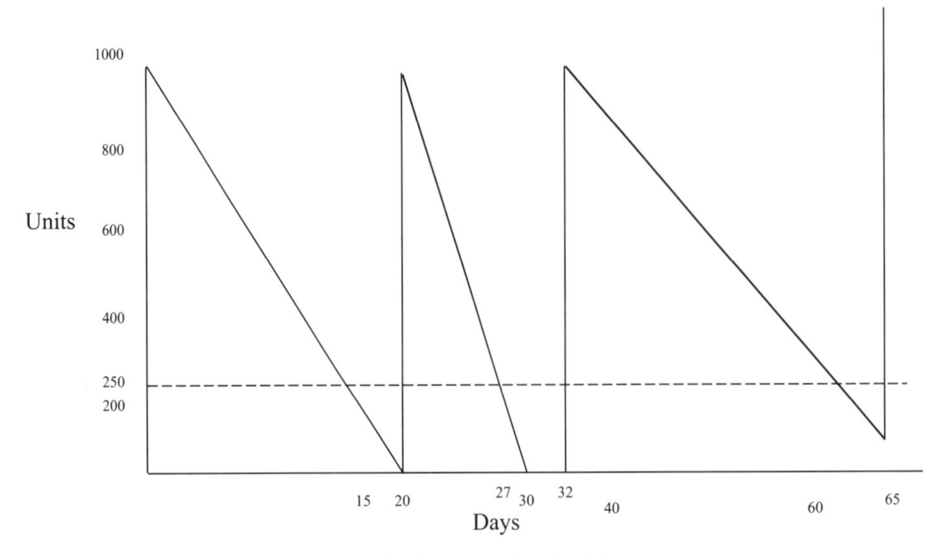

Figure 4-3 Fixed order point/fixed order quantity model

Fixed order interval model

The fixed order interval model attempts to reconcile inventory orders with forecasted sales over a specified time period. For example, figure 4-4 illustrates a 30–day order interval and assumes a five–day order cycle. Thus, on day 25, management must decide how much to reorder for days 31–60 based upon expected sales; on day 55, another order must be placed for days 61–90, and so on. This model forces management to base their ordering policies upon anticipated demand rather than EOQ alone. However, forecasts are rarely totally accurate, as figure 4-4 shows. For example, in period 2, demand exceeded forecasted levels, so a stock-out was experienced; in period 3, demand was below expectations, so additional inventory had to be stored.

Safety stock requirements

Both of these previous models illustrate the fact that even the best inventory management techniques still leave the organization somewhat vulnerable to stock-outs because both demand and lead time are inherently uncertain. (Remember that the EOQ model does not permit stock-outs.) In other words, demand and lead time will vary over a given period of time, so the question managers must answer is how much vulnerability they are willing to tolerate.

Safety stock is extra inventory that is intended to protect the organization against short-term variations in demand and lead time. Given a statistically valid sample of

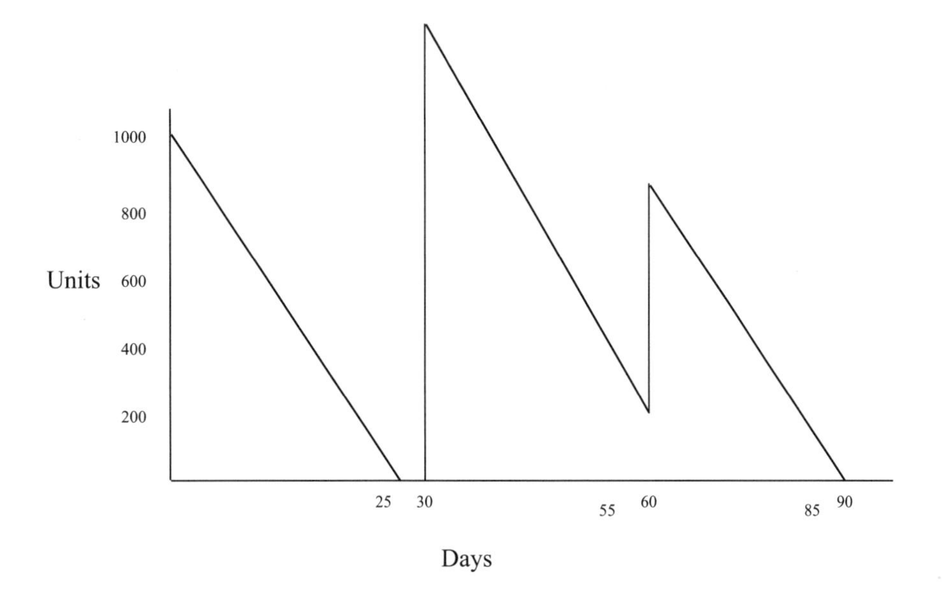

Assumptions: Order interval is 30 days; average order cycle is 5 days.

Figure 4-4 Fixed order interval model

recent sales volumes and replenishment cycles, safety stock requirements can be calculated using the following formula:

$$\sigma_{SS} = \sqrt{\bar{L}(\sigma_D)^2 + \bar{D}^2(\sigma_L)^2}$$

where: σ_{SS} = units of safety stock needed to meet demand 68% of the time (i.e. one standard deviation).
$\bar{L}$ = average lead time
σ_D = standard deviation of daily sales
$\bar{D}$ = average daily sales
σ_L = standard deviation of lead time.

For example, assume that the demand and lead-time history shown in table 4-2 has been compiled for one of the firm's markets.

From this data, the mean and standard deviation of demand can be determined as shown in table 4-3. Once the mean and standard deviation for both demand and lead time have been determined, it is a simple matter to substitute those figures back into the safety stock formula presented earlier as shown below:

$$\sigma_{SS} = \sqrt{\bar{L}(\sigma_D)^2 + \bar{D}^2(\sigma_L)^2} = \sqrt{8(222)^2 + (1200)^2(1.301)^2} =$$

$$\sqrt{8(49284) + (1440000)(1.693)} = \sqrt{394272 + 2437920} =$$

$$\sqrt{2832192} = 1682.917 \approx 1683 \text{ units}$$

Table 4-2 Sales history for market "A"

Day	*Cases sold*	*Day*	*Cases sold*
1	1,200	14	1,000
2	1,000	15	1,100
3	900	16	1,100
4	700	17	1,200
5	1,000	18	1,700
6	1,100	19	1,300
7	1,400	20	1,400
8	1,300	21	900
9	1,300	22	1,200
10	1,300	23	1,500
11	1,500	24	1,200
12	1,400	25	1,100
13	1,200		

Lead-time history for market "A"

Delivery number	*Days to arrive*	*Delivery number*	*Days to arrive*
1	6	8	8
2	7	9	9
3	9	10	6
4	8	11	7
5	10	12	8
6	9	13	10
7	8	14	7

Thus, in a situation where daily sales vary from 700 cases to 1,700 cases *and* the inventory replenishment cycle varies from 6 to 10 days, a safety stock of 1,683 cases will allow the firm to satisfy 68 percent of all demand. Two standard deviations' protection, or 3,366 units, would protect against 95 percent of all events. In setting safety stock levels, however, it is important to consider only those events that exceed the mean. As shown in figure 4-5, a safety stock level of 3,366 units actually affords protection against almost 98 percent of all possible occurrences. Given an approximately bell-shaped distribution of measurements, the mean, plus or minus one standard deviation, will contain approximately 68 percent of the measurements. This leaves 16 percent in each of the tails, which means that inventory sufficient to cover variations of one standard deviation in excess of the mean (as opposed to both above and below the mean) will actually provide an 84 percent customer service level.

Note that any safety stock calculation is based upon a given level of sales and a given lead-time history. If one or both of those changes, safety stock must be recomputed utilizing the current data.

Table 4-3 Calculating standard deviations

Sales

Daily sales (cases) (D)	*Frequency (f)*	*Deviation from mean (d)*	*Deviation squared (d^2)*	*(fd^2)*
700	1	–500	250,000	250,000
900	2	–300	90,000	18,0000
1,000	3	–200	40,000	120,000
1,100	4	–100	10,000	40,000
1,200	5	0	0	0
1,300	4	100	10,000	40,000
1,400	3	200	40,000	120,000
1,500	2	300	90,000	180,000
1,700	1	500	250,000	250,000
$\bar{D}$ = 1,200	$n = 25$			sum fd^2 = 1,180,000

The standard deviation for sales is then computed as follows:

$$\sigma_D = \sqrt{\frac{\Sigma\, fd^2}{n-1}} = \sqrt{\frac{1180000}{24}} = \sqrt{49167} = 221.74 \approx 222 \text{ cases}$$

Lead time

Lead time (Days)	*Frequency (f)*	*Deviation from mean (d)*	*Deviation squared (d^2)*	*(fd^2)*
6	2	–2	4	8
7	3	–1	1	3
8	4	0	0	0
9	3	1	1	3
10	2	2	4	8
$\bar{L} = 8$	$n = 14$			sum fd^2= 22

The standard deviation for lead time is computed as follows:

$$\sigma_L = \sqrt{\frac{\Sigma\, fd^2}{n-1}} = \sqrt{\frac{22}{13}} = \sqrt{1.692} = 1.301 \text{ days}$$

Table 4-4 Cost of holding safety stock

Service level	*Number of standard deviations*	*Safety stock Quantity (units)*[a]	*Average normal inventory*[b]	*Total average inventory (units)*	*Total Carrying Cost ($)*[c]
84.1	1.0	1,683	1,937	3,620	14,480
90.3	1.3	2,188	1,937	4,125	16,500
94.5	1.6	2,693	1,937	4,630	18,520
97.7	2.0	3,366	1,937	5,303	21,212
99.5	2.6	4,376	1,937	6,313	25,252
99.9	3.0	5,049	1,937	6,986	27,944

[a] From table 4-2.
[b] 1/2 EOQ
Assumes: average daily demand = 1,200 units
average yearly demand = 300,000 units
(1,200 × 250 days)
carrying cost = 20%
unit value = $20
ordering cost = $100
[c] $20 × .2 = $4/unit carrying cost × the number of units on hand

It is important for managers to understand that safety stock is not a panacea for other logistics problems. As shown in table 4-4, higher and higher levels of safety stock only slightly improve stock-out protection while significantly raising costs. If, for example, lead time varies owing to poor transportation support, it may make much more sense to work with the carrier to improve service (or find another hauler) rather than utilizing inventory to compensate.

Inventory Management: Signs of Trouble

- **Loss of customers.** To the extent that buyers have alternative sources for the items they demand, stock-out situations will not be tolerated for very long. Though customers may remain loyal for a while, they will eventually shift their business to the supplier that consistently has the goods demanded on hand.
- **Rising number of back-orders.** Back-orders imply that the customers must wait for their goods. As mentioned earlier, buyers, especially those in developed markets, don't want to wait. They may do it for a while, but they will find an alternative source when continually faced with having to back-order items. Thus, a growing number of back-orders could mean an increasing trend in stock-outs which will eventually result in lost sales.
- **Stable number of back-orders with a growing investment in inventory.** Clearly, if inventory is growing, back-orders should be falling. If that drop is not

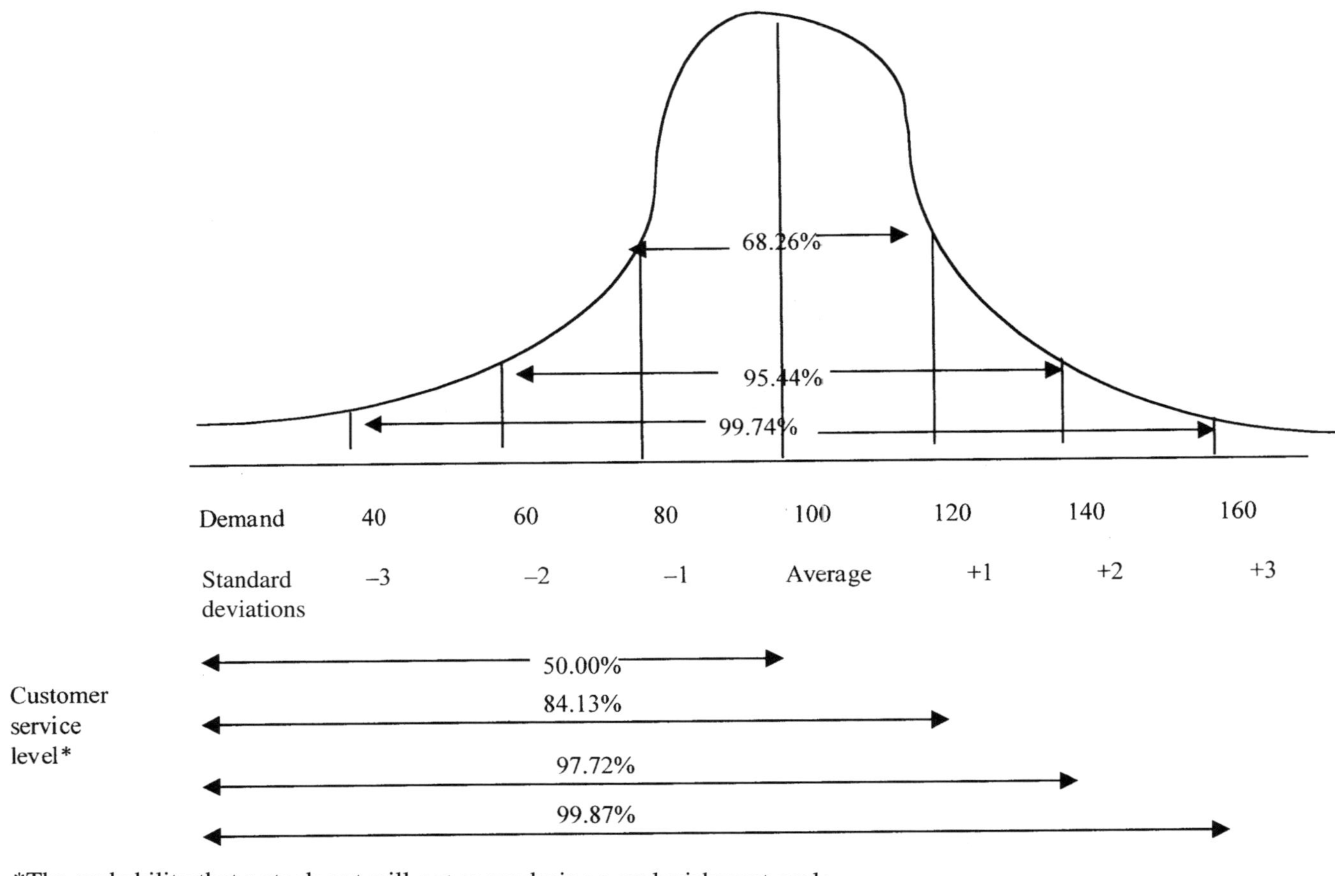

*The probability that a stock-out will *not* occur during a replenishment cycle.

Figure 4-5 A statistical presentation of safety stock

occurring, management may be holding too many of the wrong goods in inventory.

- **Periodic lack of storage space.** Getting goods early presents its own problems. There may not be room to store them and the organization will incur higher carrying costs sooner than anticipated. This situation can result from poor demand forecasting, variability elsewhere in the logistics system, or simply holding the wrong items (i.e. those with little demand) in inventory.
- **Deteriorating relationships with channel members.** If manufacturers cannot consistently provide products to their middlemen, those items will not be available when the customer wants to buy them and channel members directly serving the final consumer suffer lost sales. Repeated stock-outs or back-orders resulting from poor inventory policies could cause channel members to cancel more orders or find another supplier altogether.

Improving Inventory Management

- **Top management commitment.** As logistics profile 4-1 illustrates, key management support is essential if inventory is to be managed effectively. Because lower inventories have an impact on many different parts of the logistics system, senior leadership must ensure that all of those activities are working together to meet customer needs without the luxury of excess stock.
- **ABC analysis of all inventory items.** Management must first understand which goods in inventory are the most important in terms of their contribution to the objectives of the organization. Those few items that generate the most profits, for example, or are deemed mission-essential by the firm's most important customers would be designated "A" items and perhaps maintained at virtually 100 percent availability. The bulk of the goods in inventory would be denoted "B" items that might be supported at, for instance, 80 percent levels. Finally, there could be some low-demand items classified as "C" goods which are maintained at very low levels or possibly not stocked at all.
- **Improved performance of other logistics activities.** Managers should ensure that the rest of the logistics system is functioning efficiently. It may be that inventory policies have evolved as a way to obscure other problems that should be dealt with directly. By reviewing transportation, order processing, and warehousing functions, for example, management may find that order-cycle variability can be reduced by improving those activities that would lower the need for inventory.
- **Improved demand forecasting.** Demand forecasting is also a way of reducing variability, this time in terms of expected versus actual sales. Better forecasting techniques can be utilized to more accurately predict actual sales. Again, anything that eliminates variability allows the organization to shed inventory accordingly.
- **Inventory management software.** Software is currently available for virtually any type of inventory management situation and allows managers to track sales by item, costs, length of time in inventory, etc. Many of the more comprehensive packages are structured around some variation of material requirements

Logistics Profile 4-1
Top Management's Role in Inventory Control

One of the most powerful tools available for controlling inventory is upper management's commitment to reduce it. How do you explain it? The Nutrition and Chemical division of Syntex Agribusiness, Inc. has no complex computer-controlled inventory system, no complex material requirements planning software, no networking and no consultants. However, they have achieved remarkable inventory control including reducing their inventory by 45 percent over the last six years and lowering their raw materials inventory supply from 25 days, seven years ago, to an eight-day supply today.

Manufacturers of pharmaceutical chemicals, they are part of the Syntex Corporation, a worldwide health care products firm employing more than 10,000 people with sales of over $980 million. They began their quest to reduce inventory in a typical way by first assigning responsibility to their purchasing agents to evaluate vendors. Pharmaceutical companies occasionally use only one supplier for raw materials, so purchasing options are limited. But, in many cases, buyers are able to work with their vendors to improve delivery and dependability. Improving their flow of inventory goods from potential suppliers was one way the Nutrition and Chemical division reduced inventory levels.

Another way was through the establishment of rigorous minimum/maximum inventory levels for raw materials, packaging and finished goods inventory. The company established these limits after detailed analysis of sales for their products over a two-year period. Once minimum and maximum levels were established, they were followed by close review of actual inventory levels. Each month an operating committee composed of senior managers reviews inventory levels and takes corrective action when necessary. A report is then prepared by the finance department, which identifies products that are above the maximum or below the minimum. An asterisk is placed beside those items. Inventory that has existed longer than the maximum or is no longer in demand is either sold at bargain prices or written off. This dead inventory is the responsibility of the marketing department that must find a place to sell it. Upper management at the division recognizes that cooperation across departments is essential in order to prevent unilateral actions that could suboptimize the entire continuous improvement process. They believe it necessary to make sure everyone knows inventory control is a part of their job responsibility.

This company has had success at controlling their inventory without the computer-controlled systems one normally associates with inventory reduction. Their technique is simple. Top management is sincerely committed to controlling inventory expenses. They relentlessly emphasize the benefits and cost of inventory. Of course, it takes more than top management support to make improvements in this area. It also takes the cooperation of everyone who has inventory control responsibilities.

> Production and operations must be directly involved in reducing inventory, but others must also contribute if inventory is to be reduced. Personnel, finance and marketing meet to focus their attention on improving inventory control. Each department has something they can contribute.
>
> (**Source**: Denton, D. Keith. "Top management's role in inventory control," *Industrial Engineering*, August 1994, p. 26)

planning (MRP) or distribution requirements planning (DRP) depending on the nature of the inventory concerned. Briefly, MRP manages material and in-process inventory for production while DRP deals with finished product inventory. Together DRP and MRP provide precise control over material flow through the logistics system, from supplier to customer.[3] Both of these techniques will be explained in more detail below.

- **Postponement** involves modifying or customizing products after the main manufacturing process is complete. Final configuration of products can be delayed until the distribution cycle, or even performed after delivery. Computer products and related equipment lend themselves to this process, as is illustrated in logistics profile 4-2.

Materials Requirements Planning (MRP)

MRP deals specifically with supplying materials and component parts whose demand depends upon the demand for a specific end product. Essentially, MRP begins by determining how much of the final product customers desire, and when they need it. Then MRP breaks down the timing and need for components (all of which could have different lead times) based upon that scheduled end-product need. An MRP system consists of a set of logically related procedures, decision rules, and records designed both to translate a master production schedule into time-phased net inventory requirements and to delineate how those requirements will be satisfied. The program also replans net requirements and coverage as a result of changes in either the master production schedule, demand, inventory status, or product composition.[4] MRP minimizes inventory to the extent that the master production schedule accurately reflects what is needed to satisfy customer demand. If the production schedule does not match demand, the company will have too much of some items and too little of others. Because the master production schedule drives the need for parts, MRP is said to be a *pull* system. In other words, the production schedule "pulls" components through the system in order to meet manufacturing needs.

Logistics Profile 4-2
Reducing Inventory through Postponement

CalComp, a Lockheed company, utilizes postponement to remove inventory from their pipeline without forcing suppliers to take up the slack. CalComp ships printers in bulk to Rotterdam for European distribution. From that location, they can be customized for the country of destination to include manuals and marketing materials written in the local language and power cords compatible with each region's available electricity.

CalComp has found that postponement offers an improved match of marketing requirements and better competition against local suppliers. Furthermore, the product can be personalized either to the market or to a specific customer at their site. Finally, bulk shipping closer to the point of use results in lower transportation costs.

In the chemical industry in particular, this process can mean significant savings. Exel Logistics, a third-party service provider, receives bulk chemicals and repackages them for a particular customer. This value added service enables that customer to receive purchasing discounts for buying large quantities of raw material, and transportation savings by moving large amounts to the repackaging point. The smaller quantities of customized products are then sent on other countries. Regardless of the industry, using postponement as a strategy requires effort and cooperation. For example, shippers must share even more market and customer information with the carrier than they have in the past.

On the international scene, CalComp has subsidiaries in Europe that act as sales offices. They place purchase orders specifying exactly what the customer wants. For routine postponement products – the printers referred to earlier – coordination is controlled by the European subsidiary. For more complex orders, the goods may come from any of several European warehouses or from the US Information flows to CalComp's Southern California facility where employees determine where the goods will originate and how they will be moved. Indeed, one of the most difficult aspects of a postponement strategy is the coordination required to make it work.

(**Source**: Richardson, Helen L. "Cut inventory, postpone finishing touches," *Transportation & Distribution*, February 1994, p. 38)

Distribution Resource Planning (DRP)

DRP applies MRP principles and techniques to the flow and storage of finished products destined for the marketplace. Thus, where MRP sets a master production schedule and then breaks that down into gross and net requirements, DRP begins with customer demand and works backward toward establishing a realistic and economically justifiable systemwide plan for ordering the necessary finished products. Using the best available forecasts of finished product demand, DRP develops a time-phased plan for distributing product from plants and warehouses to points where it is available to customers. In practice, DRP allocates available inventory to meet marketplace demands; thus, it represents a *push* approach to demand satisfaction.[5]

Just-In-Time (JIT) Inventory Management

In the early 1970s, Toyota Motor Manufacturing developed a new production strategy that used little inventory, shortened cycle times, improved quality, and eliminated waste and costs in the supply chain. This just-in-time manufacturing philosophy requires manufacturers to work in concert with suppliers and transportation providers to get required items to the assembly line at the precise time they are needed for production. The concept was subsequently embraced by American and European automakers in response to the growing success of their Japanese competitors. The JIT concept then spread to other industries such as computers, and became firmly entrenched in manufacturing strategies around the world.[6]

JIT represents a move away from holding large quantities of inventory. According to JIT, to the extent that inventory is being used to compensate for other logistics difficulties, it should be eliminated and the real problems corrected. The difficulty is that inventory can be a very popular management tool: production executives like it because they can keep the line operating while storing the output; marketing managers want to have goods available to sell; and customers never want to face an empty shelf. Unfortunately, as costs have increased, so has the pressure to control them, so many firms have found that they can no longer afford the luxury of large on-hand inventories. Rather, small frequent shipments are timed to arrive on the shelf or in the bin exactly when needed by the customer.

Basic tenets of JIT

A successful JIT system is based upon the following key concepts:

- **Quality.** With JIT, the customer must receive high quality goods. One of the historical roles of inventory has been to protect the customer against defective items; if a bad product is received it can be discarded and a new one drawn from inventory. With a JIT system, however, poor quality means the production line stops or the external customer gets a defective item. There are no "extra" items to replace the poor ones.
- **Vendors as Partners.** Generally, firms using JIT rely on fewer vendors rather than more. Purchases are concentrated with a limited number of suppliers in order to give the buyer leverage with respect to quality and service. Purchasers

also include vendors in the planning process, sharing information regarding sales and production forecasts so that vendors then have a clear idea of what their customers need. At its Jeep plant in Detroit, Michigan, for example, Chrysler orders the seats for the individual Grand Cherokees being manufactured only after the bodies leave the paint shop and start down the production line. At that time, a message is sent electronically to a Johnson Controls factory – 30 minutes away – specifying the color and style of seats needed. The seats are assembled, loaded onto trucks and delivered within a few hours. The system, which helps Chrysler and Johnson Controls keep inventories at a minimum, requires and encourages close cooperation between the two companies. Chrysler, for instance, shares its production forecasts with Johnson Controls.[7] Such close collaboration allows Johnson Controls to meet Chrysler's needs while minimizing its own inventory levels. If Chrysler did not include its vendors in its production planning, firms like Johnson Controls would have to hold excess inventory to ensure they could meet unexpected changes in their customer's production. When that occurs, inventory is essentially shifted from one party (Chrysler) to another (Johnson Controls), while the overall goal should be to reduce inventory levels all together.

- **Vendor co-location with customer.** Ideally, suppliers should be located in close proximity to their customers. As the distance between vendors and buyers increases, so does the opportunity for system disruption and stock-outs. In order to minimize this risk, customers often demand that vendor facilities be co-located on the same site or at least in the same geographical area as their own.

Advantages of JIT

- **More inventory turns.** Because there is less on hand, the inventory that is maintained stays for a shorter period of time. Table 4-5 illustrates the difference between three inventory turns per year and ten in terms of average inventory on hand. It is worth mentioning, however, that inventory can be turned too fast. Theoretically, an organization utilizing 1,000 units per year could have 1,000 inventory turns if they received each item one at a time. The problem with an extremely high number of turns is that it can raise the probability of stocking out to an unacceptably high level while raising ordering costs as well.
- **Better quality.** As was mentioned earlier, high quality products must be received with a JIT system or else the entire benefit production process collapses. Customers concentrate their purchases with a small number of vendors in exchange for receiving high quality items and requisite service. The cost of failure on either count to the vendor thus becomes very high.
- **Less warehouse space needed.** When there is less inventory, fewer and/or smaller warehouses are required. Under BMW's JIT production strategy, only a minimum amount of inventory is held on the production line at its new US plant. In some cases, the time supply is a mere four hours. To ensure a reliable delivery system, the plant employs a pull strategy whereby part orders are automatically issued once the supply on the line falls below a critical level. Parts are replenished

Table 4-5 Number of inventory turns related to average inventory on hand

Yearly demand (D) (Units)	Number of inventory turns per year (T)	$\left(\frac{(D/T)}{2}\right)$ Average inventory on hand (units)	Carrying cost[a] ($)
10,000	4	1,250	12,500
10,000	10	500	5,000

[a] Assumes carrying costs of $10/unit

from a 14,000 square meter warehouse adjacent to the plant, which itself holds only three days' worth of inventory.[8]

Disadvantages of JIT

- **Risk of stock-outs.** When firms eliminate inventory, the risk of stocking out can rise. Managers attempt to minimize this occurrence by demanding very high levels of service from their vendors and logistics service providers. However, when co-location of customer and vendor is not feasible, for example, the resultant variability in the pipeline can lead to stock-outs despite management's best effort to prevent them.
- **Increased transportation costs.** Since JIT requires frequent shipments of small quantities, transportation costs almost always rise. In fact, those expenses can increase dramatically because motor carriage and air are the modes best suited to provide the necessary levels of service. As long as these costs are more than offset by the inventory savings, it is advantageous for the organization to permit them. However, it is possible to spend more on transport than is being saved with the JIT system, so management must ensure that movement expenses are closely monitored.
- **Increased purchasing costs.** As mentioned earlier, purchasing discounts are generally associated with buying large quantities at one time. Theoretically, JIT means foregoing those price-breaks in favor of obtaining smaller amounts more frequently. In actuality, there are ways to take advantage of volume discounts while still enjoying the benefits of JIT, which will be covered in a later chapter. Suffice it to say that, again, managers must make sure that purchasing costs are not rising more than inventory costs are falling.
- **Small channel members may suffer**. JIT is sometimes criticized as a system that allows strong organizations to unload their inventory on smaller firms in the channel. Theoretically, every company in the pipeline can utilize JIT; the reality, however, is that channel leaders may impose such stringent delivery criteria that vendors may feel compelled to hold inventory in order to satisfy them.
- **Environmental issues.** In a macro sense, JIT can lead to higher levels of traffic

congestion and air pollution because additional transportation is often required to maintain customer service levels in the absence of inventory. Ironically, road congestion can make sustaining a JIT system difficult in some parts of the world because vehicles simply cannot maintain reliable schedules.

JIT II/Vendor Managed Inventory (VMI)

JIT II takes the partnership idea one step farther by placing a vendor sales representative on the customer's factory floor. Also known as VMI, this approach to inventory management requires the vendor's employee to continuously and automatically replenish a trading partner's inventory. In its purest form, JIT II/VMI is automated – usually through electronic data interchange – and the partners agree at the outset on order quantities, order points, rules for replenishment, and inventory turns. The goal is to reduce redundancies and create efficiencies in the supply chain, thereby providing better service to the end user.[9] This agent can roam the plant, attend production status meetings, check on sales forecasts, and generally learn most of what there is to know about the customer's business. Based on that knowledge, the agents can then write a sales order for which the customer is billed. The representative decides what to order, when, and from whom. Therefore items may even be ordered from a competitor if it is better for the customer. JIT II can lead to even lower inventories, fewer purchasing people, and innovative solutions to supply problems. Critics say, however, that too much access to the customer's business is provided. Additionally, it can be difficult to terminate such a complicated relationship if either party's needs change.

However, VMI does help to make the administration of the delivery process more efficient. In a conventional buyer/vendor relationship, the vendor and the buyer perform many planning and administrative tasks. The vendor performs demand requirements planning while the buyer does essentially the same but calls it material requirements planning. Similarly, the buyer creates a purchase order and the vendor a sales order. With VMI it is possible to reduce administration. It is no longer necessary for the buyer to perform administrative purchasing tasks such as materials requirements planning and creating purchase orders.[10]

The reality of JIT

Some organizations have been unable to successfully adopt JIT. One reason for abandoning the apparent possible savings is that the cost of stocking out is simply too high. For example, some firms cannot risk shutting down the production line should a JIT system fail. Unfortunately, this risk of channel disruption increases when firms move to source materials and manufacture globally. Sanyo, for instance, has reduced inventory levels sharply in its major world markets since the late 1980s. However, when the Kobe earthquake struck Japan in 1995, Sanyo and many other Japanese companies found their distribution chains severely disrupted. The quake killed 5,500 people, devastated Kobe's port, wrecked major road and rail arteries, and badly damaged the local economy. In order to keep its factories around the world supplied with parts from Japan, Sanyo had to make emergency shipments by air and work closely with ocean carriers to find alternate ports. As a result, Sanyo executives are rethinking their policy on inventory to include the possibility of increasing on-hand stocks.[11]

Another factor may be that the distance between suppliers and customers is too great, a particular problem for firms serving worldwide markets. Co-location is not possible in all situations, especially when attempting to support global buyers from a domestic location. For example, Storage Technology Corporation, a US-based maker of storage devices for mainframe computers, keeps parts at seven of its European subsidiary offices so that they can reach any continental customer within four hours in an emergency. There is an inventory cost associated with their strategy, but management believes that level of performance is the only way to retain customer allegiance in the face of strong competition from IBM, Hitachi, and Digital Equipment Corporation. In Asia, Storage Technology prepositions key parts with company subsidiaries or national distributors.[12] The changing view of JIT in discussed is logistics profile 4-3.

Thus, the decision to abandon a JIT system, or simply to hold some inventory at all, really results from an appreciation for the logistics system as a whole. Some firms have realized that the costs of supporting customers without inventory are greater than the savings accrued with lower inventories alone. In other words, managers are comfortable with the idea of holding inventory because they know the system is optimized with that strategy.

Integrated Inventory Management: DRP, MRP, and JIT

DRP, MRP, and JIT can be utilized simultaneously to fully manage inventory throughout the logistics pipeline. As was mentioned earlier, DRP attempts to anticipate the need for finished goods as precisely as possible. Once that need is determined, the demand for the final product can be used as the starting point for the master production schedule that will be relied upon to manufacture those goods. MRP, in turn, relies upon the master production schedule to drive the need for component parts, raw materials, and other inputs. As MRP determines the need and time-phasing for those requirements, JIT can be then be incorporated into the management process to ensure that those needs are met without holding large amounts of inventory. Clearly, when used in concert, these three techniques allow managers to closely manage inventory at all phases of production and distribution.

Inventory Management in a Global Market

Managing inventory becomes much more complex when dealing with the distances and different customer service requirements of internationally dispersed markets. The technical side of inventory management remains the same; that is, the management techniques discussed in this chapter are equally applicable in a domestic or global setting. The challenge is that different approaches are required for

Logistics Profile 4-3
JUST-IN-TIME MIGHT (OR MIGHT NOT) DELIVER THE GOODS

Harley-Davidson Motor Company, Inc. is a big believer in the "just-in-time" theory of getting parts to the assembly line, especially for movements within the United States. But the phenomenally successful maker of motorcycles hasn't managed to make JIT work as well for international shipments. Some of Harley-Davidson's parts arrive at the plant within four hours of being put into production. Yet for material arriving from Asia, Europe, and Australia, the company is likely to have two to three weeks' worth of inventory close at hand. When it comes to international moves, product is out of the company's control for longer periods of time, says Dave Alamshah, director of transportation and general manager of Milwaukee, Wisconsin, USA-based Harley-Davidson. The company has made some important strides toward a true JIT environment. But with a stalled production line costing at least $56,000 an hour, it cannot afford to gamble on having the right part from a supplier located 10,000 miles away.

The fragility of international supply lines was emphasized in 1997, when problems with the merger of the Union Pacific and Southern Pacific railroads in the United States precipitated a backlog of import containers at the ports of Los Angeles and Long Beach that took almost a year to sort out. Some foreign suppliers attempt to minimize their exposure to disruptions by producing at least a portion of their goods domestically. But that raises overhead, and makes the supplier vulnerable to low-cost producers who source entirely outside the country. However, as Robert A. Novack, associate professor of business logistics at Pennsylvania State University, points out, "Once you start increasing distances, the complexity makes it really difficult to accomplish JIT."

(**Source**: Adapted from Bowman, Robert J. "All that it's cracked up to be?" *World Trade*, July 1998, pp. 75–6)

different markets. The long retail channels and multiple middlemen still common in Japan, for example, can necessitate the use of higher inventory levels than in Northern Europe and the United States where channels seem to be getting shorter. Supporting customers in developing nations can necessitate the placement of inventory in that country, or staging it somewhere between the point of manufacture and the point of consumption. So the reality is that an organization may have multiple inventory strategies intended to support different customers around the world. The common threads tying these policies together must be an awareness of customer needs and an appreciation for the costs of utilizing inventory to cover up other logistics problems.

Chapter Summary

Inventory is one area of logistics that has received a great deal of management attention over the past decade. Executives now realize that holding excessive stocks is simply too expensive. Therefore, a great deal of effort has been expended to eliminate unnecessary inventory without compromising customer service. However, there are numerous situations where inventory simply must be held, particularly when meeting the needs of global customers. Management's goal should be to hold only what is necessary to satisfy customer requirements and manage it effectively. This chapter discussed several approaches to inventory management, including the EOQ, fixed order point/fixed order quantity, and fixed order interval models; highlighted some potential problem areas; presented techniques for improving inventory management; and discussed the use of inventory reduction programs such as DRP, MRP, and JIT systems.

Study Questions

1. How does holding excess inventory impact the profitability of the organization?
2. How does normal inventory differ from speculative stock?
3. Briefly discuss the different costs an organization incurs when maintaining inventory.
4. How does the fixed order point/fixed order quantity model differ from the fixed order interval model?
5. How much safety stock should a company hold?
6. When should safety stock levels be recalculated?
7. Referring to logistics profile 4-1, what can senior managers do to influence a firm's inventory management policies?
8. What does logistics profile 4-3 illustrate about the realities of inventory management in general and JIT in particular?
9. How does VMI differ from JIT? How are the two philosophies similar?
10. Why have some organizations abandoned JIT?
11. What can managers do to improve their inventory management strategies?
12. Distinguish between MRP and DRP systems. How do they relate to JIT?

Notes

1. Goldberg, Aaron. *PCWeek*, March 13, 1995, p. A14.
2. Coyle, John J., Bardi, Edward J., and Langley, C. John, Jr. *The Management of Business Logistics*, 6th edn (St. Paul, MN: West Publishing Company, 1996), p. 238.
3. Schary, Philip B. *Logistics Decisions Text & Cases* (Hinsdale, IL: Dryden Press, 1984), p. 193.
4. Coyle et al., ibid, p. 98.
5. Ibid, p. 130.

6. Minahan, Tim. "JIT moves up the supply chain," *Purchasing*, September 1998, p. 46.
7. Fischer, David. "Sitting on excess supplies," *U.S. News and World Report*, Sept. 18, 1995, p. 88.
8. Auguston, Karen. "Building BMWs at a world-class JIT plant," *Modern Materials Handling*, July 1995, p. 45.
9. Fraza, Victoria. "Streamlining the channel," *Industrial Distribution*, September 1998, p. 73.
10. Holmstrom, Jan. "Implementing vendor-managed inventory the efficient way: a case study of partnership in the supply chain," *Production and Inventory Management Journal*, 3rd quarter, 1998, p. 1.
11. Magnier, Mark. "Post-quake Japan's Sanyo is rethinking its logistics," *Journal of Commerce*, April 27, 1995, p. 1A.
12. Miles, Gregory L. "Have spares, will travel," *International Business*, December 1994, p. 26.

chapter 5

Global Transportation Systems

Introduction 84
The Five Modes of Transportation 85
Deregulation and Privatization of Transportation 91
Government's Role in Transportation 94
Intermodal Transportation 96
Chapter Summary 101
Study Questions 101

Introduction

Transportation is a critical part of any global logistics effort because of the long distances that can separate a firm from its customers. As depicted in figure 5-1, decisions with respect to transportation must be made within the context of the entire logistics system. That is, transportation (both inbound and outbound), like every other logistics activity, must "fit" within that system. Historically, national governments have exercised tight economic control over transport organizations, either through direct company ownership or via laws intended to regulate the way those businesses were run. This governmental involvement in the business of transportation is gradually waning as nations move to privatize state-owned businesses and/or deregulate privately held firms. For the logistics manager, the competitive nature of goods movement today means greater opportunities for obtaining better service and/or lower costs from transport providers. This chapter will examine the various modes of transportation and how they can be utilized to support an international logistics effort.

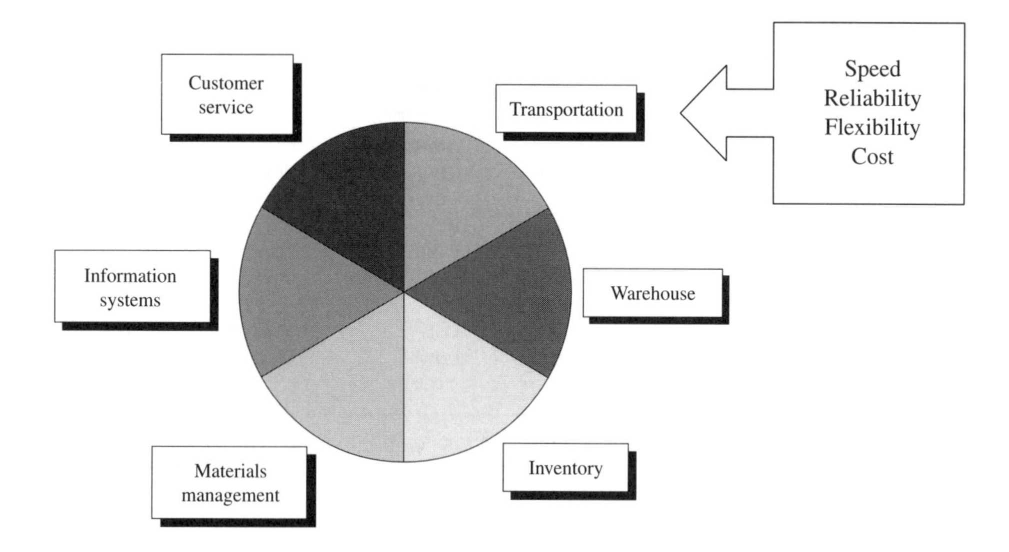

Figure 5-1 Transportation in the logistics system

The Five Modes of Transportation

The five primary modes of transportation are rail, road, pipeline, water, and air. Each has different economic and service characteristics that are summarized in table 5-1. Clearly, the logistics manager must consider a number of trade-offs when selecting a mode of transportation: cost versus speed; packaging expense versus risk of damage; flexibility versus dependability. These are all very complex issues. For example, if hazardous material is to be moved by air, it may require more and different kinds of packaging than would be required by a motor carrier. Furthermore, most movements involve the services of more than one mode of transport. For instance, an air shipment may move to and from the airport via truck, while a containerized shipment of televisions leaving Japan for a retailer in Switzerland could move by rail, truck, and ship. The challenge facing the logistics manager is that the trade-offs among the various transport modes must be evaluated within the larger framework of the logistics system as a whole. Each mode is addressed in more detail below.

Rail

Railroads offer the logistics manager cost-effective, energy-efficient transport of large quantities of goods over long distances. Though often associated with the movement of low-value/high-volume cargo like coal, railroads also move a large number of

Table 5-1 Modal service characteristics

	Rail	*Road*	*Water*	*Air*	*Pipeline*
Door	Sometimes	Yes	Sometimes	No	Sometimes
Price	Low	High	Very low	Very high	Very low
Speed	Slow	Fast	Very slow	Very fast	Slow
Reliability	Medium	Medium	Low	Very high	Very high
Packaging needs	High	Medium	High	Low	Nil
Risk of loss and damage	High	Medium	Medium	Low	Very low
Flexibility	Low	High	Low	Very low	Very low
Environmental impact	Low[a]	High[b]	Low[c]	Medium[d]	Low[e]

[a] Minimal air and noise pollution, low energy consumption per ton-kilometer traveled
[b] Air and noise pollution, traffic congestion, high energy consumption per-ton kilometer traveled.
[c] Minimal air and noise pollution, low energy consumption per ton-kilometer traveled.
[d] Air and noise pollution, very high energy consumption per ton-kilometer traveled.
[e] Pipeline rupture could result in catastrophic environmental damage.

containers in intermodal movements that will be discussed in more detail later. Rail movements are virtually unconstrained with respect to size, weight, or volume, but fixed tracks can limit their ability to provide complete customer support. For example, if both the shipper and receiver possess railroad sidings, then door-to-door service can be provided. However, if no sidings are available, the movement of goods must be completed by some other mode. Similarly, on-time delivery and frequency of service may not be as responsive as with other modes simply because multiple handlings are more common in rail movements.[1]

Because a large percentage of a railroad's total costs are, in the short run, fixed (that is, they are incurred whether or not a single train is operated), rail companies are, by definition, monopolistic. However, railroads must still cope with competition, both from other modes and, in some cases, other railroads. This tendency, though, means that most nations only have one railroad, which is often state owned. Government ownership can present problems for the global logistics executive trying to ship goods by rail across several countries. At a border crossing, goods wait while the transfer is made from one national railroad to another. In Europe, for example, the French and Spanish national railroads use different gauge (a measure of the distance between the rails), so goods must be physically moved from one railroad's equipment to another.[2] Also, voltage differences can preclude the movement of electric trains from one country to another. Similarly, safety standards for driving and signaling are not uniform. Every country has its own rules.[3]

Contrast the rail network in Europe with that found in China. The problem in China is that there are not enough railroads to support that country's economic growth. By the end of 1995, railways in operation covered 37,000 miles (59,543 km) in a country about the same size as the United States which has a rail network four times that size. Furthermore, the average speed of freight trains is 20 miles (32 km)

Logistics Profile 5-1
CHINA'S RAIL PLAN

China's Ministry of Railways (MoR) is embarking on a massive five-year 300/450 billion Yuan rail upgrade programme. In addition to the construction of 5,000 miles of new line, the project envisages double-tracking 1,700 miles of existing track. Approximately 2,600 miles of track will be electrified. In particular, new lines will be built to serve the fast-growing industrial and population centres of south western China, with a direct connection between Nanning (Guangxi province) and Kunming (Yunnan) a priority. Meanwhile, double tracking is being evaluated on lines linking Buiyang (Guizhou province) and Kunming and between Liupanshui (Guizhou) and Zhuzhou (central Hunan). Elsewhere, the MoR plans to commence preparatory work on a new high speed rail link between Shanghai and Beijing during the current five-year plan. The latest capital investment programme follows a period of rapid expansion of the country's rail system, in which more than 7,000 miles of new track have been laid since 1990. However, train scheduling difficulties and terminal congestion remain real handicaps to China's economic progress and it is something the MoR is keen to put right.

(**Source**: *Containerisation International*, March 1996, p. 39)

an hour because passenger movement has priority.[4] Despite its inadequacies, rail is the major overland hauler of cargo in China.[5] See logistics profile 5-1 for a discussion of China's plan to improve its rail system in response to the growing demand for rail transport that can meet the needs of manufacturers, importers, and exporters doing business in that country.

Road transport

Road haulage offers more flexibility and versatility to the shipper than virtually any other form of transportation. This mode tends to be used for higher-value/lower-volume cargo than that moved by rail and can offer essentially door-to-door service from seller to buyer. However, the global logistics manager will find that trucking can vary dramatically from country to country.

Western Europe, for example, has a free-market trucking industry in which price is aggressively utilized as a competitive weapon. In addition, highway systems (outside the old Eastern Bloc) are some of the best in the world. Indeed, the single-market initiative of the European Union is dissolving internal boundaries so that cross-country trucking resembles interstate transport in the United States. In fact, road freight increased by 150 percent between 1970 and 1995, while railroads saw their

Logistics Profile 5-2
A Smoother Ride on the Road to Russia

It is not often that a commercial lawyer and banker decides to run a trucking company. Even less likely is that the individual is American and the trucking company is in Russia. Gregory Glassgen, a commercial lawyer and banker from Chicago, is director and co-owner of Kareltrans Oy, a trucking company established in the Russian Republic of Karelia, located just north of St Petersburg bordering Finland to the east. Besides being the first truly private international trucking company based in that country, Kareltrans was one of the first corporations registered in northwestern Russia.

The company was founded in 1992 and now operates a fleet of 167 Swedish-built trucks and 272 chassis-and-tent trailers. About 20 of the trucks are equipped with generators that power reefer containers. Kareltrans' drivers are Russian nationals, and the fleet is registered in Russia. The company has a main office in Helsinki, Finland, and satellite offices in Moscow and St Petersburg. Kareltrans operates road freight transport services through the Gateway Finland Corridor. This is the overland route from the Baltic seaports of southern Finland to Moscow and other destinations in Russia. In 1996 the trucking company hauled 5,179 containers across the Finland/Russia border.

A wide range of products is being shipped, says Glassgen, but chief among them are name-brand consumer electronics. An increasing number of reefer units are making the journey. About 90 percent of the cargo is destined for Moscow, with the balance split between St Petersburg and other Russian destinations. Trading conditions have improved generally in the region, Glassgen claims. A newly built customs station at Torfianovka, the principal crossing point between Finland and Russia, has been allocated 200 additional agents. "While crime is a problem in Russian transport, it in no way presents the major difficulty that many Westerners perceive it to," Glassgen insists. Fraud remains an issue, he admits, and carriers have to exercise caution when delivering loads in Russia. A typical scam is for criminals to pose as customs agents and stamp the documents presented by drivers. "Six months later we get a notice from the customs authorities that the cargo has never been cleared," he explains, but the goods have disappeared without any duty being paid. Kareltrans has an elaborate system of security checks to avoid such problems. It has developed a database of 2,500 to 3,000 consignees, and keeps track of these individuals even when the names of corporations change. New consignees have to show up at the company's offices with documentation, including passports, which are photocopied.

A persistent problem is delays caused by unwieldy bureaucracies and inefficient cargo-handling operations. Conflicts between consignees and Russian customs officials, as well as the country's inadequate warehousing facilities, are common causes of delays. Kareltrans is looking to expand its services in St Petersburg and Riga, but is being held back because such a move would not make economic sense given that it can take two days or so to load and unload cargo in these places.

Considerable training and education was needed to enable the company's 400-odd drivers to transport loads internationally. Now, some of the more experienced drivers can even speak Finnish. Also, Kareltrans employs port agents who speak both Russian and Finnish to interface between port operators and the Russian truck drivers. It is the sort of service that the company has had to develop in order to survive during Russia's chaotic introduction to capitalism. "We really looked at the break-up of the Soviet Union as analogous to the dissolution of the largest corporate structure in the world," Glassgen says. Now that the dissolution is well advanced, it is more difficult to establish a company such as Kareltrans, because the regulatory regime is tighter and Moscow has become one of the most expensive cities in Europe. "If we were starting today, I have to say that I don't think we would succeed," observes Glassgen.

(**Source**: Adapted from Cottrill, Ken. "A smoother ride on the road to Russia," *Global Transport*, 1998, pp. 34–5)

traffic fall by nearly 25 percent.[6] Unfortunately, European roads are becoming increasingly saturated and there is no room to add lanes, so delays are inevitable.[7] In contrast, the global logistics manager will find dramatically different problems in China, a nation with few main highways. Though roads are paved, trucks must share them with buses, bicyclists, and horse-drawn carts. Trucking remains largely state-run, although private companies are beginning to emerge.[8] Russia presents an equally challenging environment for private operators, as is illustrated in logistics profile 5-2.

Pipelines

Pipelines are primarily used to move petroleum, natural gas, and chemicals. For suitable commodities, pipelines are the most efficient mode of transport. They offer a closed system with little risk of loss or damage to the products moved, and extremely low costs because minimal labor is involved in their operation. However, they typically serve a limited geographic area over routes that are virtually fixed. In addition, they only offer one-way service, although product can move 24 hours per day, seven days per week. Though naturally limited in their application, pipelines have been utilized to move coal and are being evaluated for other types of freight as well. Capsule and pneumatic pipelines offer the potential to diversify the types of products carried, but much additional research must be done before that capability can be fully realized.

Air

Air transport is often viewed as a premium, emergency-type service that is used when all else fails. The most expensive of all the modes, airfreight offers the logistics manager fast, on-time service, but at a relatively high price. However, for firms supporting global markets, air may in fact be the most cost-effective mode of transport when inventory and customer service issues are considered.

Air transportation is best suited to moving relatively small high-value/low-volume items long distances, although things as diverse as livestock and automobiles routinely move by air as well. Like trucking, the air transport industry is made up of many small companies dominated by a few large airlines. Many of the world's air carriers are government owned or controlled to some degree, a situation that is slowly changing as governments are moving to put their airlines into private hands.

Water carriage

Commercial water transport occurs on inland waterways (i.e. rivers, lakes, and canals) and oceans. Though slower than other modes, this form of movement is also relatively inexpensive. Traffic moving on inland waterways tends to be low value/high volume: coal, building materials, agricultural products, etc. However, in countries like Germany, with its vast network of navigable rivers, the variety of freight moved by water carriers may encompass bulk products, containers, and motor vehicles.

In general, domestic water carriers compete with railroads for freight, relying on their price advantage to offset the slow transit time. Ocean-going ships, on the other hand, carry all types of cargo, although increasingly that freight moves in containers that are stacked on top of each other aboard the vessel. Air transport competes with ocean shipping, but the high cost and limited carrying capacity make air movement prohibitive for many items. In fact, rail may also compete via land-bridge services such as that provided by the Trans Siberian railway which moves containers from the Far East across Russia to Western Europe that would otherwise go by ship.

The international maritime industry has evolved around carrier-supported organizations known as conferences. The conference system was created to link shippers and vessel operators together. Shippers agree to use only conference vessels, while the conferences agree to charge conference shippers lower rates than would be charged shippers not agreeing to use conference vessels exclusively. The conference also commits to providing regular sailings on a scheduled basis, despite the fact that during certain seasons, the total amount of cargo offered might be small.[9]

There are several hundred conferences linking the various ports of the world. Examples include Australia to Japan, or Israel to the US–North Atlantic regions. Conference lines attempt to eliminate competition among themselves as much as possible. They do this by "pooling" or sharing. An example would be for three lines to agree to sail from A to B, with the first line's vessel to leave now; line 2's ship to leave a week from now; line 3's, two weeks from now; and then repeat the sequence with line 1's vessel leaving again in three weeks. All companies would agree to charge the same rates for cargo, pay similar commissions to forwarders, etc. Nonetheless, because of vagaries in the flow of cargo, it may be that in the course of a year the traffic carried was not divided into equal thirds carried by each line. At the end of the year, the conference would examine the books of all three members and redistribute the revenues or profits according to some previously agreed upon formula.[10] The perceptive student will have realized that firms participating in a conference are basically colluding, that is, getting together to set prices and establish sailing frequencies. Since collusion is contrary to antitrust law in many countries, carriers can only participate by virtue of specific exemptions to such statutes as may apply in their home nation.

However, as their customers have become more demanding, in terms of both price and service, shippers are finding greater value in dealing with non-conference carriers willing to provide better service at lower rates than their conference counterparts. This, along with a decision by the United States to deregulate its maritime industry, is putting pressure on the conferences to permit their members to exercise some pricing freedom in order to fend off these aggressive competitors. The net result is that the conference system is weakening because those carriers simply cannot compete in an era of free trade and open markets. No longer can these conferences set non-negotiable prices for entire ocean lanes and essentially ignore the request of all but powerful corporate customers for discounts and better service. Recently, the US government, the European Union and several multinationals forced 15 carriers to disband their two-year-old trans-Atlantic steamship group, with its fixed prices and cargo volumes, and replace with a more casual alliance.[11] In other words, shipping conferences are under attack not only from government regulators, but low-priced competitors such as Evergreen of Taiwan.

Deregulation and Privatization of Transportation

Deregulation

Historically, many nations have treated transportation like a public utility similar to telephone service and electric power providers. In recent years, some countries have realized that government control and/or regulation of transportation can be inefficient and costly to customers. In general, these policies tend to raise prices and constrain service in the interest of other national priorities (employment, transport access, industry protection). Deregulation refers to a government's decision to permit market forces to replace strict controls and operating procedures. With respect to transportation, deregulation means that, within certain limits, free-market forces are permitted to govern how transport resources are allocated, the prices carriers charge, and the services that they offer. Some countries approach this on a mode-by-mode basis, while others have deregulated all forms of transportation. The end result, though, is a more efficient transport system that can be much more closely integrated with other activities in the logistics system.

However, it is important to understand that, in most cases, nations deregulate *domestic* transportation only; with the possible exception of trucking, transport between countries is still highly regulated in most cases. The exception to this practice occurs when countries join together to form an economic alliance, a situation that will be discussed below. International air services, for example, are based upon a bilateral agreement approach first promulgated in 1944. In other words, air service is negotiated between two countries; if a nation desires air links with many other countries, a separate agreement is required for each. It is worth mentioning that governments, not airlines, negotiate air transport agreements. Because air travel is usually not the only issue being discussed, diplomatic pressures may warrant giving way on air service rights in exchange for concessions on other issues. The US has long advocated open-skies agreements that guarantee each country's airlines free competitive access to the other's international air travel markets, and has recently concluded such agreements with Germany, Canada, the Netherlands, and Singapore. Countries like Australia, on the other hand, are less inclined to embrace open skies, preferring instead to pursue a shift away from the bilateral system for negotiating air rights to a multinational regime under the General Agreement on Trade in Services.[12]

As nations join other countries in forming multinational economic organizations, the issue of international transport deregulation becomes more complex. The European Union (EU), for instance, has already embarked on transport deregulation among its member states, focusing on road haulage, air and, to a lesser extent, rail. The deregulation of international road transport was agreed to by the Council of Ministers in 1987 and fully implemented in 1993. This change means that international haulers are free to adjust their fleet capacity in line with market demands and set prices accordingly.[13] Similarly, since 1997 all domestic air markets have been open to any EU-based airline that chooses to service them. Furthermore, the EU proposed that in 1998 it would start negotiating air services agreements with non-EU countries on behalf of its member nations. However, that dramatic change has yet to occur.

The crucial issue is cabotage, or the transport of domestic passengers or freight between points within a country by a foreign carrier. (An example of cabotage would be British Airways carrying revenue passengers from Frankfurt to Munich.) With respect to road haulage, as of July 1, 1998, any trucker registered in the European Union can move cargo anywhere in any EU member state. Theoretically, the result will be an open-road policy stretching over at least 15 countries and possibly more by the time the practice goes into full effect.[14] However, the European Commission has no authority to change the rules of domestic freight operation in any member nation, except if they are in breach of the Treaty of Rome. Therefore, individual countries can regulate or deregulate domestic road transport as they see fit.

Cabotage in the airline industry is still not common. However, that could change dramatically when the EU starts negotiating air agreements, effectively institutionalizing multinational (as opposed to bi-lateral) air rights. Service within the Union (between member nations) could be treated as cabotage for non-EU airlines, which would significantly weaken the bargaining position of the US because American carriers can now fly between many of these countries by virtue of rights obtained in the past. To retain those privileges, the US government could find itself forced to extend some sort of cabotage rights to foreign carriers permitting them to move passengers and/or freight between cities in America. Should the EU be successful at multilateral negotiations, similar economic unions developing in South America and the Pacific would undoubtedly follow suit.

Privatization

At the same time, some nations are selling their government-controlled airlines, ship companies, and pipelines to private interests, a move known as privatization. British Airways and Lufthansa, for example, are both privately held now. Alternatively, some governments choose to retain partial shares of national transport resources, with private interests holding the remainder. For example, the Dutch government owns 38 percent of KLM Royal Dutch Airlines, while the Mexican government controls 34 percent of its combination carrier Mexicana/Aeromexico. The transition from public to private ownership can be a traumatic one. The EU, for instance, has conditioned approval of airline subsidies on a "one-time, last-time" basis if governments vow to end such payments.[15] However, provisions for repeat requests for public support under "special circumstances" have allowed several European carriers to continue to receive subsidies even though they are by most standards of business bankrupt. Air France, for example, has received almost 18 billion francs from the French government in recent years. The fact is that many of these carriers are such high-cost, inefficient companies (sometimes as a result of their own government's imposed requirements) that they simply cannot compete in a deregulated market. As a result, they are not attractive to private investors which forces their respective governments to support them until such time as they can adapt to free-market conditions.

Efforts are also being undertaken to privatize rail operations in some areas. Several years ago, British Rail sold its national domestic freight operations to a US railroad, the Wisconsin Central, which formed a company called the English, Welsh and Scottish Railways, to develop rail freight business.[16] The EU, on the other hand, is advocating a much more radical program that calls for the division of state-owned railways into two separate entities, one dealing with infrastructure issues, the other with operational matters. The objective would be to permit any company to operate trains over any track in the EU, with the ultimate goal being the establishment of trans-European rail "freight freeways" to provide completely open access for freight services to shippers. So far the United Kingdom, Germany, Sweden, and France have taken steps to separate their railways' infrastructure and operations, while Spain, Greece, and most other countries have not.[17]

Future directions

Deregulation and privatization represent fundamental changes in the way governments view their transportation industries. However, several cautionary comments must be made. First, while deregulation is becoming more common globally, it is in fact occurring only within individual countries or alliances. Furthermore, nations attending the International Civil Aviation Organization Conference in December of 1994 only cautiously endorsed airline deregulation, clearly signaling their reluctance to commit to unfettered competition such as characterizes the air transport industry in the US. Second, multilateral transportation accords appear inevitable as countries increasingly band together to form economic unions. One result of this move away from bi-lateral negotiations will be a weakening of cabotage. The Australian government is already proposing to do away with cabotage laws affecting ocean shipping, which will allow international competition on the Australian coastline.[18] Third, deregulation does not necessarily mean abandoning all regulation and leaving resource allocation entirely to market forces. Rather, it may mean a change in the type and emphasis of regulation. While price and service controls are relaxed, additional regulation may be needed to ensure competitive forces operate satisfactorily and that customer and community interests are adequately safeguarded. Finally, privatization moves notwithstanding, governments can continue to exert control of their transport resources. Railroads, airlines, and ship lines provide a great deal of employment, are sources of national pride because of their visibility, and, in the case of air and ocean carriers, afford a nation the means to project its image globally. Furthermore, there may be military transport needs that must be met as well. Thus, a government may be tempted to step in with some sort of aid for a firm that is 100 percent private simply to keep the company operating for any or all of these reasons. In other words, deregulation and privatization both imply that a company can fail, a reality that may be politically untenable.

Government's Role in Transportation

National governments can influence their transportation systems in a number of ways. Some nations choose to rely on government-owned carriers while others depend on the private sector to meet transport needs. In the latter situation, however, governments still indirectly affect the provision of transportation by enforcing environmental laws and ensuring carrier compliance with safety requirements. Several types of governmental influences will now be explored.

Direct control and regulation of transport firms

Because of the importance of transportation to a nation's economy, some carriers are government owned or controlled. This significance goes beyond the movement of goods and people in that transport firms such as railroads may be very large employers, especially in smaller countries. Furthermore, airlines and ocean shipping provide a means of projecting an international image of progress and technical expertise that some nations find valuable. In other words, a transportation industry may fulfill multiple national objectives, some of which have little to do with goods movement.

Some countries have transport companies that are solely private with no government ownership at all. Generally in this situation the government often imposes regulations that are intended to control how the business is operated. For instance, management decisions dealing with pricing, serving new markets, route abandonment, service frequency, or customer service may require government approval before they can be implemented. This type of government intervention reflects the belief that transportation companies, if left alone, gravitate to one of two extremes: monopoly in the case of railroads and pipelines owing to their high fixed costs; destructive competition in the case of air, water, and road transport resulting from the variable-cost nature of these firms. In the former instance, companies can utilize their monopolistic power to discriminate against customers with regard to price and service; in the latter, the industries themselves can suffer from instability. Since both of these conditions are socially unacceptable (that is, either can potentially disadvantage customers, raise prices, and/or impede the flow of goods), governmental power is utilized to ameliorate those negative forces as much as possible.

When a government controls or regulates the provision of transport services, shippers generally suffer because competitive forces are reduced or non-existent. Prices are established or approved by an agency of the government which means that all carriers (assuming there is more than one) charge identical rates. Furthermore, movement alternatives can be limited since law may restrict the number of companies allowed to compete over a given route. In other words, shippers must use the carrier serving the desired route. Taken together, the inflexible pricing and reduced choice that results from government intervention in the free-market process often leads to higher costs and unsatisfactory service. For logistics managers, government involvement can mean that the benefits of transportation may not be fully realized since there are some aspects of it that cannot be manipulated.

Provision of transport infrastructure

Roads, bridges, airports, ports, and sometimes rail lines are generally built and maintained by governments at some level. Though examples of privately funded resources do exist (some roads, for example), it is in most cases simply cost prohibitive for non-governmental interests to build them. Furthermore, transport-related services such as air traffic control, weather forecasting, dredging, and navigation aids are generally provided by the government as well. In many cases, these assets are viewed as public goods available to all. Companies and individuals pay to use them, either indirectly via taxes on such things as fuel and tires, or directly via tolls.

Promulgating and enforcing environmental and safety laws

Governments enact and enforce laws relating to air, noise, and water pollution, for example, that have a direct impact on transportation. For example, many of the world's airports observe quiet hours at night, when aircraft movements are limited or forbidden altogether. Furthermore, some nations in Europe simply ban heavy truck movements on weekends and key holidays. It is probably safe to say that being environmentally responsible often leads to higher costs which are ultimately passed on to the final customer. For example, more fuel-efficient, cleaner vehicle engines cost more to buy. But the reality is that transportation harms the environment in a number of ways. Because consumers ultimately benefit from a strong transportation system, they should be willing to support efforts to minimize the negative environmental consequences that can result.

Safety is another area where governments exert a great deal of influence. Laws related to operator qualifications and hours of duty, maximum vehicle weight and length, and air traffic control procedures are just a few examples of areas in which logistics needs must be subjugated to the greater needs of society at large. In fact, safety and environmental issues become particularly sensitive in countries or states that serve as transit corridors for third-party nations (Germany and Austria in Europe or California and Texas in the US, for example). People in these areas may feel as though they are bearing a disproportionate share of the costs associated with free trade (congestion, pollution, accidents, etc.) and demand compensation through some form of taxation or direct user fees (i.e. highway tolls).

Intermodal Transportation

Intermodal transportation refers to the movement of a shipment from origin to destination utilizing two or more different modes of transport. At its heart, however, the term refers to how goods are moved between those modes. Certainly the transfer could be done by hand. That is, each individual box is unloaded from, for example, a ship, and reloaded piece by piece onto a railroad car. This manual technique is time consuming, and increases the chance of theft, loss, and damage. Today the term intermodal transportation denotes a systematic transfer of goods from one mode to another in a way that minimizes handling and total transit time. (This definition implies that freight being shifted from mode to mode in some non-systematic fashion is really not being handled intermodally; rather it is moving multi-modally via two or more different forms of transportation.) This exchange may mean placing a trailer onto a rail flatcar for onward movement, but general intermodal systems are structured around the use of containers.

A container is a metal box that resembles a trailer without wheels. It generally measures 8 feet by 8.5 feet by 20 or 40 feet, although larger containers are becoming more common. In fact the 20-foot container has become the standard unit of measure, with ship capacities, for example, quoted in terms of "TEUs" or twenty-foot equivalent units. (One 40-foot container equates to two TEUs; six 20-foot and five 40–foot containers equal 16 TEUs, and so on.) The container can be mounted onto a frame with wheels facilitating truck movement; cranes lift the container off the frame so that the boxes can then be stacked aboard ships or rail cars. The advantage of containers from the shipper's point of view is that freight can be loaded and the box sealed before it leaves the warehouse. From this point on, only the container is handled; the goods themselves are not touched again until the customer receives the container and opens it.

Containers, however, have a restricted application in inland transport. Because containers on ships must be stacked, they must be sturdy in construction. In turn, this makes them heavy – too heavy for road transport since they unduly restrict payloads. Consequently, in Europe the preferred technologies for combined transport restricted to inland movements are unaccompanied road–rail transport (trailers, semitrailers, and demountable bodies known as 'swap bodies' which resemble containers but cannot be stacked) and accompanied road–rail transport (complete vehicles comprising tractor units and semi-trailers together with drivers.[19]

The whole intent of intermodal transport is to allow the shipper to take advantage of the best characteristics of all modes: the convenience of motor freight, the long-distance movement efficiency of rail, and the capacity of ocean shipping. A brief examination of intermodal developments by mode follows.

Rail

Because rail is capable of moving such large amounts of freight at one time, it is generally considered to be the most efficient way to movc largc amounts of cargo long distances. Intermodal movements permit shippers to enjoy the flexibility of motor freight for pick-up and delivery together with the efficiencies of rail for the long-haul portion of the movement. Thus, intermodal railroad transport primarily involves the movement of containers, trucks, and truck trailers that have been loaded onto rail wagons. Two evolving services are **RoadRailer** and **double-stack** container trains. **RoadRailer** refers to truck trailers that are pulled by locomotives. Each trailer is equipped with one rail axle at the rear. The trailer is brought to the rail terminal by truck, placed over the tracks, and the rail wheels lowered to engage the rails, elevating the trailer slightly as well. One locomotive then pulls an entire train of truck trailers. The system offers tremendous operating, fuel, and environmental efficiencies by displacing an equivalent number of road power units with one locomotive. However, normal rail cars cannot be intermingled with RoadRailers because the trailers cannot take the stress. Additionally, there is a weight penalty for the highway portion of the movement because of the bulky rail axle. **Double-stack** trains are becoming common in the US market and utilize specially designed deep-welled flatcars to carry containers stacked two-high. This technique not only doubles the number of containers on a train but also halves the crew-labor cost per container.[20] However, because the stack is still higher than a normal rail car, tunnels, bridges, and other overhead obstacles must often be reworked to accommodate the taller trains. In addition, owing to prevailing cargo flows in a given market, it may be difficult to fill containers with freight for the return journey, necessitating the transfer of empty boxes back to some origin point. Recent economic problems in Asia, for example, have led to a decreased demand for US goods there. Thus, containers that arrive in the United States full of goods from Asia must be returned there empty, at a cost of approximately $300 per container.[21]

Ocean transport

Ocean vessels offer some of the most diverse forms of intermodal transportation. As discussed earlier, trans-oceanic cargo today is primarily containerized and moves via ships specifically designed to carry containers. The growing need for capacity has led companies to order larger and larger **container ships**. Sea-Land Services ordered four 4,062 TEU ships in 1996,[22] while Maersk Line has launched the *Regina Maersk*, first of 12 ships each capable of carrying 6,000 TEUs[23]. A closer look at this amazing ship is provided in Logistics Profile 5-3. Container ships offer tremendous economies over break-bulk vessels where cargo must be loaded/unloaded piece by piece. On average, container ships can be "turned" (unloaded and loaded) in a day or less, depending on port capacity, number of cranes, and crane operator skill. However, as container ships become larger they draw more water. Many ports around the world are ill prepared to cope with these deeper-draft vessels, especially since dredging is often politically unpopular. For example, access between Hamburg's terminals and the North Sea is via the River Elbe. The biggest ships have only a narrow half-hour window of opportunity twice a day when they can ride a tidal wave in and out of the port. Turnaround time can't be any less than 22 hours since ships have to come in at high tide and leave at high tide. By 1997 Hamburg hoped to expand that twice-a-day window to three hours through a special dredging project.[24]

Roll-on, roll-off (RORO) ships allow vehicles to be driven directly from the dock onto the ship, facilitating the movement of freight that cannot be containerized for some reason. LASH vessels are designed to carry barges. (A lighter is another term for a barge, so LASH is an acronym meaning lighter aboard ship.) Cargo, often in the form of a small number of containers, is loaded onto a barge that is then moved to the rear of the LASH ship where it is raised via an elevator system onto the larger vessel. At the debarkation port, the barge is offloaded and moved to its final destination where the cargo is removed. LASH services are useful in reaching water ports that may not be able to handle large ships or are inland from major ocean terminals.

Finally, bulk transports and tankers are increasingly being linked to specialized rail and port services to expedite the movement of petroleum, minerals, and grain.

Air

Almost all airfreight is intermodal in that it is picked up by truck, loaded onto an airplane, then delivered by truck to its destination. Virtually all airfreight moves in containers, although they are quite a bit different from those previously discussed. Air carrier containers are made out of fiberglass or aluminum and are shaped to conform to the contour of the aircraft. Furthermore, they are much smaller than standard containers and are not really intended for use via any mode other than for short distances because of their light construction. There has, in the past, been interest in transporting standard 20-foot containers by air, which would provide true intermodal capability between truck and air. As was noted earlier, the difficulty is

Logistics Profile 5-3
Maersk's Box Queen of the Seas

Maersk Line's newest container ship was launched in mid-January 1996. Named by Queen Ingrid of Denmark, *Regina Maersk* is the largest box carrier in the world, with a loading capacity for 6,000 TEU. Easily surpassing the 4,960 TEU rating of Orient Overseas Container Line's (OOCL) *California*-class vessels, the new ship is also top of the reefer league with electrical sockets for 700 (1,400 TEU) containers. According to Maersk, this capacity is equivalent to a massive 1.62 million cubic feet (ft^3) of refrigerated cargo space and easily exceeds (by more than 20 percent) the capacity of the largest conventional refrigerated ship afloat, *Dole Costa Rica* (1.34 million ft^3).

The huge ship is enormous in every respect, with a length of 318.2 m (almost half a mile), beam of 42.8 m and draft of 14 m. Featuring the world's largest diesel engine – a Mitsui-built Man B&W 12 cylinder 74,640 base horsepower unit – it is capable of generating sufficient power for a sustainable service speed of 25 knots, although in normal circumstances the vessel will be operated in the 22 to 23 knot speed range.

Built by the shipping line's associate company, Odense Staalskibsvaerft, the vessel features stabilizer fins, which help minimize rolling in rough seas, thereby maintaining service speed and lessening the risk of container/cargo damage. It is also equipped with stern and bow thrusters for additional maneuvrability and a fully integrated computer system. The latter allows Maersk to run the ship with an unmanned engine room and to undertake the opening and closing of valves and pumps for the ballast tanks from a single computer console.

Meanwhile, cargo-handling operations on the ship have been enhanced by the fitting of longitudinal lashing bridges which facilitate the faster and safer lashing/unlashing of containers stacked on the weatherdeck. They also relieve some weight pressure on the hatch coverings. In normal operations, the ship is capable of loading up to five tiers of boxes on the five bays immediately forward and four holds aft of the superstructure, 17 across. In the holds the double-hull structure can accommodate stows 14 wide.

The ship is also designed to sail with a single person on the bridge. However, Maersk will not implement such a procedure until a sufficient number of countries with the International Maritime Organization have approved and made recommendations on the safety of operating such a system. Obviously, with such an array of equipment and new computer technology on board, Maersk's new ships require just 13 personnel, plus a specialized reefer electrician and a second engineer, 15 in all.

Regina Maersk, which is the first in a 12–ship series, finally commenced its maiden voyage in February. The remaining 11 vessels will follow at three-monthly intervals, with the last scheduled for delivery in late 1998. Nine units are earmarked for the core Europe/Asia, but deployment of the last three ships has not been fixed.

Although Maersk refused to comment on the cost of its latest newbuild programme, industry estimates suggest that it represents a total capital investment of about US$1 billion, excluding new containers. More than 80,000 TEU will be purchased to support the new ships. These boxes will be sourced from the Container Industri factory in Tinglev in eastern Denmark.

(**Source**: "Big, blue & beautiful," *Containerisation International*, March 1996, p. 74)

that the empty container itself weighs almost 2,300 kilograms (5,000 pounds), so there is simply too much dead weight to make such a move economical.

Motor transport

Trucks provide the linkages that tie an intermodal transport system together. Trucks pick up loaded containers and deliver them to, for example, the seaport for onward movement by ship; they deliver containers to customers after the vessel has arrived and been unloaded. Trucks also shuttle containers back and forth between ocean carriers and railroads. In other words, trucks do what they do best: provide flexible, timely, and versatile relatively short-haul services supporting those modes best suited to provide long-distance transportation.

Infrastructure issues

The ability for shippers to take advantage of intermodal transport is directly dependent on the transportation infrastructure available in each market. Many developing nations, for example, lack the sophisticated port facilities needed to handle container ships. Railroads and highway systems may not be capable of supporting the surface movement of containers. In some parts of Asia, for example, 45–foot-long containers cannot be used because the road network is unable to handle boxes that long. As discussed earlier, railroad rights-of-way can require significant and costly reworking to make them suitable for double-stack container trains. In short, circumstances can conspire to render intermodal transportation infeasible in some markets.

Concluding comments

For logistics managers supporting global markets, intermodal transportation offers significant advantages over single mode alternatives. First, intermodal movement cuts down on theft, loss, and transport costs in general by eliminating virtually all handling of individual goods. Second, the entire transportation process can be expedited for the same reason, thus shortening the customer's order-cycle time. For example, in early

1995, the first container train to carry international cargo directly from China's interior to Hong Kong started operation for Orient Overseas Container Line (OOCL). The train covers the 1,122 kilometers (697 miles) between Zhengzhou and Kowloon in less than 72 hours; by truck the transit would take seven days.[25] Finally, better customer service can be provided because the goods arrive faster and damage-free. But there may be destinations that lack the resources to support some or all types of intermodal movement. Managers must then arrange the various parts of the journey on a mode by mode, country by country basis, risking higher costs and poorer service.

Chapter Summary

Transportation is one component of the logistics mix that is undergoing a great deal of change. In general, many nations are putting their various modes on a competitive footing, freeing those companies from the burdens of government ownership/operation and regulation. This policy change presents logistics managers with tremendous opportunities to obtain better movement services and lower prices than ever before. However, governments still continue to exert influence over their transport resources, some more than others. Intermodal transportation is a reflection of the changing nature of transport in general, signifying as it does the logistics manager's ability to combine the advantages of two or more modes of transport into one seamless shipment that reaches the customer faster and with less damage than a mode-by-mode routing could provide. Although still not possible in some markets, intermodal transport is clearly the choice of knowledgeable logistics managers wherever it can be utilized.

Study Questions

1. What issues should a logistics managers consider in trying to select a mode of transportation?
2. How can a government directly influence a carrier's operation?
3. How can a government indirectly influence a carrier's operation?
4. Briefly describe the concept of deregulation as it applies to transportation.
5. Briefly describe the concept of cabotage. Why is it such a sensitive subject to transport firms?
6. Does privatization lead to competitiveness in transportation? Defend your answer.
7. Differentiate between multimodal and intermodal transportation movements. How are they the same? How are they different from each other?
8. What national goals might a government rely on their transportation system to meet?
9. Refer to logistics profile 5-3. What benefits does a ship like the *Regina Maersk* offer to shippers? To the Maersk Company? What are the risks associated with operating such a large vessel?

Notes

1. Coyle, John J., Bardi, Edward J., and Cavinato, Joseph L. *Transportation*, 3rd edn (St. Paul, MN: West Publishing Company, 1990), p. 96.
2. Canna, Elizabeth. "VSA Rail shuttle," *American Shipper*, January 1995, p. 52.
3. Ibid.
4. Bangsberg, D.T. "Breakthroughs needed in train service, speed, Chinese official says," *The Journal of Commerce*, March 5, 1996, p. 4B.
5. Canna, Elizabeth. "China's intermodal boom-to-be," *American Shipper*, January 1996, p. 65.
6. Gray, Duncan. "Freeways are the only way," *Global Transport*, 1998, p. 62.
7. Strah, Thomas M. "Trucking," *Trade and Culture*, May–June 1995, p. 25.
8. Ibid, p. 26.
9. Wood, Donald F. and Johnson, James C. *Contemporary Transportation*, 2nd edn (Tulsa, OK: PennWell Publishing Company, 1983), p. 404.
10. Ibid, p. 405.
11. Miles, Gregory L. "Cheaper Sailing," *International Business*, February 1995, p. 29.
12. Jarrett, Ian. "Into a new dawn," *Asian Business*, August 1998, p. 51.
13. Cooper, James, Browne, Michael, and Peters, Melvyn. *European Logistics*, 2nd edn (Oxford: Blackwell Publishers, 1994), p. 152.
14. Canna, Elizabeth. "EU road cabotage: hazardous driving," *American Shipper*, October 1995, p. 94.
15. *The Wall Street Journal*, November 17, 1994, p. A4.
16. Banham, Russ. "Getting on track," *International Business*, March 1997, p. 18.
17. Ibid, pp. 15–16.
18. "Australia proposes shipping reform," *American Shipper*, June 1996, p. 20.
19. Cooper et al., ibid, p. 284.
20. "Moving the mostest the fastest," *International Business*, November 1995, p. 30.
21. Grant, Lorrie. "Asia crisis launching empty ships", *USA Today*, October 12, 1998, p. 6B.
22. Damas, Philip. "Maersk launches first 6,000–TEU ship," *American Shipper*, March 1996, p. 39.
23. Ibid, p. 41.
24. "Riding the wave," *American Shipper*, January 1996, p. 69.
25. "Zhengzhou container train," *American Shipper*, January 1995, p. 8–B.

chapter 6

Transportation Management Issues

Introduction	103
Developing Win/Win Shipper/Carrier Relationships	103
Transport Pricing	105
Pricing in Practice	109
Price Negotiation: The Carrier's Perspective	110
Price Negotiation: The Shipper's Perspective	110
Private Transportation	111
Other Issues Affecting Transportation Cost and Service	111
Chapter Summary	121
Study Questions	121

Introduction

There are many variables that must be considered by logistics managers as they decide which mode and/or carrier to utilize. This chapter will first examine shipper/ carrier relationships in general, highlighting issues of importance to each party. Because price is such a critical variable to both shippers and carriers, transport pricing will then be covered in some detail. Finally, the complex nature of global transport will be explored via a discussion of several issues that ultimately affect both the cost and quality of the transportation services purchased.

Developing Win/Win Shipper/Carrier Relationships

Carriers and shippers are increasingly aware that establishing a mutually beneficial relationship means both sides are better off. However, each side has issues that must be faced in order to maximize the benefits attained in any partnership.

Carriers must know their costs in order to establish an effective pricing program that will provide price stability for the shipper, volume stability for the carrier, and be easy for everyone to understand. Furthermore, carriers can improve their internal operations by computerizing all routing and equipment scheduling activities. Automating these functions leads to more efficient vehicle utilization, better customer service, and provides the capability to assess the impact of new customers, route changes, or contingencies on the total system. Carriers also need to become more customer oriented, seeking ways beyond strictly transportation to add value for their customers. Many firms are branching out into providing comprehensive logistics services such as warehousing, inventory management, and traffic management to their customers. Finally, carriers need to work at improving their productivity as a way of keeping costs down: getting more output for the same input, generating a given level of output with fewer inputs, or raising output while lowering input. The easiest way to enhance productivity in transportation is to operate bigger vehicles: trucks, airplanes, ships, etc. However, equipment in general is becoming less expensive to operate as engines become more fuel efficient, lighter construction materials are used to save weight, and computers take over many of the tasks previously done by people.

Shippers are faced with different problems. They are interested in lowering their costs while receiving better service, seemingly mutually exclusive objectives. To that end, shippers must become more sophisticated in selecting both the right mode and the right carrier to meet their transportation needs. Consistency of service (specified in terms of delivery time, damage rate, helpfulness, or some other criteria) should be the single most important criterion for evaluating transport alternatives; that is, customers must be able to depend on a shipment's arriving on time and in working order. If it does not, carrier personnel should be responsive to customer concerns and work to answer customer queries as quickly as possible. Price will be another way of evaluating alternative forms of transportation, but it should not be the only criterion. In addition, shippers should become comfortable with the idea of contracting with a carrier to guarantee a specific amount of freight in exchange for a lower rate. Not only does the shipper gain a great deal of control over transportation, but a better price as well. Finally, shippers who are operating their own vehicles may want to reexamine the use of a for-hire carrier. As free-market transportation industries become more common, it may not make continued sense to maintain an in-house transport function when a for-hire carrier can provide better service and/or lower costs.

Clearly, any transportation decision strategy must encompass several things. First, shippers should expect to pay for service; second, carriers must be willing and able to provide it while covering their costs; finally, cooperation between the two is essential to the mutual success of any successful partnership because both parties must benefit from the relationship. If one partner prospers at the expense of the other, there is little incentive to the disadvantaged firm to remain in the alliance. Figure 6-1 illustrates how Volvo's view of various transportation factors has changed over the years. Until approximately 1985, the company's main interest was in securing the lowest price possible. Today, management select carriers based on issues such as reliability (now the primary concern) and frequency/regularity of service. Pricing is still important, but within the context of obtaining requisite levels of service.

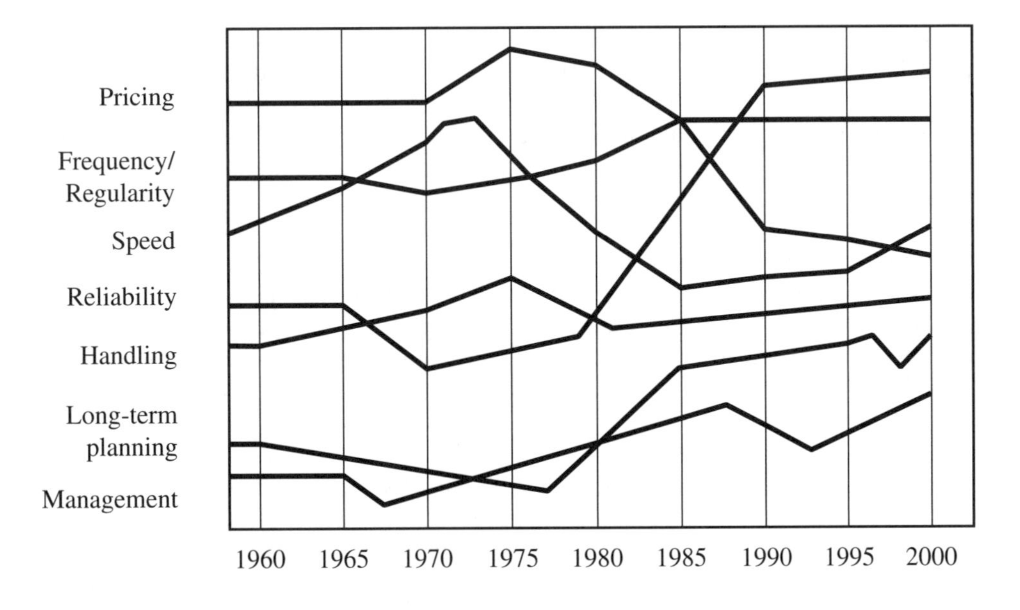

Figure 6-1 Important transportation factors for Volvo
Source: Canna, Elizabeth. "Taking JIT to new limits," *American Shipper*, February 1995, p. 54

Transport Pricing

Pricing in transportation is a function of transport market structure, shipper demand, and carrier costs. These three factors interact differently depending on the commodity being moved and the points between which it is being transported. Therefore every pricing decision is effectively unique. Following is a brief description of basic market structure models found in transportation.

Market structure models[1]

PURE COMPETITION Pure competition exists when there are a large number of buyers and sellers all of whom are so small that no one can influence prices or supply. There is unrestricted entry into the industry and the product or service being sold is homogeneous. The demand curve facing the individual firm is vertical (i.e. one of perfect elasticity), which means the producer can sell all output at the one market price, but none above that price. Although pure competition is not a predominant market structure, it is frequently used as a standard to judge optimal allocation of resources. In transportation, the road transport sector often approximates pure competition in many countries.

MONOPOLY In this situation, there is only one seller for a product or service for which there is no close substitute or competitor. The single seller is able to set the price for the service offered and can adjust the price to its advantage, given the demand curve. To remain in this situation, the single seller must be able to restrict entry. The single seller maximizes profits by equating marginal cost and marginal revenue and may make excess profit. Railroads and, in some countries, airlines would fall into this category.

OLIGOPOLY Oligopoly may be defined as competition among a "few" large sellers of a relatively homogeneous product that has enough cross-elasticity of demand (substitutability) so that each seller must, in pricing, take into account competitors' reactions. In other words, it is characterized by mutual interdependence among the various sellers. Airlines in free-market nations and ocean transportation typify this form of market structure.

MONOPOLISTIC COMPETITION In this type of market structure, there are many small sellers, but there is some differentiation of products or services. The number of sellers is great enough and the largest seller small enough that no one controls a significant portion of the market. No recognized interdependence of the related sellers' prices or price policies is usually present. Therefore, any seller may lower price to increase sales volume without necessarily eliciting a retaliatory reaction from competitors. Motor transport in the US and Great Britain falls into this classification.

Relevant market area

A general statement classifying the market structure of the entire transportation industry cannot be made because each particular movement is different. Within any mode there exists a variety of different services, involving the transportation of many different commodities between a myriad of different points, over alternate routes, and under various conditions of service. Therefore, the market structure in transportation must describe the situation at any one point, and even then the situation will differ between commodities. Thus, determining a price in transportation means describing the situation between two points for one commodity. In other words, the relevant market area for establishing prices is one commodity moving between two points.

For example, a particular railroad that provides the only rail service between points A and B (that is, the company effectively holds a rail monopoly) may find that the movement of ordinary steel approximates monopolistic competition. This condition exists because, while only one rail carrier may exist, there is likely to be a large number of other carriers, especially road haulers, that provide essentially the same service.

However, for the movement of a very large, sophisticated generator, the railroad may face an oligopolistic market on the move between A and B, because none of the motor carriers may be able to move such a large piece of equipment. Thus, the only competition may be another railroad and/or water carriers. In many countries, railroads operate in a monopolistic position because there is only one providing service. Finally, there may even be a product where the situation approaches pure competition, given the availability of alternative modes of transport. Thus, the relevant market for transportation consists of one commodity moving between two points and, perhaps, even in one direction and for particular shipment sizes (e.g. carload).

Shipper demand

Another determinant of price is the shipper's desire for the service. In other words, what is transportation in a given instance worth to the shipper, and how much are they willing to pay to obtain it? In some situations, a shipper would be willing to pay a high price. For example, a perishable commodity being moved to a market where demand is high and transportation options are limited would dictate that the buyer would be willing to pay whatever price the carrier is asking as long as it did not exceed the revenue potential resulting from selling the goods. Alternatively, a general commodity with less profit potential moving to a market served by many alternative forms of transportation might lead a shipper to seek out the lowest cost transport option among those available. In other words, the elasticities of demand for transportation are different depending on the commodities being shipped and the points between which they are being moved.

Value-of-service pricing means charging what the buyer is willing to pay. This approach represents a form of price discrimination whereby a seller sets two or more different market prices for two or more separate groups of buyers of essentially the same good or service. Though often thought of as being illegal, price discrimination is, in fact, quite common. Theater tickets are priced differently depending on seat location and timing; hotels have off-season rates; and restaurants may offer specially priced meals at different times during the day. For value-of-service pricing to work, the seller must be able to segment buyers into groups according to their different elasticities of demand. Furthermore, the seller must be able to prevent people from buying in the low-priced segment and then reselling to those in the high-priced group. In transportation, shippers are segmented according to commodities transported and points of movement. Thus, the rate paid is based on what is being shipped and where it is being moved. This means that transporting 1,000 kg of computer paper 500 km from point A to point B may not cost the same as shipping 1,000 kg of that same paper 500 km from point C to point D. Different levels of demand for the paper, together with disparate transportation markets, lead to alternative prices for the same quantity of product moving the same distance, but between different points.

The air transport companies have become very successful at value-of-service pricing, offering a price for virtually every customer need. If, for example, a shipper is willing to allow UPS to deliver the product up to two or three days later, the price may be relatively low. If the shipper wants the freight delivered tomorrow, the price will be higher. In fact, one of the newest services UPS offers in the US market is same day delivery utilizing space on scheduled passenger flights. Needless to say, the customer pays a significantly higher price for such responsiveness.

Carrier costs[2]

Simply put, the total costs of providing transport services are comprised of a fixed and a variable component. Fixed costs are constant and do not change with the volume of business. Items such as property taxes, building maintenance, management salaries, interest on debt, etc. would fall into this category. Variable costs, on the other hand, are closely related to the volume of business. The more a firm operates, the higher these costs; if all of the vehicles are parked, these obligations are not incurred at all. Fuel, tires, and engine maintenance expenses are all examples of variable costs. Railroads and pipelines have a high proportion of fixed costs, while air, motor, and water carriers tend to have a higher percentage of variable costs. As the latter produce more output (i.e. transportation), the proportion of fixed costs on each unit of freight, and thus average total cost, will be lower. So volume is a very important determinant of cost and efficiency. Furthermore, pricing the service to attract traffic is a critical factor in determining profitability, particularly where there is competition from alternate modes of transportation.

Another important cost concept is marginal cost, which is the change in total cost resulting from a one-unit change in output. Often referred to as incremental cost in the transportation industry, it can also be defined as the change in total variable cost resulting from a one-unit change in output. In other words, a change in output changes total variable cost and total cost by exactly the same amounts.

Cost-of-service pricing is difficult to implement because cost(s) relevant to the pricing issue must first be determined. As shown in figure 6-2, if the firm desired to maximize its profits, it would produce quantity O-A and charge price O-R. The firm would be making excess profits in the economic sense because the price is above average cost and the firm is not producing at a point for optimal allocation of resources. Based upon what may appear to be undesirable features, we might decide to impose regulation upon this firm. Now, if the "regulators" want to set a single price that would cover the firm's cost of production and at the same time sell all the output, then the price should be O-S and the output O-B. In this instance, we would be basing the price upon average cost. There would not be any excess profit in the economic sense, and society would be receiving more output at a lower price.

It appears that the average-cost approach is more socially desirable than the unregulated, profit-maximizing approach. What about pricing based on marginal cost? If price is set at marginal cost equal to demand, there is a higher price (O-T) and less output (O-C) than the average-cost approach yields. The advocates of an absolute marginal-cost approach argue that the output between O-C and O-B is such that the marginal cost of producing these additional units of transport is greater than what buyers are willing to pay for the extra units supplied because the marginal-cost curve is above the demand curve over this range of output.

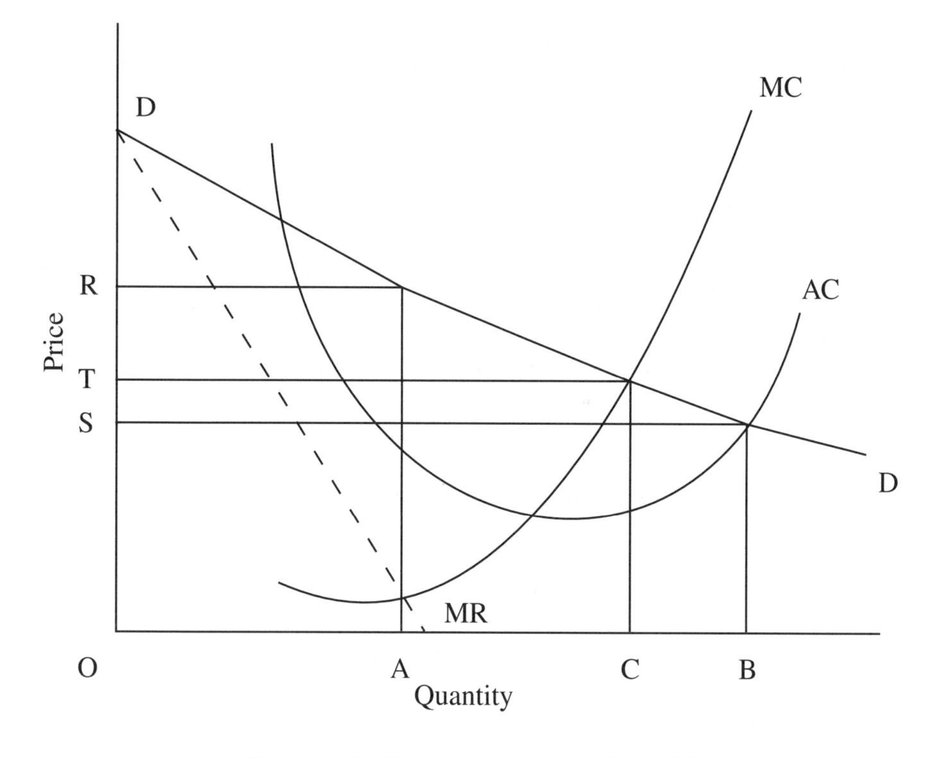

Figure 6-2 Transportation cost relationships

Pricing in Practice

In truth, both value-of-service and cost-of-service issues must be considered in determining price: the former sets the upper limit, the latter the minimum, with the actual price falling somewhere in between. In the real world, transportation prices may be established in a number of different ways. In some countries characterized by government ownership of transport resources, the rates may simply be set by decree. In situations where transportation is privately held but regulated, rates may be developed by carrier groups subject to government monitoring for fairness. These rates are then published for use by all shippers and carriers. Generally, some attempt is made to factor in value-of-service/cost-of-service considerations but, like those rates mandated by a government, the shipper has little control over what they pay. Increasingly, however, as transportation in general becomes more competitive, shippers and carriers are negotiating prices rather than relying on some preestablished published rate. Generally this practice involves the shipper guaranteeing the carrier a certain amount of freight (annually, for example) in exchange for an attractive rate. The challenges facing both parties in a negotiation are explored in more detail below.

Price Negotiation: The Carrier's Perspective

Carriers, of course, want to obtain the highest rate they can from a shipper. In order to be successful in a negotiation, carriers must be very knowledgeable about their costs. They must understand how those costs behave at different levels of output so that they can commit to a long-term contract secure in the knowledge that it will be profitable. Pricing to maximize the contribution margin keeps management focused on profitability rather than cash flow. Contribution margin represents the amount remaining after variable costs are subtracted from total revenues and is used to cover fixed costs and profit. Managers who look only at increasing total revenue may find their contribution margin drops as revenue increases because a rate was accepted that did not generate enough additional freight to offset the added costs.

Carrier managers must also be as knowledgeable as possible about their customers' needs. To be successful, they must gain some understanding of what the service is worth to the buyer so that an appropriate price can be determined based on the buyer's elasticity of demand. However, carrier executives must beware of the temptation to accept work at a price that only covers marginal cost. Clearly, a firm cannot survive for long utilizing this approach. There are related safety issues arising from this pricing strategy that will be covered in a later section.

Finally, carriers must know when to refuse to handle unprofitable traffic. If a given contribution margin is zero or, worse, negative, managers may be better off to seek other freight unless a higher rate can be negotiated. Again, it is incumbent on management to know what their costs are so that they can turn down cargo that is simply uneconomical to move. Naturally, no carrier wants to turn away business, but in some cases the carrier is much better off to do so. Only a thorough understanding of their firm's cost structure will give management the confidence to make this sort of difficult decision. There may be instances where goods may be moved at break-even (i.e. contribution margin equals zero), or possibly at a loss (i.e. contribution margin less than zero). In the former case, a load may be found for a vehicle that would otherwise return to its home-base empty; in the latter instance, maybe a valued customer is demanding some unusual service. But managers must know the true impact of these decisions, rather than mistakenly believing these kinds of services are profitable.

Price Negotiation: The Shipper's Perspective

Shippers, on the other hand, want to negotiate the lowest rate they can, while obtaining some requisite level of service. But shippers should realize that, in a competitive environment, they must be willing to pay for better service. In other words, forcing rates down below the point at which the carrier makes money can lead to unsatisfactory service in the form of late pick-ups, missed deliveries, and/or lost and damaged goods. It also behooves a shipper to be as informed as possible regarding the carrier's cost structure and financial condition so that negotiations can be conducted from a position of strength. However, the shipper must also appreciate the fact that transport firms must make a profit in order to remain in business, so forcing the price down to the point where the carrier is losing money is counterproductive for both parties.

Private Transportation

Some firms perform their own transportation utilizing their own equipment. Generally involving road transport, private transportation may occur across all modes. There are several reasons why a firm might opt for private transportation. Probably the most important is that, for some reason, they cannot get satisfactory service from for-hire firms. Perhaps specialized equipment is needed, or the firm has some unique scheduling requirements. A second reason may be that transportation costs are lower, although, as was discussed earlier, management must take care to ensure that a for-hire carrier may not present a more attractive alternative. Third, private transportation gives management total control of the transport function so that it can be more closely integrated with other corporate activities. Finally, company vehicles can provide a visible presence in the marketplace via graphics, paint-schemes, and simply having the firm's name in front of the public eye. Indeed, a recent study examining the nature of private trucking in Canada found that cost, service, and visibility were the most important factors for companies using their own fleets.[3]

There are some pitfalls that management must avoid. One is the cost of the equipment. Operating a vehicle fleet puts the firm into the transportation business regardless of what their primary purpose is. Equipment must be purchased or leased, maintained, and managed; operators must be hired, trained, and monitored for compliance with applicable laws; scheduling, routing, and tracing must be accomplished as well. Often these skills are not normally found within a firm, so employees must be hired to fulfill those duties. Another concern is that if the firm's situation changes owing to growth, contraction, or new corporate objectives, the fleet may no longer be responsive; that is, it may be too large or too small for the new conditions. Management must also consider the impact of performing in-house transportation on continued relations with commercial carriers. Most companies cannot meet all of their transport needs in-house, and must still rely on for-hire firms for some of their transportation. Negotiating for satisfactory rates may be difficult when the company is performing some of its own transportation. Finally, management must not lose sight of the possibility that, especially in light of environmental changes, for-hire carriers may simply be able to do the job better.

Other Issues Affecting Transportation Cost and Service

There are several other factors that can impact transportation services supporting international markets. Though beyond the control of the logistics manager, these issues can significantly influence the choice of transportation alternatives. Several of these concerns are discussed below.

Infrastructure availability and condition

One of the most challenging aspects of global logistics is dealing with the antiquated transportation resources that exist in many developing nations. Port facilities may be small or unable to handle large volumes of containerized freight efficiently; road systems may be sparse and unimproved; railroad service may be slow and limited in coverage; and airports may be, at best, crude compared to those found in Europe, Australia, or the "Asian Tiger" countries; at worst, they may simply not exist in areas the firm would like to reach. Germany's efforts to improve the infrastructure in the eastern part of the country illustrate the magnitude of the problem. Between 1990 and late 1997, DM 72 billion was invested in various transport-related projects. Some DM 38 billion went into the east German railways, DM 19 billion into roads and DM 1 billion into waterway development. About 5,200 km (3,231 miles) of east German rail track and 11,300 km (7,022 miles) of road have been built or improved since 1990. Half of all German transport investment in 1998 is for projects in East Germany or linking the two halves of the formerly divided nation.[4]

Coping with a substandard infrastructure at any point along the delivery route has implications for the entire logistics system. Most importantly, customer service suffers because lead times can become extremely long. Transportation costs can rise as firms attempt to circumvent bottlenecks in surface transport by utilizing air or some form of circuitous routing. More packaging may be required to ensure the product is adequately protected, while the firm may find that additional inventories must be maintained to offset the increased variability in lead times brought on by transport problems.

But problems are not confined to emerging markets alone, as illustrated in logistics profile 6-1. For example, London's Heathrow Airport is so congested that cargoes can take up to three days to clear the facility. Such delays are wreaking havoc with companies competing in a business world fixated on just-in-time delivery of goods and services.[5] In eastern Germany, the Czech Republic, and Hungary, shippers must cope with highways and railways that are primarily oriented north and east rather than west.[6] Mexico has 21 potential ports, but only four – two on the Pacific and two on the Atlantic – have container facilities.[7] Indeed, the situation at Santos, near Sao Paulo in Brazil, is typical of ports in many emerging markets. Santos was designed for a different era of cargo handling and technology, so from both an infrastructure and a management standpoint, the port is playing catch-up. There are supposed to be five or six container cranes, but at any one time there may be only four. And there is frequently insufficient space on the landside to handle the containers once they are off the ship. Carriers are responding in some cases by calling at Rio de Janeiro or Buenos Aires instead and using feeder services from there into Santos, but both of those ports are getting backed up too. In addition, the inland transportation infrastructure is poor, further impeding ground access into Santos.[8] Table 6-1 shows the largest infrastructure projects currently being planned around the world, most of which are transportation-related.

Logistics Profile 6-1
Which Intermodal Technique for Europe?

European railroads want to replicate bimodal designs already used in the US. But they also can improve performance in other ways, such as with automated loading. The European intermodal market has problems, but there is a great deal of advanced technological development going on in European rail, particularly for intermodal transport. There are some good reasons for this being so. But there are also some not so good reasons. A common characteristic of monopolies is that they are production-oriented rather than market- or customer-oriented. This is very much true of the national railways in Europe, which each have a de facto monopoly in their respective countries.

The fact that the national railways have been state-owned for most of the twentieth century has caused the states to be very protective of everything to do with railways, including the rail equipment industry. Each country has had its own industry for manufacturing rolling stock and usually locomotives, too. The national railway was generally expected to purchase all equipment from the national rail industry. The national railways tended to develop huge engineering departments that were in charge of product development and design. Since there was no market on which to compete, there was no need for the industry itself to bear the high cost of product development. This national segmentation of product development has resulted in the European railways using different systems for electric traction and for signaling. This requires costly and time-consuming changes of locomotives and crews every time a train crosses a national border. Fortunately, all this is rapidly changing now with the advent of the single market in Europe, which forbids national restrictions and discrimination. Unfortunately, however, the dominance of the "engineering mentality" has not disappeared. That is one of the reasons European railway undertakings still are motivated more by internal production concerns than by what the market really needs.

Bimodal technology

Bimodal technology has experienced some measure of success in the US, where the RoadRailer trailer, a combination rail/highway vehicle, has been used for years. The technology is very interesting from an economic point of view mainly because it drastically improves the ratio of payload to deadweight in the train. This is achieved by simply placing specially built trailers directly on single two-axle bogies, in effect eliminating the need for a second bogie and the wagon body. Instead of each trailer occupying a Tin wagon, all it needs is a five-ton bogie.

The European railways showed a keen interest in the bimodal technology in the early 1990s. But just importing the tried and tested US equipment to Europe was apparently too simple for the engineering departments of the European railways. To cut the long story short, the thing had to be re-invented in Europe – and not just a single European version. No fewer than seven different national versions were developed in collaboration between the respective national railways and national rail industries. In fairness, it should be said that there was a major European railway that opted for a non-national version in the first trial period: Germany's Deutsche Bahn.

European requirements

There are, however, some good reasons for developing new rail technology in Europe. Broadly speaking, there are two objectives: to increase speed and to bring down costs. The focus on speed may be surprising, but one of the main reasons is the fact that the European rail infrastructure is actually quite congested in certain areas. As passenger services are generally given priority, most freight trains run at night. In order to be scheduled into the high-speed daytime operations, freight trains need to be capable of top speeds of 120 kilometers per hour (75 miles per hour) or more. Today, the top speed is usually 80 to 100 kilometers per hour, but the commercial speed (end to end) may be less than half of that. The Cargo Sprinter train service developed by German industry and Deutsche Bahn is a five-wagon unit train, powered by truck engines and equipped with modern braking systems that eliminate the need for time-consuming brake tests. The wagon groups can quickly (and automatically) be coupled together into full trains on mainline runs. UPS and Deutsche Post have set up a joint venture to operate a special lightweight version at speeds up to 160 kilometers/hour (100 miles/hour). German forwarders are running trial services from Hamburg and Hannover to the Frankfurt airport with air freight.

Speed in intermodal operations also requires rapid transfer of units at terminals. The shorter the gate in/gate out time, the shorter the distance at which intermodal becomes competitive with road. Just as in the US, European intermodal is generally found to be competitive only at distances more than 500 miles. The problem for intermodal is, of course, that most container and trailer journeys are considerably less than 500 miles.

Terminal technology has been developed which can empty and reload a full train in only about one hour versus the three to four hours normally needed. The trouble with this new technology is that, although both time and cost per container are relatively low, those economies can be achieved only when total terminal throughput is very high. In other words, this approach implies a concentration of operations on a relatively small number of mega-terminals. The average pre- and post-shipment trucking distances would be increased and the mega-terminals would need to be placed in the most heavily industrialized areas. This will exacerbate congestion, which in those areas already is very serious, both on the roads and the tracks.

Automatic loading technique

The need for fast loading/unloading of trains is one reason a completely different approach is now being taken by ADtranz, a merger of the rail manufacturing divisions of Swedish/Swiss ABB and of Daimler-Benz, of Germany. The Automatic Loading System (ALS) moves trailers on modified, standard rail wagons, each of which is equipped with two caterpillar-like "robots" that lift each end of the trailer and move it between wagon and platform. Such an operation takes about three minutes and since all wagons can be emptied and reloaded simultaneously, a full train can be handled in less than 10 minutes. The ALS system provides fast loading/unloading transshipment. Unlike traditional container trains, ALS makes it possible to load and unload any number of trailers from any location in the train at each terminal stop. Other systems are basically end-to-end shuttles where the whole train is unloaded and reloaded at each end.

Other European developments

Some European railways are trying to reduce cost by following the American lead in terms of both rolling stock and infrastructure. For whatever reason, a European freight "wagon" (a freight railcar) costs about twice as much as its US counterpart. It is claimed that European wagons are over-designed, making them too heavy and too expensive. Standards are set by the International Union of Railways organization (UIC), a regulating body set up by the railways themselves. In effect, UIC approval is required for equipment to be allowed to cross borders. One of the most successful European railways in recent years has been the Swedish railway SJ. That railway recently placed a large order for bogies from NACO Inc. of Chicago to be used with US-style spine wagons for timber and other large-volume cargo flows. Another effort to bring down cost is to increase axle load. While US railways have now exceeded 35 metric tons, the standard in Europe is still only 22.5 tons, and in some regions is only 20 tons. It is estimated that an increase to just 25 tonnes will be feasible in the short term and that the savings in the form of increased payload ratio will far outweigh any increase in infrastructure maintenance costs. Except for the development of double stacking, US railroads have achieved an immense growth in profitability without major technological breakthroughs.

There is no doubt that the main reason for US railroads being vastly more efficient than their European counterparts is the competitive pressure under which they operate. The most important thing that needs to happen in Europe is for similar pressure to be created to force the railways to lower their costs, particularly manpower. Once that happens, a new technological generation will be required to handle any significant increase in cargo volumes. Operating conditions in Europe are very different from the US (higher traffic density, mixed passenger and freight operations, shorter distances). It is therefore worthwhile for European operators to explore all means by which they can become more efficient and more competitive.

(**Source**: Baasch, Henrik. "Which intermodal technique for Europe?", *American Shipper*, February1999, vol. 41, i2, p. 34(2))

Table 6-1 The biggest international infrastructure projects (Ranked by estimated dollar cost)

Rank	*Cost*	*Project name*	*Location*
1	$40 billion	New Phone System	Russia
2	$20 billion	Chek Lap Kok Airport	Hong Kong
3	$20 billion	East-West Bridge	Czech Republic
4	$20 billion	Suzhou Industrial Township	China
5	$18 Billion	Intercity High-Speed Rail	Italy
6	$17.1 billion	Mass Rapid Transit Plan	Taiwan
7	$17 billion	Three Gorges Dam	China
8	$17 billion	Swiss Metro	Switzerland
9	$17 billion	Most New Highways	Poland
10	$16.5 billion	Lyon-Turin TGV Railway Line	France/Italy
11	$15 billion	Kansai International Airport	Japan
12	$14.4 billion	Trans-Tokyo Bay Highway	Japan
13	$13.2 billion	Seoul-Pusan Rail Link	South Korea
14	$13.2 billion	Seoul Metro Airport	South Korea
15	$13 billion	New London Airport	U.K.
16	$10 billion	Poland-Russia Gas Pipeline	Poland/Russia
17	$10 billion	Bohai Bay Bridges/Tunnel	China
18	$10 billion	Beijing-Shanghai High Speel Rail Line	China
19	$9.8 billion	Rejang Hydroelectric Powerplant	Malaysia
20	$8 billion	Beijing-Hong Kong Superhighway	China

Sources: Public Works Financing International, IB Research as presented in *International Business* March 1995, p. 32.

Environmental and quality of life issues

Air pollution, noise pollution, aesthetic pollution, and traffic congestion and energy consumption are all socially unpopular by-products of transportation services. Each will be discussed below.

AIR POLLUTION Transport of both goods and passengers is considered to be a major source of carbon dioxide, accounting for 20 percent of those emissions in Europe.

Although road transport is considered to be the main source, kerosene combustion by aircraft engines also releases air pollutants. A similar effect results from rail transport, either directly through the operation of diesel-driven engines or indirectly from the burning of fossil fuels to produce electric power. In addition, the use of chlorofluorocarbons (CFCs) in air-conditioned and refrigerated freight transport vehicles is attacked by environmentalists as a leading cause of destruction of the protective ozone layer in the earth's atmosphere. In Europe, the whole issue of air pollution is being complicated by the rapid economic development of Eastern European countries.[9]

NOISE POLLUTION In such a densely populated region as Western Europe, there is considerable concern over the nuisance caused by the operations of both freight and passenger vehicles, whether by road, rail, or air transport, especially at night. EC studies have shown, for instance, that the noise of a single truck is perceived by people to be the equivalent of that from six automobiles.[10] Furthermore, the growth in commercial aviation is forcing many governments to reexamine the issue of airport expansion. For example, leaders in Great Britain, Belgium and the Netherlands are currently attempting to reconcile the need for more airport flight activity with rising citizen concerns about noise.[11]

AESTHETIC POLLUTION The public has grown increasingly sensitive to "landscape disfiguration." New logistics infrastructure projects such as the high-speed rail transport system in the south of France, the new rail line in southeast England which will connect the Channel Tunnel with London, the new airport in Munich, or more simply the construction of multi-story warehouses have stirred vigorous protest at local, regional, and even national levels. Such public concern can play a major role in thwarting companies' and governments' efforts to strike a reasonable balance between economic progress and environmental protection or to relieve pressure on logistics networks by building new manufacturing and distribution facilities or transportation infrastructure[12].

TRAFFIC CONGESTION Congestion caused by rapid increases in both passenger and freight traffic has already reached alarming levels in Western Europe. Moreover, according to a green paper published by the European Commission, road haulage (expressed in ton-kilometers) is expected to increase by 42 percent between 1990 and 2010, whereas rail transport should rise by 33 percent during the same period. Within a few years, it is estimated that 16 of 27 major airports in the European Union will reach the point of complete saturation, unable to accommodate additional flights. In addition, severe congestion will likely worsen along the main road and rail corridors and in the metropolitan centers of major European cities that have not been planned to accommodate large volumes of vehicle traffic. Clearly, these growing problems are deeply resented by the inhabitants of transit areas such as Austria, Switzerland, and the Ruhr in Germany.[13]

Rail and water transport tend to be much more environmentally friendly than the road and air modes because of the large amounts of cargo that can be moved per liter of fuel consumed. In much of the EU and Germany, in fact, there has been a

Logistics Profile 6-2
High-speed Trains: Green Aircraft of the Future

Few industries have enjoyed such continuous growth in the twentieth century as the airline and motor industries. Demand for both is forecast to continue worldwide, especially in emerging economies like China and India. Their fortunes may be about to diverge. Concerns about pollution from road transport have forced their way onto the political agenda. As the Kyoto earth summit showed in 1997, politicians have to think seriously about the problems of unrestricted car use.

The air industry deposits its main pollution out of sight and out of mind – thousands of feet above ground. Concerns about global warming and the gap in the high-level ozone layer are secondary to the concerns that have motivated protesters against factories, waste tips, new roads and opencast mining. Scientific debate is still continuing about global warming, and it is difficult to engage mass opinion with theoretical arguments and relatively little conclusive proof. Although aircraft burn far less fuel than transport and other activities on land, much of their emissions occur above the earth's surface and in very cold temperatures. Gases that contribute to global warming and ozone depletion are therefore less likely to disperse before affecting sensitive areas of the stratosphere. German researchers estimate that in 2015 aviation's effect on global warming will be equal to that of all other pollution sources put together. Part of the solution may come from another kind of aeroplane – the kind that flies on the ground. Trains like Eurostar and the French Train à Grande Vitesse are already competing with airlines between moderately spaced European cities. The concept has such enormous potential that, on a global scale, the surface is only scratched by today's high-speed services.

In environmental terms, high-speed trains have the upper hand over aircraft in that their associated emissions (at power stations) occur at ground level and their sources of energy can be varied according to economic, political and environmental criteria. All the electrified lines of the Danish rail system may soon be powered by wind generators. Potentially, a large proportion of rail services could be powered by renewables that take nothing from the earth and add nothing to its stratosphere. The concept of the modern high-speed train running on specially constructed tracks became prominent in Europe in the early 1980s, when the Paris-Sud Est TGV halved the journey time between Paris and Lyon. At two hours, the train journey was suddenly faster than the journey by air between city centres. The airline that had dominated on this corridor lost market share rapidly. In its first three years, the TGV grew to capture 57 percent of the market. Airlines can benefit from this shift as well. The Virgin Group is heavily involved in Britain's railways after privatization and the opportunity may arise in future for airlines connecting points within Europe to buy into operations of high-speed long-distance trains. Even in countries where wholesale privatization is not being contemplated, the

European Union is pressing for national rail systems to be opened up to independent operators. Infrastructure has already been separated from operation in member states. Open-access TGV services, operated and branded by established airlines, may become possible.

Freight is uncharted territory for high-speed rail. The TGVs that carry French mail are the only services using the new technology and infrastructure in Europe. Curbs on airfreight, for environmental reasons, could encourage the growth of high-speed trains for carriage of time-sensitive goods in the future. Europe is not the only region of the world where high-speed rail technology could be applied to the benefit of the environment. In the USA, the Spanish Talgo system has been tested in service, to much acclaim. Interest is growing in high-speed rail lines between major cities. New lines and services could also take the environmental sting out of economic expansion in Russia and China. High-speed lines linking St. Petersburg with Moscow and Beijing with Shanghai are in the pipeline. Another project, in China's Fujian province, is expected to employ Japanese Shinkansen technology. Further development of high-speed rail in Europe is dogged by the green lobby's bias towards the most tangible problems – not necessarily the most serious ones. People who were likely to be affected by noise pollution and property blight have fiercely opposed proposals for high-speed lines in Germany, France and Britain. A change in the balance of political and environmental priorities will be needed before high-speed rail routes are accepted as environmentally preferable to continued growth in air (and road) travel.

(**Source**: Adapted from Clark, Rhodri. "High-speed trains: green aircraft of the future," *Global Transport*, Summer 1998, pp. 101–3)

movement to get cargo off the roads and on to the rails and the canals.[14] Concerns about noise have led many airports around the world to impose quiet hours during the night, which either limit aircraft movements or preclude them altogether. Some countries limit or restrict road freight at certain times. Germany, for example, does not allow trucks to travel their autobahns on Sundays or at any time during summer weekends.[15] The future of rail as an ecologically sound form of transportation is discussed in logistics profile 6-2. While much of the current interest deals with high-speed rail passenger movements, the potential exists for moving cargo the same way.

Customs and cargo security

Global logistics managers face several other challenging transport concerns. **Customs** procedures, the advances in the EU notwithstanding, can prove to be daunting. It is not uncommon for trucks to spend two days moving from Germany into Poland, for example, because Polish officials are so thorough in their inspections.

Although situations in specific countries can change very rapidly, **cargo security** is a very real problem in certain parts of the world. One computer manufacturer utilizes secured metal trucks to move its product from Western Europe to Moscow. In Eastern Europe, especially Poland and Russia, the convoy employs shifts of drivers and stops only for gas. When it reaches Russia, carloads of armed guards accompany the truck carrying the weekly consignment of computers to Moscow.[16] Sea piracy occurs in Southeast Asia while truck hijacking is a problem in northern Mexico, but security experts regard the nations of the former Soviet Union and Eastern bloc as the most hazardous region of the world today. Organized crime cartels and poor economic conditions have made every piece of cargo including the containers themselves a potential target.[17] In response to the high risk of theft in Poland, for example, some shippers are choosing to move cargo by sea from Germany to Russia rather than cross Poland by land, which takes three days longer than truck and is much more expensive.[18]

Carrier safety

Most managers do not think of safety as a logistics issue. However, as more nations move to put their transport resources on a competitive footing, safety can become an important consideration in selecting a carrier. Critics of free-market transportation say that, as more carriers enter the market and the pressure to control costs increases, safety deteriorates for several reasons. First, there are more carriers providing service, which means more vehicles in operation. Second, competitive pressures may lead firms to operate vehicles with minor mechanical problems rather than withdrawing them from revenue service for repairs. Third, personnel reductions (as a way to lower costs) can lead to employees working longer hours. Finally, so this argument goes, the end result is more accidents. In developed markets supporting a competitive transport marketplace, shippers will not utilize carriers they perceive to be unsafe. When there is some kind of an accident, goods are damaged or destroyed, delivery dates are missed, negative publicity about the shipper can result, and sales are lost, so shippers simply will not patronize unsafe carriers. In a free market, shippers can add the carrier's safety record to the list of criteria that must be met before business is offered. In other words, hazardous operations cost the transport firm business, so there is little incentive to operate in an unsafe manner. However, in emerging nations shippers may still opt for the low-cost carrier because the less sophisticated customers in those markets may tolerate the transport disruptions that may occur. Finally, the only movement firms available may be sub-standard, so logistics managers have little choice but to use them.

Conclusions

As esoteric as factors such as security and infrastructure condition may seem from a logistics point of view, the impact on the bottom line can be quite direct. For example, a 1,000 km movement of general freight in the Former Soviet Union is estimated to cost between $370 and $498 more than an equivalent movement in Western

Europe, primarily owing to inadequate infrastructure and security risks. Furthermore, rates increase by $119 per truckload for each border crossing in Western Europe.[19] So issues that may be of little concern to a manager dealing solely with domestic transportation can directly impact both profitability and customer service when moving goods internationally.

Chapter Summary

Clearly, supporting customers around the world may require a more creative approach to transportation management than is needed to support domestic operations. Pricing issues become extremely complex as managers move to establish value/cost criteria across a wide range of industry structures and customer needs. Selecting the right mode and carrier involves difficult decisions that may include the consideration of factors managers have never dealt with before. So while the goal of obtaining requisite transport service at the lowest price is still applicable, executing that objective on a global scale can be extremely challenging.

Study Questions

1. Briefly discuss the impact of market structure on transport pricing.
2. What is value of service pricing in transportation? What circumstances must exist for this form of pricing to be successful?
3. Briefly discuss the difference between fixed and variable costs, giving transportation examples of each.
4. What are the different ways transport prices may be determined in real life?
5. Referring to logistics profile 6-2, is high-speed rail the mode of the future? Defend your answer.
6. What actions should carrier managers take in order to succeed in a competitive environment?
7. What transportation strategies should shippers implement in order to succeed in a competitive environment?
8. What are the pros and cons of a firm operating their own transport function?
9. Why should logistics managers care about the transportation infrastructure existing in various markets?
10. What sorts of transportation infrastructure problems exist in your country? How do they impact logistics?

Notes

1. Coyle, John J., Bardi, Edward J., and Cavinato, Joseph L. *Transportation*, 3rd edn (St. Paul, MN: West Publishing Company, 1990), pp. 252–4.
2. Ibid, p. 257 and pp. 268–72.
3. Harrington, Lisa. "Private fleets in Canada," *Private Carrier*, January 1996, p. 36.

4. Todd, Tom. "East German transport network takes shape," *Global Transport*, Spring 1998, p. 30.
5. Miles, Gregory L. "London's air cargo snafu," *International Business*, August 1995, p. 20.
6. Krohn, Nico. "Transportation's iron curtain," *International Business*, February 1994, p. 44.
7. Malkin, Elisabeth. "Mexico's port partners," *International Business*, February 1994, p. 38.
8. Von Oldenborg, Marita. "The world's top ports of call," *International Business*, October 1995, p. 48.
9. O'Laughlin, Kevin A., Cooper, James, and Cabocel, Eric. *Reconfiguring European Logistics Systems* (Oak Brook, IL: Council of Logistics Management, 1993), pp. 105–6.
10. Ibid, p. 106.
11. "Airport noise limits – the argument gets louder," *Global Transport*, Summer 1998, pp. 28–31.
12. Ibid.
13. Ibid.
14. Fox, Adrienne. "Gateway to the East," *International Business*, April 1996, p. 48.
15. Krohn, ibid, p. 42.
16. Ibid, p. 44.
17. Taylor, Gary. "Heist makes waste," *International Business*, October 1993, p. 30.
18. Ibid.
19. Beilock, Richard, Boneva, Paulina, Jostova, Gergana, Kostadinova, Katerina, and Vassileva, Diana. "Road conditions, border crossings and freight rates in Europe and Western Asia," *Transportation Quarterly*, vol. 50, no. 1, Winter 1996, p. 88.

chapter 7

Warehousing

Introduction	123
The Strategic Role of Warehousing in Logistics	124
Functions of Warehousing	125
Warehouse Roles	126
Warehouse Location Issues	128
Warehousing Alternatives	133
Warehousing Strategies	135
Warehousing Concerns in Overseas Markets	136
Chapter Summary	137
Study Questions	138

Introduction

A warehouse is more than just a place where inventory is stored. As shown in figure 7-1, the proper management of warehouse functions is an important ingredient of a firm's overall logistics effort. In fact, warehousing is integrally involved in four distinct supply-chain processes: sourcing/inbound logistics, processing/manufacturing, outbound distribution, and reverse logistics (returns, recycling, etc.).[1] Sites for the firm's storage facilities must be selected with due consideration being given not only to warehousing costs but to the long-term implications for customer service and transportation as well. Once placement has been determined, other decisions can be made with respect the accomplishment of day-to-day operations. Specifically, management may elect to own and operate them or they may choose to rely on a third-party provider. This chapter will briefly examine the functions of warehousing before turning to a more in-depth examination of various placement and operational concerns.

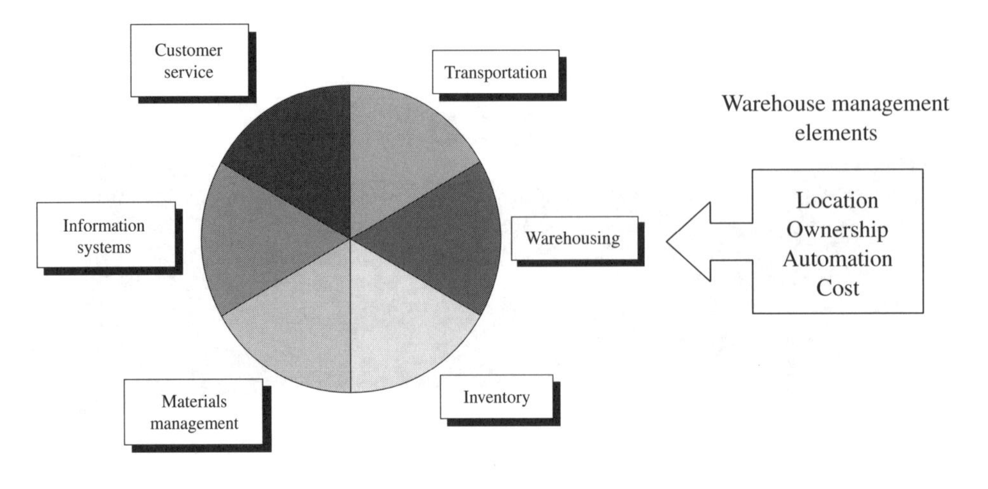

Figure 7-1 The role of warehousing within the logistics system

The Strategic Role of Warehousing in Logistics[2]

There are a number of strategic reasons to have a warehouse or distribution center today. They are to:

- **provide local inventory;** perhaps customers demand rapid service on a global basis, necessitating a network of local warehouses;
- **perform value-added services for the customer** such as labeling and ticketing of product, or the creating of in-store promotional displays;
- **operate near vital suppliers, serving as an inbound materials-control center;**
- **act as a consolidation point for orders** in a situation where multiple components of a single order are married and then shipped to the customer;
- **consolidate outbound orders for more economical transportation;**
- **protect against manufacturing lead-times;**
- **handle reverse logistics (product returns);**
- **perform quality inspections;**
- **enable manufacturing economics;** for example, keep production lines operating at a steady pace while storing finished goods in anticipation of large seasonal demand surges.
- **enable procurement efficiencies** such as buying commodity raw materials when prices drop.

As with any individual logistics activity, management must always ensure that the logistics system as a whole benefits from the chosen warehousing strategy. That is, the cost of building and maintaining the warehouse(s) must be less than the benefit the firm is receiving. For example, if warehousing costs are higher than any procurement savings received, management might be better off to simply pay a higher price for raw materials when they are needed rather than storing them in a facility.

Functions of Warehousing

The following activities are performed to some degree in all warehousing operations. However, it is possible that one or more of them do not exist in a given facility or are combined with other activities. To put these activities into perspective, each is numbered and keyed to the generic warehouse shown in figure 7-2.[3]

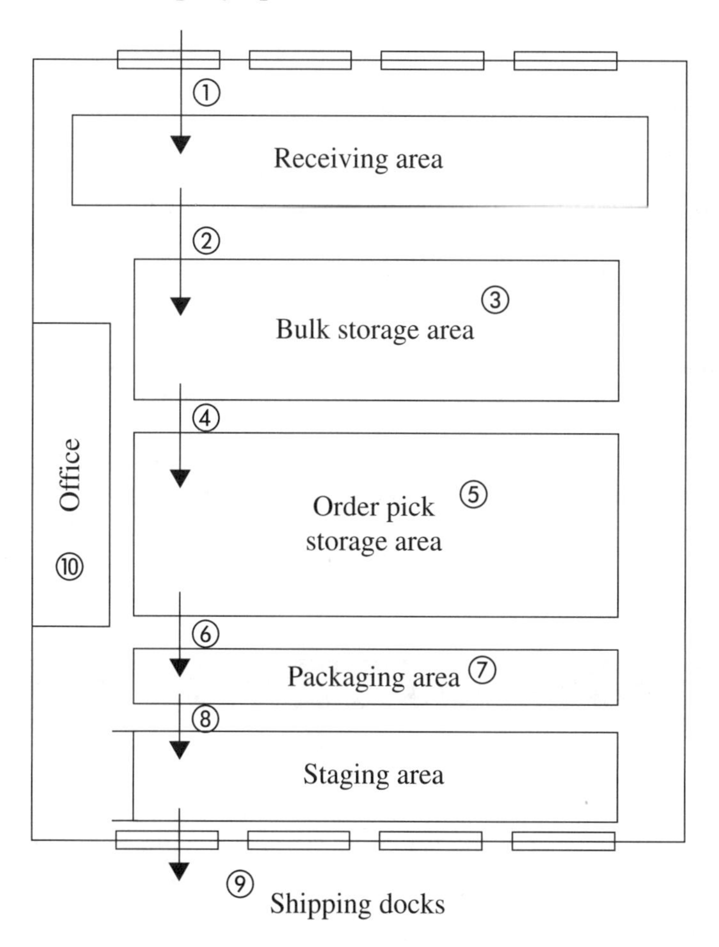

Figure 7-2 Basic warehousing functions
Source: Byrne, Patrick M. *Improving Quality and Productivity in the Logistics Process* (Oak Brook, IL: Council of Logistics Management, 1991), p. 318.

1. **Receiving** involves physically accepting material, unloading it from the inbound transportation mode, verifying quantity and condition of the material, and documenting this information as required.
2. **Put-Away** means removing the goods from the receiving dock, transporting them to a storage area, moving them to a specific location and recording this movement, and identifying where the material has been placed.
3. **Storage** is the retention of products for future use or shipment. Other than occasional inventory verification or physical transfers within the storage area along with documentation of the transfer, there is usually no labor involved in this activity.
4. **Replenishment** occurs when material is relocated from storage to a temporary resupply area from which orders are directly filled.
5. **Order selection** involves picking the required quantity of specific products for movement to a packing area.
6. **Checking** means verifying and documenting order selection in terms of product number and quantity.
7. **Packing and marking** refers to placing one or more items of an order into an appropriate container and labeling that container with customer shipping destination data as well as other handling information that may be required.
8. **Staging and consolidation** means physically moving material from the packing zone to a shipping area based on a prescribed set of instructions related to a particular outbound vehicle or delivery route.
9. **Shipping** involves loading an outbound vehicle with material from the staging area and completing the documentation associated with the movement.
10. **Clerical/Office administration** refers to all of the tasks associated with keeping track of items as they move into, through, and out of the warehouse.

With the exception of storage and clerical, all of these activities involve movement in some way. Indeed, as firms strive to eliminate inventory, movement can become the primary activity of a warehouse as goods remain there for shorter periods of time. At one extreme, goods flow directly from the receiving area to the shipping dock, a process known as cross-docking.

Warehouse Roles

Warehouses can serve a variety of roles in a firm's logistics system. Figure 7-3 depicts warehouses serving as gathering facilities, breakdown centers, and in a multifunctional role embracing both. For some organizations, the warehouse serves as a **gathering** or consolidation point. For example, small quantities of multiple products may be received into a warehouse from a variety of vendors via less-than-full-load shipments. At the facility, the various items are then combined into an assortment of goods based upon customer orders and shipped to the customer in full-load quantities. For example, a manufacturer might buy components from multiple vendors that are combined into truck-load shipments at the warehouse for movement to the assembly plants. In this application, the intent is to utilize the warehouse as a means

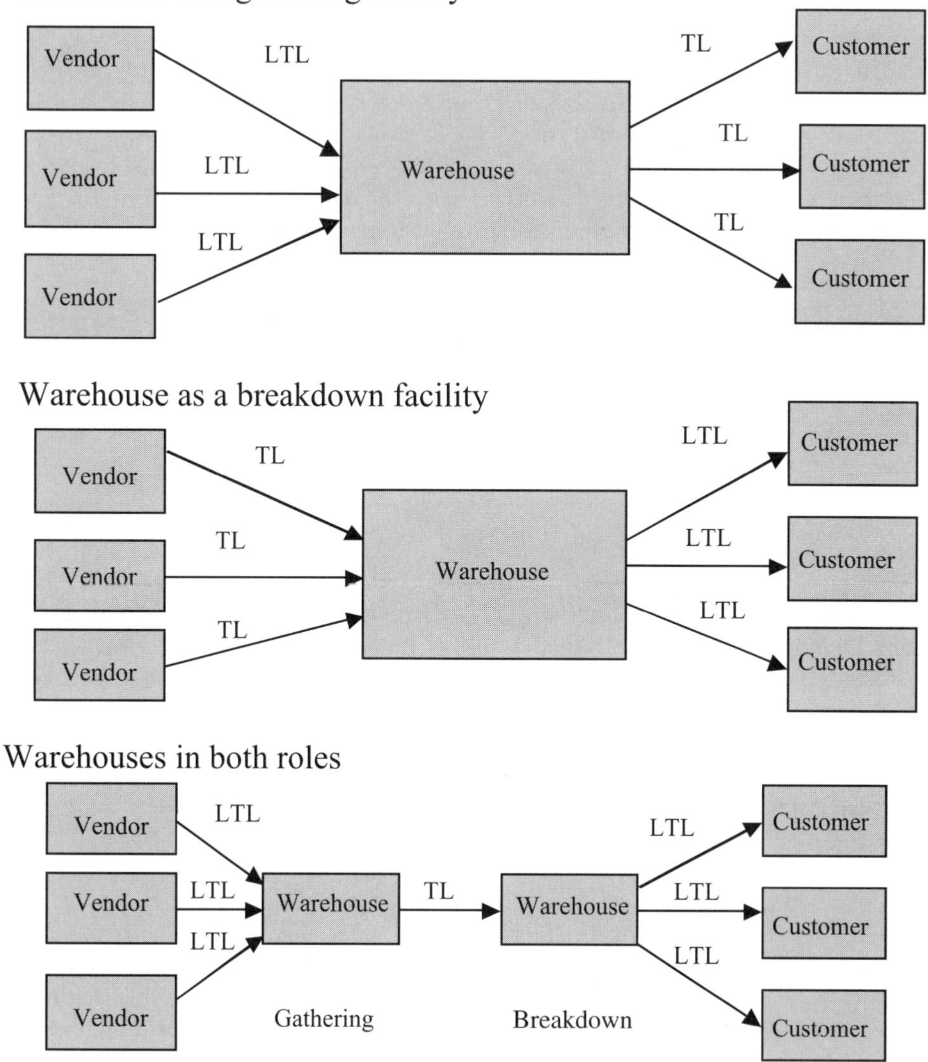

Figure 7-3 Warehousing's role in the logistics system

of minimizing the distance that expensive less-than-full-load shipments must be moved. Alternatively, the warehouse may perform a **breakdown** function, where large quantities or goods come in from suppliers via full-load transport and are broken down into smaller lots that are then shipped out to customers in less-than-full-load shipments. Retail grocery chains, for example, typically purchase large quantities of the goods they sell. These products are received by the truckload into a warehouse where they are broken down into the smaller quantities required by each store. Again, the objective is to minimize less-than-full-load transportation. Note that, while the vehicle moving goods from the warehouse to the retailer may be fully loaded, the products have come from many different suppliers. Thus, the movement becomes essentially less-than-truckload. Firms serving global markets often find they must use warehouses in **both roles**. Goods are gathered together in a domestic warehouse in order to achieve, for example, full container loads. Multiple containers can then be shipped together to a warehouse in the overseas market where the goods are broken down for onward movement to customers.

Warehouse Location Issues

Centralized versus decentralized warehouses

Managers serving international customers must decide whether to support multiple markets from one centralized warehouse or place a facility in each market. There are several advantages in centralizing inventory, including simplified order processing, elimination of nationally based warehouse operations, reduced need for working capital and inventory holding, lower outbound transport costs (assuming load consolidation), and potentially better use of intermodal capabilities. However, the disadvantages must also be weighed. They include increased inbound transport costs, as well as perceptions by customers and internal sales and marketing managers who may react negatively to the fact that products are shipped from outside their own countries.[4] Finally, a centralized facility may need to be larger and more sophisticated in order to handle the inventory needs of multiple countries or markets.

Traditionally, for example, most companies have organized their European distribution on a national, rather than a regional basis. Each distribution area operated more or less independently of the others. The company would have a warehouse in each country to receive incoming products then distribute them locally within national boundaries. This kind of distribution pattern had a logic to it because distribution was often very closely tied to the marketing function, and marketing is usually nationally focused in order to cope with things such as differences in taste and language. But organizing warehousing on a country-by-country basis assumes that national borders and patterns of demand coincide which, or course, they may not.[5] Nike, for example, had 25 warehouses scattered around Europe supporting various subsidiaries. Stock would be left unsold in Germany while there was demand for it in France. Production planners had to cope with at least a dozen individual forecasts.[6]

Centralizing, on the other hand, tends to cut inventory-holding costs. The square-root law of inventory illustrates how if the number of warehouses is cut, the amount of safety stock in the warehouse system as a whole drops dramatically. The law states that total inventories in a future number of facilities can be approximated by multiplying the total amount of inventory at existing facilities by the square root of the number of future facilities divided by the number of existing warehouses. The formula for this computation is presented here:[7]

$$X_2 = X_1\sqrt{\frac{n_2}{n_1}}$$

where n_1 = number of existing facilities
n_2 = number of future facilities
X_1 = total inventory in existing facilities
X_2 = total inventory in future facilities.

For example, replacing four warehouses each handling 250,000 units a year with one facility would require system inventory of only 500,000 versus the 1,000,000 units maintained under the old system. (The student can verify the savings by substituting those figures into the formula.) The lower inventory level comes about primarily due to the simpler and more accurate forecasting (and resultant reduction in variation) that is possible when a single facility is being utilized versus multiple ones. The more forecasts there are, the greater the opportunities for error which must be covered with safety stock.[8]

Centralization may not always work, however. For example, products may be country specific because of safety requirements or technical specifications, which means that products cannot be combined into a common inventory. For example, French consumers prefer front-loading washing machines while Germans have a penchant for top-loading ones. Average customers in the UK and Benelux countries appear to be more sensitive to price, while in other countries they may pay more attention to brands.[9] But many companies that have historically utilized country-based warehousing in Europe, for example, are discovering that the inventory costs are simply too high. External developments, particularly the move to a single European market, present such firms an ideal opportunity to rationalize and reduce inventory through regionalized warehousing across Europe. Bosch-Siemens, a manufacturer of household appliances with headquarters in Munich, recently shrunk its Scandinavian warehousing operations. Previously, it had a nationally focused distribution center in each of three Scandinavian countries (Finland, Norway, and Sweden). Today, it has consolidated these into one center based between Stockholm and Malo, distributing to other Nordic countries from that single location. This development necessitated a fundamental realignment of relationships among distribution, sales, and marketing.[10]

The process of rationalization poses both operational and organizational challenges. Sales and marketing managers may be uncomfortable with the prospect of sourcing products from distant foreign countries and dealing with associates who speak other languages. When Valeo, a French automotive parts distributor, attempted to reduce its Belgian and German warehouses, sales executives in both Germany and Belgium feared that service levels would suffer. Eventually, however, they discovered that their customers could be served even better from the centralized warehouses. Clearly, companies find that it is not often an easy management task to make the transition from a national to a European focus in warehousing for finished products.[11] Such a move may necessitate the cooperation of other channel members as well. Whirlpool's pan-European consolidation of its spare parts warehouses was facilitated by an agreement with wholesalers that accepted the addition of 2,000 parts to their own inventories, to give better "off-the-shelf" parts service to their own customers, compensating for the closing of Whirlpool's UK warehouse.[12]

Selecting specific sites

Once the larger question of centralization has been addressed, the firm must still consider many variables in deciding specifically where to put their warehouse or warehouses. For logistics networks that span the globe, the problem of location may involve hundreds of products moving to thousands of customers from hundreds of potential warehouses, plants, and vendors by means of multiple transportation services. The questions that must be answered include:

- How many warehouses should there be, where should they be located, and what size should they be?
- How should customer demand be allocated to each warehouse?
- How should vendor/supplier output (i.e. products) be allocated to each?[13]

Much early work in location theory centered around placing a facility so as to minimize transportation costs alone. In fact, there are techniques that require no more than a hand calculator to locate a single warehouse, given knowledge of inbound and outbound flows and their associated transportation costs. However, logistics executives supporting far-flung global markets must concern themselves with more than just transportation costs. Rather, the impact on the entire logistics system must be assessed.

Most comprehensive facility-location techniques fall into one of three categories: optimizations, simulations, or heuristics. **Optimization** models are based on a mathematical structure that can be solved to provide (or at least converge on) an optimum solution within the parameters specified. Linear programming and mixed-integer linear programming are examples of optimization techniques. The major advantage of utilizing this kind of model is that it provides an optimal location. The disadvantages are that it becomes computationally burdensome very quickly, requiring a lot of computer time to run, and it limits the number of variables that may be utilized to specify the model. Thus, the "optimum" solution may be based upon the analysis of a relatively small number of variables. **Simulations** are mathematical representations of the logistics system that can be manipulated with a computer. Simulations are popular because data can be changed and the model rerun to answer management questions and study the costs of alternative choices. Unlike optimizations, simulations do not guarantee an optimum solution; one might result, but the analyst would not necessarily know it. **Heuristics** attempt to limit the search before analysis begins by calling upon management to bound the process at the outset. In other words, only those locations with a reasonable chance of acceptance are considered. While allowing the manager to specify that, for example, an optimal location must be within 20 miles of a major seaport, and 3 miles of a major roadway, heuristic approaches do raise the possibility that a "good" solution may be omitted from the solution set. Thus, an optimal solution is not guaranteed.

There are a number of software programs available (many PC-based) that will consider transportation costs throughout a given shipping network, warehouse storage and handling costs, facility fixed costs, and production or purchase costs in arriving at a "best" although not necessarily optimal, location for a warehouse. But these packages have shortcomings as well, that illustrate the complexity of the whole location problem. First, establishing accurate relationships between network design (customer service) and the contribution to revenue that a particular design can generate is very difficult. Second, even though a few include multiple time periods for the purpose of handling seasonality, existing models do not directly treat the dynamic warehouse location problem. Third, issues associated with customer service such as delivery times and product selection are only crudely treated at best. Fourth, inventory, purchasing, and production-lot sizing and their timing are not well handled. Finally, the use of private as opposed to for-hire transportation in location analysis is poorly represented.[14]

The solutions that emerge from the location search process, however, can be fairly general in nature; that is, they may specify a location in a geographic location that will still require management to pick a site within that area. If management desires to own their own facility, selecting a specific location will involve assessing, among other things, the quality and variety of transportation modes serving the site; the quality, quantity and cost of available labor; land availability and cost; tax issues; construction costs; and the potential for expansion. If a third-party provider is to be utilized, available facilities and the services offered by each must be considered, along with more general concerns regarding transport access and customer service.

The issue of warehouse location has a direct impact on the entire logistics system. For example, inventory decisions are affected in several ways. First, the number of warehouses influences the overall level of safety stock in the system. As the number of warehouses increases, the safety stock at each warehouse decreases, but the total system safety stock increases. Second, the allocation of markets to warehouses affects the sizes of inventories at various warehouses. Finally, the number and locations of the warehouses affect the distances between plants and warehouses. Longer distances between plants and warehouses imply longer replenishment lead times and greater variance of those lead times, both of which lead to increased levels of safety stocks at the warehouses. Inventory decisions have the reverse effect on warehouse location decisions. For instance, a decision to reduce the overall level of inventory in the system, particularly the level of safety stock, would lead to inventory consolidation and therefore fewer established warehouses.[15]

Most importantly, warehouse location directly affects customer service. For instance, warehouse placements determine the distance between warehouses and markets that directly affect order-cycle times. Longer delivery distances would result in longer, and more variable order-cycle times. Warehouse location decisions also affect product availability because they determine the distances from plants and warehouses. Greater distances imply longer average replenishment lead times and more variability in those lead times. These factors, in turn, increase the variability of demand during replenishment lead time at the warehouses, thereby reducing

Logistics Profile 7-1
Virtual Realty: Web Firms Go on Warehouse Building Boom

The Internet's top retailers aren't sneering at giant warehouses anymore – they are building them. This wasn't supposed to happen. Much of the early excitement about electronic commerce involved the belief that companies could serve millions of customers without needing anything approaching the infrastructure of a Sears or Wal-Mart. E-commerce companies were supposed to be incredibly efficient clusters of computer programmers, who used outside subcontractors to handle such dreary tasks as keeping inventory, filling orders and handling customer-service issues. But now online merchants are discovering that if they don't control their own warehouses and shipping, their reliability ratings with customers can turn dismal. Amazon.com, for example, is in the midst of a $300 million distribution-center initiative that involves building giant facilities in Nevada, Kentucky and Kansas to handle its inventory of books, music, videos, toys and electronics. An online grocery retailer, Webvan Group Inc. has placed a $1 billion order with Bechtel Group for giant warehouses in 26 cities across the US. And other electronic merchants such as eToys Inc. and Barnesandnoble.com are pushing ahead with big warehouse projects as well.

Such investments may be essential if e-commerce companies hope to build up a base of loyal customers, says Steve Johnson, co-director of the e-commerce program at Andersen Consulting. "Customer acquisition costs are quite high for these companies, and the only way to get a payoff is if you get a lot of repeat business from people," he says. "One bad experience, and you have blown it forever." But Internet companies face a steep learning curve as they try to master the shipping and warehouse business. Books and compact disks can be shunted through a warehouse without much trouble, but bulky, odd-size items such as toys and electronics are a lot more difficult. Also, customer return rates can be as high as 30 percent in categories such as apparel, posing big challenges in handling such merchandise. What's more, the make-it-up-as-we-go along culture of many Internet companies may mesh badly with the logistics industry's need for careful, precise planning. In a recent interview, Webvan's chief executive officer, Lewis Borders, said: "You would laugh at some of our early design errors." Heavy equipment targeted for a corner of Webvan's Oakland, California warehouse site had to be relocated after it was discovered that poor soil couldn't support the load, he said.

Some e-commerce companies delegate warehousing and shipping to specialists in that area. But some of the most ambitious Internet retailers argue that, for all the additional headaches, it is still worth going into these logistics businesses themselves. "The closer we are to the customers, the more we can build up the lifetime value of our relationships with them," says Jonathan Bulkeley, CEO of

Barnesandnoble.com. To oversee these facilities, e-commerce companies are recruiting executives who have plenty of experience in the heavy-lifting end of the business. With some effort, the Internet and logistics cultures are trying to blend together.

(**Source**: Anders, George. "Virtual realty: Web firms go on warehouse building boom," *The Wall Street Journal*, September 8, 1999, p. B1)

product availability for any pre-specified levels of safety stock at the warehouses.[16] The consequences of failing to understand this relationship between warehousing and customer service are discussed in logistics profile 7-1.

Warehousing Alternatives

Private warehousing

Private warehousing is owned and operated by the company whose goods are stored in the building.[17] The major advantage is that the facility can be custom designed to meet the organization's needs. Owning the facility also permits management total control over the warehousing function and its integration into the overall logistics system. There is also the possibility that the facility can be utilized to house other corporate functions such as a sales office or a retail outlet. Finally, a company warehouse does convey a commitment to the marketplace that is reassuring to customers.

Unfortunately these benefits come at a high cost, in terms of both the initial investment required to build the facility and the long-term obligations associated with maintaining it. Furthermore, the risk of suboptimization is higher than if a public facility is being used. If demand increases or decreases, the facility may be too large or too small; if the market disappears entirely, the firm may be left with a building that it cannot use and is unable to sell because it was custom designed to support specific products.

Contract warehousing

A contract warehouse is operated by a third party that dedicates resources to the company owning the goods in storage.[18] Although similar to public facilities, contract providers offer their customers specialized services that typically cannot be obtained at a public warehouse. For example, they may be equipped to handle specialized types of products; perform various functions such as packaging, labeling, or billing; or dedicate personnel to support a given customer's needs. In exchange for such tailored support, the customer contractually commits to utilize these services for a specified period of time. In essence, a contract warehouse offers the customer benefits approaching those found in a private facility, but at a lower cost. Disadvantages are somewhat less control than would be possible in a company-owned facility, the necessity for sharing confidential customer information with the warehouse operator, and the risk of the relationship proving unsatisfactory before the contract period is completed.

Public warehouses

A public warehouse is operated by a third party that stores goods for multiple shippers/owners.[19] There are several advantages to using the services of a public warehouse. First, management only utilize (and pay for) the space they need. Should their storage needs change during the year, they can rent more or less space as required. In addition, there is no capital outlay required to erect a building. Furthermore, the upkeep of the facility is the responsibility of the warehouse owner, not the user. There is also the benefit of knowing exactly what storage costs are being incurred each month in the sense that a bill is received from the warehousing company.

The disadvantages of using a public facility include relinquishing control of the warehousing operation to the service provider. In addition, merely leasing space in a public warehouse may imply an impermanence some customers might find disturbing. Furthermore, operating costs tend to be higher owing to the inclusion of profit and overhead components in the warehouse operator's monthly charge. Another concern is that the building design may not be optimal for the user's products or needs. Finally, administering the warehousing function may be more complicated by virtue of having to work with a third party.

The line between private, contract, and public is becoming increasing blurred. Public warehousing firms, rather than serving merely as storage areas, are offering more and diverse services to attract customers. Yamatane Corporation is, among other things, one of the top ten warehouse companies in Japan. Concentrated around the nation's largest markets of Tokyo and Osaka, Yamatane's integrated warehousing and logistics operations are geared to one objective: customer satisfaction. Logistics services extend from warehousing to international freight forwarding and customs clearance as well as providing linkages to overseas affiliates and associates that offer product delivery services around the globe. Furthermore, the firm has developed a highly sophisticated computerized logistics control system to integrate warehousing, inventory management, and delivery activities for its customers.[20]

In fact, the UK National Association of Warehouse Keepers lists the following as major services being offered by their membership: break-bulk, cold storage, cool storage, container facilities, customs, export packaging, heated storage, high security, open storage, and rail and waterborne access.[21] Alternatively, the shipper may own the warehouse, but contract out its entire operation to a third party. Finally, some firms may desire a contract operator that will assume responsibility for the entire function, to include providing the building. Hoechst-Celanese, for instance, is moving into a new warehouse outside of Charlotte, North Carolina that is operated by a third-party company that owns the building and all the materials handling equipment. In addition, this third-party firm provides all of the labor as well.

Warehousing Strategies

Management's decision to utilize private, contract, or public warehousing (or some combination) flows from an analysis of the costs and benefits associated with each. A research effort was recently conducted to identify important service and cost considerations across those three options. A survey was sent to 488 managers in consumer goods companies, chemical companies, health care firms, and automotive industry companies. Out of that group, 105 usable surveys were returned. Respondents were asked to rank each warehousing type on its ability to deliver certain benefits. Possible rankings were excellent, good, fair, and poor. Table 7-1 shows the mean rating assigned to each type of warehousing on all 13 expected benefits. Asterisks in the table denote statistically different ratings versus private warehousing. The pattern is striking in that contract warehousing is always rated between public and private. Also, private facilities are consistently rated better on service attributes than both contract and public. In fact, private warehouses perform better than third parties even on such noncore services as JIT transportation and new-product distribution. On the other hand, the respondents recognize

Table 7-1 Expected benefit by warehouse type

Benefit	*Public*	*Contract*	*Private*
Most responsive to management requests	2.5**	1.9**	1.3
Best customer service	2.4**	1.9**	1.4
Most reliable delivery service	2.3**	1.9**	1.5
Quickest emergency deliveries	2.3**	1.9**	1.4
Best transportation capability for JIT	2.3**	2.1**	1.8
Best way to distribute new products	2.1**	2.1**	1.7
Widest range of logistics capabilities	1.8*	2.0*	2.3
Easiest "sell" to upper management	1.9**	2.3**	2.7
Fewest labor problems	2.0**	2.0**	2.4
Joint planning and forecasting with shipper	2.7**	1.9**	1.4
Sharing benefits/burdens of shipper–warehouse relationship	2.6**	1.9	1.9
Lowest upfront investment	1.2**	2.1**	3.5
Lowest delivered cost to customer	2.3	2.2	2.0

*Significant at p<.05
**Significant at p<.01
Note: Excellent = 1; Good = 2; Fair = 3, Poor = 4
Source: Maltz, Arnold B. "The relative importance of cost and quality in the outsourcing of warehousing," *Journal of Business Logistics*, vol. 15, no. 2, 1994, p. 51

the third-party advantage in strategic areas such as upfront investment and labor problems.[22]

Initially the firm must assess its ability to perform the warehousing function in-house. Issues of concern include unique customer service requirements, cost, control, convenience, internal capacity and capabilities, and control of quality. Private warehousing can then be compared to services available externally across such factors as cost, ability to meet customer needs, control, environmental concerns, secrecy, market conditions, and supply assurance.[23] Should management decide to outsource the storage activity, then a choice must be made between public and contract warehousing. Again, each option can be considered with respect to cost, control, additional logistics services required, and duration of need. If, for example, a swimsuit manufacturer desired to maintain a seasonal inventory for a few months, public warehousing may offer the best alternative. On the other hand, should managers be considering a longer-term relationship (such as the one envisioned by Hoechst-Celanese) involving the performance of additional tasks such as order picking, packing and labeling, then contract warehousing will offer the ability to establish a partnership arrangement that will provide the additional control needed to ensure customer satisfaction.

Warehousing Concerns in Overseas Markets

Managers supporting global logistics networks must confront a myriad of issues with respect to warehousing. In many emerging markets, merely finding even marginal facilities may be a challenge. Existing buildings may not offer the size, level of security, climate control, or transport access needed to meet the firm's needs, so erecting their own facility may be the only option. In some countries, however, ownership may not be possible which forces management to increase their use of transportation as a way of minimizing the need for warehousing. Should the use of substandard facilities be the only option for at least some inventory, management may have to consider various alternatives to compensate for whatever warehousing deficiencies may exist. For example, additional packaging may offset the higher risk of damage during manual handling, while holding less inventory for shorter periods of time may decrease losses due to theft.

Even in developed markets, however, warehousing concerns abound. For instance, the attractiveness of warehousing automation differs widely across Europe. Costs of labor and land, as well as social legislation (for example, rules affecting working hours) vary greatly from country to country. Where multiple-shift operations are permitted for example, as in the United Kingdom, investments in capital-intensive warehousing technologies may be easier to justify than in those areas such as Scandinavia where operations are limited to single shifts.[24] In other parts of the world, political issues such as a government's long-term stability or its attitude toward foreign trade must also be considered along with the above factors. So a firm that has successfully utilized one warehousing strategy for its domestic market may find that strategy unworkable as it expands overseas. In fact, multiple approaches may be required to meet the needs of customers in very different markets. Hewlett-

Logistics Profile 7-2
HEWLETT-PACKARD'S EUROPEAN PRINTER BUSINESS

Many companies have become frustrated by their inability to predict what the consumer will buy from day to day. Hewlett-Packard Company (HP) addressed this issue in their European printer business through postponement or building products with modular format assemblies that can be completed in the marketplace within an acceptable order-cycle time.

HP was having problems trying to supply printers to Europe because of the nature of the marketplace – country differences necessitated different power supplies, different language manuals, and different machine configurations. It tried to forecast country-specific demand and was inevitably off the mark. "The Germans would order more than expected, the Italians would order less," says Richard Dawe, executive coordinator at the Fritz Institute of Global Logistics, Concord, California, USA. You couldn't take an Italian machine to Germany, so HP had the worst of both worlds – frequent stock-outs and high inventory." HP's solution was to modularize its product, set up several distribution centers (DCs) in Europe, and use them to configure generic printers to their specific markets as orders were received. As soon as HP received an order for a machine from Germany, the DC would configure the printer for that market (plug in the correct power supply, attach the right literature, etc.) and ship it out. This approach eliminated the stock-out/high-inventory problem.

(**Source**: Harrington, Lisa H. "The new warehousing," *Industry Week*, July 20, 1998, p. 54)

Packard's innovative use of warehousing to meet the varied needs of its European customers is discussed in logistics profile 7-2.

Chapter Summary

The warehousing function is a very important component of the firm's logistics system, not only on a day-to-day basis, but because the decisions surrounding warehousing have crucial long-term costs and customer-service implications. Warehouses must be located to optimally serve the company's customers. Once each facility is placed, management must decide how it should be managed: in-house, by a third-party, or utilizing some combination thereof. These issues become extremely complex and multifaceted for a firm supporting a global logistics effort, because different markets require different approaches. As with any component of the firm's logistics systems, the costs and benefits associated with various warehousing options must be carefully weighed to ensure that customer needs are being met at the lowest possible cost.

Study Questions

1. How does utilizing a warehouse as a gathering point differ from using it as a breakdown facility?
2. Referring back to the chapter, briefly summarize why Nike changed their European warehousing strategy. Would that same strategy work in Asia? Why or why not?
3. Why would a firm decentralize their warehousing?
4. Briefly discuss the advantages and disadvantages of optimization-type facility location models.
5. Briefly discuss the advantages and disadvantages of simulations.
6. Briefly discuss the advantages and disadvantages of heuristics.
7. How does the warehouse location decision affect the rest of the logistics system?
8. Discuss the three approaches to warehouse operation: private, public, and contract. What criteria should managers use to evaluate them?
9. What are some of the warehousing issues that could confront a logistics manager pondering an international expansion?

Notes

1. Harrington, Lisa H. "The new warehousing," *Industry Week*, July 20, 1998, p. 54.
2. Ibid.
3. Byrne, Patrick M. and Markham, William J. *Improving Quality and Productivity In The Logistics Process* (Oak Brook, IL: Council of Logistics Management, 1991), pp. 318–19.
4. O'Laughlin, Kevin A., Cooper, James, and Cabocel, Eric. *Reconfiguring European Logistics Systems* (Oak Brook, IL: Council of Logistics Management, 1993), p. 232.
5. Brown, Malcom. "All change in Europe," *Management Today*, April 1994, p. 83.
6. Mottley, Robert. "Nike's European 'hot banana'," *American Shipper*, September 1995, p. 52.
7. Coyle, John J., Bardi, Edward J., and Langley, C. John Jr. *The Management of Business Logistics*, 6th edn (Minneapolis/St. Paul, MN: West Publishing Company, 1996), p. 212.
8. Brown, ibid.
9. O'Laughlin et al., ibid, p. 178.
10. Ibid, p. 263.
11. Ibid.
12. Ibid, p. 176.
13. Ballou, Ronald H. and Masters, James M. "Commercial software for locating warehouses and other facilities," *Journal of Business Logistics*, vol. 14, no. 2, 1993, p. 73.
14. Ibid, p. 91.
15. Ho, Peng-Kuan and Perl, Jossef. "Warehouse location under service-sensitive demand,"

Journal of Business Logistics, vol. 16, no. 1, 1995, pp. 135–7.
16. Ibid, p. 137.
17. Maltz, Arnold B. "The relative importance of cost and quality in the outsourcing of warehousing," *Journal of Business Logistics*, vol. 15, no. 2., 1994, p. 48.
18. Ibid.
19. Ibid.
20. Yamatane Corporation informational brochure, pp. 2–5.
21. O'Laughlin et al., ibid, p. 75.
22. Maltz, ibid, pp. 49–50.
23. Rogers, Dale S. and Daugherty, Patricia J. "Warehousing firms: the impact of alliance involvement," *Journal of Business Logistics*, vol. 16, no. 2, 1995, p. 250.
24. O'Laughlin et al., ibid, p. 286.

chapter 8

Materials Handling and Packaging

Introduction	140
Basic Warehouse Design	140
Manual Versus Automated Materials Handling Systems	141
Trends in Material Handling	146
Product Packaging	149
Chapter Summary	155
Study Questions	157

Introduction

Planning for the utilization of space within the warehouse is a crucial task that holds important implications for other logistics activities as well. A poorly designed facility slows the movement of goods, raises both inventory and storage costs, and adversely affects customer service. In order to optimize the use of available space, management must evaluate different forms of materials handling systems, specifically addressing the trade-offs between automated and manual alternatives. Placement of goods within a warehouse based upon sales demand must also be considered, especially in situations in which the storage function is not automated. After examining these points relating to warehouse management, the chapter will then turn to the issue of packaging and its role in the logistics system.

Basic Warehouse Design[1]

A shown in figure 8-1, there are several general principles that guide the layout of any warehouse. First, use a one-story facility wherever possible, because it usually provides more usable space for the money and is less expensive to construct. Second, use straight-line or direct flow of goods into and out of the warehouse, to avoid backtracking and inefficiency.

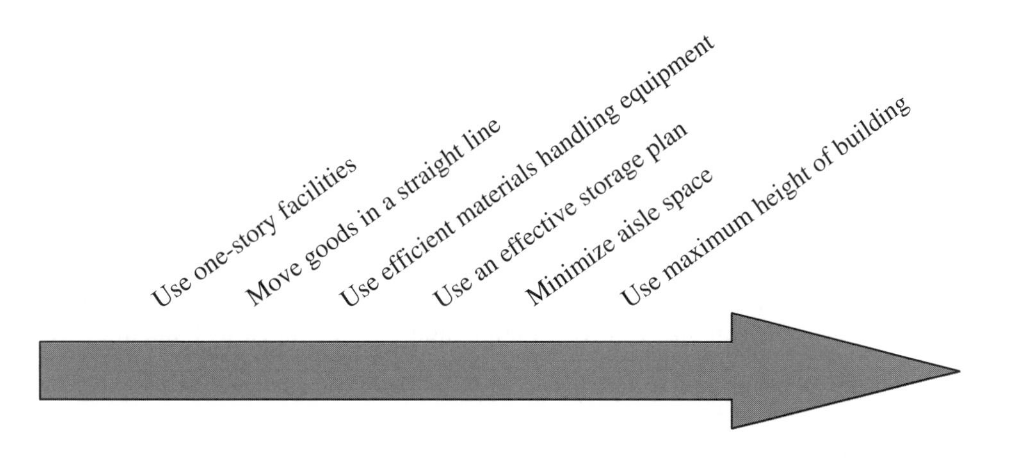

Figure 8-1 Principles of warehouse layout design
Source: Coyle, John J., Bardi, Edward J., and Langley, C. John Jr. *The Management of Business Logistics* (St. Paul, MN: West Publishing Company, 1996), p. 257.

Third, use efficient materials handling resources and operations to improve warehouse productivity. Fourth, develop an effective storage plan that will promote complete and effective use of existing space while providing adequate accessibility and protection for goods. Fifth, minimize aisle space within the constraints imposed by materials handling equipment and the products being stored. Finally, make maximum use of the building's height to utilize all available space. Clearly, these axioms are interrelated, their relative importance being determined by local business conditions, the type of products being housed, and management's strategic vision. For example, a logistics manager in Hong Kong may have to utilize multi-story warehouses simply because land shortages preclude building a large sprawling single-level facility. Similarly, one of the big decisions warehouse managers must face in establishing a facility is how much to automate materials handling operations, a topic that will be addressed in more detail in the next section.

Manual Versus Automated Materials Handling Systems

Manual warehouses

Manual handling systems typically require a great deal of labor. Warehouses utilizing a non-automated approach generally rely on relatively simple systems of racks and shelves for goods storage. Operators place or remove goods either by hand or via some sort of motorized equipment such as a forklift. Manual systems require fairly wide aisles to accommodate these vehicles and are limited in vertical storage because all items must be within reach of the laborer or the forklift. Manual systems tend to work best where there is either very high or very low demand for the goods stored within. They provide a great deal of versatility in order fulfillment, since they use the most flexible handling system around: a person.[2]

However, a labor-intensive warehouse can be extremely costly if local wages are high. Furthermore, people can place items in the wrong place, incorrectly record location data, damage goods, and incorrectly pick the customer's order. Many of these errors can be eliminated through automation of the materials handling function.

Automated warehouses

Warehouse automation attempts to improve productivity and efficiency by mechanizing labor-intensive storage activities. Table 8-1 shows the distribution of automation devices reported by logistics/warehousing executives responding to a survey conducted in 1991. The most common automation device in use today is the hybrid lift truck, reported by slightly less than half of the responding firms (47.6 percent). The next most commonly used systems are improved horizontal systems such as conveyor belts or carousels (41.2 percent), automated storage and retrieval systems (AS/RS) (39 percent), high-speed sorting or screening systems (30.1 percent), driveless and automatic or semi-automatic loading and unloading devices (28.1 percent) and item picking devices (15.9 percent).[3] The responses summarized in table 8-2 indicate that the focus of automation is largely in the following areas: horizontal movement within the warehouse

Table 8-1 Warehousing automation systems in use[a]

Type of mechanization	*Percent of respondents using a system*
Hybrid lift trucks	47.6
Automatic storage and retrieval systems (AS/RS)	39.0
Improved horizontal movement systems	41.2
Driveless and automatic or semi-automatic loading and unloading devices	28.1
High-speed sorting/screening system	30.1
Item-picking systems (i.e vertical and horizontal carousel systems controlled by computer)	15.9
Stationary robots	8.5
Robot vehicles	13.4
Other robots	8.5

[a] $n = 82$ corporate warehouse automated systems
(*Source*: Dadzie, Kofi Q. and Johnston, Wesley J. "Innovative automation technology in corporate warehousing logistics," *Journal of Business Logistics*, vol 12, no. 1, 1991, p. 70.)

Table 8-2 Warehousing activities automated as cited by warehousing executives

Activity	*Percent of respondents automating each activity*
Horizontal movements	63.4
Storage and retrieval	40.3
Inventory scanning/live updating	29.3
Item-picking for orders	25.6
Warehouse transportation	19.5
Cargo handling	10.9
Palletizing	9.8
De-palletizing	12.2
Inspection operations	9.6
Other activities	14.6

(*Source*: Dadzie, Kofi Q. and Johnston, Wesley J. "Innovative automation technology in corporate warehousing logistics," *Journal of Business Logistics*, vol. 12, no. 1, 1991, p. 71)

(63.4 percent); storage and retrieval (40.3 percent); inventory handling, including scanning and updating (29.3 percent); item picking for orders (25.6 percent); palletizing/de-palletizing (22.08 percent); transportation (19.5 percent); cargo handling (10.9 percent); inspection (9.6 percent); and other warehouse activities (14.6 percent).[4]

It is important to understand that these tables represent aggregate responses. As will be discussed later, deciding which functions to automate and how that process should best be accomplished involves the consideration of many company-specific issues. For example, inventory handling may be the critical activity to one firm, while another might view storage and retrieval as being more important and worthy of automation.

Manual versus automated: making the choice

There are some issues that must be considered before moving to an automated system. One is the initial cost of buying the equipment and changing the operation over to the new system. Another major problem can be the retraining of those people whose jobs have been eliminated in the automation process. Other concerns exist as well. Equipment reliability is extremely important because maintenance problems can result in the entire system being shut down. In addition, warehouse management software should be compatible with the firm's existing management information systems. Management must also worry about capacity under-utilization and integrating automation devices into existing equipment. Finally, the fixed nature of an automated system can impede the firm's ability to respond to changing conditions once the manual system is replaced.[5]

Generally, the benefits received from lower operating costs and greater efficiencies outweigh these disadvantages. However, in countries where labor is plentiful and inexpensive, replacing people with equipment may not be as economical as it is in locations where wages are high. Thus, managers must evaluate manual versus automated warehouse systems based upon an assessment of the overall benefit provided by one option over another. In some situations, a manual system might best serve the needs of the firm's logistics system. The optimum storage scheme depends on types of products handled, demand requirements, building design and staffing levels.[6]

Conventional storage layouts typically use aisle widths of 144 inches (365 cm) and a stacking height of between 5 and 10 meters (16.4 and 36 feet) encompassing either four or five shelves. This sort of rack configuration is designed to be used with standard four-wheel counterbalanced sit-down fork trucks that require a large amount of room to maneuver. To translate this into storage positions, a rack configuration that holds 1,000 pallets will require 10,000 square feet (929 sq.m) of floor space.[7] Alternatively, adopting a narrow-aisle (NA) storage configuration increases the number of pallet positions by at least 50 percent (i.e. 6,470 square feet (601 sq.m)) because aisle widths of only 96 inches (244 cm) are required versus the traditional 144 inches. However, different materials handling vehicles must be purchased because the aisles are now too narrow to accommodate conventional forklifts. Very Narrow Aisle (VNA) designs shrink aisle width still further, down to 66 (168 cm) inches, but require highly specialized vehicles. The advantage is that now only 3,070 square feet (285 sq.m) are required to store the same 1,000 pallets.[8]

Fully automated warehouses rely on some sort of automated storage and retrieval system (AS/RS) that is computer-controlled. Bar coding (which will be discussed in more detail later) or radio-controlled devices on each box or stock-keeping unit (SKU) permit the system to automatically store, monitor, and retrieve each item as necessary. Items can be placed wherever there is an open space; because the computer tracks everything, storage can be essentially random. Scattering items throughout the storage area also ensures that if one portion of the materials handling system is not functioning for some reason (e.g. maintenance), SKUs remain accessible at other locations in the facility. These sophisticated systems operate with little direct human contact and provide very high storage density together with near flawless inventory control. However, should mechanical problems occur, goods may simply be unreachable because manual access is not possible given the system's design. Furthermore, should the computer fail, the entire process stops until the malfunction is repaired. However, a state-of-the-art automated warehousing system can offer management a significant competitive advantage and, as discussed in logistics profile 8-1, is especially essential for firms engaged in e-commerce.

Thus, management must weigh a number of variables in deciding how much to automate the warehouse, if at all. The characteristics of the goods being handled, desired throughput rates, building size and shape, labor availability, and the initial costs of mechanized materials handling systems are only some of the factors that must be considered. Indeed, the optimal solution might involve both manual and mechanized components. Agfa-Gevaert NV, the Belgian producer of digital and photochemical products and systems, palletizes nearly all of its air freight shipments at its warehouse in Mostel, Belgium. As the products arrive from the company's European plants, each item is bar-coded so that a computer can monitor its location in the warehouse. When an order by airfreight is made, the products are picked and shuttled mechanically to the consolidation floor. There, Agfa employees stack the freight on wooden pallets instead of traditional flat aluminum airline pallets because

Logistics Profile 8-1

BEHIND DOORS OF A WAREHOUSE: HEAVY LIFTING OF E-COMMERCE

At a sprawling warehouse in St. Cloud, Minnesota, USA, hundreds of employees whiz through the warehouse aisles on forklifts and cargo haulers, filling orders for the Web sites of Wal-Mart, eToys, Fingerhut, and other online retailers. The workers snatch goods off thousands of shelves and deliver them to an army of packers, who box the orders and drop them on conveyor belts. Every item has a special code to speed up the packing: a big-screen television takes an X1, indicating the item is heavy and must be shipped by itself. Lighter-weight valuable items, like VCRs, take a 200 code. That means it requires an additional layer of wrapping paper to help disguise it on a customer's doorstep. Red lasers scan each package as it zips by on the conveyor belt. If the weight of the box doesn't match the specifications on the label, the package is automatically shunted aside so a human inspector can make sure items weren't incorrectly added or omitted. The result: a high-tech, militarized operation that has become one of the Internet's biggest and most admired distribution centers. Vernon Nies, who runs the warehouse for Fingerhut Companies, boasts that his employees can process as many as 30,000 items an hour.

Fingerhut's warehouse illustrates a fact of life on the Internet: While anyone with a computer and an Internet connection can open up a "store" in cyberspace, delivering the goods to consumers has proven to be a much more complicated task. Major retailers, from traditional store chains such as Macy's to Web powerhouse Amazon.com Inc., learned that lesson the hard way during the Christmas season of 1998, when an unexpected surge of online orders left thousands of irritated customers who didn't get their gifts in time for the holidays. Retailers have all had to rethink their packing and delivery strategies. Delivery companies from FedEx to UPS are vying for that business, but Fingerhut's expertise has helped it score some of the biggest coups by concluding arrangements to handle the e-commerce shipments for such mammoth retailers as Wal-Mart and eToys Inc.

The St. Cloud center is computerized down to the minutest detail. As many as 100 trailer loads of goods arrive each day at the facility. Every item's location in the warehouse is precisely charted. Green and white bed sheets, for instance, recently occupied bin YH959 on the second shelf of aisle 52 in building 23A. Customer orders – which come in either via the phone, mail or Internet – pour into Fingerhut's big mainframe computer. It sorts them into groups ordering similar goods and sends them electronically to a printing center. Computers scan each customer's order, checking the dimensions of every item on the list to calculate the smallest possible box that can be used for shipping. "If we can reduce air space in each box so that we can get 1,500 packages on a truck instead of 1,000, in a year's time we have reduced our transportation cost by 50 percent," says Mike Murray, vice president of distribution at Fingerhut. "It ends up to be worth significant amounts of money."

Packages that pass inspection are then routed to one of 38 bays at the shipping dock, where trucks await to haul the goods away for mailing points all over America. A dedicated fleet of trucks departs daily to local post offices throughout the country. By paying local postage fees, Fingerhut significantly reduces their shipping costs.

(**Source**: Quick, Rebecca. "Behind doors of a warehouse: heavy lifting of e-commerce," *The Wall Street Journal*, September 3, 1999, p. B1)

the company prefers to use conventional forklifts. Otherwise, Agfa would have to incur the expense of installing a rollerbed floor in its warehouse. Management did not like that idea because of its permanence and the fact that some trucks serving the warehouse lacked rollerbed equipment on their trailers.[9] Thus, their semi-automated system solved the problem even though some additional handling became necessary.

Trends in Material Handling

There are several important trends in material handling that should guide managers as they examine their warehousing needs:[10] reliability, total integration, flexibility and modularity, upgradeability, automated identification, ease of use, and maintainability. Each of these will now be examined in more detail.

Reliability

In the future, material handling systems will join the entire operation together in an interrelated network. A failure in one area could bring the entire facility to a halt. In the past, "work arounds" usually involved having people move material from one point to another. Today, and more so in the future, facilities will have few – if any – people who can be spared to move material. There will be even less work in process inventory than today, and there certainly will not be enough to permit even partial operation during material handling system failure. Thus, the road to reliability will follow the same path as today. Reliability will require the proper mix of robust equipment and systems fault tolerance, and redundancy. The selection of material handling systems will evolve from selecting the low-cost bidder to picking the most durable equipment available. Managers will analyze each component to determine the failure rate and the impact of the failure upon the entire system. Based upon this analysis, the designer will determine which components require redundancy or duplicated capability that permits the failed segment to be isolated and repaired without shutting down the entire system.[11]

Total integration

The forces of the marketplace in the twenty-first century will require that material handling systems are integrated with all of the equipment in the warehouse. More importantly, the material handling systems will need to be integrated into the entire organization. Equipment will have to be able to move items to and from a wide variety of other stations and equipment types. The material handling system of the twenty-first century will be designed from the ground up so that it provides data to and receives instructions from a wide variety of enterprise-wide computer systems.[12]

Flexibility and modularity

Facilities will be making or handling one product one day and another the next. Managers of the future enterprise will need to be able to make decisions without considering whether or not the material handling equipment can do the job. They will need to be assured that once a new path forward is selected, the material handling equipment will be able to handle the challenge.[13]

Upgradeability

Flexibility and modularity involve being able to handle changes in requirements. Upgradeability is the ability to incorporate advances in equipment and technology. Organizations will be unwilling and/or unable to throw away their material handling equipment with every new advance. As each new improvement comes along, material handling systems will be required to upgrade without replacing major subsystems. In other words, material handling systems will be designed so that improved components can be substituted for old ones.

Automated identification

In order to keep track of a wide variety of products, the material handling system of the future will have to be able to identify each item and take appropriate action as needed. This capability will go far beyond bar coding. Many applications will have the ability to identify objects at a distance, and to instantaneously obtain large amounts of information about a particular item. These requirements, coupled with decreasing chip costs, will result in the wide-scale application of radio frequency (RF) technology. RF chips will be inserted in an object at the beginning of the production cycle. These chips can be queried at any time to identify and provide information about the object or item through-out the entire manufacturing/distribution cycle.[14] In fact, a series of tamper-indicating shipping boxes is now available in sizes from hand-held to large 40-foot-long intermodal containers. The composite material boxes and retrofit liners use embedded fiber optics to determine if security has been breached. The self-contained units continuously monitor fiber-optic loops incorporated in the container frame, door, or hasp and record any activity. Temperature, pressure, GPS position, moisture, light, and other sensors also can be added and monitored, as well as movement of specially tagged items in and out of the container. The boxes can operate passively, with data download to a palm-sized computer, or be modified to be capable of real-time communications.[15]

Ease of use

Material handling will become part of a broader operation. Managers of the overall operation won't have the time or skills to operate difficult-to-use systems. As material handling requirements change, the material handling computer system will modify itself to account for these changes. The system will constantly track material handling performance and will modify itself to increase overall material handling efficiency. Voice recognition and response will become standard whereby operators will be able to instruct and provide information to the system using normal speech.[16]

Maintainability

Several factors will increase the need for maintainability in the future. First, more operations will function around the clock, seven days a week. Thus, there will be little time for planned maintenance. Second, cost considerations will require that material handling system operate with minimum-sized crews. These two factors will result in operators maintaining all or part of the system themselves. Furthermore, the advanced computer systems of the future will be able to detect indications of potential failures before they occur, which will make it possible to schedule maintenance while problems are easy to repair.

Conclusions

While material handling systems of the future will resemble those of today, they will use advanced technology to accomplish their functions faster, better, and at lower cost. Clearly, many managers, especially those in emerging markets, will still find advantages in manual material handling techniques. However, automated systems offer benefits not only in product handling, but in information management, item tracking, and inventory management as well. In addition, environmental issues will demand attention regardless of the scenario selected, as illustrated in logistics profile 8-2. Managers will have to closely analyze the costs and benefits of alternative approaches in order to come up with the material handling system that best meets the needs of customers while supporting the overall logistics process.

Logistics Profile 8-2
LEGO CONSTRUCTS A "GREEN" WAREHOUSE – BLOCK BY BLOCK

As most warehouses are just beginning to ponder the issues involved in obtaining ISO 14000 certification, the environmental management standard, the crew at the LEGO Distribution Center (DC) is already environmentally sound. Construction of the 225,000-square foot building in Enfield, Connecticut took place just three years ago, allowing the company the opportunity to plan an environmentally friendly facility.

Take the DC's ongoing noise control program. "We worked with acoustic engineering students at the University of Hartford to define our noise levels and set up a program to reduce it," says Roger Vogt, director of physical distribution. "We changed the speed on our conveyors and put up barriers around them. Altogether, we reduced the noise level by six or seven decibels." The noise level is so low that LEGO has been able to eliminate the use of ear protection. The company tests employee hearing annually to ensure no one's hearing is harmed. The DC also has an all-electric policy, resulting in the use of electric forklifts exclusively. Air quality is further enhanced by high-tech air handling units and 50-foot ceilings, and is tested on a regular basis.

Because LEGO generates a lot of corrugated cardboard, the staff bundles and recycles it, along with any other paper products. Spills are prevented from damaging the environment through the use of pumps, traps and drains built into the floor. An on-site retention pond lets water run off at the appropriate rate. "We did the right things up front," says Vogt. "We designed the building with both the interior and exterior environment in mind."

(**Source**: "The environment's legal connection," *Warehousing Management*, Sep./Oct. 1996, p. 25)

Product Packaging

Packaging is a topic receiving increased attention around the world. For example, under China's previous planned economy, Shanghai's production sector placed major emphasis on the quality of products and paid little attention to packaging. Shanghai commodities on both the domestic and world markets were often said to display "first-class quality, second-class packaging and third-class pricing." Shanghai lagged far behind developed countries and other coastal areas of China in terms of packaged goods. Over the past two years, Shanghai has earmarked increased investment for its packaging industry in order to ensure that its packaged products meet the demands of consumers for damage-free goods. Manufacturers have come to realize that the improved packaging of commodities can significantly increase the added value of products.[17]

Types of packaging

There are two basic kinds of packages: the consumer package and the industrial package. The former is also referred to as the interior, or marketing, package, because it is what the customer sees when the product is on the shelf. The interior package generally falls under the purview of the marketing department because it is designed to appeal to and inform the final customer. The industrial package is also known as the exterior package, and is primarily a logistics responsibility. The main purpose of the outer package is to protect the goods while facilitating their journey through the logistics pipeline. Often, this package is discarded before the items are placed on the shelf, so customers may never even see this material. What they *do* see if the item is packaged properly is a product that is damage-free and in working order.

Organizational influences on packaging

Many diverse parts of the organization have an interest in packaging for various reasons. As was mentioned earlier, **marketing** cares about packaging because of the role it plays in capturing and retaining customers. **Logistics** is concerned with packaging that will protect the product and make it easier to handle. **Production** must deal with getting each product into its respective package(s). **Legal** must consider packaging from the standpoint of product safety issues and legal requirements to impart certain types of information about the product to the customer. Finally, the **customer** worries about packaging because he or she must handle, store, and use the product before also facing the issue of package disposal.

Clearly, these different views of packaging can conflict for various reasons. **Marketing**, for example, wants an inner package that supports the product, appeals to the target customer, and conveys an appropriate message about the firm and what it stands for. Thus, a company like Chanel, for example, might want to package its newest perfume in a tall triangular bottle made out of Lalique crystal. **Logistics**, on the other hand, would prefer that the perfume was placed into a square container made out of some highly durable and damage-resistant material. The fact is that the logistics world is cubic: intermodal containers, railcars, and warehouse pallets are all rectangular or square. Furthermore, the process of moving products from manufacturer to consumer can be harsh and may result in goods being damaged. So the challenge from a logistics point of view is to take the marketing package and place it in an exterior package that is square and offers sufficient protection from the rigors of the logistics system. The goal, of course, is for the customer to receive a pristine example of Chanel's latest offering.

The role of packaging

One important purpose of packaging is to convey information. This information may be in the form of instructions on how to use, store, and dispose of the product, or it could be guidance on how to handle items during transit. In the former case, the information tends to be written, while pictographs are often utilized to illustrate such handling requirements as the need to protect from weather, stack only to a certain height, or treat with care. In many cases, legal requirements dictate that product ingredients, manufacturing location, and sell/use by date also be provided.

A second critical function is that of protection. This role may involve protection from damage while in the warehouse or en route to the customer, security from tampering or contamination by other products, or shielding from weather.

Finally, packaging facilitates the efficient handling and movement of products by making them physically easier to manipulate. For example, as was discussed earlier, inner packages that may be shaped in an unusual manner for marketing purposes can be made cubic for logistics purposes. Packaging also facilitates unitization or the creation of sensible unit loads for logistics purposes. For instance, fragile perfume bottles can be placed in larger shipping containers so that only one case of 24 needs to be shipped instead of 24 individual items. A number of those cases can then be built up onto a pallet that can then be loaded into a truck or container. Thus, a forklift can handle (assuming 30 cases to a pallet) 720 bottles (24 bottles/case × 30 cases) at one time.

Logistics packaging materials

Historically, most logistics packaging was made out of wood or metal, but both of these tend to add a great deal of weight and cost. Today, however, cardboard is still the primary material for most outer shipping containers. Plastic and other synthetic materials in various forms have become the choice for packing products within those larger boxes. Styrofoam, bubble wrap, plastic wrap, and foam rubber are used extensively because they are inexpensive and offer high levels of protection. Unfortunately, there are environmental considerations associated with these substances which will be considered in the next section.

Some firms are embracing the use of reusable packaging. Mercedes-Benz US International, Inc. (MBUSI), for instance, relies on reusable containers to reduce its manufacturing costs and maintain its commitment to protecting the environment at its new assembly plant in Tuscaloosa County, Alabama, USA. To facilitate JIT manufacturing, MBUSI requires that suppliers use, in addition to several part-specific racks, standard reusable containers to ship components to the plant. Approximately 4,000 standard forklift-type containers in two sizes are utilized. When the loaded containers arrive at MBUSI's receiving dock, their contents are entered into the plant's inventory by using a bar code scanner to record the part number and description from the container. The containers are then moved a short distance to an intermediate holding area. From this holding area, components are delivered to the line just in time, and in sequence, for assembly. Indirect labor costs are reduced because there is no need to cut open boxes or repackage the components for delivery to the line. Furthermore, less space is required for inventory, reducing those costs as well. Once the containers are empty, they can be quickly collapsed and returned to the supplier on the same trucks that have just unloaded full containers.[18]

Environmental issues

Packaging has come under increasing scrutiny in recent years because of the reality that every piece eventually ends up as waste. Unfortunately, many of the materials that are best for packaging (i.e. those made from plastic) essentially never degrade once they are discarded. As consumers and governments become more concerned with environmental issues, firms have had to redesign packages in order to make them biodegradable. McDonald's, for example, used to sell many of their food items in individual Styrofoam containers. These packages not only kept the food hot, but protected it from being crushed. Unfortunately, when thrown away, these food cartons were very slow to decompose. McDonald's tried recycling them into plastic furniture, but was largely unsuccessful because so many of the boxes were discarded away from the restaurants. The company then moved to wrapping most of their products in layers of paper, but this approach failed to both retain heat and prevent damage from occurring if one product was stacked on another. Finally, McDonald's adopted boxes made out of a more friendly cardboard-like material that met both customer and environmental needs.

As products have proliferated in recent years, so has packaging and, by implication, waste. Several nations around the world are becoming concerned enough about the problem of waste that their governments are enacting laws to address packaging issues. In February 1995, the European Union enacted a directive on packaging waste, requiring that all member countries recycle a minimum of 25 percent of their packaging by 2001.[19] The goal then is to harmonize European packaging standards and symbols in order to facilitate the free flow of goods within the Union, while simultaneously maximizing the environmental benefits of various national waste management systems through increased coordination.[20]

Germany is perhaps the farthest along in dealing with the environmental impacts of packaging. Their *Ordinance on the Avoidance of Packaging Waste*, passed into law in 1991, places on industry the sole responsibility for managing packaging waste, including the costs of collecting, sorting, and recycling packages after use.[21] Other European nations such as Austria and the Netherlands have similar approaches either in place or pending. In the United Kingdom, a Landfill Tax enacted in 1997 makes the disposal of solid waste much more expensive then was previously the case, a situation that will no doubt lead to higher levels of consumer recycling. In Canada, a set of voluntary guidelines for the management of industrial, commercial, and household packaging has been developed as opposed to legislation.[22] Even in Asia, where the environmental impact of packaging issues is of less concern, the percentage of recycled packaging is growing at a rapid rate.[23] The governments of countries such as Singapore, Australia, and New Zealand, for example, have all adopted legislation intended to curb waste and address consumer concerns regarding environmental issues.

This increasingly tough stance on packaging waste has profound implications for product exporters. They will have to conform their product packaging to meet the most demanding importing country's standards.[24] If that means the exporter must collect and dispose of used material, managers will have to incorporate those requirements into their overall logistics plan. As was discussed earlier, reusable packaging helps address environmental concerns by reducing solid waste and the various forms of transport-generated pollution.

Packaging for global markets

Supporting global markets presents some unique packaging problems. Shipping internationally requires that products be packaged to withstand the worst possible conditions that might be encountered in the pipeline. For example, moving goods from Germany to markets in rural China could involve a journey that begins with sophisticated, automated logistics systems and ends with manual ones. Transportation might range from trucks to aircraft to bicycles, while warehouses could be mechanized in Germany but manual in China. Thus, in order to ensure that items arrive undamaged, they must be essentially over-packaged for much of their journey.

Another issue is that the inner, or marketing, package may differ from country to country. For example, condiments such as mustard or mayonnaise are sold in glass or plastic jars in the United States whereas in parts of Europe these same products are sold in tubes which necessitates an entirely different outer package. Thus, a packaging strategy that works in one region may have to be totally redesigned to meet the needs of other markets.

A third concern deals with identifying packaging problems when they occur in global settings. Often, customer complaints of goods received in a damaged condition are what alert management to the possibility that deficiencies in packaging may exist. This problem is especially worrisome because the pipeline may be full of goods in transit that are packed exactly the same way. Furthermore, discovering the flaw resulting in the damage can be extremely difficult. Is the carton being dropped or crushed? Is the damage being caused by vibration or is it weather-related somehow? And where in the channel is the abuse occurring?

Fortunately, there are ways to identify the source of damage and in what part of the logistics process it is occurring. Instruments that measure time and impact forces can be packaged identically to, or even with, the product and sent through the pipeline. The data can then be analyzed to isolate the source of the mishandling. For example, it may be that most instances of damage are occurring in a certain warehouse during a specific time frame. Once that discovery is made, personnel can be retrained to handle items more carefully or a mechanized system evaluated to replace one that is mainly manual.

Occasionally the problem may be one that is not so easily traced. For example, management may experience a rash of consumer complaints regarding items that do not work when a buyer gets them home. The products may appear undamaged, but that is small consolation to the user. Vibrations that occur only when certain modes of transportation are utilized may cause the defects. Test equipment is available that simulates the vibration and jostling a product experiences when it is moving, for example, on a truck over a rough road at 100 km (62.1 miles) per hour. This equipment can replicate the conditions experienced with other modes as well. Once the cause of the problem is identified, the packaging (or perhaps the product) can be redesigned to eliminate the damage.

Bar coding

For a number of years, retail packages have displayed bar codes that appear as a series of parallel black and white lines. These lines are of varying widths and represent letters and numbers when read by appropriate scanning devices. Increasingly, bar codes are being utilized on the outer logistics package as well to convey information such as product type, shipment origin and destination, weight, and other data pertinent to the item and its handling. In fact, multi-dimensional bar codes are now being used to impart greater amounts of information.

Bar code scanners fall into two main categories: automatic and handheld. Automatic scanners are in a fixed position and scan packages as they move on a conveyor belt. In contrast, a worker can carry the portable handheld scanner or wand throughout the warehouse. In order to read bar codes, these optical scanners emit light beams and translate the reflections bouncing off the lines into electrical signals. These electrical impulses, which the scanner records as binary digits of 1s and 0s, form the code.[25]

Bar codes facilitate the automation of the entire logistics process. When utilized on the outer package, bar codes convey information needed to store, handle, and transport the goods. Thus, upon entering the warehouse, the bar code can be scanned automatically and the freight entered into the logistics system by the computer. The boxes are then moved to a storage location via the automated materials handling system. The computer records each storage site so that when an order comes in the items can be pulled automatically and sent to the appropriate outbound shipping location. The boxes are scanned again as they are loaded to verify order correctness, create a transportation manifest, and update inventory levels. When included on the inner package, bar codes allow retail checkout to occur much more quickly. The goods can be scanned at the cash register and the price captured instantaneously. In addition, that one scan can also update store inventory levels and sales. In a fully integrated system, the data scanned at the checkout counter initiates the entire logistics process. Store inventories are monitored and, when stock drops to a certain level, a replacement order can automatically be sent to the supplier. This order then starts the replenishment process by directing the materials handling system to find the requisite items in the warehouse, pull them, and move them to the appropriate warehouse location for outbound transport. If both supplier and customer are automated, the entire reorder cycle can be accomplished by the computer without human intervention. Bar-coding is what makes automated order process possible.

Developments in packaging

Much of the work in packaging and package design centers on maintaining (or increasing) protection levels while lowering costs and enhancing disposability. Plastics, styrofoam, cellophane, and other man-made substances are still the primary materials used in packaging because they provide high levels of protection at modest costs. Unfortunately, their very durability makes them unsatisfactory from an environmental point of view. Natural materials such as popcorn and cornstarch are also being turned into packaging that decomposes very quickly once it is discarded and exposed to the elements. Another way to address many of the environmental issues discussed earlier is to utilize reusable containers. Mercedes-Benz's work in this area was previously noted. McDonald's, too, ships products such as ketchup to their restaurants in reusable crates and encourages suppliers to use more durable pallets.[26] Finally, Philips also has developed a reusable and inflatable polystyrene bag to use for packaging products.[27]

Trade-offs with other components of the logistics system

Packaging costs increase directly with the level of protection desired. As shown in figure 8-2, losses from damaged goods fall as the amount spent on packaging increases. In theory, items could be packaged to withstand virtually any shock whatsoever; however, the cost would be prohibitive. Figure 8-2 also reflects the relationship between packaging and transportation costs. The less expensive modes of transport require better packaging because goods are more susceptible to damage. On the other hand, using airfreight means that less can be spent on packaging because items are subjected to fewer shocks and are handled more carefully. A similar trade-off exists with warehousing and is also depicted in figure 8-2. Moving goods through a manual warehouse would require that more be spent on packaging because the handling tends to be rougher and damage more likely. Automated facilities, on the other hand, treat goods more gently, which means that less expensive packaging can be used.

Chapter Summary

The trade-off between a manual versus an automated warehouse can be a difficult one. Mechanized material handling systems offer tremendous opportunities to improve the flow of goods through the facility while enhancing inventory control and minimizing damage. Unfortunately, the initial investment can be quite high and the fixed nature of the system may make it relatively inflexible. Manual systems, on the other hand, are much simpler, easier to adapt to changing conditions, and do not require a large initial outlay of capital. Managers must evaluate each market to determine which is the best approach given local conditions and customer service needs.

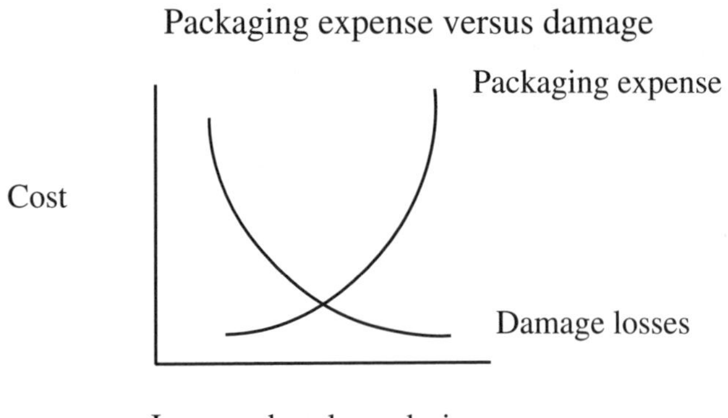

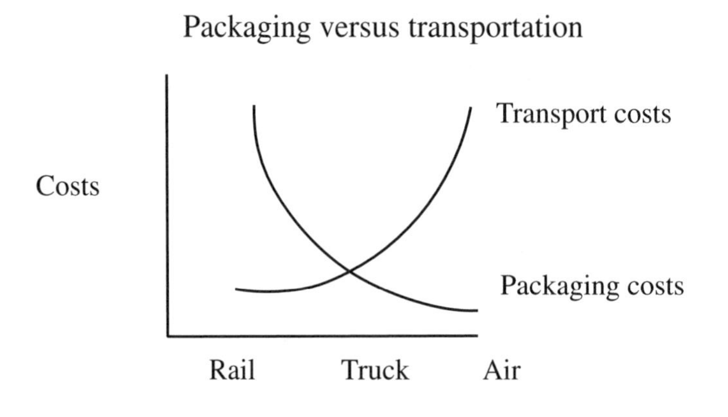

Packaging versus warehousing

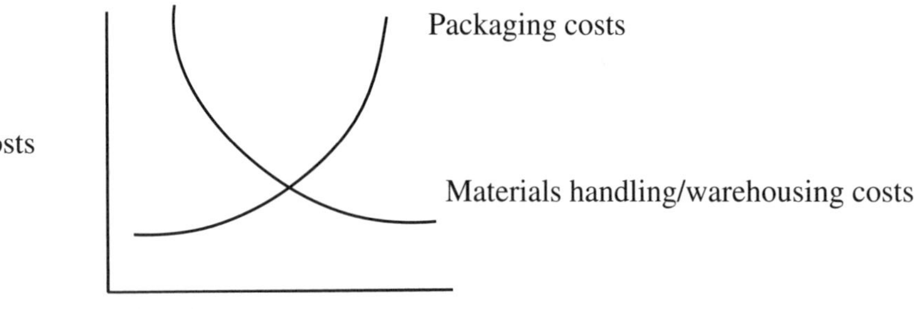

Improved package design

Figure 8-2 Packaging trade-offs

Packaging is an area that is assuming a greater role in logistics as managers attempt to meet their global customers' demands for undamaged goods with packing material that is both environmentally friendly and low cost. In addition, it is now being viewed as an active contributor to overall logistics system efficiency by virtue of the automation made possible with bar coding.

Study Questions

1. Briefly discuss the general principles that managers must consider in designing a warehouse.
2. What are the advantages and disadvantages of a manual warehouse?
3. What are the advantages and disadvantages of an automated warehouse?
4. What variables should managers weigh in deciding how much to automate the warehouse?
5. What environmental factors must be considered in designing a warehouse?
6. Briefly distinguish between the marketing package and the logistics package.
7. How might marketing's view of packaging conflict with that held by the logistics department?
8. Refer to logistics profile 8-1 and the conceptual model presented initially as figure 1-6. Why would a firm develop a "green" warehouse? What customer benefit is being provided?
9. How are countries dealing with the environmental implications of packaging?
10. Describe some of the packaging issues management must deal with when selling to global markets.
11. What is bar coding? How does it facilitate the logistics process?
12. Briefly describe some of the trade-offs between packaging and other components of the logistics system.
13. Give an example of a product that has excessive amounts of packaging. How do you think the packaging could be improved?

Notes

1. Coyle. John J., Bardi, Edward J., and Langley, C. John, Jr. *The Management of Business Logistics* (St. Paul, MN: West Publishing Company, 1996), pp. 257–8.
2. "Storage equipment for the warehouse," *Modern Materials Handling*, 1985 Warehousing Guidebook, Spring 1985, p. 51.
3. Dadzie, Kofi Q. and Johnston, Wesley J. "Innovative automation technology in corporate warehousing logistics," *Journal of Business Logistics*, vol. 12, no. 1, 1991, p. 67.
4. Ibid.
5. Ibid, p. 71.
6. "Plan Ahead To Optimize Your Storage," *Modern Materials Handling*, May 1996, p. 12.
7. Ibid, p. 13.
8. Ibid, p. 15.
9. Gillis, Chris. "'We're not Santa Claus for the forwarder'," *American Shipper*, February 1997, pp. 31–2.

10. Tompkins, James A. and Schaffer, Burt. "High performance material handling trends," *IIE Solutions*, April 1996, p. 16.
11. Ibid.
12. Ibid, p. 17.
13. Ibid.
14. Ibid, p. 18.
15. "Smart containers," *Aviation Week and Space Technology*, January 18, 1999, p. 13.
16. Ibid.
17. Liao Ye, "Packaging and printing in Shanghai," *Beijing Review*, April 25–May 1, 1994, p. 14.
18. "Mercedes-Benz saves on costs, time, and space with returnables," *Modern Materials Handling*, May 1998, pp. 44–7.
19. Buxbaum, Peter A. "European packaging confusion: Europe may give the appearance of being unified, but on packaging, it's a mixed bag," *Transportation and Distribution*, April 1995, p. 63.
20. "Going green in Europe," *Global Trade and Transportation*, May 1993, p. 6.
21. Russo, Ada S. and Shah, Shvetank P. "Packaging taxes and recycling incentives: the German Green Dot Program," *National Tax Journal*, September 1994, p. 689.
22. Ibid, p. 696.
23. "Southeast Asia promises demand for board," *Paperboard Packaging*, May 1996, p. 20.
24. Russo and Shah, ibid, p. 700.
25. Coyle et al., ibid, p. 312.
26. O'Laughlin, Kevin, Cooper, James, and Cabocel, Eric. *Reconfiguring European Logistics Systems* (Oak Brook, IL: Council of Logistics Management, 1993), p. 143.
27. Ibid, p. 175.

chapter 9

Managing Logistics Information

Introduction	159
The Order Processing System	160
Logistics Information Systems	161
Forecasting Methods	163
Using Information to Link a Global Logistics System Together	165
Developments in Logistics Information Systems	170
Chapter Summary	175
Study Questions	175

Introduction

As depicted in figure 9-1, information is a crucial component of any logistics system because it acts as the glue holding that system together. To a greater extent than ever before, large companies view the world more in terms of regions rather than as individual countries. For example, from a logistics standpoint, Norway, Sweden, Denmark, and Finland are looked upon as a single entity, or as the Scandinavian region. From the perspective of sales and marketing, however, they are treated as autonomous countries, i.e. business is local. Behind the scenes there are powerful information systems that make it possible to combine different pricing (sales prices and internal prices), exchange rates, warehouses, suppliers, factories, and supply modes for the same customer order.[1]

The organization's order processing system is the source for a great deal of data, so the nature of that system has far-reaching implications for the entire logistics process. How information is handled within the firm is equally important, with decision support systems becoming more common as a means of rendering information from all parts of the company more useable for managerial decision making. The rapid growth of the Internet as a business tool is forcing firms to reexamine how information flows across the entire supply chain as well. In this chapter, the order processing system will be examined, both in its role as an individual logistics activity

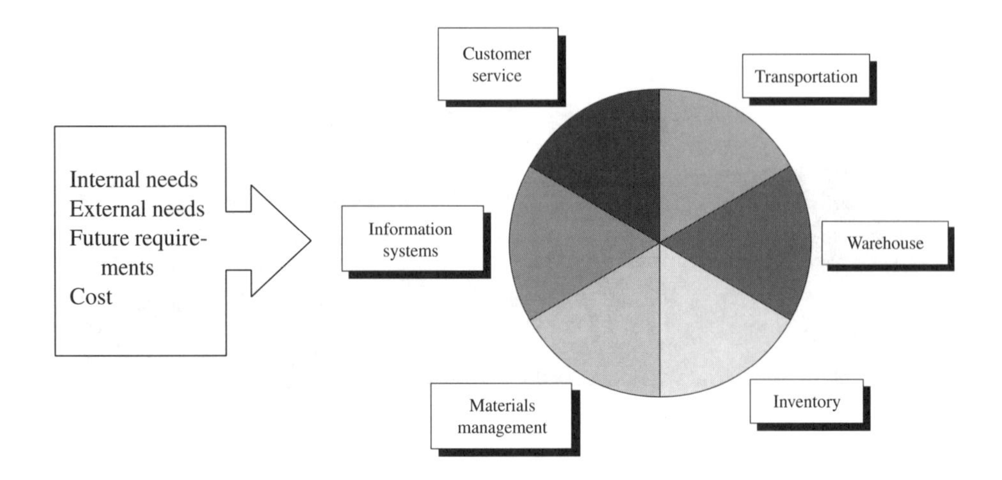

Figure 9-1 Information management within the logistics system

and as the source for much of the information that drives the logistics system as a whole. Then decision support systems will be discussed, as will several emerging issues in logistics information management.

The Order Processing System

One way that an order can be placed is for the customer to write it up by hand and mail or give it to a sales representative who takes it back to the firm. Alternatively, the buyer could fax or telephone the order to a clerk who then writes it. Another approach is for the customer to place his or her order over the phone to a salesperson who simultaneously inputs it directly into the computer. Finally, by utilizing some preprogrammed criteria, orders can be placed automatically by the buyer's computer directly to the seller's system without human involvement. There are clear trade-offs in each situation between cost and information quality. When the ordering process is completely manual, the cost is relatively low but the procedure is slow and prone to errors. As the order placement activity becomes more automated, customer requests can be handled more quickly and with fewer mistakes, but the initial costs increase with the sophistication of the system.

Automating the order processing function offers significant advantages to the firm. First and foremost is that customer service improves because orders can be handled much faster and with fewer errors. By improving the speed and accuracy with which the customer's order is handled, order-cycle time can be reduced which means that customers do not need to hold so much safety stock. Employees handling the computerized ordering process can also advise customers immediately as to item availability, shipping dates, and credit availability. Once the order is accepted, inventory levels can be updated and outbound movement activities initiated. If the item is not in stock, reordering or production activities can be initiated and the customer advised of the product's estimated delivery date. It is worth emphasizing that all of these actions can be accomplished while the sales representative is talking with the customer.

Other benefits accrue to the firm as well. Fewer people are required to perform order-handling functions because these activities are now largely computerized. Cash flow can often be accelerated because of the system's ability to generate customer invoices on the same day as the shipment is made. Finally, there are fewer billing errors and clerical mistakes.

Unfortunately, the more sophisticated the communications system becomes, the more vulnerable the company is to any disruption in the ordering process. Customers do not want to be told that their orders cannot be taken because the computer is not working. In addition, customers may feel more vulnerable to service interruptions because shorter cycle times mean firms hold less safety stock which increases the likelihood of stocking out. However, these disadvantages seem relatively minor in light of the benefits that can result from automating the order processing system.

Logistics Information Systems

As important as the order processing system is, it is but one component of the firm's logistics information system (LIS). Indeed, as businesses adopt a more global posture, the need for an LIS is being recognized as an essential ingredient for success in today's marketplace. Unfortunately, managers often find that logistics information can only be obtained by contributions from several rather poorly integrated information systems. However, as logistics channels become longer and more complicated, involving more channel members, efficient coordination becomes the key to effectiveness.[2] The integration of information from varied sources within the firm is a goal that many companies are establishing. Information integration makes available to management multiple bits of information that previously were generated, analyzed, and stored by many throughout the organization. This integrated information source permits managers to examine the operation of the organization in total, rather than in a fragmented, functionally isolated way.[3] In fact, the whole idea behind a decision support system (DSS) is that making data available to managers will enable them to make better decisions. Thus, a logistics decision support system includes appropriate information files from across the logistics function, but more importantly the linking of these through a database system with access to appropriate modeling software.[4]

The intent of any LIS is to link all facets of the firm's operation together into a cohesive whole so information flows freely to all of the managers who need it. Sanyo has made it a priority to complete a global electronic data-interchange system that will connect all of its 116 companies in 28 countries worldwide. Their goal is to accept and place orders, process delivery information, control manufacturing and inventory, confirm delivery, extend shipping instructions, and provide data to offices around the globe.[5] Not only will this LIS result in more efficient internal operations, but it will provide customers with better information on order status and shipments location.

Environmental scanning

Managers also require information from outside the firm, so any LIS must have the ability to bring in pertinent data from beyond the boundaries of the organization. Environmental scanning is the process by which the company links its environments to its strategic decision making. Operationally, it is the process that identifies and evaluates environmental events and interrelationships for the purpose of improving logistics decision making. Sometimes this activity is **irregular** or reactive; that is, managers attempt to identify the implications of an event that has already taken place. This approach tends to focus on immediate responses to occurrences, without identifying and evaluating future environmental trends and events. Alternatively, **regular scanning** is anticipatory rather than reactionary, and is done systematically but not necessarily continuously. It is up to management to decide how much time and money to devote to the scanning process short of dedicating people to the task full-time. **Continuous scanning** is long term and ongoing, and is often accomplished by employees or an entire department dedicated to the task. Continuous scanning is the best type of environmental observation because the organization is able to identify, evaluate, and respond to forces in the environment much sooner. Clearly, accessing internal data alone is not enough; environmental events must also be considered and corporate resources marshaled based upon occurrences that can positively or negatively impact the attainment of organization objectives.

LIS and information management

One of the by-products of the computer era is that managers are often faced with more information than can be effectively used for decisions. This abundance of data has several detrimental effects, among which are slower decisions, confused decisions, and the obscuring of important information. Consider, for example, a warehouse manager at a consumer products company receiving weekly reports from corporate management. If a computer output of great bulk is delivered with important and unimportant information mixed, inexpert managers will have difficulty finding the data that they really need. Expert managers will find the decision-relevant information, but will lose time developing the search expertise to do so. Both novice and experienced managers may simply stack the report in a corner of the office, to read when they have time. Of course, the managers will continue making decisions based on some other source of information and when reading time becomes available much of the formerly relevant information will be obsolete. Giving managers more than they need to know can be very dangerous when it keeps them from effectively receiving and using the information relevant to their current problems. Decision support systems screen out irrelevant information so it cannot be misused or merely slow down use of the important data.[6] In other words, managers can have the precise data they need to deal with the issue at hand without examining a lot of extraneous and irrelevant information.

Forecasting Methods[7]

One management task that is greatly aided by an LIS is forecasting. By having better data available, analysts can generate more timely and accurate forecasts that more closely reflect environmental realities. A number of standardized forecasting methods are available. These have been categorized into three groups: qualitative, historical projection, and causal. Each group differs in terms of the relative accuracy in forecasting over the long run versus the short run, the level of quantitative sophistication used, and the logic base (historical data, expert opinion, or surveys) from which the forecast is derived. A brief description of each category is presented below.

Qualitative forecasts

Qualitative methods are those that use judgment, intuition, surveys, or comparative techniques to produce quantitative estimates about the future. Sometimes these forecasts emerge from an individual. For example, a manager who has worked for a company for a long period of time may feel as though he "knows" what next year's sales will be. That is, he can observe the market over time; interact with his sales force, channel members, and even competitors informally; and then, based on his experience, come up with a sales forecast for the coming period. Alternatively, a panel of experts (business consultants, academic researchers, or corporate executives) may be brought together to pool their individual opinions into an organizational forecast. Individual assessments may be based on various insights ranging from respective experts' time-honed personal experiences in industry to econometric analyses. Then, once their individual cases have been confirmed (or at least discussed), a corporate forecast emerges and is agreed upon.[8] (Clearly, the value of these future estimates, whether developed individually or collectively, depends on the quality of the people deriving them.) The information relating to the factors affecting the forecast are typically nonquantitative, soft, and subjective. Historical data may not be available or is of little relevance to the forecast at hand. The nonscientific nature of the methods makes them difficult to standardize and validate for accuracy. However, these approaches may be all that is available when trying to predict the success of new products, government policy changes, or the impact of new technology. They are likely to be methods of choice for medium to long-range forecasting.

Time-series methods

When a reasonable amount of historical data is available, and the trend and seasonable variations in the time series are stable and well defined, projecting these data into the future can be an effective way of forecasting for the short term. The basic premise is that the future time pattern will be a replication of the past, at least in large part. The quantitative nature of the time series encourages the use of mathematical and statistical models as the primary forecasting tools. The accuracy that can be achieved for a forecasted time period of less than six months is usually quite good. These models work well simply because of the inherent stability of the time series in the short run.

Time-series models are reactive in nature, tracking change by being updated as new data become available. This feature allows them to adapt to changes in trend and seasonal patterns. However, if the change is rapid, the models will not signal the shift until after it has occurred. Thus, projections by these models are said to lag fundamental changes in the time series and are weak in signaling turning points before they take place. This limitation may not be serious when forecasts are made over short time horizons unless changes are particularly dramatic. However, because these estimates are based on historical data, they can be easily distorted. Several years ago, Motorola, contrary to the guidance provided by historical data and trends, substantially increased its production based on the orders of its distributors. The distributors, fearing that Motorola would once again fail to keep up with demand during the Christmas holidays, ordered extra supplies. By the time Motorola figured out what was happening it was too late. The resulting oversupply in inventory cost the firm 9 percent of its first-quarter 1995 profits.[9]

Causal methods

The basic premise on which causal models for forecasting are built is that the level of the forecast variable is derived from the level of other related variables. For example, if customer service is known to have a positive effect on sales, then by knowing the level of customer service provided, the level of sales can be projected. We might say that service "causes" sales. To the extent that good cause-and-effect relationships can be described, causal models can be quite good at anticipating major changes and forecasting accurately over the medium to long-range period.

Causal models come in a variety of forms. **Statistical** forms such as regression and econometric models provide a figure, for example, of expected sales, that is based upon other numbers input into the model. **Descriptive** approaches such as input–output, life cycle, and computer simulation models provide more of a picture of the future from which an outcome (i.e. sales, deliveries, etc.) can be estimated. Each model derives its validity from historical data patterns that establish the association between the predicting variables and the variable to be forecasted.

A major problem with this class of forecasting models is that truly causal variables are often difficult to find. When they are found, their association with the variable to be forecasted is often disturbingly low. Causal variables whose behavior leads the forecasted variable in time are even more difficult to find. The period needed to acquire data for the leading variables too often uses up all or a substantial portion of the one to six months that such variables are found to be leading the variable to be forecasted. In reality, models based on regression and economic techniques may experience substantial forecasting error because of these problems.

Forecasting logistics needs

Generally, the logistician need not be directly concerned with the broad spectrum of available forecasting techniques. Because forecasted information, especially the sales forecast, is needed by various segments of the organization, the forecasting activity is often centralized in the marketing, planning, or business analysis area of the firm. Forecasts of medium- or long-term time periods usually are provided to the logistician. Unless there is a need to develop specific long-term forecasts, the logistician's need is limited to the short-term forecasts that assist in inventory control, shipment scheduling, warehouse load planning, etc. Indeed, "simple" models of the time-series variety often predict as well or better than more sophisticated complex versions.[10]

Selecting the right forecasting technique

Managers must ensure that they select a forecasting method appropriate to the problem, the data, and the objects of the organization. As mentioned earlier, techniques such as time-series models are better suited for short-range problems, while causal models work best for medium to long-range time periods. Sometimes the analyst becomes comfortable with a certain approach, and attempts to use it for every situation. For example, a catastrophic event such as the Kobe earthquake that struck Japan in 1995 can cause a dramatic drop in sales that will not be immediately identified by and accounted for in a time-series model. Continued use of that technique would be unwise, as it will present management with an erroneous estimate until such time as the model assimilates the effects of the random event. Rather, the technique used should be the one that will generate the best forecast. A "good" forecast displays certain characteristics. First, the forecast should be **computationally efficient** which means that it must be able to handle the data efficiently. Second, the forecast should be **robust**, which means that it should be relatively insensitive to minor errors in the input data. Finally, the forecast should **strike a balance** between responsiveness and stability by responding to meaningful changes in the data without overreacting to slight variations in the data. Utilizing the technique appropriate for the situation will lead to a forecast that generates meaningful results.

Using Information to Link a Global Logistics System Together

Electronic data interchange (EDI)

Managing a global logistics operation requires a huge amount of information. Much of this data was (and still is) in the form of paper documents. However, the growth of electronic data interchange (EDI) has made it possible to send "documents"

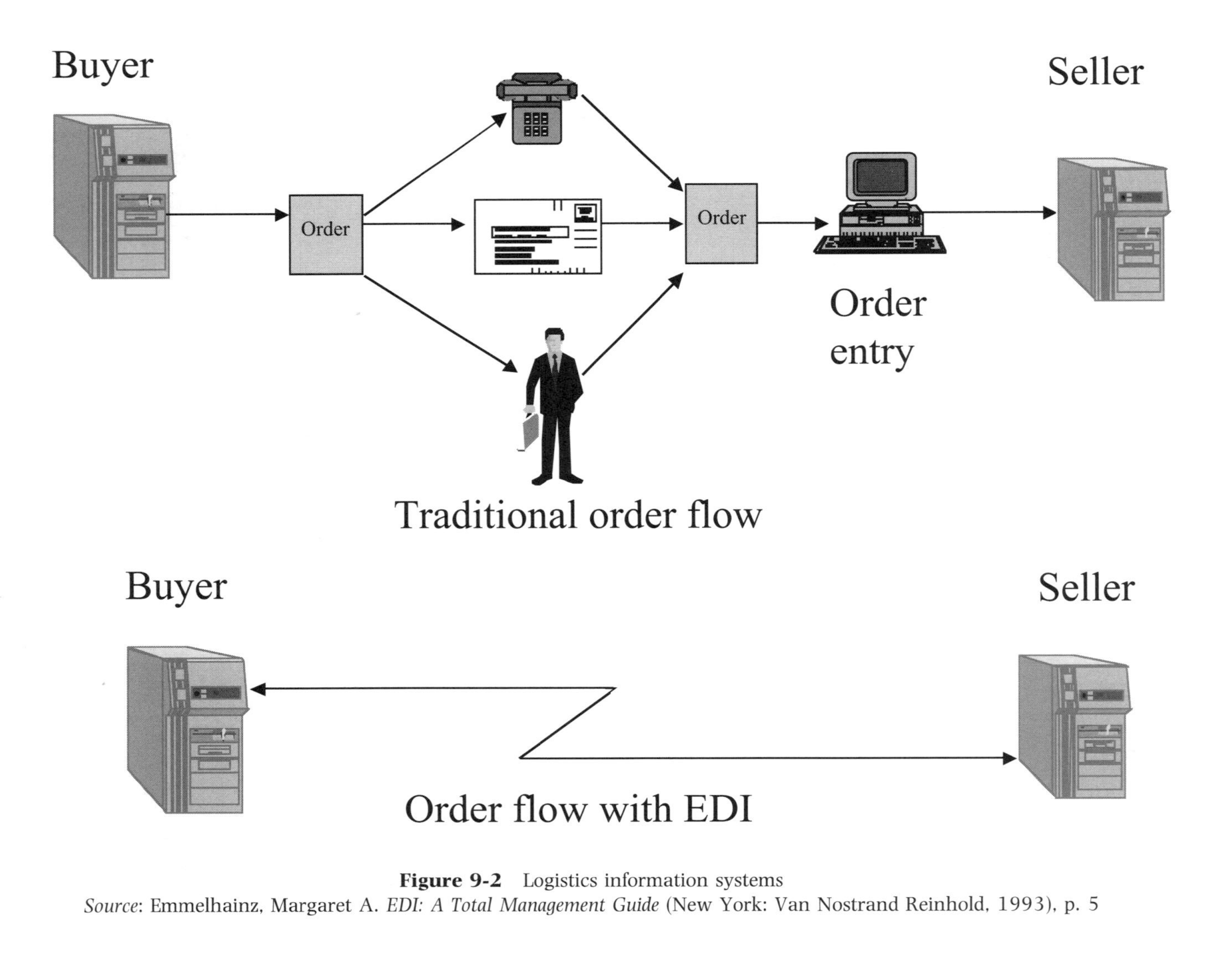

Figure 9-2 Logistics information systems
Source: Emmelhainz, Margaret A. *EDI: A Total Management Guide* (New York: Van Nostrand Reinhold, 1993), p. 5

instantaneously from one computer to another. EDI is the inter-organizational, computer-to-computer exchange of business documentation in a standard, machine-processable format. EDI is intended to allow the receiving computer to "read" and process data without additional human intervention.[11]

The difficulty is that, while an order-entry clerk can review two completely different purchase orders and abstract the pertinent information from each with relative ease, a computer cannot do the same. Although a computer is incredibly efficient and accurate, it cannot equate similar information that is in different formats or in different positions. Therefore, the computer must be programmed, in advance, to receive specific information in a designated format, and then the information must be transmitted in that prescribed manner. EDI standards provide the structure required for computers to be able to read, understand, and process business documentation.[12]

To engage in EDI, business partners must add three components to their existing computer systems: EDI standards, EDI translation software, and some sort of transmission capability. Figure 9-2 shows the order fulfillment process with and without EDI. To illustrate the underlying concept, Emmelhainz provides the analogy of an American dealing by mail with a trading partner in Germany. To communicate successfully, the parties would require a letter written in "generally accepted business format," translation capability from English to German, and a mail service or other method of transmission. With an electronic transfer, EDI standards furnish the format, EDI software provides the translation, and either direct links or value-added networks (VANs) are utilized for transmission.[13] Steady and significant growth is predicted based upon plans of major companies and their suppliers and customers to incorporate EDI.[14]

The advantage of computer-to-computer transfer between companies has been well recognized and developed by progressive organizations in competitive industries. During the 1970s, suppliers and customers began linking computers to facilitate direct data exchange. Suppliers could receive and fill orders without a paper purchase request from the customer. Data from the inventory tracking and production systems could be transmitted to the supplier through EDI communication links. A purchase order could be automatically submitted. Invoices could be sent and payments made through electronic funds transfer (EFT).

Given the rapid growth of global trade and all of the attendant documentation that goes along with it, moving to electronic commerce becomes almost mandatory at least within developed countries. For example, government figures show that about 250 million documents change hands annually in the Hong Kong business community, among 14,000 trading companies, 42,000 manufacturers, 44,000 shippers, 800 freight forwarders, 250 ocean carriers, and their trading partners. The cost of paper-based trade is estimated at some 77 billion Hong Kong dollars (US$9.9 billion) or 5 percent of the city's total trade.[15] EDI offers the ability to convey requisite information without incurring all of the costs that go along with imparting that same data on paper.

In fact, transportation activities benefit dramatically from EDI. Freight forwarders and shippers can now access airline, rail, ship, and truck schedules permitting them to electronically book cargo movements directly with a carrier.[16] In addition, as global trade has increased, so has the need for international transportation. EDI makes it easier to cope with the documentation required to support those shipments. In order to comply with all of the regulations imposed by various governments on shippers, carriers, other intermediaries, and the customers receiving the goods, up to 42 different trade or movement documents (usually in paper form) may be required for an international containerized shipment of goods. A "typical shipment," however, involves an average of six or seven paper documents – including items such as bill of lading, commercial invoice, purchase order, certificate of origin, quota visa, insurance certificate, packing list, health certificate, and documentary letter of credit.[17] To the extent that some or all of these documents can be handled electronically, accuracy improves, costs fall, and the entire transport process becomes much smoother.

One of the biggest constraints affecting EDI growth is the lack of a single EDI standard or language. Internationally, UN/EDIFACT is the standard. (UN/EDIFACT stands for United Nations/EDI for Administration, Commerce, and Transport.),[18] while in North America, the most commonly used format of EDI is the ANSI ASC X12 standard promulgated by the American National Standards Institute.[19] In addition, there are numerous industry-specific "standards" that have evolved over the years. In transportation, two of the most common are Cargo Interchange Message Procedure (CARGO-IMP) in aviation (developed by the International Air Transport Association) and TDCC for the surface modes (TDCC stands for Transportation Data Coordinating Committee which was the group that first developed EDI standards for transportation in the late 1960s and early 1970s).[20] Finally, companies have developed their own proprietary systems over the years that do not utilize any of the previous standards mentioned. Thus, while EDIFACT seems to be emerging as *the* worldwide standard, that process is still far from complete.[21] In order to cope with the plethora of formats that exist, community systems comprised of neutral software are being created that serve as translation buffers between formats. For example, Spectrum, the system utilized by the Cargo Community Network in Singapore, provides a link between shippers, airlines, and freight forwarders. One of the services it provides is translation capability between Cargo-IMP, EDIFACT, and ANSI X-12.[22] However, the widespread use of proprietary systems by many organizations makes it virtually impossible to develop a community system that can translate everything.

Unfortunately, the physical movement of goods today is often still impeded by antiquated information flows that have not kept pace with developments in logistics technology. Especially with regard to transportation, the implication is that, while EDI offers the ability to move information as rapidly as cargo, its use is far from widespread. For example, transport firms have found that documentation in support of intermodal shipments is especially difficult to handle via EDI when multiple carriers are involved. Problems arise because different modes utilize different documents and/or different information within common documents. These issues become especially complex with international movements. For instance, shipments might be tracked one way by a road haulage company, another way by a railroad, and still a third by an ocean carrier. As a result EDI between modes operated by different companies is not common. In fact, while several firms are designing software to address this problem, neutral software that allows for intermodal transportation tracking is still not widely available.[23]

Today's most sophisticated intermodal information systems are those maintained by the so-called integrated carriers such as FedEx and United Parcel Service (UPS). These arrangements often include two-way communication systems that allow drivers and depots to transmit delivery information on a virtually continuous basis. In addition, FedEx and UPS give computer terminals to their customers that connect them directly to the carrier's systems. Shippers can enter package information, track cargo, and check rates without intervention by the carrier's personnel. FedEx has given out 26,500 "PowerShips" costing several thousand dollars each, while UPS has placed 15,000 similar units with its customers. The tracking systems are often real-time for packages that are currently in the transportation pipeline. For items already delivered, daily batch updates with online inquiry are used for historical tracking. The tracking system may also be integrated with the warehouse management systems that support the storage, retrieval, and reconciliation of packages held in bonded warehouses.[24]

EDI use is not restricted to carriers and shippers. Euromar, an association launched in February 1996 by the ports of Genoa, Marseilles, and Valencia, plans an electronic data interchange network between and among Mediterranean ports and shipping lines. Called MARNET, the two-year project intends to create a "multinational real-time logistics network" by linking existing port community information systems. MARNET will also introduce less technologically advanced ports into the network through a series of "technological building blocks" in the form of compatible software. The EDI plan is expected to provide training and software packages to Mediterranean-European, North African, and Mideast ports and transport operators.[25]

Impediments to global implementation of EDI procedures

Perhaps the single biggest drawback to widespread use of EDI is that there simply is no "generally accepted business format" for logistics documentation, especially in a global sense. Although the world is gravitating towards EDIFACT as a standard EDI language, users must still contend with other standards and proprietary conventions. Furthermore, even when a common language is in use, data may be interpreted differently between EDI partners (i.e. does the number shown represent kilograms or pounds?). Another concern is that some countries require paper copies of certain transportation and customs documents that could otherwise be sent electronically. Add to these issues problems associated with formatting errors (data is entered incorrectly, typographical mistakes, etc.) and the costs (both direct and indirect) of implementing a system, and the lack of widespread reliance on EDI as a competitive logistics variable becomes clear.[26]

The reality is that the greatest barriers to the future success of EDI in a global logistics system are not solely technical ones. For example, many emerging markets may lack the electronic infrastructure to handle EDI transactions, necessitating a totally manual approach to information management when doing business in those areas. Alternatively, organizational issues with respect to finances, employees, or other matters may raise barriers to the successful implementation of an EDI system.

However, information technology will continue to advance, allowing greater functionality at lower levels of cost and complexity. Indeed, it can be comfortably assumed that technology will exist to support a paperless and seamless logistics system. Unfortunately, overcoming specific business issues unrelated to technological capabilities will prove to be the greater challenge.[27]

Developments in Logistics Information Systems

Logistics information systems will benefit from advances being made in a number of different areas.

The Internet and electronic commerce

The use of the Internet to conduct electronic commerce is the natural outgrowth of the integration of information technology in corporate operations. As security issues are resolved, it is becoming more common for firms to use the net for logistics purposes such as EDI transmissions, ordering and payment services, and shipment tracking. In fact, the conducting of buying and selling over digital networks is clearly the wave of the future as evidenced by the fact that US companies alone are currently spending nearly $9 billion to lay the infrastructure for electronic commerce. In the process, they are fundamentally changing the way consumers and companies interact, as well as transforming business-to-business supply chains. By 2000, it is projected that nearly $120 billion worth of goods and services will be transacted over digital networks.[28]

Clearly, logistics systems will be affected dramatically by the move to electronic commerce. Companies, suppliers, partners, and banks will all be tied together resulting in streamlined support operations, reduced manufacturing and distribution costs, and increased outsourcing of non-core functions.[29] In fact, information can be updated in real-time all along the supply chain, which will result in shorter order-cycle times, better speed and service quality, and an enhanced ability to handle complexity without errors.[30] For several years, Texas Instruments (TI) has used digital technologies to link its global manufacturing, engineering, and product development operations on three continents, so that they can run 24 hours a day, seven days a week. As a result, product cycles have been slashed, and dramatic cost efficiencies have been gained. Many more companies will follow TI's example: Business-to-business commerce over the Internet is expected to grow to $66 billion dollars within three years.[31]

Electronic commerce is still in its infancy, but the implications are staggering. Manufacturers, suppliers, logistics intermediaries, and customers will all be tied more closely together, permitting the tight integration of all phases of the business cycle: pre-sale marketing, order entry, manufacturing, inventory management, and post-sale delivery. Such control will provide all members of the supply chain with the ability to be more responsive to their customers while improving their own productivity and lowering their costs.[32] As noted earlier, UPS lets customers track the status of deliveries, calculate rates and taxes, and dispatch couriers. Furthermore, UPS

Logistics Profile 9-1
VIRTUAL SHOPPING, REAL DISTRIBUTION

An Internet-based system launched by Federal Express last year opens new opportunities for electronic commerce by linking online shopping directly with express transportation. The system enables shippers to set up an online catalog through which customers can order goods by simply visiting a web site, choosing the required items, and paying by credit card. But VirtualOrder goes one step beyond the static web-site stage, and connects that same online catalog directly to the FedEx transportation network. That means that as soon as an order is made, FedEx is alerted and the shipping process starts. If all goes according to plan, the integrated carrier delivers the purchase within 48 hours.

To speed delivery of goods, FedEx pre-positions an inventory of commodities available through online catalogs in what the integrator calls Express distribution Centers. These are located in destinations around the world, including FedEx's hub sites at Subic Bay, Philippines; Paris; Dubai; and Memphis. Deciding where to position inventory depends on where demand for the product is. "If a UK company delivers mostly to Japan, for example, then we might place stock in Subic Bay or Tokyo," said Antony Francis, vice president of FedEx logistics and electronic commerce in Europe, Mideast and Africa. "Alternatively, we could hold all the stock in the UK and use the FedEx network to get the goods to Japan in 48 hours." FedEx systems are fully integrated with those of the shipper, so all the information needed to anticipate when inventory stocks need replenishing is immediately available to both the integrator and the shipper as soon as on-line orders are made. FedEx can then prepare the replenishment requirement and request those stocks from the shipper. Depending on what the shipper chooses, transportation of replacement inventory to the FedEx distribution center can be handled by either FedEx itself or a third-party provider. Shippers can also opt to handle warehousing themselves, relying on FedEx only for online order-processing and subsequent transportation requirements.

FedEx has targeted the VirtualOrder system at the business-to-business market primarily, although it is also available for businesses selling to the general public. There are two options available for companies that want to sell their goods to other business customers. The first is to create an open access web site that allows anyone to view the on-line catalog, requiring him or her to register only when they make an order. A variation of that option requires customers to register in order to view the web site. VirtualOrder is aimed at the kind of high-value, low-weight commodities normally shipped by FedEx as an express transportation provider. In the business field that means electronic and medical products, but in the consumer field FedEx is looking at other items, such as luxury products. Francis admits that FedEx is still learning about the potential offered by the VirtualOrder system, particularly when it comes to offering shippers customized versions of the products. VirtualOrder is currently available only in the US and for US export, but Francis said the company plans an international version. The latter would need to make provision for factors such as different transportation rates and varying customs regulations.

(**Source**: "Virtual shopping, real distribution," *American Shipper*, April 1998, pp. 31–2)

tracking functionality is also integrated into the sites of the three major Internet search engines: InfoSeek, Lycos, and Yahoo.[33] FedEx has recently introduced an Internet-based shopping system that is described in logistics profile 9-1.

Open-systems computer networks

Multiple vendor, multiple operating system environments are becoming more common as firms move toward the use of computers running a variety of operating systems. These machines are connected via local area networks (LANS) which are in turn connected through bridges or routers to wide area networks (WANS) covering vast geographic regions.[34] Because LANS and WANS provide connectivity between these disparate systems, issues regarding such things as multiple EDI "standards" can be handled.

Wireless communication

Wireless technology will redefine logistics information systems in general. For example, a wireless modem has recently been introduced which provides connectivity of serial input–output devices, in any combination, to a host computer. Fixed scanners, weight scales, remote printers, batch terminals, point-of-sale terminals, PCs running dedicated applications, and PCs running terminal emulation programs can be integrated into this wireless data communication system.[35]

Two-dimensional bar codes

As was noted in the previous chapter, two-dimensional bar codes contain significantly more information than the standard flat bar codes commonly used today. Where scanners previously read only across relatively thin bars of slightly varied width, now the bars are thicker and are read both horizontally and vertically. This additional capacity is sufficient to permit the coding of, for example, an entire freight waybill, on a one-inch (2.5cm) square.[36]

Logistics Profile 9-2
MAKING PALLETS TALK

Today's shorter product life cycles and just-in-time (JIT) orders are challenging warehouse managers to reconsider traditional order fulfillment systems. A new "smartpallet" system, based on Texas Instruments' TIRIS Radio Frequency Identification (RFIT) Technology, eliminates repetitive handling and compresses delivery lead times using automated processing.

At Unilever Italia, one of the first companies in the world to use this system, order fulfillment takes 20 percent less time and requires one-third the manpower. Unilever, the 25th largest company in the world, manufactures shampoo, toothpaste, laundry detergents, cosmetics, floor care, and a variety of other consumer products. Before installing a RFIT system, processing 200 pallets daily at Unilever's Elida-Gibbs plant took three workers. Today, one warehouse worker can expedite 350 plus pallets a day. One entire step, in which pallets were stacked and reloaded as an employee prepared the final loading list, has been eliminated.

TI and Sinformat SRI, a computer engineering company, teamed up to create Unilever's system. The system was installed in June 1995 at their Gaggiano plant, located near Milan. Sinformat SRI designed the Windows-based computing system, EASYSEND. TI developed the low-frequency RFID system that controls product movement, records its whereabouts, and activates weighing and labeling operations. Shipments are whisked through the warehouse by lift trucks equipped with radio frequency readers. These readers signal the status of every pallet to transponders at each gate. Information is transmitted to a warehouse computer that knows the location of any order at any time. The TIRIS system, which combines semiconductor technology, microelectronic packaging and computer systems design, consists of three components: a transponder, a computerized reader, and an antenna. Transponders are attached to gates in the warehouse through which pallets pass; the reader and antenna are on the lift truck.

At Unilever's high-tech warehouse each pallet is assigned a bar code that is scanned into the warehouse's programmable logic controller. Along with the bar code, the computer stores a description of the pallet: how many boxes it holds, where the order is bound, and what product is being shipped. A pallet might contain 2,000 bottles of shampoo or 10,000 tubes of toothpaste. Before it passes through the first gate, it is film wrapped and weighed. That weight is compared at the last gate to ensure accuracy. Pallets are handled on a First-In First-Out (FIFO) basis. Their queue order goes into the computer's memory. As a pallet is being moved to the loading bay, a TIRIS reader on the lift truck interrogates the disk-shaped transponder on the gate with a burst of radio frequency energy. The same energy powers the transponder to return a signal of its own. That signal transmits the gate's location, simultaneously pinpointing the pallet's location. When the pallet reaches the loading bay, another transponder alerts the computer of which trailer the pallet has entered. When a trailer is full, the truck scale automatically compares the total weight of its load, along with the individual pallet weights from the computer's memory. This comparison signals any discrepancies in the system.

Since pallet data are transmitted electronically, the system eliminates manual entry and paperwork. A loading list is automatically printed for each trailer shipment. Delivery forms at the loading bay are electronically stamped. The database of information created by the computer also helps the warehouse better manage its operations. Unilever hopes to network its loading dock with its distributor in Melzo, allowing information about truck trailer loads to leave the computer as the truck departs the loading dock. The distribution facility could have its warehouse pre-organized to accommodate the incoming load by its arrival time. "With this system, it is possible to know, in real-time, what and how much we are producing and sending," says Renzo Codeca, industrial engineering manager at this warehouse. "The principal advantages include better security of the stock and elimination of rehandling, both of which save time, errors, and, by implication, drive costs up". Thus, the company is saving both time and money!

(**Source**: Dawe, Richard L. "Tackle 21st century technology today," *Transportation and Distribution*, Oct. 1996, vol. 37, no. 10, p. 113–14)

Radio frequency identification (RFID) technology

RFID refers to the electronic tagging of boxes, pallets, or equipment with a device that utilizes a radio signal to transmit information regarding location, contents, and/or movement. These transmissions can be read at any point in the shipping process to provide instantaneous, real-time information about the status of the items from which they are emanating. The implications for use on ocean containers, for instance, are staggering. Not only could specific containers be located quickly (for example, a message could be sent asking, "Where is box number 3256?" and the box will answer, "Here I am, Row 3, Column 6, on the bottom."), but the contents of each unit could be ascertained as well.[37] Logistics profile 9-2 explores the possibilities inherent in RFID applications.

Other advances in communications

There are other developments that will profoundly impact logistics as well. Global positioning system (GPS) technology is already being applied to vehicle tracking and monitoring applications as well as to scheduling and routing software. Vehicles can be located immediately, allowing managers to keep their customers informed as to shipment location and anticipated delivery time. Sensitive shipments can be tracked continuously if need be, while trucks can also be rerouted to fulfill last-minute pick-up or urgent delivery requests. Similarly, on-board computers and evolving cellular telephone technology combine to keep drivers in constant touch with dispatchers. Downtime is therefore reduced while customer service is improved.

Chapter Summary

Advances in information systems are transforming the way logistics is managed. Automating the order processing function leads to better customer service and the capture of more information for later analysis. The growing use of decision support systems in logistics is helping managers to improve both their decision-making and forecasting capabilities. Electronic data interchange offers firms the means to transmit logistics information throughout the channel with more precision and at lower cost than comparable manual systems. Finally, technological advances in various types of hardware will continue to enhance the quality of information available to managers, improve customer service, and lower response times.

Study Questions

1. What is the impact of an automated order processing system on customer service?
2. How can a logistics information system contribute to improved management decision-making?
3. Differentiate between the three types of environmental scanning.
4. What is a qualitative forecast based on? Does it have value as a predictive tool? Defend your answer.
5. Describe time series forecasting techniques. What are the advantages/disadvantages of using these models?
6. From the analyst's point of view, what constitutes a "good" forecast?
7. What is EDI? How can it improve logistics processes?
8. What problems must be overcome before the benefits of EDI can be fully realized?
9. The text discusses a number of innovations or developments occurring in logistics information systems. How will these advances work together to improve customer service and/or reduce costs?
10. Referring to logistics profile 9-2, how might "talking" pallets impact the rest of the firm's logistics system? the firm's customers?

Notes

1. Carlberg, Ulf Caster. "Information systems must offer customized logistics and increased profitability," *Industrial Engineering*, June 1994, vol. 26, no. 6, p. 24.
2. Bardi, Edward J., Raghunathan, T. S., and Bagchi, Prabir K. "Logistics information systems: the strategic role for top management," *Journal of Business Logistics*, vol. 15, no. 1, 1994, p. 72.
3. Ibid, pp. 72–3.

4. Bookbinder, James H. and Dilts, David M. "Logistics information systems in a just-in-time environment," *Journal of Business Logistics*, vol. 10, no. 1, 1989, p. 52.
5. Magnier, Mark. "Post-quake Japan's Sanyo is rethinking its logistics," *The Journal of Commerce*, April 27, 1995, p. 8A.
6. LeMay, Stephen A. and Wood, Wallace R. "Developing logistics decision support systems," *Journal of Business Logistics*, vol. 10, no. 2, 1989, p. 8.
7. Adapted from Ballou, Ronald H. *Business Logistics Management*, 4th edn, (Upper Saddle River, NJ: Prentice-Hall, Inc., 1999), pp. 277–94.
8. Ibid, p. 175.
9. Czinkota, Michael R., Kotabe, Masaaki, and Mercer, David. *Marketing Management*. (Cambridge, MA: Blackwell Publishers, Inc., 1997), p. 166.
10. Ibid, p. 117.
11. Emmelhainz, Margaret A. *EDI: A Total Management Guide* (New York: Van Nostrand, 1993), p. 53.
12. Ibid.
13. Ibid, p. 13.
14. Ibid, p. 3.
15. Bangsberg, P. T. "EDS deal seen spurring Hong Kong EDI," *Journal of Commerce*, March 19, 1996, p. 1B.
16. Gourdin, Kent N. and Clarke, Richard L. "An update on the status of EDI in transportation," *Journal of Transportation Management*, vol. +VI, no. 2, Fall 1994, pp. 111–12.
17. Damas, Philip. "Balero EDI clearinghouse," *American Shipper*, January 1997, p. 42.
18. Ibid, p. 69.
19. Ibid, p. 53.
20. Ibid, p. 67.
21. Gourdin and Clarke, ibid, p. 113.
22. Gourdin , Kent N. and Andersen Consulting. Unpublished research report entitled *Intermodal Information*, Research Project H, Air Cargo Manufacturing Facility Study, FAA Research Grant 93–G-022, October 1993, p. 7–5.
23. Ibid, p. 134.
24. Grossman, Laurie. "Federal Express, UPS face off on computers," *The Wall Street Journal*, September 17, 1993, p. B1.
25. *American Shipper News Wire*, vol. 2, no. 36, February 20, 1997, pp. 2–3.
26. Gourdin and Clarke, ibid, p. 137.
27. Ibid, p. 138.
28. Alden, John. "What in the world drives UPS?" *International Business*, March/April 1998, p. 7.
29. Ibid.
30. "The warehouse: making reality a dream," *Inbound Logistics*, May 1998, p. 28.
31. Alden, ibid.
32. Ibid, p. 26.
33. Ibid.
34. Dawe, Richard L. "Tackle 21st century technology today," *Transportation and Distribution*, October 1996, vol. 37, no. 10, p. 112.
35. Andel, Tom. "Technology's challenge: fast but flexible," *Transportation and Distribution*, January 1996, vol. 37, no. 1, p. 72.
36. Lamb, J. J., "Whiz-bang!," *World Trade*, June 1995, p. 66.
37. Ibid.

chapter 10

Inbound Logistics and Purchasing

Introduction	177
The Growing Importance of Inbound Logistics	177
Inbound Logistics Activities	178
Purchasing	182
Management Techniques for Improving Materials Management	190
Chapter Summary	190
Study Questions	190

Introduction

Inbound logistics embraces the flow of raw materials, component parts, and supplies into the production process. Often referred to as materials management, inbound logistics issues are frequently viewed as sub-areas of production since manufacturing is, in some sense, the customer. However, this narrow perspective ignores the reality that, as illustrated in figure 10-1, decisions made with respect to purchasing and obtaining raw materials affect the finished good and thus can have a direct impact on the final consumer. This chapter will first examine the activities that make up the firm's inbound logistics system. Then the similarities and differences that exist between those tasks as performed on the outbound (or finished goods) side of the production line will be presented. Finally, the purchasing function will be explored in more detail.

The Growing Importance of Inbound Logistics

The objective of logistics management on the inbound side of the production line is virtually the same as it is on the outbound side: to provide a given level of customer service at the lowest total cost. However, the changing nature of global competition is forcing firms to pay more attention to materials management than ever before.

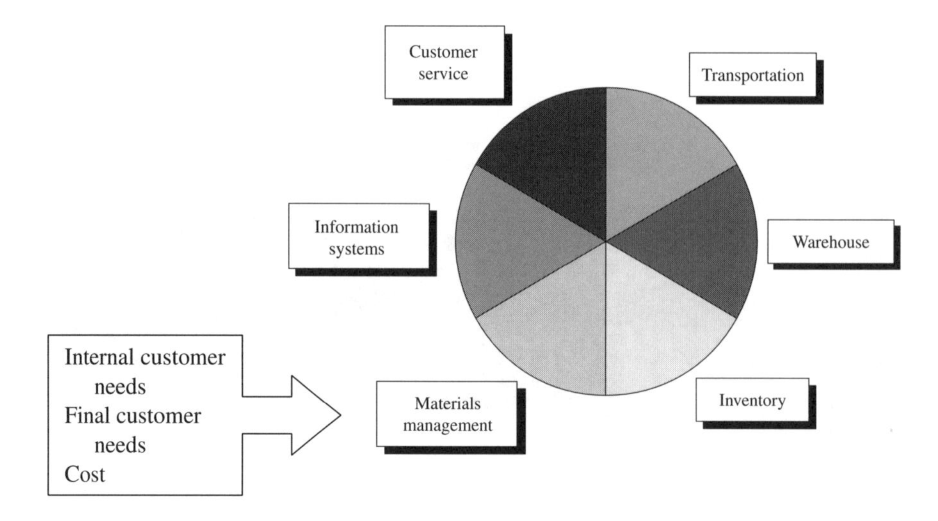

Figure 10-1 Materials management within the logistics system

Ten to 15 years ago, most European products, for example, were manufactured locally for local distribution. Today, components and finished products may come from many different sources. For instance, because the vast majority of portable audio products sold in Europe are now imported, the "economical" size of plants has increased dramatically. According to estimates by Philips, the Dutch electronics giant, the optimal output for their TV-set factory should be around 2 million units per year; for VCR recording heads, it would be near 5 million. As a result, the company has gradually decreased the number of manufacturing sites for finished products and components in Europe from 50 in 1972 to fewer than 20 today.[1]

Sourcing is becoming increasingly global. The more mature a product, the more standardized its production becomes. As this process occurs, it is common for manufacturing to move from, say, one site in Northern Europe to a plant in Southern Europe, and from there to Far Eastern locations such as Singapore and Malaysia. Philips, for example, has on average a three-week order cycle between its central warehouse and European plants, compared to three-month lead times for goods manufactured in the Far East. New entrants such as Japanese manufacturers, which used to import all their products from Far Eastern plants, face a similar challenge of coordinating inbound flows of parts and components as they develop a manufacturing base in Europe.[2] The potential for smoothing the entire process is illustrated by Saturn's experience, detailed in logistics profile 10-1.

Inbound Logistics Activities

Despite the generally similar nature of inbound and outbound logistics operations, there are some significant differences that warrant a brief examination of the specific activities that could comprise a firm's inbound logistics system.

Logistics Profile 10-1
SATURN INTEGRATES ITS INBOUND LOGISTICS

A great many supply chain management practices converge at the Saturn operation in Spring Hill, Tennessee, USA. So adroitly does the automaker manage its supply chain that in four years it has had to halt production just once – for only 18 minutes – because the right part was not delivered at the right time. Saturn maintains almost no inventory of components. Instead, a central computer directs trucks to deliver pre-inspected and presorted parts at precise times to the factory's 56 receiving docks, 21 hours a day, six days a week. Especially striking about this just-in-time system is that most of Saturn's 339 suppliers are not located anywhere near the plant. They are in 39 states and an average of 550 miles (916 kilometers) away from Spring Hill.

Charged with making the Saturn network run on schedule is Ryder Systems, the Miami, Florida (USA) transportation services company that has become the biggest logistics management firm in the US. Ryder's mandate is to keep parts, people, and trucks in nearly constant motion. Tractors, pulling trailers that are, on average, 90 percent full (an exceptionally high ratio), arrive daily at Ryder's command post some two miles from the Saturn factory. There the drivers uncouple the trailers. Specially designed shuttle tractors then take the trailers, which contain bar-coded, reusable plastic bins full of parts, and deliver them to the plant.

The long-distance drivers, meanwhile, connect their trucks, the most expensive part of Ryder's $32 million of assets, up to other waiting trailers, which are stocked with empty bins to be hauled back to suppliers. In a first for the auto industry, the trucks also carry boxes of service parts to be delivered to Saturn dealers. The truck drivers plug a plastic key, loaded with electronic data, into an on-board computer. The screen then tells them exactly where to go, which route to take, and how much time to spend getting there.

(**Source**: Henkoff, Ronald. "Delivering the goods," *Fortune*, November 28, 1994, pp. 76–8)

Customer service

Customer service is somewhat multi-dimensional because, in one sense, the firm is the customer. That is, the company is purchasing raw materials, component parts, etc. for transformation into finished goods. Thus, the organization is receiving customer service rather than providing it. However, management must keep in mind that decisions made regarding flows into the production process also impact the final customer in terms of the cost, quality, and availability of the finished product. In other words, customer service is just as important a variable on the inbound side as it is on the outbound side.

Transportation

There are several significant differences between the movement of raw materials, component parts, and subassemblies inbound and finished goods outbound. First, basic differences in the nature of the items moved often necessitate the use of different equipment inbound as opposed to outbound. For example, sheet steel used in the manufacture of washing machines may be delivered to the plant via railroad or flatbed (i.e. open-sided) trucks. The finished appliances, however, may depart the factory in vans (i.e. enclosed trailers) for delivery to retail stores. Second, firms often exercise less control over their inbound transport because delivery is included in the price of the goods and is under the control of the seller. Finally, the demand for inbound transportation tends to be more stable than the requirement for finished goods movement because production rather than inherently variable market forces dictate the need for raw materials.

Inventory management

Inventory concerns are virtually the same whether dealing with raw materials or finished goods. Managers want to meet customer needs while minimizing the cost of holding inventory. With raw materials, the firm itself is the customer, but, of course, decisions made also have an impact on the final consumer as was noted earlier. Because stock-outs on the inbound side bring the production line to a halt, the cost of holding inventory must be balanced against the cost of not having inputs on hand when the manufacturing process requires them.

Essentially, the expenses incurred in stopping production are the costs that result when a stock-out occurs. These costs can be very high, as the General Motors Corporation found out several years ago when a key body and stamping plant went on strike. The factory was the sole supplier for about 300 Saturn parts, so the entire GM Saturn division was forced to shut down because it operated on a just-in-time inventory system and had no stockpile of parts. That closure quickly rippled back through the corporation, forcing eight more GM plants to stop production at a daily cost to GM of between $8 and $10 million in pretax profits.[3]

Warehousing and storage

Raw materials must be stored on, or very close to, the manufacturing site whereas finished goods can often be positioned closer to the market. As was mentioned earlier, handling and storage requirements for raw materials tend to be quite different from those of finished goods. Indeed, while a warehouse is usually thought of as a building with walls and a ceiling, it may be nothing more than an open field depending on the commodity being housed. However, despite the requirement for less sophisticated facilities, costs are still a concern on the inbound side because the products themselves are often of little value. Steel used in the manufacture of appliances, for example, costs very little to buy and can be stored outside. Even though storage expenses are relatively low, they still make up a large percentage of the product's value because the steel is so inexpensive. In other words, as a percentage of product value, warehousing expenses comprise a larger proportion of total product cost on the inbound side.

Maintenance

Maintenance refers to all of the activities associated with the servicing and repair of equipment. Maintenance may comprise a large part of a service firm's inbound logistics system; indeed, maintenance to some companies is what production is to others. An airline, for example, cannot move people unless the airplanes are maintained. Even in a manufacturing firm, the assembly lines must be serviced and maintained, although maintenance here tends to be a much smaller part of the organization's overall logistics effort.

Information management

Clearly, information management is equally important to both inbound and outbound logistics managers. In the former instance, managers collect and utilize information to smooth the flow of raw material into the production process. However, much of the data that is initially captured on the inbound side (raw materials costs, production schedules, etc.) will be repeatedly utilized throughout the organization as various analyses, forecasts, and other unforeseen problems are dealt with. Thus, the quality of the data coming in has a profound and lasting effect on the entire logistics system, not just the materials management portion.

Salvage and waste disposal

As firms and their customers become more concerned about environmental issues, managers must ensure that production by-products are handled in a socially responsible manner. Sometimes there may be a market for the company's waste. Two Japanese firms have developed a melting furnace designed to recycle ash generated by municipal waste incinerators so it can be converted into such things as road bed materials, fired tiles, and ballast for heavy machinery applications.[4] However, in the absence of such good fortune, management can expect to incur whatever costs are necessary to dispose of waste in a way that does not harm the environment. This task can be extremely complicated and expensive if the waste is hazardous because specialized equipment and handling may be required.

Production

Production turns raw materials into the finished goods customers desire. Thus it has a direct impact on not only the organization's demand for raw material and component parts, but also the level of customer satisfaction the firm is able to deliver. Because of its overall importance, production has been, and often still is, viewed as the most important part of any organization. Every other corporate function may be seen as secondary to supporting the manufacturing line. Increasingly, however, managers are realizing that customer needs should drive the organization's efforts, not production.

Summary

All of these functions will not occur in every company. But managing the flow of component parts, subassemblies and raw materials into the production process requires the same systematic approach advocated for handling finished goods. By viewing inbound activities as pieces of a larger inbound logistics system with the firm as the customer, management can maximize the value they obtain from their suppliers which, in turn, means greater value for the final consumer.

In fact, having a common senior manager oversee both inbound and outbound logistics activities offers some significant opportunities for service improvement and cost savings. First, a single manager can keep the entire logistics effort focused on delivering value to the final customer. When viewed as two distinct functions, materials management and physical distribution activities may come into conflict without a common leader to maintain the customer's point of view. Second, there are economies of scale that may be obtained. For example, it may be possible to use vehicles transporting component parts into the production process to move finished goods to the marketplace. Similarly, warehousing space may be used to store both raw materials and finished goods. In reality, the different nature and handling characteristics of raw materials versus finished goods often makes such sharing impossible. However, an astute manager may still realize that the same transport company could be utilized for both inbound and outbound movement requirements. Though probably requiring the use of different equipment, such an alliance should result in lower costs and better service than would be possible if one company was used for inbound transport and another for outbound.

Purchasing

Over the past three decades, increasing global competition has caused a dramatic increase in the outsourcing of materials. Firms are demanding the best value for all components used in the finished product. Parts that were once produced in-house as a matter of corporate policy are being purchased from suppliers around the world. For a typical manufacturing firm, the share of finished product cost that is

Logistics Profile 10-2
HOW THE GAP FILLS ITS GAPS IN LOGISTICS

The Gap, a specialty retailer of clothing and other merchandise, has almost 1,900 stores worldwide, including Gap Kids, Banana Republic, and Old Navy. There are 900 Gap stores in the US, 91 in Canada, 70 in the United Kingdom, 17 in France, nine in Japan, and eight in Germany. In the US, there are 450 Gap Kids stores, 210 Banana Republic Stores, and 140 Old Navy Stores.

Each division has a different pitch. The Gap offers clothes for the masses. According to Ro Leaphart, senior director of logistics, Banana Republic sells "a higher end of garment product, while Old Navy is a department store concept offering a variety of merchandise." "We have waves of freight moving worldwide every hour of the day. When back-to-school happens, our volumes increase fourfold. We love our clothes to be there on time, which requires a flexible supply system."

The Gap and its divisions source product in more than 50 countrics. "Abroad, Asia is our heaviest sourcing area," Leaphart said, with Hong Kong alone accounting for 25 percent of the company total. In the US, 500 factories account for 35 percent of sourcing. "As much as we are a retailer, we're not buying wholesale," Leaphart said. "We go directly to the factories and place orders, and we have them shipped from the factory to The Gap. Then, we disperse them to our stores and distributors."

In contrast, Levi-Strauss sells its products to other parties, which then distribute them (The Gap itself distributed Levi-Strauss's goods until 1991). But The Gap owns its products from the time they enter its supply chain. "We have new logistics every day," she said. "We have to source product, get it from wherever we can find it at the price point available, and move it to its destination on time, every time." For example, "if customers want jeans in very small sizes in Tokyo on a certain date, they are going to get them. Our stores in Japan are compact, so we feed in the right amount of product on a daily basis. That's a very expensive distribution of just-in-time inventory."

(**Source**: Mottley, Robert. "How The Gap fills its gaps in logistics," *American Shipper*, January 1997, pp. 36–9)

represented by purchased parts (as opposed to those made in-house) can range from 40 to 60 percent.[5] As a result, purchasing is becoming a key success factor and the current movement towards even greater trade internationally will only increase its importance.[6] Logistics profile 10-2 provides some insight into the magnitude of the challenge.

Purchasing refers to all of the activities associated with the buying process. Indeed, it can be argued that purchasing starts the organization's entire need-satisfaction process. Initiating and maintaining a steady inbound flow of raw materials, parts, and services has become especially daunting as companies have decentralized their manufacturing processes. Consider the web of international transactions that are required to obtain and assemble all of the parts that make up a personal computer. The hard disk drive may be made in Singapore by the offshore plant of a German company. The microprocessor is made in the US by a US company. The keyboard comes from a Taiwanese company that recently moved production to China to get cheaper labor. The floppy disk drive is supplied by a Japanese firm that stays competitive by manufacturing in Thailand. And the whole thing is assembled in Mexico by a Taiwanese computer maker working under contract to the US company whose name is on the box.[7]

This convoluted sourcing path illustrates one of the most important trends in global business: as manufacturers concentrate on core competencies and outsource everything else, suppliers are responsible for an ever-larger share of the final product. At Mercedes-Benz's new French production facility only 20 percent of their new micro-car will be made in-house, compared to the company's usual 45 percent. Across the world, in Silicon Valley, California, outside components account for nearly 75 percent of the cost of Conner Peripherals Inc.'s computer disk drives.[8] Clearly, purchasing's task has become much more important and, at the same time, complex than ever before.

Goals of purchasing

Above all else, purchasing must ensure that raw material, supplies, and services come into the firm so that finished goods can go out. However, that flow must be maintained while addressing other issues as well. First, purchasing must be sensitive to management concerns regarding **excess inventory**. Large quantities of goods bought at a discount may lead to inventory carrying cost increases that are greater than the amount saved. Second, the products/services purchased must adhere to some **quality standards** as defined by top management. Third, those items should be obtained at the lowest **cost** possible consistent with quality needs. Fourth, company **leverage** should be exercised to the maximum extent possible, either by standardizing the items purchased or by buying multiple things from a single vendor. Finally, like other functional tasks, purchasing should maintain a **systems view** regarding the logistics system in general and how buying decisions have an impact on other functions within that system.

Purchasing tasks

There are a number of different facets to the purchasing activity, some of which are discussed in detail below.

SUPPLIER SELECTION One of the most difficult challenges is selecting the vendors that the firm will patronize. Typically this decision rests upon a number of variables that are weighted based upon the specific situation at hand. Product cost is certainly a critical factor; indeed, cost has historically been *the* most important concern. However, other factors are now just as crucial if not more so, than cost alone. Product quality and conformance to specifications, delivery reliability (the degree to which the supplier is able to consistently deliver an accurate shipment on time), and product availability were all ranked higher than cost in a recent survey of purchasing managers.[9] Furthermore, respondents noted that other criteria, while less important than quality or cost, may also be considered. Sophisticated buyers now seek suppliers that will work very closely with customers to raise performance levels, contain costs, and develop leading edge technologies. They also want vendors who will share data, resources, and people to overcome obstacles that stand in the way of mutually agreed-up goals. Finally, smart managers value suppliers that can identify aspects of the buyer's operations that can be improved and that are willing and able to respond quickly to problems and emergencies.[10]

However, the extent to which these factors are considered is a function of two things: the item being purchased and how the purchase is being accomplished. Selecting a vendor for a small and/or recurring transaction may involve nothing more than reordering from the supplier that has been used in the past. As long as the buyer–seller relationship has not changed to any significant degree, purchasing may see little reason to go to the time and expense of considering all potential suppliers every time a reorder is needed. Alternatively, a large and/or infrequent purchase may necessitate a lengthy search involving an in-depth evaluation of many vendors across the factors noted above. Furthermore, what one firm considers a routine reordering situation another might view as a one-time buy involving a great deal of supplier research. In other words, the nature of the supplier selection process tends to be very situation and buyer specific.

QUALITY MANAGEMENT Purchasing wants to provide the organization with as much value as possible. As simple as that statement seems, the reality necessitates a constant balancing act between price and quality. When the buying process is cost-driven, the materials obtained are often of very low quality. Alternatively, obtaining very high-quality items drives costs up. Today, purchasing managers realize that buying inexpensive, but poor-quality items often leads to production disruptions, more rework, and a higher percentage of defective finished goods, all of which increase costs. Indeed, when the cost of customer dissatisfaction is included, the negative impact of buying poor-quality material tends to be much greater than what was "saved" on the purchase.

On the other hand, buying material of higher quality than customers need is wasteful because it fails to add value in the buyer's mind. When Toyota redesigned their Camry model in 1996, they were able to actually reduce the price of the new car versus the previous one by substituting less expensive components and processes for higher-priced ones in areas where customers would not notice. Thus, in virtually every meaningful way, buyers are offered a better automobile at a lower price; in other words, they receive more value from the new car than the old.

FORWARD BUYING Forward buying refers to obtaining materials well before they are needed to satisfy customer demand. Firms might elect to stockpile items for several reasons. First, managers may fear that a commodity may not be available at some future date or in sufficient quantities to meet production needs. Purchasing would then buy enough to continue manufacturing finished products until the shortage ends. Another argument for forward buying exists when a future price increase is anticipated, leading management to amass the resource affected in order to procure it at the lower price. Finally, purchasing and/or transportation discounts offered in exchange for a large-volume order may provide an incentive to forward-buy as well.

There are, however, some risks associated with forward buying. First, events may not occur as anticipated. Availability may not be a problem or prices may not go up (they might even fall). Should either of these events occur, management would have wasted corporate resources in two ways. First, unneeded items will have been purchased; second, these items will have been stored as inventory thereby incurring carrying costs. Another danger is that management fails to consider the total cost of forward buying. For example, the discount received for buying in large quantities may be more than offset by the carrying costs associated with holding the goods in inventory. It is, then, incumbent on managers to ensure that environmental conditions truly warrant forward buying and that the total costs associated with that decision are lower as a result.

INTERACTION WITH OTHER CORPORATE DEPARTMENTS Once viewed as largely a subunit of inbound logistics, purchasing now finds itself interacting with many diverse parts of the organization. As purchasing has become a more visible and important activity, managers must deal with their counterparts from marketing, finance, operations and, of course, production. Some firms have developed a procurement organization that integrates purchasing individuals into product teams. For example, at Quantum Corporation, a California-based manufacturer of disk drives and mass storage devices, purchasing acts as a liaison between engineering and suppliers to help determine the feasibility of a new design and influence the design team into the most effective choices of suppliers and materials. Because purchasing professionals have an in-depth knowledge of the supply base and its cost drivers, they are able to guide design engineers toward new sources of supply and move them away from parts with questionable quality or suppliers that could pose capacity problems during full production.[11] Not only does this provide the purchasing activity with more credibility, but it also keeps their people involved in all phases of a product's development, marketing, and sales.

The linkage between purchasing (and inbound logistics in general) and marketing is becoming especially critical because of the role both have in providing final customer satisfaction. Purchasing must understand the needs of the ultimate consumer so that supplier relationships can be developed that do, in fact, enhance end-buyer satisfaction. In fact, managers are increasingly aware of the fact that every aspect of the firm's efforts should be focused on the final customer, but it is production, marketing, and logistics that constitute the primary value creation chain in most firms.[12] These three components of the organization must work in concert if the total value delivered by the firm is to be maximized.

Improving purchasing productivity

Like every other component of the logistics system, the purchasing activity must constantly seek ways to add value to the organization. Several possibilities include developing enhanced internal management procedures, utilizing technology to deal with suppliers, strengthening the firm's ties with its vendors, and reorganizing the purchasing function to reflect its importance to overall customer satisfaction.

DAY-TO-DAY MANAGEMENT TECHNIQUES Purchasing managers must always look for opportunities to substitute less expensive items for costlier alternatives when quality levels do not suffer. Standardizing acquisitions can also lead to lower costs, as can buying in large quantities. Furthermore, price changes must be aggressively managed to ensure they are justified. For example, Olivetti, the Italian manufacturer of business equipment, negotiates prices with its suppliers at least every three months, but it also renegotiates prices on orders already issued if the need arises.[13] Contracts that combine purchases over time or that reflect the purchase of multiple items from the same vendor can be used to increase leverage. Similarly, stockless purchasing can be utilized to support the firm's JIT system while still taking advantage of volume discounts. Here, one large order is placed but delivery deferred to coincide with the "as-needed" demand for smaller quantities of raw materials into the production process.

ELECTRONIC DATA INTERCHANGE (EDI) One technology that can be used to tighten the linkages between purchasing and its suppliers is EDI. As discussed earlier, EDI allows for the electronic transfer of business documents between or within firms without being rekeyed. When EDI is implemented between vendors and their customers, purchasing typically experiences increased productivity by virtue of the reduced need for labor-intensive manual data transfer activities. Furthermore, costs fall and external relations with suppliers improve. For example, in 1988 British retailer Marks & Spencer (M&S) began sending orders to suppliers via EDI. The firm gained significant productivity improvements by eliminating the masses of paperwork that previously characterized its ordering process. Rekeying of data, high error rates, slow transfer of information, and high labor costs were all problems that disappeared with the adoption of EDI. Aided in part by better management of inbound operations, M&S has become the largest provider of fresh-packed food in the UK.[14]

British retailers in general are leaders in applications of EDI. Sainsbury, having implemented a system that integrates its scanned data and computer facilities with suppliers' systems, reports a decrease in order-cycle time from two weeks to one. L'Oreal (UK), which supplies more than 70 percent of the largest retail chains, has also enjoyed several advantages from EDI, including faster order transaction times, reduction of administrative costs, and better relationships with retailers. However, cross-border EDI transmission of information is not accomplished on a large scale in Europe because of inconsistent data and communications protocols. If the EDIFACT protocol is established as a universal standard in the future, though, the technology will likely spread rapidly throughout the retail market.[15] Thus, despite the tremendous potential offered by EDI, it is not yet widely used in purchasing, for many of the same reasons delineated in chapter 9: lack of a common EDI language, data being interpreted in different ways by partner firms, and cost issues related to EDI start-up.[16]

IMPROVING EXTERNAL RELATIONSHIPS In addition to developing EDI procedures, purchasing must further strengthen its external relationships. Within some firms, closer partner relationships are being developed and suppliers are becoming involved in internal teams. Such actions enable purchasing to involve suppliers in design issues and obtain information about the supply market, thereby enhancing the ability of the purchasing function to perform its long-term strategic planning role. Critical to the development of strong external relationships is the reduction of the supply base to allow for long-term agreements with single sources where possible. High-performing firms are reducing their supply base but many companies still single source only an average of 34.3 percent of all purchased items (excluding maintenance, repair, and operating supplies). In addition to allowing the nurturing of good relationships, single sourcing can provide many other benefits. For example, Xerox, since beginning its move towards single sourcing in 1980 has, as of 1990, obtained a 50 percent reduction in material costs, a 66 percent reduction in overhead materials costs, and a drop in defects from 10,000 to 25,000 per million to about 350 per million.[17] These improvements directly result from the fact that each partner wants the other to succeed. In other words, the fortunes of each are linked together, so that if one firm does well, the other also benefits.

ORGANIZE FOR ENHANCED PRODUCTIVITY The firm must have an organizational structure that supports the ability of purchasing personnel to create value for the firm. Traditionally, organizations have used a functional structure in which individuals are organized by specialty. Though still very common, such a structure can inhibit horizontal communication and coordination, leading to inaccurate and slow decision making.[18] The purchasing component in this situation has often been centralized and then organized by task, i.e. buyer, expediter, manager. The buyers are then most frequently organized by commodity. In many firms, this organizational design based on specialization is being phased out and replaced with one that entails a merging of functions, such as the jobs of the buyer and the production control materials scheduler, creating a new function often described as a "buyer/planner." This individual handles daily interaction with the supplier and production, prepares master production schedules, determines order quantities, and expedites materials while a buyer or team performs the strategic procurement functions like supplier selection, partnering, certification, and negotiation. Firms adopting this approach report smoother materials flow, improved coordination with key suppliers, and increased productivity.[19] Some organizations have developed a procurement organization that goes further to support value-based management: the integration of procurement individuals into product teams. Purchasing individuals are becoming increasingly involved in teams throughout the organization and this team responsibility is expected to increase.[20]

To enhance the ability of purchasing individuals to contribute to the cross-functional teams' goals, procurement may need to be elevated to a level equivalent to its counterpart functions. They may also need to receive additional tools, resources, and training because they generally do not have the status, means, and training possessed by other functional areas.[21] Participation in cross-functional teams is becoming more common for purchasing individuals but if teams are not yet part of the firm's structure, the manager of procurement may wish to develop them within procurement to perform negotiation, sourcing, or specific problem solving. Teaming would encourage interaction, develop procurement individuals with greater awareness and skills, and prepare these people for further company-wide teams.[22]

Furthermore, the decision to centralize or decentralize has not been a uniform one. A recent study indicates that 59 percent of firms use a combined centralized/decentralized form of procurement organization; 28 percent a centralized approach, and 13 percent a straight decentralized structure.[23] These numbers show an increase in completely centralized procurement from an earlier study,[24] with most of the change coming from a reduction in combined centralized/decentralized organizations. However, although centralization has increased from the past, another study shows expected movement towards greater decentralization in the future, with the reasons cited being cost pressures to reduce staff and the need to place decision making closer to the design and manufacturing centers.[25] These reasons are consistent with those driving value-based management and based on the value framework, decentralized procurement would better meet the needs of value-based management, especially as the product becomes more technically complex or the supply environment more uncertain. Select centralization of common requirements initially may provide benefits in economies of scale but this decision may be evaluated periodically because, over time, the development of supplier relations and increased information flow from a decentralized structure might more than offset the savings. In either case, whether the function is centralized or decentralized, taut linkages with providers and customers must still be developed.[26]

For example, General Motors (GM) recently consolidated its 27 relatively autonomous purchasing groups into a single organization that uses the same processes and measurements around the globe. What emerged was a worldwide purchasing group that trades GM's traditional hierarchy and independent buying camps for a process-driven, grid-shaped organization that leverages the company's size and knowledge base to make sourcing decisions on a global basis. The new organization divides purchasing by commodity groups (chemicals, metallic, electrical, and machinery and equipment) and operating divisions (North America, Europe, Latin America, and Asia-Pacific). The commodity group leaders, also known as commodity executives, are responsible for knowing everything GM is doing with a particular part or system around the world. They also are in charge of developing and pushing common sourcing, quality, and benchmarking processes throughout the company. Purchasing heads in each of GM's four operating divisions see to it that these processes are implemented within their own divisions.[27]

In sum, the purchasing activity must be structured to enhance coordination and information flow by minimizing the number of levels in the hierarchy, identifying key suppliers with whom the firm can develop strategic partnerships, modifying supplier selection and evaluation criteria to include areas critical to the firm's performance, and sharing information with "partners" through EDI, teams, or mutual education and training.[28]

Management Techniques for Improving Materials Management

As was discussed in chapter 4, there are a number of computer-based packages to assist in managing the flow of inbound material. Materials requirements planning (MRP I) is a computer-based production and inventory control system that attempts to minimize inventories while maintaining adequate materials for the production process. Manufacturing resource planning (MRP II) broadens the analysis by adding financial, marketing, and purchasing aspects to what was essentially a production-based orientation of MRP I.[29] Distribution requirements planning (DRP I) takes the concept still further by integrating supply scheduling throughout the entire logistics channel, from suppliers to customers.[30] Distribution resource planning (DRP II) extends DRP I to include the planning of key resources in a logistics system – warehouse space, manpower levels, transport capacity, and financial flows.[31] Finally, as was noted earlier, just-in-time (JIT) inventory management techniques were primarily developed to improve the materials management process. In fact, JIT systems are usually combined with other systems that plan and control materials flows into, within, and out of the organization. MRP and DRP are often used to implement the JIT philosophy.[32]

Chapter Summary

Often ignored, inbound logistics activities in fact add value to the finished product by ensuring that high-quality raw materials continually flow into the production process at a reasonable cost. Purchasing is one of the most important components of an inbound logistics activity and is becoming more so as firms search globally for their suppliers. The challenge of finding and retaining reliable vendors of quality goods and services has taken on a whole new dimension, as global competition has become more acute. In reality, the sourcing and obtaining of production inputs involve many decisions that ultimately have an impact on both the prices of finished goods and customer satisfaction.

Study Questions

1. How can the performance of inbound logistics activities have an impact on the final customer?
2. How does inbound transportation differ from outbound transport?
3. Explain the role of maintenance as an inbound logistics function.
4. For what reasons should a single manager oversee both inbound and out-

bound logistics functions?
5. Why is the purchasing activity becoming more important to global firms?
6. What factors determine how extensive a supplier selection process might be?
7. What trade-offs must the purchasing manager consider when evaluating quality levels of the goods offered by different vendors?
8. When might a firm engage in forward buying? What trade-offs must be considered in making the decision to forward-buy?
9. Why is it important that there be a sound linkage between the purchasing and marketing departments?
10. How can electronic data interchange be utilized to improve purchasing productivity?
11. What organizational changes must take place if purchasing is to truly add value to the organization?
12. What advantages are possible as a result of reducing the number of vendors supplying the organization?
13. How does Saturn's integration of inbound flows impact the automobile buyer?

Notes

1. O'Laughlin, Kevin A., Cooper, James and Cabocel, Eric. *Reconfiguring European Logistics Systems* (Oak Brook, IL: Council of Logistics Management, 1993), p. 172.
2. Ibid.
3. Epps, Ruth. "Just-in-time inventory management: implementation of a successful program," *Review of Business*, Fall 1995, vol. 17, no. 1, p. 40(5).
4. "Melt furnace recycles ash from incinerators," *American Metal Market*, January 12, 1994, vol. 102, no. 8, p. 14.
5. Ballou, Ronald H. *Business Logistics Management*, 4th edn (Upper Saddle River, NJ: Prentice-Hall, Inc., 1999), p. 415.
6. Fawcett, S. E. and Birou, L. M. "Exploring the logistics interface between global and JIT sourcing," *International Journal of Physical Distribution and Logistics Management*, vol. 22, no. 1, 1992, pp. 3–14.
7. Carey, Patricia M. "Currencies, free markets and sourcing," *International Business*, May 1995, p. 55.
8. Ibid, pp. 55–6.
9. Fitzgerald, Kevin R. "What makes a superior supplier?" *Purchasing*, November 19, 1998, p. 21.
10. Ibid, p. 20
11. Minahan, Tim. "Is this the future of purchasing?" *Purchasing*, March 12, 1998, p. 42.
12. Carter, Joseph R. and Narasimhan, Ram. "The role of purchasing and materials management in total quality management and customer satisfaction," *International Journal of Purchasing and Materials Management*, Summer 1994, vol. 30, no. 3, pp. 3–15.
13. O'Laughlin et. al., p. 193.
14. Ibid, p. 138.
15. Ibid, p. 139.
16. Sriram, V. and Banerjee, S. "Electronic data interchange: does its adoption change purchasing policies and procedures?" *International Journal of Purchasing and Materials Management*, vol. 30, no. 1, Winter 1994.

17. Drumond, Ellen J. "Applying value-based management to procurement," *International Journal of Physical Distribution and Logistics Management*, January 1996, vol. 26, no. 1, pp. 5–25.
18. Vondermebse, Mark, Tracey, Michael, Tan, Chong Leng and Bardi, Edward J. "Current Purchasing Practices and JIT: Some of the Effects on Inbound Logistics," *International Journal of Physical Distribution and Logistics*, March 1995, vol. 25, no. 3, p. 41.
19. Dumond, E. J. and Newman, W. "Closing the gap between buyer and vendor," *Production and Inventory Management Journal*, vol. 31, no. 4, 1990, pp. 13–17.
20. Trent, R. J. and Monczka, R. M. "Effective cross-functional sourcing teams: critical success factors," *International Journal of Purchasing and Materials Management*, vol. 30, no. 4, Fall 1994, pp. 2–11.
21. Mendez, E. and Pearson, J. "Purchasing's role in product development: the case for time-based strategies," *International Journal of Purchasing and Materials Management*, vol. 30, no. 1, Winter 1991, pp. 2–12.
22. Drumond, ibid.
23. Kolchin, M. G. and Giunipero, L. *Purchasing Education and Training: Requirements & Resources* (Tempe, AZ: *Center for Advanced Purchasing Studies*, 1993).
24. Fearon, H. *Purchasing Organizational Relationships* (Tempe, AZ: NAPM, Inc., 1988).
25. Egan, D., "Cost-reduction pressures prompt shift in purchasing authority," *Electronic Buyers' News*, May 22, 1995, p. 2.
26. Drumond, ibid.
27. Minahan, Tim. "Is Harold Kutner GM's comeback kid?" *Purchasing*, August 15, 1996, vol. 121, no. 2, p. 40(4).
28. Ibid.
29. Lambert, Douglas M., Stock, James R., and Ellram, Lisa M. *Fundamentals of Logistics Management* (New York: Irwin-McGraw Hill, 1998), p. 203.
30. Ballou, ibid, p. 411.
31. Lambert et. al, ibid, p. 207.
32. Ibid, p. 201.

chapter 11

The Global Logistics Environment

Introduction	193
The Global Supply Chain	194
Changing Market Opportunities	194
Cultural Issues in Logistics	198
Alternative Global Distribution Strategies	199
International Documentation	200
Customs Regulations	202
Foreign Trade Zones	203
Logistics Intermediaries and Facilitators	204
Controlling the Global Logistics System	206
Chapter Summary	207
Study Questions	209

Introduction

When the World Trade Organization (WTO) replaced the General Agreement on Tariffs and Trade (GATT) secretariat in 1995 and began to administer the system of international trade law, conducting business on a global basis became much easier to do. The WTO is committed to simplifying international business and has already orchestrated the liberalization of the world's telecommunications business.[1] As the WTO's efforts continue, global business opportunities will continue to grow. Clearly, managers today must look beyond their home borders for sales. While opportunities may exist in markets that are stable and closely resemble the firm's domestic sales area in many ways, other new customers may be in politically unstable regions that are culturally quite different from the organization's present buyers. Management's challenge is to evaluate the environmental and cultural make-up of each prospective market and then develop a logistics system that will meet what may be radically different customers' needs. As already mentioned, logistics becomes even more critical to the firm's success globally than it is domestically. Extended supply chains, multiple languages, different channel members, distinct regulations, and a myriad of cultural factors all combine to make the entire logistics process much more complex than managers may be used to.[2] Ironically, as the logistics system becomes more complicated, managers may feel as though they are losing a substantial portion of control and familiarity. That is, providing customer value in new overseas markets requires an appreciation for cultural diversity, currency exchange fluctuations, and other matters that managers may not have dealt with in the past. This chapter will first examine the changing nature of global markets. Then alternative strategies for servicing different international markets will be presented. Finally, several structural issues that can have an impact on the firm's global logistics system will be reviewed.

The Global Supply Chain

It is important to remember that global logistics embraces the firm's entire supply chain. As was discussed in an earlier chapter, the supply chain represents all of the actors involved in conveying something of value to the final consumer. Thus, it includes vendors, producers, intermediaries, and logistics service providers, all working together to ensure the customers receive more value then they might from a competing supply chain.[3] Many of the issues already presented in earlier chapters must be considered simultaneously as firms evaluate the risks and potential profits awaiting them in overseas markets. The result is that a great deal of money is spent on logistics. Indeed, in an aggregate sense, the numbers are staggering. According to a recent study, a conservative estimate of worldwide logistics costs for 1996 is $3.4 trillion, broken down by geographic area as follows: the 12 original European Union members had total logistics expenditures of approximately $941 billion; North America spent almost $919 billion; Asian/Pacific nations $652 billion; and all remaining nations $916 billion.[4]

Changing Market Opportunities

Emerging nations

The growth of new markets in developing nations offers much sales potential although with some risk. At current economic growth projections, the emerging markets will command a larger share of global economic output than the industrialized world early in the next decade. For example, China is now emerging as a global economic leader, and it could eventually supplant the United States as the largest economy. By 2020, nine of today's developing economies will be among the world's 15 largest markets. Following China, some predict, will be the United States and Japan, then India, Indonesia, Germany, South Korea, Thailand, France, Taiwan, Brazil, Italy, Russia, Britain, and Mexico. Logistics profile 11-1 discusses the changing nature of distribution in China in more detail. The reasons for the phenomenal

Logistics Profile 11-1
THE CHINA CHALLENGE

Arguably, China has the most inefficient distribution system in all of Asia. Transport is poor, regulations unclear, and distribution systems are undergoing major upheaval. Although state-owned distribution systems remain prevalent particularly in inland regions, they are slowly being complemented by distribution networks built from scratch by local companies (often profit-making spin-offs from state-owned companies) and multinationals eager to satisfy China's 1.2 billion consumers.

For example, economic reforms in the 1980s had a huge impact on traditional food distribution systems. Formerly, all food was distributed through state-run distribution groups under different ministries with each ministry responsible for a particular category of foodstuffs. The Grain Bureau was responsible for distribution of rice; the Ministry of Commerce's Non-Staple Food Company handled meats and processed foods; and the Ministry of Light Industry's Sugar, Cigarette, and Wine Corporation handled sweets, tobacco, and liquor.

During the 1980s, this system was effectively dismantled. Distributors at every level of the system could buy from any supplier and sell to any customer. Over time, the national distribution system evolved into a patchwork of local networks with wholesalers (both old and new) competing for the same product and customers.

Not surprisingly, transportation in China is also a problem. China's per capita road and rail capacity is lower than other countries of comparable size – such as India and Russia. Shipments by air and rail are unreliable and slow; port bottlenecks are common and imports are often delayed because of obsessive government regulations.

Enter foreign companies

Breaking into China's evolving distribution system is a major problem for foreign companies. Weak control over distributors, poor transport, piracy, and high logistics costs top the list of complaints. However, aggressive players are working hard to develop innovative solutions. For example, many foreign companies have invested in their own truck fleets and distribution centers to control the delivery of products and ensure that items arrive in good condition. Some desperate companies are even considering establishing their own freight forwarding businesses to handle third-party shipments as well as their own products. In addition, a group of six consumer product companies are consolidating shipments of 35 products to reduce logistics costs, increase bargaining power, and improve control over the distribution process. Finally, Asian companies are joining forces to create one-stop shipping for the retail trade. Mitsubishi, Lucky Goldstar, and Hong Kong's Li & Fung Group are building a cash-and-carry distribution center in Guangzhou for retailers. In addition to consortium members' products, the distribution center will be open to other manufacturers of consumer products trying to control distribution to retailers.

Opportunities for third parties

Freight forwarders and carriers able to provide customers with turnkey distribution solutions will find receptive buyers in China. In fact, a number of third-party transportation and distribution companies active in China – such as Schenker/TNT, DHL, SeaLand, and Inchcape – are currently negotiating with the center government to provide integrated services to China. Going it alone is difficult, though, due in great part to current regulations prohibiting foreign companies from acting as wholesalers in China. This could gradually change, however. The Chinese government is experimenting with the idea of foreign wholesalers in China. Mitsubishi recently received an experimental wholesaler's license and other foreign distributors have also been granted licenses to set up wholly owned distribution operations in Shanghai.

Based on current experience, a more likely formula for success is to form close working partnerships with entrenched local companies anxious to upgrade their capabilities and expand their international networks. Local candidates include regional stores and trading corporations, transportation companies, regional government wholesalers and distributors, and large department stores that also distribute to small shops.

(**Source**: Zubrod, Justin, Tasiaux, Robert, and Beebe, Alan. "The challenges of logistics within Asia", *Transportation and Distribution*, February 1996, vol. 37, no. 2, p. 81(3))

growth are the immense surge in world population, particularly in the developing world over the last 100 years, together with an increase in the living standards and per capita income, the tremendous increase in trade and financial flows during the post-World War II period, and the nearly universal acceptance of the liberal economic model to organize economic activity.[5]

Multi-lateral trade organizations

Regional economic integration is another phenomenon affecting international business. More and more, countries engage in economic cooperation to use their respective resources more efficiently and to provide larger markets for member-nation producers. Integration efforts have facilitated marketing activities across borders but, on occasion, inhibited them between trading blocs. The emergence of regional economic agreements such as the European Union (EU), the North American Free

Table 11.1 Members of the European Union and year of admittance

1958	*1973*	*1981*	*1986*	*1995*
Belgium	Denmark	Greece	Portugal	Austria
France	Ireland		Spain	Finland
Germany (west)	United Kingdom			Sweden
Italy				
Luxembourg				
Netherlands				

(*Source*: World Bank Atlas 1997 (Washington, DC: World Bank, 1997), p. 17, as presented in Ball, Donald M. McCulloch, Wendell H. Jnr., *International Business*, 7th edn (New York: Irwin/McGraw-Hill, 1999), p. 142).

Table 11.2 Members of the Association of Southeast Asian Nations (ASEAN)

Brunei	The Philippines
Burma	Singapore
(now called by the ruling junta Myanmar)	Thailand
Indonesia	Vietnam
Malaysia	

(*Source*: Ball, Donald M. and McCulloch, Wendell H. Jr. *International Business*, 7th edn (New York: Irwin/McGraw-Hill, 1999), p. 145.)

Trade Agreement (NAFTA) between the United States, Canada, and Mexico, Mercosur in Latin America (comprised of Brazil, Uruguay, Paraguay, and Argentina),[6] and ASEAN in Asia are profoundly changing the way global trade is accomplished. The members of the EU and ASEAN are presented in tables 11-1 and 11-2, respectively. Often these changes mean that a company has to do business within a given bloc in order to remain competitive. At the same time, global integration has also successfully reduced red tape, documentation hassles, and transportation difficulties. Harmonization of rules and standards has made the achievement of economies of scale easier, especially in logistics. By reducing the barriers between markets, such integration has also increased the levels of efficiency and competition – a boon for customers and for managers on the cutting edge but the bane of traditionalists who long to keep doing things the old-fashioned way.[7]

Indeed, while new markets are emerging at an unprecedented rate, supporting existing international customers is becoming more difficult as well. The pattern seems to be that the more things people have, the more they want. In the early 1990s when many Eastern European nations were first shaking off the fetters of communism, a consumer in what was the German Democratic Republic might have been astounded to enter a food store and have a choice between four brands of mustard. Today, that same customer can select from three different flavors, all of which are available in five alternative packages representing six brands. Clearly, satisfying that same buyer today requires a radically different logistics strategy than the one that would have met his or her needs five years ago.

Global sourcing

The availability of cheap and efficient labor and transportation services has made it economical for companies to source parts, components, and finished goods from every corner of the Asian continent. Although discussed in chapter 10, vendor selection and management is crucially important to a successful global logistics effort. Not only must suitable suppliers be found, but also they must be managed on a day-to-day basis as well, often from half a world away. Many firms rely on middlemen, often agents, to act in their stead overseas.[8] Agents not only handle the freight itself, but also have responsibility for collecting, managing, and transmitting information to the buyer. Essentially, these agents connect suppliers, carriers, customs, and buyers together in order to minimize the effects of distance and cultural differences on the satisfaction provided to the firm's ultimate customer.

Cultural Issues in Logistics

To successfully exploit new business opportunities, logistics managers must understand the cultural make-up of the customers that comprise those markets. This sensitivity is especially crucial in a global setting because buyers can differ widely in preferences and receptiveness to alternative forms of marketing stimuli. For example, buyers in Japan are used to dealing with logistics channels that are longer, more complex, and, by implication, more costly than customers might tolerate in other countries. Efforts to bypass the numerous middlemen and small retailers by building large stand-alone stores served by shorter more direct distribution channels have not been very successful, not only because of government protection of small retailers but because Japanese consumers prefer the present system. The reason for that preference is that Japan is an intensely relationship-oriented society. Personal connections are the very essence of doing business so that customers view sellers as friends as well as providers of goods. So what appears to be a costly and inefficient channel, in a Western sense, suits the Japanese perfectly.[9]

Buyer shopping habits impact other areas of logistics as well. Customers in many parts of the world purchase things like food and personal items on a daily or as needed basis rather than buying, for instance, a week's worth at one time. People in Germany, for example, have less storage space at home and tend to walk or rely on public transport more than consumers in the United States. Thus, goods must come in small packages that can be easily carried on the bus and stored in an apartment. A package of laundry detergent that weighs 5 kilos simply won't sell in that market because it is too large for customers to conveniently transport and store. In another market where consumers rely more on personal automobiles and have more living space, the economies of buying such a large package may be attractive. As always, understanding the needs of the customers in each market is essential so that a logistics system can be developed that respects, and doesn't clash with, the cultural make-up of those buyers. A strategy that is highly successful in one country may fail dismally in another if management ignores the importance of cultural differences in providing customer satisfaction and value.

Alternative Global Distribution Strategies

When assessing how to best satisfy customers in an overseas market, management must consider the trade-off between the risk of asset loss on the one hand and operational control of the foreign enterprise on the other. For example, market research may uncover significant opportunities in a country with a very unstable government. Exploiting those markets may require a strategy that minimizes the firm's exposure to risk at the expense of relinquishing direct control over the foreign business. Alternatively, customers in a stable, established, low-risk market may be served with a more structured channel that provides the company with a maximum amount of control. Several different channel alternatives are discussed below.

Exporting occurs when the firm engages the services of a middleman to sell its products overseas. This middleman may simply buy the goods from the manufacturer directly, then resell them in some attractive market of the former's choosing. Alternatively, the intermediary may act as a broker, searching for a foreign buyer and putting them in contact with the seller. An exporting strategy is extremely popular with firms entering the global arena for the first time, as it requires very little knowledge about the specific workings of international trade. In addition, it is a great way for management to begin serving markets outside their own country while simultaneously learning about the intricacies of foreign business.

One advantage of an exporting strategy is that the firm has total flexibility since there are usually no monetary or contractual ties in the foreign market. Management can terminate the effort quickly if sales do not materialize, or expand distribution as dictated by customer demand. In addition, because the company has no investment in another country, risk is minimal. Furthermore, in some cases the firm has already been paid for its goods by the middleman, so sales in any subsequent market are of little immediate concern. The major disadvantage is that managers have very little control over how their product is handled. Markets, pricing, promotion, and distribution are all determined by the middleman who might make decisions that have an adverse impact on the domestic seller over the long term. In essence, the firm must rely on the expertise and capabilities of the exporting intermediary to sell the product.

Licensing is a strategy that provides a bit more control over the marketing process without a substantial increase in risk. With a license, a company in one country (the licensor) permits a firm in another (the licensee) to make a product, utilize a recipe, or employ some other process that belongs to the first party. The control comes from the licensing agreement, which is essentially a contract. Minimal risk results because there are no large capital requirements imposed on the licensor. Unfortunately, that same contract can make terminating the arrangement difficult should the relationship falter. In addition, the licensee always has the potential of becoming a competitor. McDonald's used licensing arrangements early in their international expansion, finding a local company in a new market to basically act like McDonald's. That is, the licensee would offer customers the usual McDonald's menu in a restaurant situated, designed and decorated with guidance from McDonald's while utilizing the trademark "golden arches" to reassure customers that they were patronizing a "real" McDonald's. In some instances, however, the licensee would fail to maintain McDonald's standards with respect to cleanliness, food quality, etc. In those cases, the only recourse McDonald's had was to withdraw from the market, leaving the local firm to continue operating under a (sometimes only slightly) different name.

Joint ventures occur when one company buys an ownership interest in another firm. The investor can now exert much more control via direct managerial input owing to its financial partnership. Joint ventures also allow the investing firm to utilize the specialized skills of its local partner as well as have immediate access to a local distribution system. Finally, in countries that prohibit outright ownership of domestic firms, a joint venture may be as much control as the foreign partner can exert over operations. Disadvantages of this approach are that risk is higher and flexibility lower because an equity position has been established in the partner. Furthermore, it is often the local firm that enjoys the benefits of majority ownership at the expense of the foreign partner. McDonald's now utilizes this approach in many global markets. For example, its restaurants in Moscow are operated through a joint venture between McDonald's of Canada and the City of Moscow.

Ownership of a foreign subsidiary provides a firm the highest degree of control over its international marketing effort, but with higher levels of risk. Indeed, ownership offers essentially total control, permitting management to operate without the need to accommodate a partner. In addition, customs duties and other import taxes may be eliminated since the subsidiary is, for all intents and purposes, a domestic entity in that country. However, flexibility is lost because the firm has made a substantial long-term commitment to the foreign market. Finally, there is always some risk of government nationalization of foreign-owned businesses.

The appropriateness of each strategy depends on the conditions encountered in each market, management's tolerance for risk, and the degree of control desired. An initial marketing effort into an emerging market characterized by rapid change and accompanying political instability might best be supported by an exporting strategy. Expanding in a stable country where the firm has accumulated some selling experience might call for a joint venture or even direct ownership. Clearly, different approaches work best in different markets. Once the overall channel strategy has been determined, the logistics system can be assembled to support it.

International Documentation

One of the most intimidating aspects of moving goods internationally is the whole area of documentation. It tends to be much more complex than is required for purely domestic movement and varies from country to country. The big problem is that absolute accuracy is essential because errors can delay shipments or result in penalties being assessed by the importing country. In addition, documents must often be completed in the language of both the origin and destination countries. Unfortunately, incorrect documentation may not become apparent until the customer complains that the goods have not arrived. The shipment must then be traced, the goods located, and the problem(s) corrected. And while all of this remedial activity is going on, a replacement shipment will have been expedited to the customer in an attempt to recover from the dissatisfaction generated as a result of the initial documentation mistakes.

A study conducted in Canada found that a single international shipment will typically generate 46 separate documents with 360 copies that require up to 46 person-hours to process. In extreme cases, the number could be as high as 158 documents with 790 copies.[10] Many documents convey the same types of data but are uncoordinated and require special procedures, because they serve different purposes in the transaction. In addition to the necessary financial documents and transportation forms, there are documents designed for customs clearance and import/export control. Finally, there are collection documents that are submitted to customers for payment.[11]

Concerted efforts are being made by both governments and private industry groups to simplify and reduce the cost of transactions as well as to increase the speed with which they are accomplished. These streamlining efforts are particularly far along within the established trade alliances such as the EU and NAFTA where aligned documents containing standard information can be utilized to speed the movement of goods between member nations. As the use of electronic data interchange (EDI) in logistics continues to evolve, the number of paper international shipping documents should continue to decrease.

As discussed in chapter 9, there are still a number of hurdles to overcome before a truly paperless logistics environment can become a reality. As was mentioned earlier, EDIFACT is evolving as the major international, cross-industry, general business standard for EDI data transmission. While a number of industry-specific standards are in use, they are starting to converge on EDIFACT as the common message set.[12] However, advances are being made. The Port of Hamburg now accepts shipping information from forwarders, liner agents, and exporters electronically through its new ZAPP system. While original documents of export papers for goods of European Union origin still must be sent to Hamburg's Main Free Port Customs Office within a reasonable time after data input, ZAPP guarantees that shippers can get their cargo loaded, because documents don't need to arrive before the goods can be shipped.[13] (Ironically, data cannot be transmitted directly from the Port of Hamburg to the Main Free Port Customs Office because it is not linked to the ZAPP computer.[14])

The United States Customs Service is striving for completely paperless import customs declarations for cargo within the next decade. Their Automated Manifest System (AMS) allows shippers to advise Customs of inbound shipments before they arrive at the US port of entry. Shippers can then be notified which material Customs needs to inspect. Since this determination can occur via AMS before the cargo actually reaches the port, material routing can be pre-designated to maximize process efficiency. Once the material has been inspected, the status can be electronically transmitted along with appropriate actions necessary for final clearance.[15]

US Customs also offers an Automated Brokerage Interface (ABI) that will allow for direct messaging between Customs and whomever is facilitating a shipment's customs clearance. By replacing numerous paper transactions with direct messaging, shippers can know even before freight arrives whether or not it has been cleared by Customs for onward movement. If goods must be inspected, their status in the process can be checked, inquiries made, and protests filed, all electronically. In short, an efficient documentation process translates directly into faster service. As an example, the carrier can be directed to a specific off-load location, Customs officials can prepare for immediate inspection, intermodal unloading and loading personnel can be allocated, and the connecting carrier can arrive just in time for pick-up.[16]

In a real example of connectivity, foreign customs offices can connect to the US Customs system to check the status of inbound shipments and invoices. Schiphol airport, in the Netherlands, has an agreement that if the importer does not receive inspection notification within 30 minutes from the time the manifest is electronically received by Netherlands Customs, it can be assumed the cargo has clearance.[17]

Customs Regulations

A nation utilizes customs laws to accomplish three things: generate revenue, protect domestic industry, and prevent the entry of prohibited items into the country. Revenue is provided via the collection of import taxes, more commonly known as duties. These assessments may be based on a percentage of the item's value, a fixed amount per unit, or some combination of the two. Generally, duties are collected when the goods arrive in a country. Duties, together with other restrictive requirements such as quotas, can also serve as a mechanism for protecting domestic industries by making the importing cost of competing goods extremely high. Finally, items such as illegal drugs, weapons, and articles that do not meet national standards must be stopped before they enter the country.[18] Items in the latter category could include various food products, electrical components, or even automobiles, which often must comply with engine emissions and safety laws that can vary from nation to nation.

As with documentation, customs laws and procedures vary from country to country. Indeed, learning the requirements for each market served can be an extremely daunting task. However, ignoring or misinterpreting customs regulations can lead to stranded goods, higher costs, and dissatisfied customers. Again, a buyer complaining of non-delivery may be the first indication of trouble. Then the goods must be found and the error(s) corrected. At times, local customs rules can seem arbitrary and capricious, but that doesn't make them any less enforceable. A thorough comprehension of the customs regulations in all export markets is absolutely essential to a successful global marketing effort. Unfortunately, this understanding may be almost impossible to attain. A report published in 1997 by global integrator DHL noted that customs rules and regulations are by far the biggest problem Western European multinationals face when doing business with Central and Eastern European countries. The report went on to say that customs demands in some countries can change virtually on a daily basis, costing companies lost revenue and even contracts.[19]

Efforts are being made, however, to speed up the customs clearance process by pre-inspecting goods in the exporter's country rather than at the port of entry in the importer's country. This procedure starts with the overseas importer notifying the liaison office of the inspection company (such as the Societe Generale de Surveillance, a Swiss firm doing 2.5 million such inspections annually) about the need to physically inspect a shipment at a location of the exporter's choice in the exporting country. After the inspection, the contents are verified, the import duty is assessed, necessary documents prepared, and the shipment is sealed. Pre-inspection dramatically cuts inspection time – down to two or three days instead of weeks in Indonesia, for example. And because it can be done while the order is being readied for shipment, additional timesavings occur.[20]

Foreign Trade Zones

Foreign trade zones (FTZs) were specifically created to smooth the flow of goods into a country by easing the impact of customs regulations. FTZs are designated areas within a country that are treated as foreign territory by the local Customs service. Though generally comprised of several warehouses on a dedicated site, an FTZ might also be a corner of a large manufacturer's plant. In fact, an FTZ can be any secure area that is so designated by local Customs officials. Goods can be landed, stored, and processed within an FTZ without incurring any import duties or domestic taxes. Of course, these fees are not eliminated; they must be paid when the items *leave* the FTZ and enter the importing country. Utilizing an FTZ means that management can bring in goods in large quantities to take advantage of transportation or purchasing discounts without having to pay duty all at once. Rather, payments are made in smaller increments as the goods are sold and shipped out of the FTZ to customers. Work such as assembly, repackaging, and testing can be done in the FTZ, which might allow a firm to take advantage of the lower labor costs available in that country. Furthermore, goods that are stored in an FTZ incur lower carrying costs because duty has not yet been assessed. In fact, firms can use the FTZ for product manufacture as well. The producer can purchase raw materials or component parts at the lowest price on the world market and bring them into the FTZ. The finished product can then be reexported or else imported using the duty on either the components or the final product, whichever is more advantageous to the importer. In addition, the manufacturer pays no duties on waste or by-products from the production process, realizing even more savings.[21] In other words, the sole purpose of a foreign trade zone is to facilitate international business by making the importing process a little easier. The Jebel Ali Free Zone Authority in Dubai, for example, offers numerous incentives to lure foreign firms into their FTZ: 100 percent foreign ownership (unlike anywhere else in Dubai, where foreign ownership is limited to 49 percent); a 15-year tax exemption renewable for an additional 15 years; no personal income taxes; no currency restrictions; and no unions.[22]

China established 13 FTZs in the early 1990s specifically to make doing business in China easier for foreign firms. Most of the FTZs are located in small port or border areas of the country and all have clearly demarcated boundaries and controlled access for both people and goods. Trade activities that take place in these zones are exempt from PRC trade laws. Foreign goods imported into the FTZs require no license or quota documents, and are not subject to import tariffs or taxes. Goods remain duty-free while in storage or being processed for export in FTZ territory. When they exit the FTZ into China proper, goods are considered "exported" to China and become subject to tariffs, taxes, and any applicable license or quota documentation. Furthermore, firms can also import, label, package, and transship products to such landlocked countries as Mongolia and Kazakhstan without paying Chinese taxes. The FTZs have numerous showrooms displaying imported furniture, automobiles, construction materials, and other imported goods that companies hope to sell to the Chinese market. As no duties are levied until the products are sold, many companies encourage agents to set up dealerships or showrooms in an FTZ. An auto manufacturer, for instance, may arrange with a Taiwan- or Hong Kong-owned dealership to set up shop in an FTZ and market its vehicles on the mainland. Mercedes-Benz AG has a dealership owned by Southern Star Automobile Company in the Guangzhou FTZ while Ford Motor Company has a dealership owned by MTI Inc. in the Tianjin FTZ.[23]

Logistics Intermediaries and Facilitators

Some firms may have the skill and expertise to perform all of the tasks required to reach overseas customers themselves. Such a commitment requires that a great deal of knowledge, effort, and manpower be committed to each market in which the organization does or wants to do business. However, many companies that have heretofore concentrated solely on a domestic market may have management that lack the experience or confidence to launch and support a global marketing effort on their own. Rather, they rely on different kinds of intermediaries and facilitators to help them (for a fee) reach international markets. While they may be called by different names in different countries, the intermediaries exist virtually everywhere in some form.

International freight forwarders focus primarily on arranging international transportation. Their task is to combine many small shipments into a single large one that then qualifies for a lower transportation rate. The rate charged to each shipper is less than they would have paid to move their individual small orders, but higher than that paid by the forwarder to the carrier. The difference between the two fees goes to the forwarder for providing the consolidation service. From the shipper's point of view, forwarders take care of everything: mode and carrier selection, documentation, payment, etc. Customers merely turn their freight over to the forwarder and rely on them to do the rest.

Alstrom, a French paper manufacturer with ten plants in France and Belgium, uses two forwarders with which it has worked for years and which it regards as partners. The company feels that forwarders have the information to do a better job of selecting carriers than Alstrom could while still permitting management to retain control over costs. Alstrom and its forwarders collaborate on carrier selection, the latter recommending which carriers to use while leaving ultimate approval up to the former. Alstrom also lets its forwarders handle customs declarations and clearance.[24] Similarly, Hong Kong-based China Light & Power Ltd. has outsourced its ocean-shipping activities to Panalpina and Kuhne & Nagel. In addition to providing lower transportation costs, these forwarders are able to improve consolidation operations and have more flexibility in schedules. They decide whether to consolidate cargoes for shipment as full containerloads, or to send them as less-than-containerload shipments. In addition, China Light & Power is considering outsourcing its customs declaration and clearance work to them as well.[25]

Non vessel-owning common carriers (NVOCCs) specialize in less-than-containerload ocean shipments and perform some of the same functions as ocean freight forwarders. Unlike freight forwarders, who usually act as a shipper's agent, NVOCCs are common carriers utilizing containers rather than vehicles or vessels. In fact, freight forwarders can be an NVOCC's biggest customers. For example, a freight forwarder may have a partial containerload of goods moving from Hamburg to Singapore. An NVOCC would take this shipment and combine it with other goods going to Singapore in order to achieve a full container. The container would then be given to, for instance, an ocean carrier for movement to Singapore. Upon arrival, the NVOCC would receive the container at the dock and deliver the contents to each individual shipper or forwarder.

NVOCCs also work hard to find backloads for empty containers that are being returned from inland locations. Often, surface transport firms charge the same to move an empty container as a full one, so NVOCCs attempt to reduce those unloaded miles by obtaining revenue-generating return shipments. In essence, NVOCCs perform a container management function for carriers as much as a transportation service for shippers.[26]

Export management companies (EMCs) are used when a firm wishes to sell its products in a foreign market but lacks the resources or expertise to conduct the business itself. EMCs function like external export departments, acting as agents for domestic firms in overseas markets by either selling a product themselves or taking orders for their clients' products. Companies venturing into the international arena for the first time or entering new but risky markets may choose to rely on the knowledge and global business acumen provided by the EMC rather than attempt to do business overseas on their own. EMCs often specialize in a specific type of product or in a particular market so that they understand in detail local customer needs.

Export trading companies are in the business of exporting goods and services. They locate overseas buyers and handle most of the export arrangements, including documentation, inland and overseas transportation, and the meeting of foreign government regulations. In essence, they attempt to combine all facets of international business: sales, finance, communications, and logistics.[27] Perhaps the best-known export trading companies are the *sogo shosha* of Japan. Their worldwide operations, combined with an information network that provides market knowledge and links to capital resources throughout the world, make them major trading organizations in a great many markets. A recent trend for *sogo shosha* is to reach beyond their traditional functions and become involved in direct investment: for example, Mitsui, the fourth largest exporter of grain from the United States, considered buying established US food businesses like Sara Lee.[28]

Export packers supply packaging services for overseas shipments when the shipper lacks the equipment or the expertise to do it itself. The benefits these intermediaries provide are adequate protection for the product and compliance with all packaging regulations throughout the channel. In the first instance, the length and complexity of the channel, transit time, and the sophistication of the entire logistics system must be considered. For example, goods may have to be packaged to withstand movement over poor roadways, rough handling in a manual warehouse, and even prolonged exposure to the weather. Furthermore, various countries along the route may require specific labels, handling instructions, or that special packaging material is used.

Sound export packing is not just the operation of putting a piece of merchandise into a container so that it will arrive at its destination in good condition. Additional objectives are to economize shipping space, to save expense by employing economical packing materials, to prevent pilferage, and to ensure the lowest assessable customs duties. For example, one US exporter used heavy paper cartons to ship electric refrigerators with enamel exteriors to the West Coast of South America. This is virtually a contradiction of every rule of sound packing, but it was successful because the amount saved in packing materials and in shipping space far outweighed the losses that occurred owing to the fragility of the packing.[29] Thus, rather than attempting to cope with all of these requirements in-house, management may prefer to rely on the expert staff provided by the export packer.

Customs brokers shepherd goods through the customs process. They ensure compliance with all local laws, that documentation is correctly completed, and that any disputes that may arise are resolved quickly in as favorable a manner to the shipper as possible. For many firms, the task of handling the many documents and forms that accompany an international shipment can be overwhelming. Together with the variety of customs procedures, restrictions, and requirements that differ in each country, the job of facilitating export shipments across international borders requires a specialist – the customs broker. In general, if a company is exporting to a number of countries with different import requirements or if the company has a large number of items in its product line (e.g. automotive parts, electronic components, food products), a customs broker should be a part of the firm's global distribution network.[30]

The common thread running through all of these intermediaries is that they allow the firm to enter, or conduct business in, global markets without having a lot of knowledge or expertise in doing it themselves. The trade-off is the cost of the services provided and the lost of control that can result relative to how the firm's products are handled. However, like other intermediaries in the channel, logistics service providers will only be used to the extent that they add value to the customer. Ten years ago, Agfa-Gevaert NV, the Belgian producer of digital and photochemical products and systems, relied on forwarders to handle all of the company's airfreight business. Today, after deciding that it could do the work more efficiently in-house, Agfa handles 65 percent of its airfreight itself. Management say that by negotiating directly with carriers and producing their own shipping paperwork by computer, they have cut freight costs by 15 percent a shipment.[31] Thus, as firms seek to integrate their worldwide supply chains, intermediaries such as those just discussed are assuming broader logistics responsibilities as a way of adding value to the channel leader. Those firms failing to add value will eventually be eliminated from the channel.

Controlling the Global Logistics System

Effective control of the firm's global logistics effort can best be accomplished by centralizing some functions while localizing others. A highly centralized logistics function offers some economies of scale and does facilitate the implementation of a unified global logistics strategy, but at the expense of less sensitivity to changing customer needs in country-specific markets. On the other hand, a purely decentralized approach, while highly customer centered, can make it difficult to coordinate a unified corporate logistics strategy worldwide. Many firms are finding a balance by centralizing the overall control of logistics while simultaneously localizing customer service-related issues to ensure that competitive advantage is gained and maintained.[32]

If the potential trade-offs in rationalizing sourcing, production, and transportation across national boundaries are to be achieved, it is essential that a central decision-making structure for logistics be established. Many companies that are active on an international basis find that they are constrained in their search for global optimization by strongly entrenched local systems and structures. Only through centralized planning and coordination of logistics can the organization hope to achieve the twin goals of cost minimization and service maximization.[33] On the other hand, local markets have their own specific characteristics and needs, so there is considerable advantage to be achieved by shaping marketing strategies locally – albeit within overall global guidelines. This is particularly true of customer service management, in which the opportunities for tailoring service against individual buyer requirements are great. The management of customer service involves the monitoring of service needs as well as performance and extends to the management of the entire order fulfillment process – from order placement through delivery. Although order fulfillment systems are increasingly global and centrally managed, the need for strong local customer service management will always remain.[34]

Hoffman-La Roche, the Swiss multinational, has given responsibility for distribution and inventories of finished products to the area managers who are responsible for marketing. At the same time, the company has kept carrier selection, rate negotiation, raw-materials supply, and intra-company shipments at the Basel headquarters. The company has found that its "localized" global distribution system is a way to stay close to the customer without surrendering the economies of central control.[35] Logistics profile 11-2 explores its strategy in more detail.

Chapter Summary

Global expansion is the key to success for many firms today. Exploiting those opportunities may be relatively easy in some cases, extremely difficult in others. As a result, management may find that one marketing strategy works well in one market, while a totally different one is most effective in another. However, the objective of any marketing approach must be the same: to provide more customer satisfaction and value than the competition. Because of the additional complexities resulting from issues related to customs and documentation, managers may feel more comfortable using one or more intermediaries to assist in performing some or all of the processes needed to expedite and smooth the flow of goods to distant customers. But whether value delivery processes are performed in-house or with the benefit of intermediaries, an effective logistics system is absolutely essential to the success of a global marketing effort.

Logistics Profile 11-2
"Localized" Global Distribution

Hoffman-La Roche has steered a middle course between centralized and decentralized control of logistics for its vitamins and fine-chemicals unit. Marketing responsibility for customer satisfaction has been given to area managers while the company has retained decision-making authority for system-wide activities such as carrier selection and procurement. "Area managers say that distribution is one of the key functions to serve customers," said Roman Kamber, the unit's global logistics services manager. Kamber said area managers could provide more personalized service through what he calls "fine distribution." With the new structure of distribution responsibilities, area managers will have flexibility and will not be measured against identical benchmarks applied to all areas. In Europe, for example, movement from the area distribution center to customers is usually by truck and takes only one day at the vitamins and fine-chemicals division. But in Asia, where ocean transportation is used, area distribution can take up to two weeks.

Decentralizing area distribution is the final stage of a five-year supply-chain restructuring. Five years ago, the division set up its global distribution center in Venlo, Netherlands and three area distribution centers in Village-Neuf, France; Belvidere, New Jersey, USA; and Singapore, while simultaneously dispensing with a network of multiple national warehouses. Kamber said reorganizing the warehouse and logistics information networks helped reduce inventory levels and finance costs. "Before, we had a lot of inventory in many countries," he said. He acknowledged that having just one distribution center for Europe has lengthened delivery times for certain countries. But he said this choice has paid off. "We had discussions with customers to see if they really needed deliveries within two hours and discovered that some did not. It's a question of not being too early nor too late – we want to hit the target. Often customers have special requirements in terms of packaging or other things which are more important than two-hour delivery availability," he said.

While warehousing was converted to the centralized area distribution center system, order processing was computerized to cut response times. Previously, about 30 order-processing staffers were based at the company's head office to process paper orders from local offices and feed them into the logistics system. Local offices now take and process orders at source and enter them into the company's order system, which has a direct, electronic link to the area distribution centers. Since the new setup five years ago, the global distribution center has been divided into two parts: Global Distribution and European Distribution, which has taken over the North Europe distribution activities of the European area center based in France. Management of the global distribution center's warehousing operations was, from the outset, contracted out to a specialized European warehousing company, Vitess. However, Hoffmann-La Roche has its own staff on the second floor of the center to manage other distribution operations in-house such as freight documentation.

(**Source**: Damas, Philip. "'Localized' global distribution", *American Shipper*, February 1997, pp. 36–8)

Study Questions

1. What are some of the factors management must consider in selecting an international channel strategy?
2. Give examples of a situation where a firm would utilize an exporting strategy.
3. Contrast an ownership strategy with the joint venture. Why would management choose one over the other?
4. Why is international documentation more difficult to manage than that required for domestic shipments?
5. What is being done to improve the flow of international documentation?
6. Why do governments establish customs regulations?
7. Discuss a scenario where foreign trade zones might no longer be needed.
8. Briefly describe the functions of an international freight forwarder.
9. Compare and contrast export management companies with export trading companies.
10. Discuss the role of the export packer. Why is packing/packaging so important in an international logistics system?
11. Contrast a centralized global logistics function with a decentralized one.
12. Discuss the concept of "localized" global distribution and how it can improve customer satisfaction.
13. Reviewing logistics profile 11-1, what sort of distribution approach will be the most effective one for China today? In your opinion, what is/are the biggest impediment(s) to logistics in China?

Notes

1. Ball, Donald M. and McCulloch, Wendell H. Jr. *International Business*, 7th edn (New York: Irwin/McGraw-Hill, 1999), pp. 134–5.
2. Zubrod, Justin. "How important is local culture to global logistics?" *Transportation and Distribution*, December 1996, vol. 37, no. 12, pp. 61–3.
3. Quinn, Francis J. "Building a world-class supply chain," *Logistics Management*, June 1998, p. 38.
4. "Study pegs global logistics market at $3.43 trillion," *Logistics Management*, August 1998, p. 20.
5. Ibid.
6. Robb, Drew. "A hot market's hottest trading bloc," *World Trade*, June 1998, p. 34.

7. Czinkota, Michael R., Kotable, Masaki, and Mercer, David. *Marketing Management: Text and Cases*, (Cambridge, MA: Blackwell Publishers, Inc., 1997), p. 71.
8. Gooley, Toby B. "Keeping an eye on Asia," *Logistics Management*, May 1998, p. 83.
9. Rosenbloom, Bert. *Marketing Channels*, 6th edn (Fort Worth, TX: The Dryden Press, 1999), p. 531.
10. Schary, Philip B. *Logistics Decisions* (New York: CBS College Publishing, 1984), p. 405.
11. Ibid, pp. 405–6.
12. O'Laughlin, Kevin A., Cooper, James, and Cabocel, Eric. *Reconfiguring European Logistics Systems* (Oak Brook, IL: Council of Logistics Management, 1993), p. 90.
13. "'Paperless' exporting at Port of Hamburg", *American Shipper*, August 1997, p. 62.
14. Ibid.
15. Gourdin, Kent N. and Andersen Consulting, Air Cargo Manufacturing Facility Study (FAA Research Grant 93–G-022), Research Project H: Intermodal Information, unpublished, 1993, p. 8–1.
16. Ibid, pp. 8–2&3.
17. Armbruster, William. "UPS one step away from complete link to Customs' automated manifest system," *The Journal of Commerce*, May 24, 1993.
18. Coyle, John J., Bardi, Edward J., and Langley, C. John Jr. *The Management of Business Logistics* (St. Paul, MN: West Publishing Company, 1996), pp. 512–13.
19. Hastings, Phillip. "Obstacles on the road east," *Global Transport*, Summer 1998, p. 68.
20. Hise, Richard T. "The implications of time-based competition on international logistics strategies," *Business Horizons*, Sept.–Oct. 1995, vol. 38, no. 5, pp. 39–46.
21. Ibid.
22. McConville, Daniel J. "Racing the clock," *World Trade*, February 1998, p. 35.
23. Stevenson-Yang, Anne. "Quiet incursions: China's free-trade zones are oases of relative freedom for foreign business," *The China Business Review*, Sep.–Oct. 1996, vol. 23, no. 5, p. 36(6).
24. Gillis, Chris, and Damas, Philip. "What should you outsource?" *American Shipper*, January 1997, pp. 25–31.
25. Ibid.
26. Coyle et al., ibid, p. 505.
27. Johnson, James C. and Wood, Donald F. *Contemporary Logistics*, 6th edn (Upper Saddle River, NJ: Prentice Hall, 1996), p. 413.
28. Dahringer, Lee D. and Muhlbacher, Hans. *International Marketing, A Global Perspective* (Reading MA: Addison-Wesley Publishing Company, Inc., 1991), pp. 312–13.
29. Albaum, Gerald, Strandskov, Jesper, Duerr, Edwin, and Dowd, Laurence. *International Marketing and Export Management* (Wokingham, England: Addison-Wesley Publishing Company, 1989), p. 374.
30. Lambert, Douglas M. and Stock, James R. *Strategic Logistics Management*, 3rd edn (Homewood, IL: Richard D. Irwin, Inc., 1993), p. 697.
31. Gillis, Chris. "'We're not Santa Claus for the forwarder'," *American Shipper*, February 1997, pp. 31–4.
32. Christopher, Martin. *Logistics and Supply Chain Management* (London: Richard D. Irwin, Inc., 1994), pp. 105–6.
33. Ibid, p. 106.
34. Ibid, p. 107.
35. Damas, Philip. "'Localized' global distribution," *American Shipper*, February 1997, pp. 36–8.

chapter 12

Logistics Strategies

Introduction	211
Corporate Strategic Planning	211
Formulating Logistics Strategy	214
Integrating the Logistics Channel	216
Implementing Logistics Strategies	218
Future Issues That Will Affect Logistics	223
Implications for Logistics Managers	226
Chapter Summary	227
Study Questions	227

Introduction

Logistics is becoming an increasingly important and visible component of the firm's corporate strategy. Indeed, to realize the full value of logistics as a source of competitive differentiation requires that managers develop and implement strategies that are increasingly more complex, longer lasting, more difficult to reverse, and riskier than ever before.[1] Ironically, an even greater risk may lie in failing to develop a logistics strategy responsive to the rapid pace of environmental change. However, many decisions must be made by the organization's senior leaders before a logistics strategy can be promulgated. This chapter will begin by examining the corporate strategic planning process. Next, the formulation of logistics strategies within that corporate framework will be discussed and several current approaches to logistics management presented. Finally, the impact of environmental change on logistics strategy development will be addressed.

Corporate Strategic Planning[2]

Corporate strategy is made up of two parts: critical elements and planning. Critical elements refer to areas of the business for which options are evaluated and decisions

Table 12.1 Elements of corporate strategy and examples

Lines of business	Mercedes and BMW entered the sport utility vehicle (SUV) market.
	Mazda withdrew from the high-priced luxury car business.
Geographical scope	Fujitsu entered, abandoned, and re-entered the US supercomputer business.
	FedEx ceased serving Europe through its own fleet.
Growth strategy	Boeing merged with McDonnell Douglas.
Stakeholder commitments	The Body Shop's dedication to being environmentally responsible.
Core competencies	Sony used miniaturization technology across its products.
	BMW emphasizes its engine and suspension technology.

(*Source*: Rao, Kant, Stenger, Alan J., and Wu, Haw-Jan. "Training future logistics managers: logistics strategies within the corporate planning framework," *Journal of Business Logistics*, vol. 15, no. 2, 1994, p. 253)

made. These factors include selecting the line(s) of business the firm will pursue, geographical market coverage, growth strategies, stakeholder commitments, and which core competencies to exploit. Decisions made regarding any of these areas set the tone for the enterprise and dictate the choices and evaluation criteria for more detailed decisions at the lower functional levels of the organization. Specific examples illustrating the types of choices management might make are depicted in table 12-1.

The corporate strategic planning process typically starts with a vision, a mission statement, and a set of objectives that the firm wants to achieve to satisfy its stakeholders: customers, suppliers, employees, shareholders, or the public at large. Next, the firm assesses the resources available to it by cataloging its strengths and weaknesses in both internal operations and its channel relationships. In addition, the external threats and opportunities that will have an impact on the company's performance in the future are also identified. In this analysis of strengths, weaknesses, opportunities, and threats (SWOT), the firm must detect both ongoing and potential changes in its surroundings which are relevant – including shifts in social, demographic, behavioral, and environmental variables – as well as both societal and governmental responses to these changes, such as the adjustments in taxes, services, and regulatory policies. The market and the competitors are also studied to see how they might respond to the changes and where the company should position itself against competitors in the market.

The external and internal environment analysis described above is sometimes referred to as environmental scanning. Senior management need to monitor events occurring beyond the boundaries of the corporation so that major strategies can be developed that will allow corporate leaders to anticipate and respond to meaningful change. The firm also needs to know the resources that are available and use them fully to achieve desired objectives. Analyzing their strengths and weaknesses gives management insight into the firm's overall health in comparison to its competitors.

Next, the company needs to develop several corporate strategies that could realistically be used to attain desired goals and then select the one that best fits the company's mission, objectives, and operating environment. Later, functional strategies in marketing, operations, finance, and logistics are developed following the same model employed to develop the strategic plan. The planning process keeps moving down through the management hierarchy until all strategic, tactical, and operational plans have been developed. Strategic plans are fairly long term in nature (three to five years or longer) and provide the overall framework within which the firm conducts business. Tactical plans cover a shorter time period (usually one year) and focus on implementing strategic initiatives. Operational or action plans specify how the business should be run on a day-to-day basis. In addition, action plans also close the loop in the strategic planning process by providing feedback and enabling corrective actions to be taken in response to changes in the marketplace.

The decisions at the corporate level on the various elements of corporate strategy, coupled with the planning process, provide the structure within which functional strategies can be formulated and linked to each other. For example, a corporate decision to manufacture multinationally or to source globally would lead to a dramatically different logistics network than otherwise. Similarly, a corporate decision to seek significant export sales would require a greater attention being paid to aspects of international logistics than perhaps was done in the past. The implication here is that logistics managers must be well attuned to their firm's corporate strategies and to its key business processes and practices. Experience and insight are necessary to develop good judgment about what logistics strategies are likely to work and contribute to the attainment of company objectives. The corporate planning process is summarized in figure 12-1.

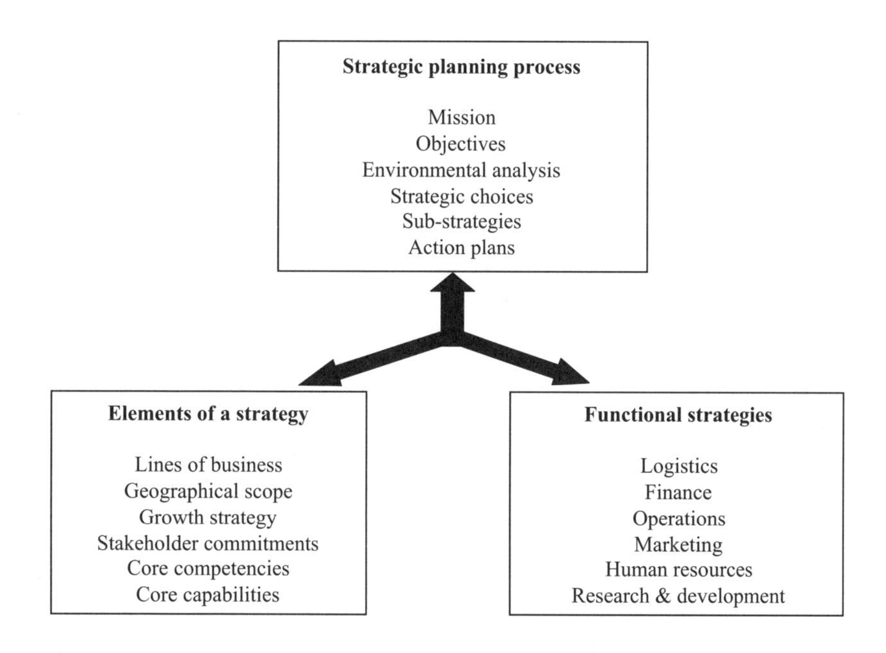

Figure 12-1 Corporate strategy formulation
Source: Rao, Kant, Stenger, Alan J., and Wu, Haw-Jan. "Training future logistics managers: logistics strategies within the corporate planning framework," *Journal of Business Logistics*, Vol. 15, No, 2, 1994, p. 255

Formulating Logistics Strategy[3]

Logistics strategies must be developed within the context of corporate strategy and consider not only larger organizational objectives but also the relevant strategies of other functional areas such as manufacturing, marketing, and finance. For example, issues regarding manufacturing capacity available and the firm's marketing mix must be factored into the logistics planning process. The growing visibility of logistics is at least partly due to the pervasive nature of logistics' interaction across the functional spectrum of the firm. The challenge to logistics managers is how to develop a coordinated logistics approach in a time of increasing uncertainty. The answer lies in some form of supply chain integration.

The term "supply chain" denotes the channel of firms and intermediaries through which a product (or group of products) moves from the original sources of its basic raw materials through conversion/manufacture and then distribution in its finished form to the ultimate consumer. The premise espoused throughout this text is that integrated supply chain management will result in logistical system performance in the channel of distribution (or supply) superior to that of channels not employing such integrating approaches. The means for achieving integration typically involves the sharing of information, particularly with regard to projected demands and planned production. In addition, integration requires a comprehensive look at a number of critical elements as described below.

- **Customer service levels** This element involves determining the appropriate levels of customer service for the target product–market combination. In order to evaluate strategic options, customers must be surveyed and studied, opportunities for differentiation determined, and the performance of competitors analyzed. Finally, the costs associated with offering various service levels through alternative network options must be calculated so that the "best" choice (from the customer's viewpoint) can be made.
- **Channels of supply and distribution** How many channel members should there be and what should be the working relationships with them? As has been previously discussed, firms are moving to reduce the number of suppliers, carriers, and middlemen they do business with and bolster their relationships with those remaining, often entering into long-term contractual and partnership arrangements. 3M is one of the few firms to formalize this strategy. Calling it their "Channel Approach," managers have identified five logistics channels to serve 80 separate businesses and have established teams to develop customized logistics strategies for each channel.
- **Facility locations** What raw material supply sources, supply consolidation points, distribution facilities, and field service centers should be part of the logistics network? What should be their capabilities and responsibilities? Answering these questions involves close liaison with manufacturing and marketing departments so that the whole supply chain is working in a satisfactory manner.
- **Allocations** These strategies involve determining the best use for the facilities identified above. How should raw material supplies be deployed to meet

manufacturing needs and how should plant output be allocated to distribution centers and eventually to customer locations?

- **Inventories** What should be the inventory management system, how much inventory should be carried, of what products, and where should they be maintained? As the hidden cost of large inventories has become better understood, there has been a move to reduce these assets, requiring a much more coordinated operation to manage product and goods flows.
- **Transportation** What modes of transportation should be used? What carriers and shipment sizes are most appropriate? Who should make the transportation decision, shippers or receivers? As was discussed earlier, the move toward deregulation worldwide has opened this area as a major opportunity for cost savings and quality improvement.
- **Information Management** What planning, operation, and control systems are appropriate, and what type of telecommunication systems are needed to track product flows throughout the logistics pipeline? The rapid growth of bar-coding and other forms of automatic identification, electronic data interchange (EDI), and imaging facilitating transaction processing and communications as well as sophisticated decision support and expert systems for planning attest to the significant role of information in the logistics process.
- **Organization** The structure of the logistics organization in terms of line and staff and the degree of centralization versus decentralization are important issues to be addressed for a well-functioning operation. The interrelationship of the logistics organization to the rest of the firm is also critical, if logistics is to realize its full potential as a source of competitive advantage.

Developing a successful logistics strategy, then, is really a two-part process. First, as shown in figure 12-2, firms must integrate their own logistics activities, adopting a systems view and understanding the trade-offs inherent in any logistics decision. Secondly, managers must find a way to integrate their logistics systems with those of their channel members because the supply chain is only as strong as its weakest link. All of management's best efforts will be wasted if a weak middleman can subvert the entire process, so there are two dominant objectives that must be met if a supply chain is to be successful. First, there is a need to maximize the value added to each activity or member organization in the supply chain for both customers and suppliers. Second, synergies must be achieved that improve the aggregate performance of the supply chain in such areas as reducing total cycle times, reducing system inventory, and taking costs out of the whole supply chain.[4] Each organization, then, needs to examine its individual supply chain in terms of its major products and services and its competitive challenges. Each needs to decide where it can differentiate products and services by capitalizing on supply chain capabilities and resources to bring products and services to market – faster, at the lowest possible cost, with the appropriate product/service features, and with better overall value.[5] Airbus Industrie's partners, for example, are rapidly boosting production, shortening cycles, and cutting costs with a significantly leaner supply chain. European and overseas subcontractors, vendors, and suppliers are being tightly monitored in an effort to rapidly identify or prevent delays and component shortages that could endanger on-time deliveries. In 1998, Airbus delivered

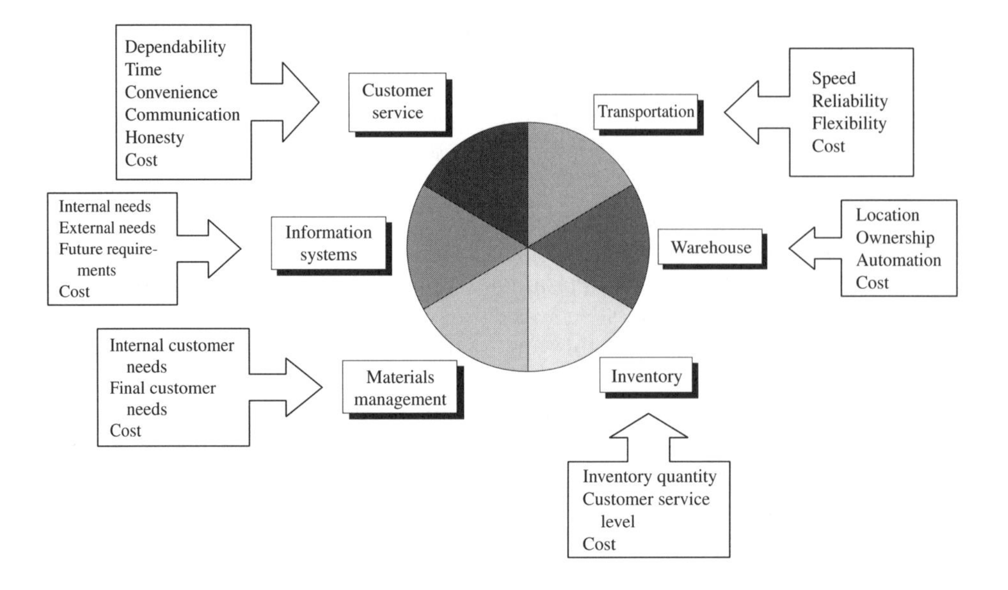

Figure 12-2 Putting the pieces together to create a logistics strategy

230 aircraft, up from 182 during 1997. It is scheduled to deliver 285 commercial transports in 1999 and 334 in 2000. The single-aisle A320 family's production rate, which currently averages 18 aircraft/month, is scheduled to increase to 22 aircraft/month by mid-2000 – by far the highest production rate ever achieved for European commercial transports. In addition, one aircraft can be built in 12 months today, down from nearly two years in 1990.[6] The overriding goal for any firm, then, must be to offer higher levels of customer satisfaction to end-users than they receive from the competition. Several alternative approaches will be discussed below.

Integrating the Logistics Channel

Four major options are available, and are depicted in figure 12-3. These approaches vary by the size of the firm wishing to pursue such strategies and the size of that company's channel partners. The most important thing illustrated in figure 12-3 is that an organization need not be large to benefit from the development and implementation of a systematic logistics strategy. The options illustrated are discussed in more detail below.

- **Implement channel integration strategies** This approach works best when large manufacturers, distributors, or retailers deal with other large manufacturers, retailers, or middlemen. The idea here is that the two large channel members will integrate the channel however they see fit: establish common inventory

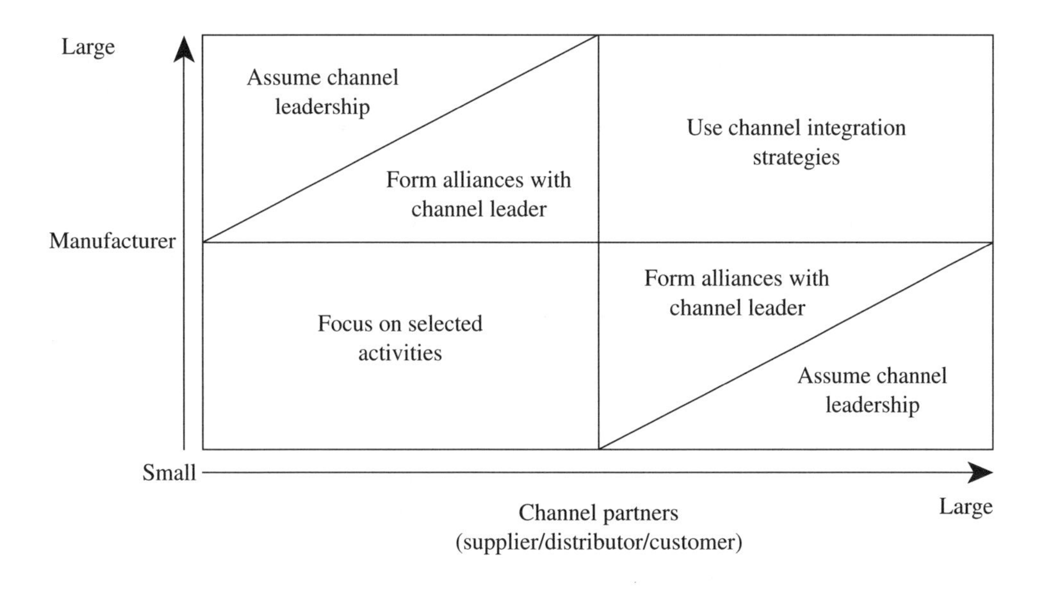

Figure 12-3 Integrated channel management strategies
Source: Copacino, William C. and Lambert, Douglas M. "Integrated channel management," unpublished manuscript, 1992, as presented in Lambert, Douglas M. and Stock, James R., *Strategic Logistics Management* (Homewood, IL: Irwin, 1993), p. 748

management policies, share transportation management duties, implement full EDI for billing and reordering, etc. Other smaller members of the channel may have to modify their procedures in order to participate. For instance, BMW and Michelin may utilize EDI to track the movement of tires to the automaker's plants. Transportation firms and other intermediaries would be expected to adopt the same system if they want to participate in the channel.

- **Assume channel leadership** This strategy is most appropriate when one large firm is dealing with smaller partners. Here, the channel leader focuses on strategies that improve profitability for the company and its channel partners by sharing information, providing value-added services, and implementing productivity improvements. Toyota, for example, exerts virtually total control over its channel, directing that events be handled in specific ways. However, by sharing automotive production information with its suppliers, Toyota enables those vendors to improve their planning so as to better meet the needs of both Toyota and any other customers that seller may supply.
- **Form alliances with the channel leader** When a small firm is dealing with large channel partners, it should identify the channel leader's goals and present alternative methods of achieving them. This strategy provides a way for smaller firms to take advantage of the relative strength of the dominant channel member by facilitating the attainment of its objectives. Thus a small company that supplies

machined parts to Toyota might look for ways to add value (either by improving the quality of the parts supplied for the same money or by offering some innovative order fulfillment program) to Toyota, thereby helping both parties to attain their objectives.
- **Focus on selective activities** When a firm participates in a channel comprised of small firms competing with larger and more powerful channels, management should focus on selected activities that build the relationship at low cost and with low levels of investment. For example, channel members can share business plans, cooperate to reduce order-cycle times, or establish common inventory management practices. The objective would be for the small channel to be able to compete on the basis of one or more important customer variables. Safmarine, a South African ocean transport firm, has been very successful with this strategy, as is explained in logistics profile 12-1.

It is important to understand that small companies as well as large ones can benefit from the implementation of channel integration strategies. Much discussion centers on the successful strategies of large firms and how they are able to leverage their buying power and their size to create fortress channels. Organizations with less clout can succeed as well, but they cannot expect to do it in the same way as their large competitors. Rather, managers of smaller channel members must formulate strategies that either assist the channel leader in meeting its objectives or, depending on the situation, offer some noticeable advantage to the customer that is not available elsewhere.

For example, Habitat, the European home furnishings and accessories retailer, is implementing a system to improve the visibility of its inventory and imported goods. Working together with LEP, its third-party forwarder, Habitat has started implementing the first phase of the new event-tracking system designed by LEP, called Purchase Order Management System (POMS). This system manages and tracks purchase orders and uses electronic data interchange to transfer data between commercial, transport, or logistics parties. Habitat operates a network of 102 owned and franchised stores in the United Kingdom, Germany, France, Spain, Italy, and the Netherlands. It designs and imports a large range of goods, many of which are sourced from Asia and include a large range of exclusive products, sometimes ordered in relatively small production runs. POMS will link Habitat, its overseas buying agents, suppliers, and LEP as the freight forwarder and will cover the entire order cycle, from purchasing to warehousing, through shipping. The whole purpose of this integration effort is to provide better visibility of products moving through the channel which will, in turn, improve lead times, lower inventory levels, and lessen the requirement for warehouse capacity. Indeed, Habitat's management are more concerned with improving lead-time certainty rather than lead-time speed by utilizing POMS to more closely orchestrate channel activities.[7]

Implementing Logistics Strategies

Once management has selected an appropriate logistics strategy or strategies (depending on market conditions, product sectors, customer groups, etc.), implementation

Logistics Profile 12-1
SAFMARINE FINDS NORTH/SOUTH PARTNERS

South African carrier Safmarine believes in "strategic" alliances, but not "global" ones. Where is the nuance in these terminologies? The focus of the strategic alliances sought by Safmarine is on "basic areas and niches where we are strong – Africa and north/south trades," explained Anthony Z. Farr, managing director of Safmarine. "It is difficult for a single entity to operate without entering into a strategic alliance," he conceded. "Safmarine as a container operator is relatively small by international standards."

The specialized strategic alliance as defined by Safmarine, in common with the global alliances, intends to maximize economies of scale and synergies through cooperation. But Safmarine's liner shipping alliance, SCL (Safmarine CMBT Lines), has no interest in competing against global competitors in east/west trades, Farr said. SCL was established in January to merge the liner interests of Safmarine and Belgium's CMB Transport, in which Safmarine already had a 49 percent stake. Farr said CMB Transport carried around 250,000 full containers a year and Safmarine 200,000. With total annual revenues in excess of $1 billion, the combined 450,000 box-a-year operation puts Safmarine "in a new lead," according to Farr. "It is one of the largest liner shipping operations in the north/south trades, and certainly the largest to and from Africa," he said.

Farr views the creation of SCL as Safmarine's most significant strategic step in the development of its liner shipping business since the company adopted containerization. Yet Farr said Safmarine's equity link with CMB Transport did not preclude it from entering additional alliances with other carriers. Safmarine subsidiary Universal Reefers recently implemented an agreement with Outspan and Unifruco, two South African fruit companies. Under the arrangement, the fleet of Universal Reefers incorporated the refrigerated ships of the two fruit companies. The enlarged Universal Reefers is expected to handle 1 million pallets of uncontainerized fruit annually from South Africa. Following expansionary moves such as its purchase of a 49 percent stake in CMB Transport in 1991, Safmarine believes it no longer relies on South Africa as its primary market.

(**Source**: Damas, Philip. "Safmarine finds north/south partners," *American Shipper*, September 1996, p. 90)

issues must then be addressed. There are several issues that must be considered because they can have a significant impact on the structure of the firm's logistics system. These include evaluating the merits of a centralized versus a decentralized system, assessing the use of outside third parties to perform some or all logistics activities versus in-house personnel, and ensuring that a chosen strategy meshes with other functional areas within the firm.

Centralization of logistics activities versus decentralization

A **centralized** logistics operation means that resources are reduced to achieve more efficient and cost-effective operations. This would imply fewer warehouses serving more customers over a wider geographic area. A **decentralized** approach refers to coordinating logistics across geographic boundaries, perhaps distributing products from warehouses in multiple countries or regions. In practice, most companies' strategies include both of these approaches. For example, a food manufacturer that operates manufacturing plants and distribution centers in each of the European Union countries decides to reorganize. Having determined that centralized oversight of operations would keep administrative and distribution costs down, company management considers closing all 12 distribution centers and consolidation operations in a single location. But several factors conspire to make regional warehouses necessary (decentralization). First, transportation costs for frequent, small shipments from a single location to the farthest corner of the EU would rise unacceptably. Furthermore, customer demand for second-day delivery and the perishable nature of some products mean that a single, central warehouse is impractical. The final decision is to create a European headquarters overseeing three regional manufacturing/distribution sites.[8]

Clearly, there are important trade-offs to consider. A centralized approach can lead to reduced costs (owing to economies of scale) while providing managers greater control of the entire logistics systems. Decentralized, on the other hand, allows management to provide better customer service albeit with less total control. Historically, companies operating in Europe utilized a very decentralized approach consisting of separate sales, production, warehousing, and transportation organizations in each country. Each national division also had its own inventory and managed it independently. Now, thanks to new laws, companies can more easily manage manufacturing and logistics operations on a regional or centralized basis should they decide to do so.[9] In actuality, a firm might use a decentralized approach in one area, a centralized scheme in another, and something in between in a third market depending on how their customers' needs can best be served.

Third-party service providers

Often, company personnel perform all or most logistics activities in-house. Historically, the use of third parties (i.e. freight forwarders) for international shipments involving ocean or air transport was quite common. However, increasing corporate emphasis on such concepts as reengineering and supply chain management has led many companies to consider outsourcing the entire logistics process or, more commonly, selected activities within that process.[10] Of course, utilizing third parties does not absolve management from their responsibility to ensure customer satisfaction is maintained at desired levels. Indeed, customers may not even be aware that the company has outsourced some of its logistics tasks and probably don't care even if they do know.

In an effort to assess the extent of third-party involvement in logistics, a survey was sent to the 500 largest manufacturers in the United States. Based upon the 92 completed questionnaires that were returned, some interesting findings emerged. As might be expected, the initial consideration of third-party logistics providers as substitutes for in-house job performance may make managers nervous. The study found that the three most common concerns are the potential loss of direct control of logistics activities, uncertainties about the service levels to be provided by the outside company, and questions concerning the true costs of using a third party. Other concerns expressed included job security, data security, the questionable expertise of third-party companies, and the difficulties inherent in attempting to build new working relationships.[11]

Once the decision to outsource is made, implementation may prove troublesome as well. Typical start-up problems include overcoming resistance to change, difficulties encountered in teaching third-party personnel about the company's business requirements and systems, cultural differences between the firms, and the need to integrate computer and information systems. Furthermore, a lack of clear performance criteria, the need to communicate internal expectations, and slow reactions by third-party providers to rapidly changing customer needs are also issues that may require management's attention.[12]

In determining whether or not to utilize third parties in the logistics process, management must decide where the greatest value to the customer lies. Will outsourcing a particular task lead to better customer service, lower costs, or provide some other meaningful benefit? If not, that activity should probably remain in-house. Table 12-2 shows the functions most often performed by third parties while table 12-3 depicts the benefits outsourcing provided to survey respondents.

Supporting results were found by similar research conducted in Australia. There the majority of respondents to a survey investigating outsourcing among the country's largest corporations reported that their organizations use third-party logistics services. The services commonly contracted included fleet management, warehouse management, shipment consolidation, order fulfillment, and product returns. Those same respondents were almost unanimous in claiming that outsourcing had positive effects on logistics costs, logistics systems performance, customer satisfaction, and employee morale.[13]

However management choose to perform the logistics function, customer satisfaction levels must be monitored on a continuous basis. It may be that services outsourced at one time may be brought back in-house at a later date, depending on changing customer needs and environmental factors. Similarly, tasks performed by company personnel may be given to a third party for the same reasons. It is true, though, that some decisions have longer-term implications than others. For example, should the firm enter into a relationship whereby a third party builds and staffs a warehouse for the company alone, terminating that agreement may be difficult if not impossible. The point is that the outsourcing decision should not be taken lightly.

Table 12.2 The most frequently used third-party logistics services

Logistics function	*% citing use – 1995*	*% citing use – 1994*	*% citing use – 1991*
Warehouse management	36	44	49
Shipment consolidation	33	37	45
Logistics information systems	29	33	32
Fleet management/operations	22	26	28
Rate negotiation	22	26	21
Carrier selection	33	23	21
Order fulfillment	9	16	26
Import/export		10	
Product returns	11	7	2
Order processing	6	5	6
Product assembly/installation	11	2	6
Customer spare parts	7		
Inventory replenishment	6		

(*Source*: Lieb, Robert C. and Randall, Hugh L. "A comparison of the use of third party logistics services by large American manufacturers, 1991, 1994, and 1995, "*Journal of Business Logistics*, vol. 17, no. 1, 1996, p. 310)

Table 12.3 Most frequently cited benefits related to use of third party logistics services, 1995

Benefits	*% of respondents indicating that benefit*
Lower cost	38
Improved expertise/market knowledge and access to data	24
Improved operational efficiency	11
Improved customer service	9
Ability to focus on core business	7
Greater flexibility	5

(*Source*: Lieb, Robert C. and Randall, Hugh L. "A comparison of the use of third party logistics services by large American manufacturers, 1991, 1994, and 1995," *Journal of Business Logistics*, vol. 17, no. 1, 1996, p. 310)

While it can offer a number of advantages to the firm, outsourcing can lead to large changes in personnel and physical plant that may be hard to replace should management change their minds at a later date.

General Motors, for example, took the radical step of creating a single logistics strategy for parts moving to its assembly plants throughout the world. Previously, GM had allowed its various divisions to handle their own distribution. The result was a plethora of carriers serving hundreds of suppliers under a myriad of contracts. In order to better integrate inbound supply channels, the firm divided the world into regional blocs and assigned contracts to each of these blocs. Burlington Air Express oversees parts movement between North America and Europe, while Air

Express International is responsible for parts movement between North and Latin America, and between North America and Asia Pacific. The task these third-party service providers face is daunting because a part might wind its way back and forth between continents before ending up on the assembly line. For instance, Burlington moves raw materials for fuel injectors from the United States to the parts manufacturer in Vienna, Austria. From there, the part returns to the United States for a quick quality check and minor subassembly at GM's Delphi engine management plant in Rochester, New York. Then the part is moved again, this time to a final assembly plant in the United States or Canada. Similar challenges exist in Asia, where GM has assembly plants or vendors in China, Japan, South Korea, Singapore, Indonesia, Australia, and New Zealand, among other places. Indeed, in Asia parts shift between vendor and manufacturer in the same complicated pattern as between Europe and North America.[14]

Logistics strategy and improved corporate performance

As was mentioned earlier, logistics functions within the framework established by corporate policy. Logistics managers, then, must be cognizant of how a given strategy will impact overall corporate performance. For example, the potential cost benefits of redesigning European logistics systems in light of the changes occurring there can be surprising in their magnitude. The authors of the Council of Logistics Management's *Reconfiguring European Logistics* study report that the 150 companies they surveyed often realized total logistics-cost savings of as much as 40 to 50 percent. By reducing the number of distribution centers and support staff required to serve customers throughout Europe and managing logistics strategies and expenditures on a regional or pan-European basis, these companies have experienced extraordinary savings.[15]

But there are trade-offs involved as well. Although many companies have simplified their manufacturing and distribution operations, that simplification has made life more complicated for logistics managers. Serving more markets from fewer locations means more cross-border trade, more traffic lanes, and greater complexity. Furthermore, the days of a "one-size-fits-all" logistics strategy in Europe are over. What works for a manufacturer selling high-value electronics in 12 countries isn't necessarily the right strategy for a company selling low-value construction supplies in two countries. An added complication is that the stagnant Eastern European economies are likely to become important markets in the future, so any logistics system should be flexible enough to take advantage of that growth as well as any other opportunities that may emerge over time.[16]

Future Issues That Will Affect Logistics

One of the primary purposes of the planning process is to equip managers to deal proactively with changes in their environment. Although it would be impossible to address (or even anticipate) every important future event, the importance of sound planning can best be illustrated by examining some challenges managers are facing today.

Continued expansion of global business

Many emerging nations produce food for export and/or sell relatively sophisticated manufactured goods to the developed countries. Current economic problems notwithstanding, consumers in Asia, as well as those in Latin America and parts of Africa are earning more and demanding goods once considered out of their reach.[17] Managers must continue to develop logistics systems that are capable of exploiting both emerging consumer markets and new sources of supply. As was mentioned in a previous chapter, political instability and strife mark some nations, so that taking advantage of growth opportunities may require that the firm incur some risk. In these unstable situations, sound planning becomes especially critical.

Environmental and ecological issues

Many logistics activities will be affected by the growing need to conduct business in an environmentally sensitive way. New forms of packaging will have to be developed that offer acceptable levels of protection while either being recyclable or biodegradable; transportation will have to be accomplished in ways that reduce energy consumption and minimize pollution; reverse logistics channels will have to be established to return greater numbers of defective and worn-out products to some designated point for recycling. Logistics impacts the environment in a myriad of ways; the challenge will be to minimize those negative effects while continuing to reduce costs and improve service.

Transport infrastructure condition and capacity

Transport infrastructure issues were presented in an earlier chapter. However, it is worth reiterating that increases in global trade will inevitably lead to greater demands being placed on available roads, bridges, airport, harbors, railroads, and canals. Over time, these assets will start to wear out, resulting in slower, more damage-prone transportation services. Indeed, in a worst case scenario, access to certain markets could even become a problem. This issue is discussed from the European point of view in logistics profile 12-2.

Transportation deregulation

As nations continue to deregulate transportation, logistics managers will find continued opportunities for improving service and reducing costs, both between carriers and across modes. However, the onus will be on management to have a precise understanding of their shipping needs as well as a working knowledge of the transportation systems in every part of their global network. Unfortunately, the reality of the free market means that less astute managers will find they are paying higher prices and/or receiving unsatisfactory service.

Logistics Profile 12-2
LOOKING DOWN A CROWDED ROAD

A major worry in the European Union is the future of mobility. Ever-growing trade, and slowly but ever-growing populations, are already causing serious obstructions of road transport. Not only the main motorways are congested, but also access ways to cities, ports, airports, industrial and agricultural centers where cargo must be collected and delivered. In a smallish country like the Netherlands or Belgium, road congestion reports broadcast every hour are frightening. Between 10 and 20 traffic jams in each of the countries have become routine rush hour events. In Germany, alternate routes are numbered and sign-posted along the motorways to enable drivers to get around a clog.

Many very expensive solutions, such as doubling bridges over rivers, adding lanes to motorways, digging more tunnels under rivers and through mountains, and building new passes over mountains simply displace the routine congestion a few kilometers further away. Moreover, these solutions attract even more cars and trucks. Environmentalists predict road traffic will double within the next 25 years or so. At the same time, their tolerance of the side effects of increased road traffic (i.e. noxious fumes, acid rain, alteration of landscapes to accommodate new roads) is diminishing. The younger generation, especially, is more often voting "green."

The problem is not just with road congestion. At the same time, ports and airports never appear content with their size and capacity. They move heaven and earth (literally) to enlarge to meet present and future demands and growing cargo flows. They do not accept that part of future demand and growth of cargo movement originates from their attempts to expand. It never occurs to any of their managers that full is full and enough is enough and eventually an overflow will have to go elsewhere. The very thought of ships and boxes having to shift to some other port is unbearable to them. Especially in the Netherlands, extensions are proposed to be constructed even in the North Sea on artificial isles or peninsulas, ultimately aggravating the problems on the access ways.

In sum, in the interest of their long-term strategies and planning, exporters to Europe would be well advised to study the cost, ways and means to get their goods where they want them to go over the next 10 or 20 years. The most promising markets are worthless if they cannot be reached at an acceptable cost and on schedule.

(**Source**: Verhaar, Gerard. "Looking down a crowded road," *American Shipper*, December 1995, p. 26)

Government regulations

Despite the increasingly free market in transportation, governments continue to influence the conduct of global business in a great number of ways. Companies selling goods in different countries are confronted with a varied and often confusing array of laws, rules, and even customs that all must be obeyed if the marketing effort is going to succeed. The demise of the Soviet Union and the opening of Eastern Europe illustrate just how quickly things can change and how important it is that managers to able to react to a new reality.

Consumerism

Free enterprise has become the rule rather than the exception, even in once staunchly socialist nations like India, China, and Russia.[18] One of the axioms of the free market seems to be that the more people have, the more they want. Customers simply are becoming more demanding with regard to where, when, and in what quantities products are available. Similarly, those items must arrive in the consumer's hands undamaged and at a reasonable cost. Global companies will find themselves dealing with customers in radically different stages of the free market. Customers' needs will change as markets grow and prosper. Keeping up with that evolutionary process is perhaps management's greatest challenge.

Technological advances

The ongoing refinements in computers and information systems in general will make it possible for a firm to offer better customer service while simultaneously managing the entire logistics effort more effectively. Transport vehicles will become more economical to operate while mechanized materials handling systems will become more elaborate and comprehensive. However, all of this state-of-the-art equipment will come at a cost; the task for management is to determine when the situation warrants the investment and when a simpler, more manual approach to logistics is most appropriate.

Implications for Logistics Managers

The impacts of environmental change are magnified for companies serving global markets. Management must adopt a systems approach in order to best serve the needs of their widely diverse customer base. With respect to **customer service**, creative responses are required to ensure that the requisite levels of service are provided at the lowest possible cost. **Transportation** decisions must be made such that equipment utilization is maximized while energy consumption and pollution are minimized. Furthermore, managers will find themselves increasingly able to improve service and lower costs, as transport deregulation becomes more widespread. **Inventory management** offers great potential for cost reduction, although growing levels of consumerism may lead to the adoption of higher service levels that necessitate holding more inventories. Advances in **information systems** offer significant opportunities for reduced order-cycle times, better customer service, and improved control over the entire logistics system. **Warehousing** can add value to the customer through location and improvements that will reduce the cost per unit of handling goods as they move through the storage facility. **Packaging** is assuming a more important and multifaceted role in the logistics process, both as a marketing tool to differentiate products on increasingly crowded shelves and as a protective resource to ensure the product reaches the consumer in working order.

In sum, all parts of the logistics system are affected by change. Management's task, then, is twofold. First, a strategic planning system must be established that will provide the information necessary for managers to anticipate significant environmental change. Secondly, the logistics system must be managed so as to be able to exploit opportunities and protect the organization against threats. Thus, the impact of change on both individual logistics activities and the system as a whole must be considered so that appropriate courses of action can be developed that will help the firm achieve its overall corporate objectives.

Chapter Summary

The development of a sound and responsive logistics strategy is crucial to the overall success of the organization. Increasingly, firms are looking for ways to integrate their logistics activities both internally and externally with their channel members. An organization's chosen logistics strategy is based upon its size, strength in its supply chain, and many hard decisions regarding cost and customer service objectives. But any size firm can, and must, develop a flexible, long-term plan for utilizing the power of logistics to increase the delivered value offered to customers. Flexibility is a key concept because management must be able to anticipate or react to changes in the environment and modify their strategy accordingly.

Study Questions

1. Briefly discuss the two components of corporate strategic planning, giving examples of each.
2. Outline the strategic planning process. How does logistics fit into corporate planning effort?
3. Discuss the concept of the firm's "supply chain." Why is integrating the supply chain so important?
4. Utilizing figure 12-3, discuss what actions a small retailer participating in a channel dominated by a large manufacturer might take to optimize its relative position within that channel.

5. How might two large channel members work together to integrate their logistics channel? What are the implications for the smaller channel members participating with them?
6. Discuss some environmental changes impacting logistics in your country or region over the next ten years.
7. When should a firm utilize third-party providers for some or all of its logistics activities? Discuss the pros and cons of outsourcing.
8. Discuss the pros and cons of having a centralized logistics operation serving multiple markets in Europe, and in Asia.
9. What issues will impact the provision of transport services in the future?
10. How does the changing nature of consumerism impact a company's logistics strategy?

Notes

1. Rao, Kant, Stenger, Alan J., and Wu, Haw-Jan. "Training future logistics managers: logistics strategies within the corporate planning framework," *Journal of Business Logistics*, vol. 15, no. 2, 1994, pp. 249–72.
2. Adapted from Rao et al., pp. 250–6.
3. Ibid, pp. 256–9.
4. Monczka, Robert M. and Morgan, Jim. "What will happen and what you should know," *Purchasing*, January 18, 1998, p. 78.
5. Ibid, p. 79.
6. Sparaco, Pierre. "Airbus' partners shorten supply chain," *Aviation Week and Space Technology*, January 4, 1999, p. 35.
7. Damas, Philip. "Habitat integrates logistics flows," *American Shipper*, July 1997, pp. 34–7.
8. "Logistics strategies for a 'new Europe'," *Traffic Management*, August 1997, vol. 33, no. 8, August 1994, p. 49A(3).
9. Ibid.
10. Lieb, Robert C. and Randall, Hugh L. "A comparison of the use of third-party logistics services by large American manufacturers, 1991, 1994, and 1995," *Journal of Business Logistics*, vol. 17, no. 1, 1996, p. 305.
11. Ibid, p. 311.
12. Ibid, pp. 311–12.
13. Dapiran, Peter, Lieb, Robert, Millen, Robert and Sohal, Amrik. "Third party logistics services usage by large Australian firms," *International Journal of Physical Distribution and Logistics Management*, October 1996, vol. 26, no. 10, p. 36(10).
14. Bowman, Robert J. "The 12,000 mile pipeline," *Distribution*, vol. 96, no. 7, June 1996, pp. 46–8.
15. "Logistics strategies for a 'New Europe'," ibid.
16. Ibid.
17. Martin, Kathleen. "Worldly desires," *International Business*, January/February 1998, pp. 10–11.
18. Ibid, p. 11.

chapter 13

Developing High-Quality Logistics Systems

Introduction	229
Basic Quality Concepts: The Internal Perspective	230
Basic Quality Concepts: The External View	232
The Service Quality Model	233
Total Quality Management (TQM) in Logistics	237
Developing a Formal Quality Process	238
Quality Process Success Factors for Logistics Management	240
ISO 9000: The International Quality Standard	241
The Cost of Quality	243
Chapter Summary	243
Study Questions	244

Introduction

Logistics managers must provide their internal and external customers with quality service. However, determining exactly what quality service is can be very difficult for several reasons. First, quality means different things to different customers. Second, service providers may have their own ideas regarding the nature of quality service that may be totally different from the view held by their customers. When these two parties do not agree on what constitutes quality service, conflict and customer dissatisfaction inevitably result. Finally, supporting diverse global markets with their different cultures and customs means that the characteristics of quality logistics services will also differ between countries or regions. This chapter will first examine various philosophical approaches to quality management in general. The application of these same quality precepts to logistics functions specifically will then be addressed, as will some of the organizational issues that can arise as managers move to formulate high-quality logistics strategies. The international quality standard known as ISO 9000 will be briefly presented, as will a short discussion of the costs related to improving logistics quality.

Basic Quality Concepts: The Internal Perspective[1]

Recent emphasis on work improvement has focused more on internal (to the organization) processes rather than functional effectiveness, through total quality management (TQM) and reengineering programs. TQM's origins can be traced to a committee of the Union of Japanese Scientists and Engineers, formed in 1949 to improve productivity and enhance the postwar quality of life in Japan.[2] The committee developed a statistical quality control course and worked to disseminate the evolving Deming philosophy among Japanese manufacturers.[3] Deming broadened and expanded his early emphasis on statistical methods, to 14 points necessary to achieve superior quality management. The Deming framework focused on organizational processes rather than individuals or functions and stressed the importance of leadership, teamwork, and the need to reduce process variation.[4]

Several other theorists have offered alternatives to the Deming framework. Juran, for example, presented a trilogy of activities (quality planning, control, and improvement) that emphasized a customer orientation, performance evaluation, and coordinated skilled efforts. Crosby's 14 quality steps emphasized zero-defects through management commitment, teamwork, training, and adequate measurement.[5] In 1990, Hammer articulated six principles of reengineering which emphasized business processes, information technology, and employee empowerment.[6] The stated objectives of reengineering are to achieve improvements in critical measures of performance, such as cost, quality, service, and speed, by fundamental rethinking and radical redesign of business processes.[7] The fundamental rethinking part of reengineering has contributed to the extensive downsizing and outsourcing activities of the 1990s. In fact, Kodak was considering laying off as many as 20,000 employees in an effort to cut $1 billion from its $4.5 billion annual expenses.[8] One of the greatest challenges any firm faces in a reengineering effort of that magnitude is to maintain and even improve customer satisfaction with fewer resources. So, while reengineering was originally positioned as relatively unique and separate from TQM, it may be more appropriately considered a continuation of an organization's TQM efforts.

Both the TQM and reengineering movements suggest that organizational work should be defined and supported by senior leadership and accomplished from cooperative processes to yield desirable employee and customer outcomes. Although Deming, Juran, Crosby, and Hammer differ in semantics and somewhat on the relative importance of quality elements, there is a great deal of similarity across their respective philosophies. Each work improvement advocate, either explicitly or implicitly, is concerned with the quality management concepts of leadership, cooperation, learning, process management, employee outcomes, and organizational performances.

Leadership

The leadership concept is defined by two quality management factors: vision and commitment. The central role of senior executives in defining, communicating, and motivating quality management efforts has been widely recognized. It is the responsibility of senior leaders to articulate a realistic, credible, attractive future, currently labeled as vision. The influence of an organizational vision on logistics processes and outcomes is indicated, in part, by the extent to which logistics is viewed as a key capability and as a contributor to growth and returns expectations. The commitment of senior management to the philosophy of work improvement is necessary to achieve progress in cost and delivery performances.[9] This commitment is a form of transformational leadership, requiring communication and reinforcement efforts to implement the work improvement philosophy.

Cooperation

Cooperation, the degree of internal and external collaboration, is a dominant concept in the quality literature. Internal cooperation is defined in terms of two related factors: teamwork and employee involvement. The teamwork factor measures the usage of work teams empowered to improve work performance. Canadian Airlines utilized employee teams as a part of management's Service Quality process begun in 1990. These teams were instrumental in making both corporate and frontline improvements that, among other things, reduced the amount of mishandled or delayed baggage by 75 percent and increased the speed of telephone response time by 79 percent. The end result was that Canadian Airlines was ranked first in independent customer service surveys of airlines based in Canada in 1995.[10]

Indicators of the employee involvement factor include the degree of participation in planning and decision making. Supplier management is the factor used to define external collaboration. The contributing role of the supplier in quality management initiatives has also been widely recognized in the purchasing literature.[11] Juran, for example, has recommended that long-term partnerships with suppliers be established.[12]

Learning

Organizational learning is most directly reflected by the training efforts of the firm. Employee training in work improvement concepts and tools is necessary for understanding of quality-related issues and for stimulating a greater level of participation.[13] Efforts to improve specific work skills, management commitment, and resource availability are indicators of the learning factor.

Process management

The set of practices that combine methodological approaches with human resource management has been labeled the process management concept.[14] The key defining factors that provide identification, information, and analysis of processes are benchmarking, data availability, and statistics usage. Benchmarking involves identifying best practices and making comparisons with key competitors.[15] The firm then attempts to raise the function being benchmarked to the same level as that maintained by the selected company. Adequate, accurate, and timely information on warehousing, inventory, and order processing are taken as indicators of the data availability factor. Decision support systems have significantly enhanced data availability by providing access to, and information from, all corporate activities. The application of quantitative and graphical methods is an indicator of the statistics usage factor. These will be discussed more fully in a later section.

Employee outcomes

The employee outcomes concept is defined by three factors that measure the results of the work effort to those employed by the firm: fulfillment, stress, and economics. Fulfillment is indicated by the degree of morale and company loyalty on the part of managers and non-supervisory employees. Stress is indicated by the degree of work-induced strain, and measures of monetary rewards reflect the economics factor. In general, the three outcomes are taken as measurements of the degree to which an organization satisfies employee needs.

Organization performances

The factors of the organizational performances concept measure the end value of work improvement efforts. Such efforts should produce improvements in the key logistics performance factors of cost, speed, dependability, and customer needs. Ordering, inventory, and transit performances are indicators of the cost, speed, and dependability factors. Abilities to handle unique customer requirements and to expedite orders are indicators of meeting customer needs. Performances in relation to key competitors should also be affected by work improvement efforts. Indicators of competitive performance include cost, transaction processes, order-cycle time, delivery, availability, flexibility, and assessment ability.

In summary, it is worth pointing out that all of these factors illustrate management approaches to providing quality logistics services. As such, they may be characterized as representing the *internal* (to the producer or service provider) perspective to quality.

Basic Quality Concepts: The External View

Customers, on the other hand, typically define quality as value or fitness for use. That is, they have expectations for the product or service that must be met. However, these expectations may embrace several different aspects of quality, some of which are totally unrelated to the production process. While product/service performance may be paramount, the customer may also look at other things such as the cleanliness of the vehicle delivering the goods, after-sales service, the number of errors in the bill, time spent on the telephone waiting for assistance, salesperson knowledge or even employee courtesy. Thus, a customer may be very satisfied with the performance of the product or service, for example, but may be put off by the rude behavior or unkempt appearance of the person delivering it.

The challenge from the organization's point of view is to reconcile both the internal and external views of quality so that the customer is truly satisfied. Unfortunately, sometimes management believe that they are providing a quality service when, from the customer's perspective, they are not. VIA Rail of Canada, for example, thought they were giving very good customer service. The truth was that they did give good service some of the time. A passenger could get on a train in Montreal and get absolutely wonderful service to Toronto, but, on the return trip, get terrible service. VIA was creating expectations for customers that it didn't always live up to, which created even more problems. In order to preclude customer dissatisfaction, Terry Ivany, President and CEO, empowered employees to ask the question, "Does this add value for my customer?" and make any necessary improvements. To facilitate the move to a more customer focus, employees receive continuous training in such topics as achieving excellence in customer service.[16]

This conflict between internal and external view of quality is especially troublesome in logistics because, as with any service, the benefit provided to the customer is largely intangible. That is, buyers cannot see or touch what they are buying. Because quality began in, and is still largely associated with, manufacturing, much of the improvement comes from monitoring the production process by measuring parts and assemblies. Defects are identified immediately and corrected so that the finished product leaves the factory free from defects. The challenge is to bring these same TQM ideas to bear on the logistics system so that the service provided to customers is as free from defects as the products being delivered.

The Service Quality Model

Because logistics processes provide services to customers (both internal and external), the service quality model is useful in examining the factors that can cause them to be unhappy. The service quality model is presented in figure 13-1 and illustrates how customer dissatisfaction can develop in a service encounter. Ignoring the arrows, the model represents the basic marketing process. That is, the chart is divided into two parts: customers are on the top, management on the bottom. Managers must first learn what customers expect in terms of service. Once management understand their customers' needs they can put together a service mix that will satisfy them. The customer benefits offered by the firm must be communicated to the buyers so that they understand why the firm provides more value than a competitor. That value must then be delivered to the customers in a way that meets their expectations. If the service the buyers receive meets their expectations, then they will be satisfied.

The arrows, or service quality gaps, depicted in the model represent potential sources of customer dissatisfaction. Each of these gaps will be explained below.

- **Gap 5** is the most critical opening, because it reflects a situation in which the service received by customers is different than what they expected. Buyers are dissatisfied because their actual experience was less than what they anticipated.

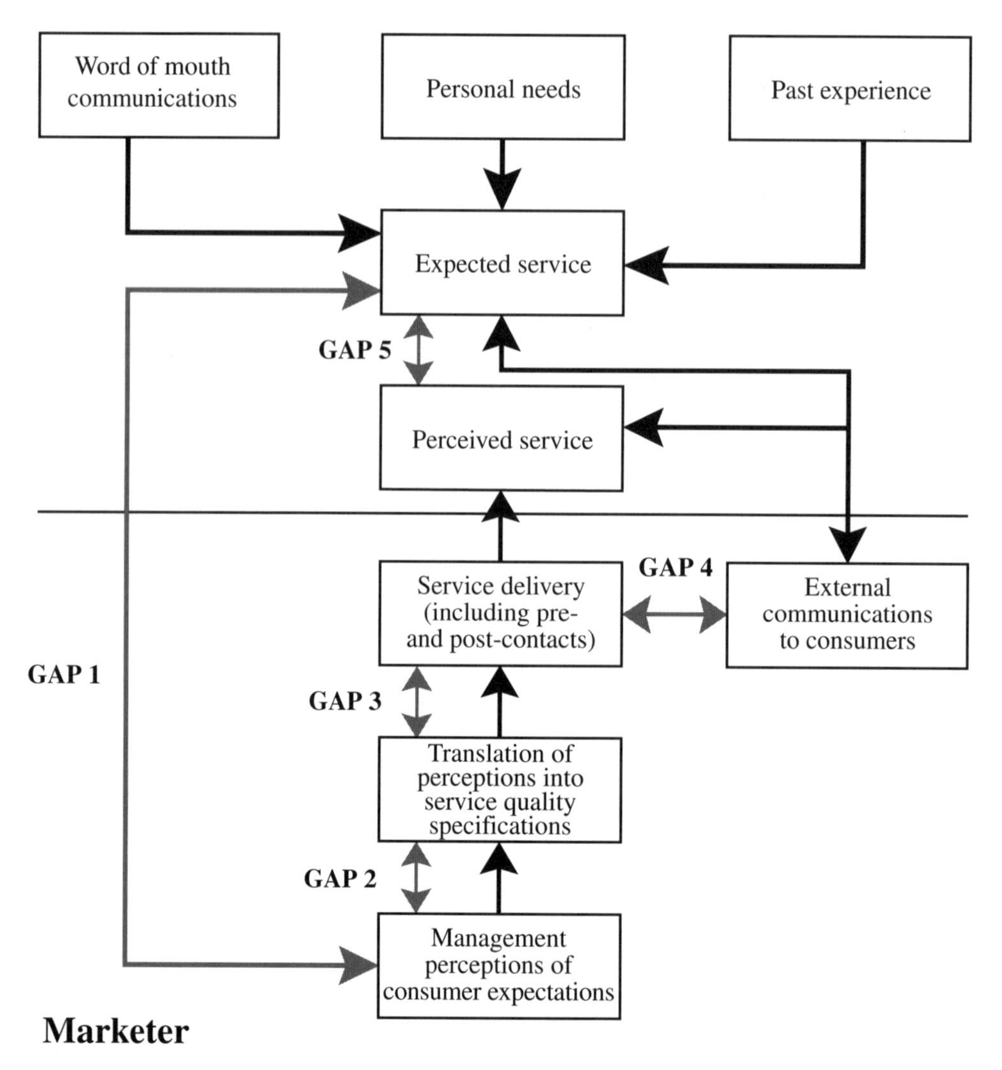

Figure 13-1 Service quality model

Source: Zeithaml, V. A., Berry, L. L., and Parasuraman, A. "Communications and control processes in the delivery of service quality," *Journal of Marketing*, Vol. 52, April 1998, p. 36

However, the customers may have actually experienced better service than what they were prepared for. As discussed in chapter 3, this situation presents its own challenges. First, the customers' expectations will be raised for the next encounter, so the opportunity for dissatisfaction is greater unless the experience can be replicated. Second, costs are higher because the buyers would have been content with less service. Third, the additional service beyond what the customers were expecting might even be offensive.

Gap 5 also results when any of the other four gaps open.

- **Gap 1** illustrates the situation when management do not really understand their customers' needs. For example, managers might assume that customers desire overnight product delivery when, in fact, they do not. Either insufficient market research has been performed or the results have been misinterpreted. Whatever the reason, management cannot hope to design and deliver quality service if they do not completely understand what their customers want.
- **Gap 2** opens when management does know what their customers desire (i.e. Gap 1 does not exist) but are unwilling or unable to satisfy their needs. Perhaps customer expectations are too high or the firm simply lacks the resources to adequately meet them. Alternatively, customers may not be sufficiently aware of their "true" logistics needs so that their stated desires are inconsistent with their actual requirements. Again, the service mix developed and offered to customers does not meet their expectations, and dissatisfaction results.
- **Gap 3** is an especially troubling one because it signifies the situation where managers know what customers want and have developed a high-value service to meet those needs, but that service is poorly delivered. For example, the customer may receive his or her goods on the promised delivery day, but the truck driver is rude and has lost a required piece of documentation. Thus, the customer is dissatisfied with the whole encounter (Gap 5). Often the difficulty is that the only company employee the customer comes into contact with is the truck driver, order clerk, or customer service representative. If this person is upset for some reason or simply disinterested, he or she can undermine all of management's best efforts to provide quality service.
- **Gap 4** is created when the organization promises something to the customer that is subsequently not provided. For example, the salesperson promises next-day delivery; the goods actually arrive in three days. The three-day delivery may not be a problem; the broken promise, on the other hand, is, because the customer was expecting his or her order to arrive and it did not. Again, Gap 5 results.

Gap 5 may also open by itself. As shown in figure 13-2, the services marketing model is somewhat different than the product marketing mix. Note that satisfactory performance results from the interaction of factors that the managers can control (the physical layout of a facility, employees) and those that they cannot (other customers, the buyer himself). Thus, a customer dining in a crowded, noisy restaurant may be unhappy with the experience even if the service and food are excellent. Similarly, a person who is unhappy, irritated, or simply having a bad day may be disposed to find fault with very minor provider mistakes.

External forces (i.e. laws, governmental regulations, etc.) can also have an impact

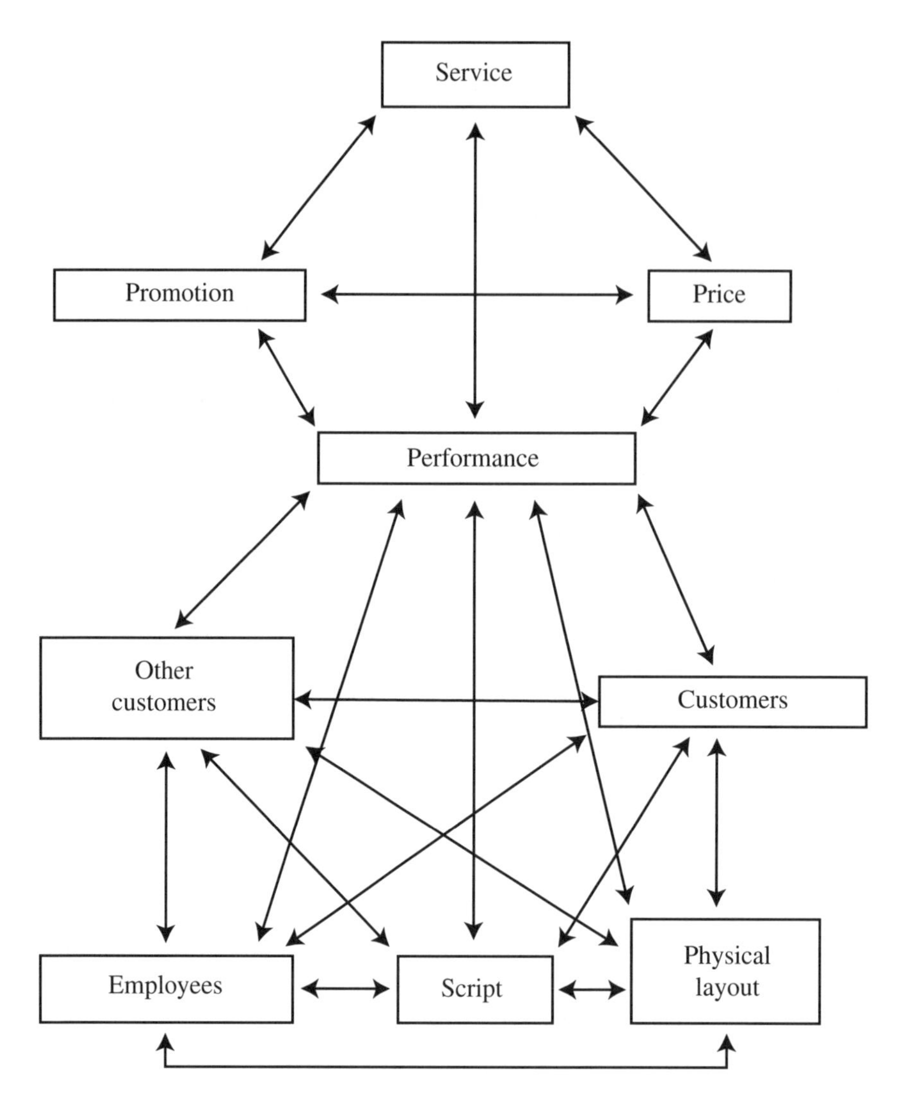

Figure 13-2 Services marketing model

on the level of service provided by a firm. For example, many countries limit the hours retail establishments may be open. In addition, several European nations restrict or even prohibit the movement of trucks on weekends or public holidays. Naturally, limitations such as these can have a profound impact on customer service even though the company has no control over them. The challenge for managers is to minimize the size and occurrence of service quality gaps by understanding the needs of customers, providing a service mix that meets those needs better than the competition, and constantly monitoring customer satisfaction so that corrective action can be taken immediately if required.

Table 13.1 Implementation stages in a quality process

Stage	*Characteristics*
Quality control (QC)	Defect-free services management driven
Quality assurance (QA)	100% satisfied customer Customer driven
Total quality management (TQM)	Significant competitive advantage Management, employees, customers, vendors, channel members work toward a common goal
Customer value	Emphasis on providing best comparative net value for the customer

(*Source*: Coyle, John J., Bardi, Edward J.and Langley, C. John Jr. *The Management of Business Logistics* (St. Paul, MN: West Publishing Company, 1996), p. 537)

Total Quality Management (TQM) in Logistics

More firms are moving to identify and implement quality improvement processes in logistics as a way to reduce cost, enhance service, and increase customer satisfaction.[17] As organizations embrace quality initiatives in a formal manner, four sequential phases occur in the evolution of that overall effort, and are depicted in table 13–1. Quality control (QC) exemplifies the internal view of quality, relying as it does on defect-free services (or products) as defined by management. Quality assurance (QA) shifts towards the external view by emphasizing customer satisfaction. Total quality management (TQM) embraces quality as a source of competitive advantage and enlists all channel participants to work towards a common goal rather than relying on the firm itself. Finally, customer value reflects the need to do things that create the best comparative net value for the customer.[18]

While individual companies will search for different ways to characterize their particular commitments to quality, there are a number of elements that seem to be common to many formally stated quality processes. They include:[19]

- emphasis on customer requirements and expectations;
- concern for the logistics process, in addition to the measurable results of the process;
- continuous improvement;
- elimination of waste and rework;
- measurement and concern for variability;
- total organizational commitment; and
- dedication to a formal quality process.

Developing a Formal Quality Process

While some firms have maintained an excellent reputation for product and service quality in the eyes of the customer, adherence to a formal quality process will be accompanied by a greater likelihood of long-term, sustainable improvement. Figure 13-3 shows the six major steps in the development of a logistics quality process, each of which will be discussed in more detail below.[20]

STEP 1: MAKE AN ORGANIZATIONAL COMMITMENT Top management must be the driving force behind the commitment to quality. This responsibility falls not to corporate general management, but also to the chief logistics administrator as well.

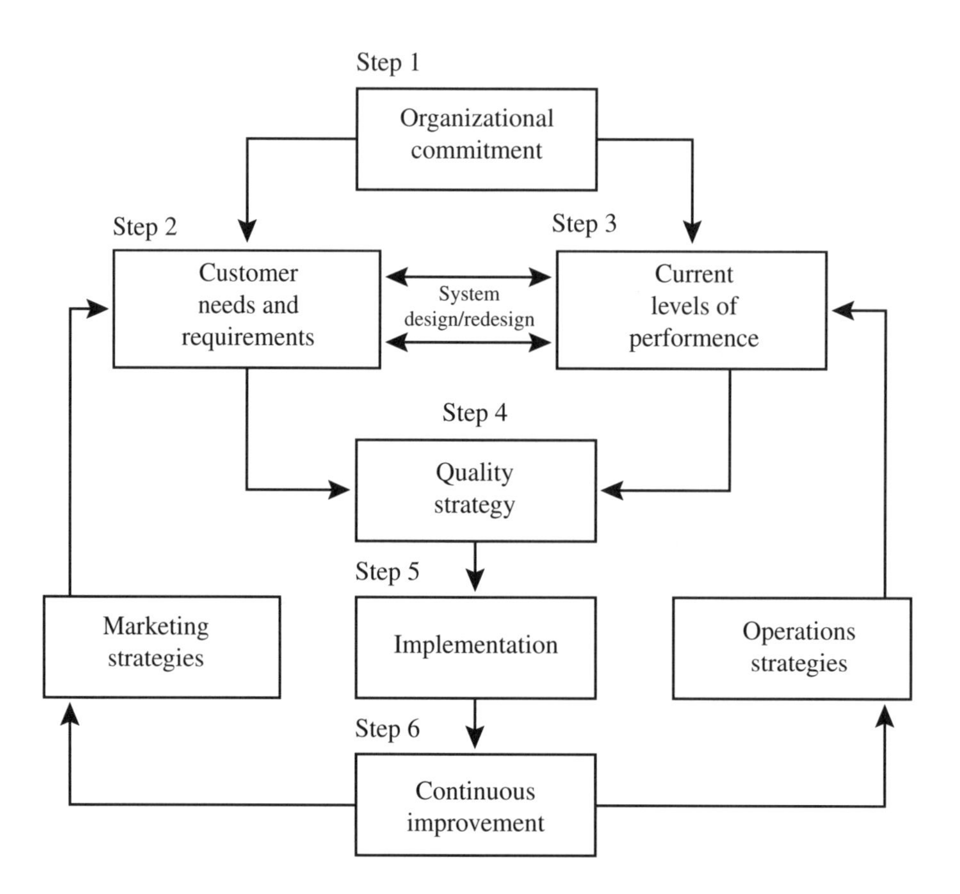

Figure 13-3 Logistics quality process
Source: Langley, C. John Jr. "Quality in logistics: a competitive advantage," *Proceedings – R. Hadly Waters Logistics and Transportation Symposium* (University Park, PA: Pennsylvania State University, The Center for Logistics Research, 1990)

People at these senior levels must be fully dedicated to the objectives they must meet and the actions they must take. Also, these executives must provide the resources and encouragement their people need to produce tangible results from the commitment to quality.

Quality processes commonly fail due to a lack of commitment by top management. An unwillingness to sacrifice short-term financial results or productivity, for example, may imply that management will resist needed improvement efforts. Instead, a logistics process that is able to leverage managerial commitment can usually achieve improvements through quality, and, by adhering to a formal quality process, actually lower the cost of doing business. At the outset of a formal quality process, the logistics organization should have meaningful, well-developed statements of mission, goals, and objectives. This step helps logistics to assume leadership with regard to the quality area.

STEP 2: UNDERSTAND CUSTOMER NEEDS AND REQUIREMENTS The emphasis in this step is on specifically and scientifically understanding the needs and requirements of the customers of the logistics process. Identifying customer needs and requirements is not always easy. More often than not, this step requires a rigorous examination of customers and their needs. Firms desiring a successful quality process should think of their suppliers, vendors, and channel partners as "customers," understanding their needs as well those of the final customer. Firms throughout a truly integrated supply chain must share significant coordination and singularity of purpose. A shortsighted firm's failure to view these other entities as customers will prove detrimental to the total quality effort.

STEP 3: MEASURE CURRENT LEVELS OF PERFORMANCE For this information to be valid and useful, a firm must acquire it specifically and scientifically. The use of statistical process control techniques, which for years have been utilized to monitor manufacturing quality, can prove invaluable in logistics as well. The lack of something tangible to measure can prove daunting, however. Management's task is to identify suitable performance measures in key areas such as customer service, transportation, inventory management, warehousing, information processing, and packaging that can be measured and monitored to ensure quality service is being provided throughout the logistics system. The astute reader will note that Steps 2 and 3 closely relate to the Service Quality Model presented earlier. Before moving on, management must make sure that none of the gaps depicted in that model are open.

STEP 4: DEVELOP A QUALITY STRATEGY The term "quality strategy" refers to the specific initiatives selected for inclusion in the logistics quality process. Perhaps the first significant step is to study the teachings and philosophies of several of the quality experts discussed earlier. While the organization should consider many approaches, the ultimate priorities should focus on understanding the customer's needs, appropriate initiatives for education and training, measuring performance levels and monitoring variability, and overall organizational commitment.

STEP 5: IMPLEMENT THE QUALITY PROCESS Effective implementation is essential for success and must be accomplished smoothly. Many of the more important people to include in the quality process are inventory control specialists, warehouse employees, vehicle drivers, product packaging personnel, and order-entry clerks. These workers, any of whom can easily affect the service levels experienced by the firm's internal and external customers, are in a position to make a truly positive contribution to the overall quality process. A meaningful implementation plan should also include a timetable and a comprehensive list of necessary resources. These will help to assure the success of a well-conceived and well-executed quality process.

STEP 6: CONTINUALLY IMPROVE THE PROCESS The final major step is that of process improvement and the recognition that results should include both continuous as well as breakthrough improvement. While the former should represent a daily pursuit for those involved in the logistics quality process, the accomplishment of the latter can vault the organization ahead of the competition by radically changing the way the logistics system operates. Although identified as the last step in the process, meaningful quality programs really have no end as such. Management must constantly monitor customer satisfaction to ensure that quality service is being provided and to identify quickly those instances where it is not so that changes can be made to bring the logistics system back into compliance with quality criteria.

While each of these steps is important, the objective of continuous improvement will be advanced most through the changing of marketing and operating strategies as the firm's quality process takes hold.

Quality Process Success Factors for Logistics Management

Within the context of the model presented in figure 13-3, certain things must occur if the quality process is to become institutionalized. First, as was mentioned in Step 1, senior logistics managers must believe in the program, commit to it, and fully expect to change the way they manage. In short, providing quality logistics service must become a way of doing business. Second, every employee in the logistics organization must accept responsibility for performing quality work. Third, management must gain that commitment by "selling" the benefits from one layer of the logistics organization to the one below. A quality program cannot be mandated; to do so creates the impression that quality is the current "hot topic" or slogan of the day. Rather, employees must embrace the idea that the quality logistics processes will lead to increased sales and, by implication, greater benefits to the workers themselves.

Fourth, errors must be caught and corrected immediately, stopping the process if necessary. Fifth, because delaying an aircraft departure or halting a warehouse package conveyor to correct a discrepancy can be extremely disruptive in the short term, employees must feel free to make those decisions without fear of losing their jobs. Again, this goes back to the need for top management to foster an environment in which workers will report major problems, correct minor deficiencies immediately, and recommend improvements that will lead to higher quality service. Sixth, each logistics activity must be thought of as a process that has measurable inputs and outputs to facilitate the use of statistical process control techniques such as check sheets, Pareto charts, histograms, and control charts. Utilizing these tools to monitor a work process gives management the information needed to immediately identify, measure, and determine the cause of each process error. Furthermore, these techniques also aid in the identification of employees who need training and the type of training that is required in order to prevent those mistakes from recurring. Finally, everyone must understand that a successful quality program takes time to establish. Executives at Australia-New Zealand Direct Line (ANZDL), for example, acknowledge that their initial quality efforts in 1990 were made in response to customer complaints and without management's being totally convinced of its value. Their half-hearted approach led to some mediocre performance ratings by key shippers that, in 1993, forced the implementation of a more serious and rigorous program that has been very successful. The firm initially shunned the more arcane statistical concepts, focusing instead on simple measurements and basic ideas of customer satisfaction. In 1993, it moved toward a more rigorous system of statistical process controls that contributed to the attainment of ISO 9002 accreditation in Australia, New Zealand, and at its Long Beach, California office.[21] Another transport company, TNT Express Worldwide (now a subsidiary of the Dutch-based TNT Post Group),[22] developed a strong quality program as well. Their experience is discussed in logistics profile 13-1.

ISO 9000: The International Quality Standard[23]

Many logistics operations are faced with little choice about adopting quality standards. As more global competitors achieve registration under ISO 9000, those that have yet to do so are feeling the pressure to start the process. The international quality standard series, ISO 9000, was made available in 1987. Based on the UK quality standard series BS5750, this standard was developed as a result of the demand for a set of requirements that would reach beyond a single industry and could be used as a quality model by all companies. Briefly, the ISO 9000 Series of Standards are based on sound business practice. They are models or frameworks and are nonprescriptive. This point mystified many firms who expect to be told exactly what to do. The Standards, developed by the International Standards Organization (ISO), recognize that every company is unique and, as such, will have their own unique way of complying. To date, ISO 9000 has been adopted by approximately 100 countries and almost three-quarters of a million firms are registered to the standard. The benefits that an ISO 9000 compliant logistics system can bring include:

- improved discipline – individuals within the organization become more conscious of their activities and contribution;
- continuous improvement in logistics processes;
- process analysis and reengineering as appropriate;
- identification and elimination of redundant procedures and routines;
- structured training for new employees and cross-training for existing workers;
- improving the customer value added by all logistics activities.

Logistics Profile 13-1
TNT EXPRESS WORLDWIDE

Air cargo shippers pay more for transportation – and expect more in return. That's one reason why quality has taken off among the premium-service integrators. TNT Express Worldwide, the joint venture of (then) Australia's TNT Group and five national postal services, launched its quality program in mid-1991. Within two years, TNT's operations in the United Kingdom had achieved certification under ISO 9002, a set of quality standards promulgated by the Geneva, Switzerland-based International Standards Organization.

TNT Express looked to outside consultants for initial guidance and studied the quality efforts of many non-transportation entities. Following an in-depth diagnosis of performance levels, the company put together a series of workshops to establish targets for improvement. TNT focused in on how it could retain both customers and employees. The targets were 98 percent on-time delivery and 5 percent employee turnover. Management admits the company has a way to go yet: Its on-time record is in the low- to mid-90th percentile, and turnover hovers between 15 and 20 percent a year. TNT recently implemented a new program to boost employee morale and cut the cost of worker replacement. In addition, TNT is aiming for same-day response – in most cases, three hours – to all customer queries. According to management, the company is approaching that goal now. Whenever possible, service representatives now have the power to resolve problems immediately.

When quality efforts fail, studies show that top management is usually to blame. Often, it hasn't instilled quality throughout the organization on a day-to-day basis. A second mistake, tied closely to the first, is the failure to impress upon workers the need for radical change. Thus, employees don't accept the program as completely as they should. Transportation companies are becoming more aware of the need for quality, but they still have a long way to go. "There's no final chapter," says a senior executive. "You have to continue to rewrite the book." For TNT, the next step is to conduct surveys with a significant portion of its customer base.

(**Source**: "Eye on the prize," *World Trade*, January/February 1995, pp. 76–8)

The danger is that management may view ISO 9000 certification merely as a way to placate customers. The entire process can be time consuming and costly as well. A recent study of Belgian firms that had implemented ISO 9000 showed that, on average, implementation time ran to 608 days and cost $75,000 to complete.[24] In other words, while keeping existing customers happy is important, the real benefit should be internal in the form of operational improvements, energized employees, and better training programs. The Belgian firms bore out this contention, noting that the single most important reason they adopted the standards was to improve internal efficiency and control. Interestingly, the second most important reason noted was requests/demands from customers for the certification.[25] These changes to the way logistics is performed will, in turn, lead to better customer service, market advantage, and, by implication, higher profits.

The Cost of Quality

When the work system, comprised of people and equipment, is being used consistently in the best way possible, then the system is said to be stable. In other words, improving the quality level would require a substantial investment in new equipment and retraining. On the other hand, reducing the number of mistakes in an existing operation may be possible with virtually no out-of-pocket expenses by increased employee awareness, minimal retraining, minor procedural changes, etc. This, in turn, would result in lower costs and higher-quality service. There are three types of costs associated with any quality program: failure, prevention, and appraisal.

- Cost of failure, which really addresses the losses that result from not having a quality program. These expenses are reflected in after-sales product repairs, exchanges, returns, and subsequent lost sales that result from customer dissatisfaction.
- Cost of prevention measures the impact of, for example, delaying a ship to correct an improperly loaded container or taking the time to check a customer's order before it leaves the warehouse. These expenses occur when the process must be halted in order to correct some discrepancy.
- Cost of appraisal addresses the expenses incurred to inspect, measure, and monitor the logistics process. Random sampling of a day's worth of orders to check completeness, monitoring transit-time for containers moving over certain traffic lanes, and evaluating the daily performance of customer service personnel are all examples of monitoring activities.

Thus, when management is contemplating the adoption of a formal quality process, these are the costs must be considered in order to arrive at a true measure of what that change will involve. Essentially, the cost of failure represents the status quo, while the costs of prevention and appraisal measure the impact of change. Thus, increasing the latter two should decrease the former.

Chapter Summary

Quality has become the management quest of the 1990s. While based upon statistical process control techniques originally involving the measurement of product assemblies, similar philosophies and tools can be brought to bear on the provision of logistics and other services. Management must first determine what types and levels of service their customers desire and then develop a logistics mix to consistently deliver that service to buyers. Institutionalizing quality logistics service in the form of a TQM program must involve every single person in the organization. Each employee must truly believe that providing quality customer satisfaction is his or her responsibility, otherwise the program will ultimately fail. While instituting quality improvements can be costly in some situations, minimal retraining, increased employee concern, and more attention to detail can often realize significant benefits.

Study Questions

1. Briefly discuss the role of leadership in fostering the establishment of quality programs.
2. Discuss the importance of employee involvement in the quality improvement process.
3. Distinguish between the internal view of quality and the external. What happens when the two do not agree?
4. Utilizing the service quality model, give an example of poor service that you experienced and identify the service quality gap that was the primary cause of your dissatisfaction. What other gaps contributed to the situation?
5. Briefly explain how Gap 5 might open without the existence of any other Gap.
6. What are some external (i.e. outside the organization) factors that can influence the quality of logistics services customers receive?
7. Briefly outline the steps required to develop a logistics quality process.
8. Why is it important that employees willingly commit (i.e. "buy in" to the program) to supporting quality initiatives? What can happen if management attempt to mandate that acceptance?
9. Briefly describe ISO 9000. What is it? Why have firms adopted it?
10. What are some of the costs that management must evaluate in deciding how much to invest in a TQM program?

Notes

1. Adapted from Anderson, Ronald D., Crum, Michael R., and Jerman, Roger E. "Relationships of work improvement program experience and logistics quality management factors," *Transportation Journal*, Fall 1996, vol. 36 no. 1, p. 20(15).
2. Powell, Thomas C. "Total quality management as competitive advantage: a review and empirical study," *Strategic Management Journal*, vol. 16, 1995, pp. 26–7.
3. Walton, M. *The Deming Management Method* (New York: Pedigree, 1986).
4. Deming, W. E. *Quality, Productivity and Competitive Position* (Cambridge: MIT, Center for Advanced Engineering Study, 1982); Deming, W. E. *Out of the Crisis* (Cambridge: MIT, Center for Advanced Engineering Study, 1986).
5. Juran, J. M. *Juran on Quality by Design* (New York: The Free Press, 1992); Crosby, P. B. *Quality is Free* (New York: Mentor Publishing, 1979); George, S. *The Baldridge Quality System* (New York: Wiley, 1992).
6. Hammer, M. "Re-engineering work–don't automate, obliterate, *Harvard Business Review*, July–August, 1990.
7. Hammer, M. and Champy, J. *Re-engineering the Corporation – A Manifesto for Business Revolution* (New York: Harper Business, 1993).

8. Smith, Geoffrey. "Can George Fisher fix Kodak?" *Business Week*, October 20, 1997, p. 118.
9. Garvin, D. A. "Japanese quality management," *Columbia Journal of World Business*, vol. 19, no. 3, 1984, pp. 3–12.
10. Bemowski, Karen. "Quality is helping Canadian Airlines International get off the ground," *Quality Progress*, October 1995, p. 33.
11. Newman, R. G. "Insuring quality: purchasing's role," *Journal of Purchasing and Materials Management*, vol. 24, no. 3, 1988, pp. 14–21; Giunipero, L. C. and Brewer, D. J. "Performance based evaluation systems under total quality management," *International Journal of Purchasing and Materials Management*, vol. 29, no. 1, 1993, pp. 35–41.
12. Juran, J. M. "Product quality: a prescription for the West (Part I)," *Management Review*, vol. 70, no. 6, 1981, pp. 8–14. Juran, J. M. "Product quality: a prescription for the West (Part II)," *Management Review*, vol. 70, no. 7, 1981, pp. 57–61.
13. Galagan, P. A. "How to get your TQM training on track," *Nation's Business*, 1992, pp. 24–8. Garvin, D. A. "Building a learning organization," *Harvard Business Review*, 1993, pp. 78–91.
14. Anderson, J. C., Rungtusanatham, M., and Schroeder, R. G. "A theory of quality management underlying the Deming management method," *Academy of Management Review*, vol. 19, no. 3, 1994, pp. 472–509.
15. Kamp, R. C. *Benchmarking* (Milwaukee, WI: ASQC Quality Press, 1989).
16. Bemowski, Karen. "VIA Rail puts the brakes on runaway operations," *Quality Progress*, October 1996, p. 38.
17. Langley, C. John, Jr. and Holcomb, Mary C. "Creating logistics customer value," *Journal of Business Logistics*, vol. 13, no. 1, 1992, p. 18.
18. Coyle, John J., Bardi, Edward J., and Langley, C. John Jr. The *Management of Business Logistics*, 6th edn (St. Paul, MN: West Publishing Company, 1996), p. 537.
19. Langley and Holcomb, ibid, pp. 18–19.
20. Coyle et al., Ibid, pp. 540–4.
21. "Eye on the prize," *World Trade*, January/February 1995, p. 78.
22. TNT Postal Group homepage, www.tntpost-group.com
23. Adapted from Jackson, Lindsay. "Is a quality standard the vehicle for satisfying customers?" *Transportation and Distribution*, June 1996, vol. 37, no. 61, p. 62(2).
24. "Implementing the ISO 9000 Standards in Belgium," *Quality Progress*, June 1996, p. 46.
25. Ibid.

chapter 14

Improving Logistics Performance

Introduction 246
Improving Organizational Performance 246
Basic Tools for Improving Logistics Performance 249
Effecting Meaningful Change 258
Impediments to Improved Logistics Performance 260
Creating a World-Class Logistics System 264
Chapter Summary 265
Study Questions 265

Introduction

Managers today must constantly strive to improve the operating performance of their organizations. Logistics managers are under particular pressure to deliver more customer value in the face of growing competitive threats, escalating global demand, and rising costs. Despite the attention given to process improvement in the manufacturing sector, logistics has been slow to benefit from the techniques developed for and applied to production. This chapter will first examine process improvement issues in general before discussing various ways that logistics activities specifically can be enhanced. Finally, various impediments to the successful implementation of performance improvement methodologies will be presented.

Improving Organizational Performance[1]

In the 1950s, W. Edwards Deming popularized an improvement process framework built around four basic steps. He advised companies to *plan* improvements, execute the plan (*do*), *check* whether the desired improvement was realized, and *act* by adjusting the plan if improvements fail to accrue or by institutionalizing the actions if improvements do materialize. This approach is known as the Deming wheel, the

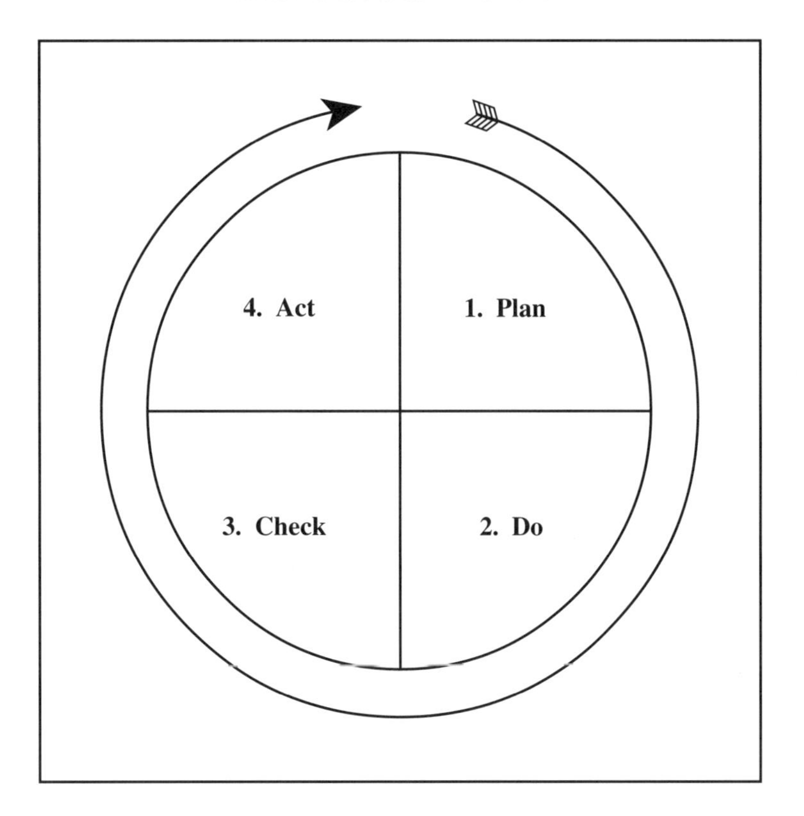

Figure 14-1 PDCA cycle of improvement
Source: Byrne, Patrick M. and Markham, William J. *Improving Quality and Productivity in Logistics* (Oak Brook, IL: Council of Logistics Management, 1991), p. 110

Deming cycle, or simply the PDCA cycle. Figure 14-1 illustrates the PDCA cycle as a continuous process of questioning current performance and developing plans to derive additional improvement.

Briefly, in the *plan* step, two activities occur: evaluation of present practices and action planning. Evaluation represents management efforts to assess how well functions are being accomplished under current conditions. At the same time, managers want to uncover potential problems or opportunities that may indicate the need for improvements. At this point, the organization might assemble an improvement team to investigate the situation. The team's job is to understand the problem using process analysis techniques, then use statistical analysis to identify the underlying issues causing the problem. (Both methodologies will be discussed later.) The team's next task is to identify alternatives for improvement, after which action can be planned. For instance, specific improvements can be selected, measures established, and goals for improvement set.

Affecting improvement actions represents the *do* step. Implementation often involves making changes to processes, techniques, work flows, equipment, and methods. These changes frequently necessitate significant training for the people that will carry out the changed activity.

The *check* step comes next. During this phase, the improvement team uses measures, on-site inspection, and employee input to answer three key questions:

- Was change implemented as planned?
- Were desired results achieved?
- What corrective actions are required?

While the *check* and *evaluation* steps may seem similar, the former deals with monitoring change activity that has been initiated while the latter is a more global assessment of the process in general.

The answers to these questions drive the fourth step in the process – *act*. If the implementation of desired change does not go as planned or fails to achieve the desired results, this step reorients the process by recycling through PDCA. If implementation succeeds, the improvement team acts to standardize and institutionalize the improvements elsewhere. Many companies successfully use the PDCA cycle to drive quality and productivity improvement in logistics.

Continuous and breakthrough improvements[2]

The PDCA cycle is key to a continuous improvement effort. Continuous improvements often come about from altering the existing process and generally occur within functions. However, continuous improvement is not the only way to move ahead. Under certain conditions, breakthroughs occur as a result of trigger points. A trigger point is an event that shakes a company to its foundation and forces management to fundamentally rethink its way of doing business. A trigger point may take the form of a new competitor, a merger, a major quality failure, or political change. For example, as discussed in chapter 6, the deregulation of transportation industries forces both shippers and carriers to totally rethink the way they conduct business. The old rules simply do not apply any longer. Both parties must see themselves as partners rather than adversaries, and focus on developing mutually beneficial relationships. Similarly, a trigger point may come in the form of a major customer demand such as requiring that all vendors adopt EDI ordering procedures as a condition of sale.

Breakthroughs, in contrast to continuous improvements, involve major process changes that often are cross-functional or cross-organizational in nature. The continuous improvement process demands no special action on the part of senior management except to nurture it and maintain momentum. Breakthroughs, on the other hand, are the product of challenging tradition and undertaking risk. With few exceptions, their success hinges on senior management involvement and cross-functional cooperation. A successful improvement process incorporates a means to ensure continuous improvement and the ability to capitalize on trigger points to achieve breakthroughs.

Basic Tools for Improving Logistics Performance[3]

There are a number of useful tools available for logistics managers intent on improving the operational effectiveness of their units. These techniques can be used to help explain how a particular logistics process works, identify possible causes of problems, and suggest ways to improve.

Process analysis tools

Process analysis tools allow people to understand how a process works so they can look for ways to improve it. **Cause-and-effect diagrams** illustrate the relationship of potential causes (reasons that a situation occurs) to an existing effect (the situation being analyzed). Sometimes referred to as a fishbone diagram because of its shape, a general cause-and-effect model is illustrated in figure 14-2. Note that the causes of the effect being examined are clustered together along a specific branch of the diagram denoting a specific category of causes. For example, the effect in question might be holding inventory; the causes (reasons for maintaining inventory) might result from corporate policy, customer requirements, process variability, or other concerns.

Flow charts provide a pictorial display of the steps in a process. Figure 14-3 depicts a simple order-fulfillment process from order entry to delivery. Flow-charting helps define the processing steps and logic flow for carrying out an activity. Its

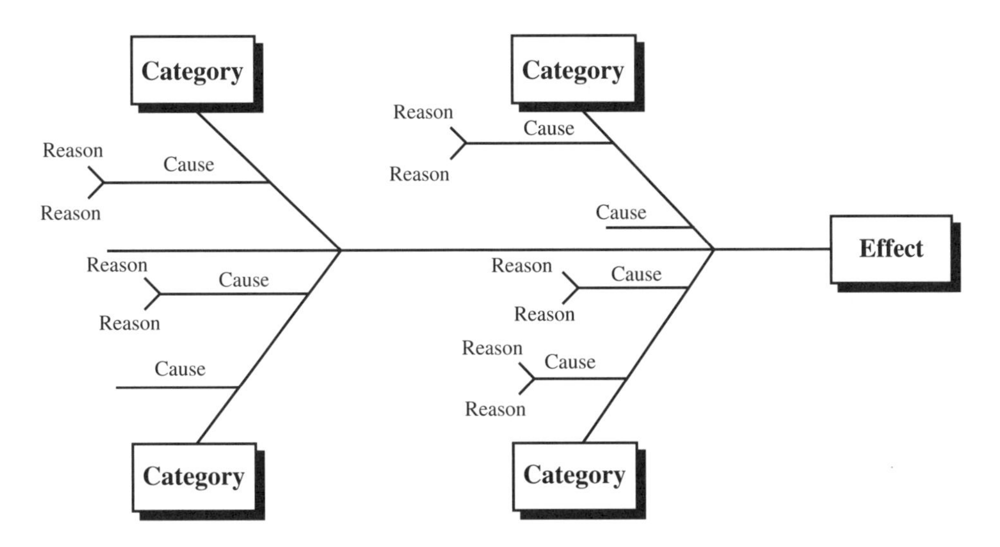

Figure 14-2 General structure of a cause-and-effect diagram
Source: Byrne, Patrick M. and Markham, William J. *Improving Quality and Productivity in Logistics* (Oak Brook, IL: Council of Logistics Management, 1991), p. 117

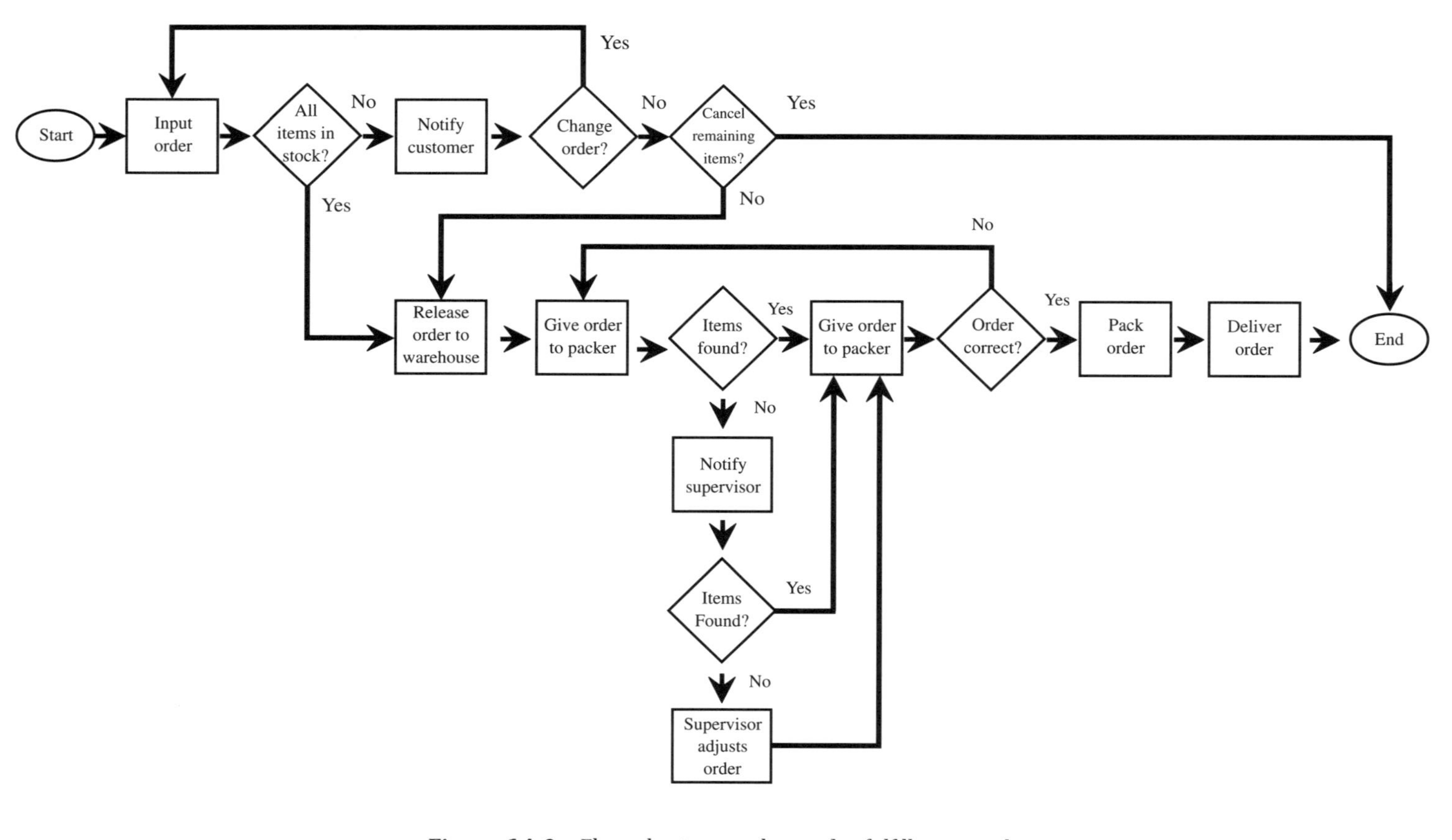

Figure 14-3 Flow chart example – order fulfillment cycle
Source: Byrne, Patrick M. and Markham, William J. *Improving Quality and Productivity in Logistics* (Oak Brook, IL: Council of Logistics Management, 1991), p. 121

pictorial nature encourages a common understanding of how the process works. Flow-charting also helps identify weaknesses in a process such as bottlenecks, redundancies, gaps, and ambiguities. And finally, flow-charting assists in developing, describing, and documenting improvements to the process.

Brainstorming is a technique for quickly generating ideas in a group setting. It helps identify problems, pinpoint reasons for the problems, develop potential improvements, and plan the actions necessary to implement the improvements. Some brainstorming techniques are highly structured (each group member takes a turn contributing an idea in sequence) while other approaches are unstructured whereby participants call out ideas as they occur.

Statistical analysis tools

Statistical analysis tools supplement process analysis methods by actually measuring what is happening in the process. Statistical analysis is used with two basic kinds of data: attributes data and variables data. Attributes data refer to simple information that counts things, e.g. measurements such as yes/no, good/bad, pass/fail, etc. Variables data represent broader measures of things, e.g. frequency, quantity, time, and money. Attributes data are generally easier to obtain than variables data. However, for attributes to be useful, management must clearly define what is acceptable and what is not. Examples of statistical analysis tools include check sheets (which are used to keep track of things), run charts (designed to track the output of a process), histograms (which follow the frequency distribution of data across a range), and control charts (which measure the variation of a process).

Benchmarking

Benchmarking is a process for identifying "best" practices by comparing key performance indicators (KPI) for a specific activity across organizations and using those performance levels as inputs to corporate goal setting. (Best practice is defined as meeting customer required service levels, delivered at minimal cost to the logistics provider.[4]) The unit selected as the benchmark may be within the same corporate structure or outside; it may be a customer, competitor, non-competitor, or supplier; it might be in a totally unrelated industry and/or in a different market. The only criterion is that the organization chosen be generally acknowledged for accomplishing the tasks in question better than anyone else.[5] In a logistics setting, for example, the areas to be benchmarked might be warehouse operations, order processing, mode and carrier selection, packaging, and forecasting. The benchmarking process should include the following steps: define the present performance level for the activity to be benchmarked; determine the level of performance that is desired in the given activity; determine how and what type of improvement is implemented to achieve stated targets, and establish a process time frame.[6]

The process should start with an in-depth service market audit that involves both an internal survey of operations and an external survey of customers. By analyzing and evaluating the results of those surveys, management can compare, for example, their transportation management activity to the one identified as the "best." Operating strategies, tactics, and systems improvements can then be developed to close the gap between the firm's present performance levels and those of the benchmarked organization. The external survey could also provide special customer benchmark targets that need to be met based upon the requirement of the specific buyers or buyer segments.[7]

A measurement and data collection system to be used to analyze and evaluate service performance against those performance targets needs to be designed and implemented. The continuing comparison of performance against targets point out whether or not the logistics activity in question is complying with the targets. The lack of compliance with the benchmark standards should lead to changes or improvements in strategy and operational practices. This process should continue with a performance audit of the activity being carried out on a regular cyclical basis at least every one to two years.[8] However, managers must remember that benchmarking against competitors only tells you where the competitor is today – not where it will be tomorrow. To gain competitive advantage, therefore, the company must aim ahead of the competition at the target set by its customers.[9] Another thing management must understand is that fundamental differences in industries, customers, or markets may temper the ability of the aspiring firm to completely reach a desired level of success simply by copying the benchmark's ways. Rather, the knowledge obtained from the benchmarking process must be modified to fit with the company's individual situation.

One way to maximize the benefits of benchmarking is to link it with networking and face-to-face discussions with managers in similar organizations. A benchmarking network can embrace several non-competitor organizations that have common business processes that come together for mutual gain. For example, one such group is a retail supplier network in Australia whose members include Carlton & United Breweries (CUB), The Smith's Snackfood Company, Nestle Confectionery, Streets Ice Cream (Unilever), Shell Lubricants, Sunicrust Bakeries (Bunge), Queensland Independent Wholesalers, Hilton Hosiery (Sara Lee), Arnott's Biscuits (Campbells), and the Boots Healthcare Company. This network is focused on benchmarking the supply chain.[10] In contrast there is another benchmarking group focused on transport management whose members include BP, the Cootes Transport Group, Bunge, Elgas, CSR Readymix, Murphy's Transport, Kalari, Associated Dairies, Australia Post, Pioneer, L.S. Booth, and FBT Operations. Because the focus is on a network of companies, the range of commonalties, which link the organizations together, can be broader than if there were a specific focus in the benchmarking project. The networks are all non-competitive and the objective is mutual gain, whereby organizations' representatives can be involved in frank discussion about current business processes and their outcomes.[11] Benefits to network participants include quantifying best practice logistics; understanding and believing in the strategic direction of logistics; improvement of individual logistics processes; management and cultural change; and reduction in costs.[12] Logistics profile 14-1 illustrates how this networking arrangement works.

Logistics Profile 14-1
The Benchmarking Process

Management at a transport company believed that current performance of 9 cents per kilometer traveled for tire costs was very good. Managers believed this because the supplier confirmed their perception. In order to determine whether they (and the supplier) were correct, they decided to benchmark the tire management process with a noncompetitive benchmarking network. The steps in benchmarking this activity occurred over a 6 to 12 month period. Initially tire costs and tire management was highlighted as a critical factor in the successful management of a transport fleet. The eight senior managers who were members of the network defined the performance measure of tire costs as the total tire costs divided by kilometers traveled. To ensure the performance comparison across the eight companies was valid and relevant, face-to-face discussions over a 6 to 12 month period occurred. This ensured that all benchmarking partners were measuring the same process and that similar costs were included in the analysis.

The first round of this iterative performance comparison process identified a significant spread between tire costs of 4.6 cents per kilometer traveled and 11 cents. The members saw this as a surprising outcome given that the fleets of trucks being compared were similar. The initial reaction was disbelief and questions were asked about how members were measuring the costs. After all, how could a professional well-managed transport company have tire costs of 11 cents while another organization has costs of 4.6 cents? The benchmarking process is very personal when it involves face-to-face network meetings. After a six-month period where data were normalized, a similar performance gap existed. Discussion about the tire management process highlighted significant improvement opportunities by better managing the tire process. The organization with 4.6 cents per kilometer traveled detailed the tire management process to other benchmarking partners who absorbed this relatively sophisticated process, and then embraced process improvement within their own organization.

After introducing policy and process changes, the partners saw a significant improvement in tire costs. When spread over a fleet of 100 vehicles, all traveling 150,000 kilometers per annum, the cost savings associated with a two-cent cost reduction amounts to hundreds or thousands of dollars. In the transport-benchmarking group, the site with the highest tire costs was declared best practice, highlighting that best practice is not necessarily tied to the lowest cost. The higher costs were explained by different operating characteristics. Benchmarking must focus on improvement opportunity and not solely on performance measures as an end in themselves.

(**Source**: Hanman, Stephen. "Benchmarking your firm's performance with best practice," *The International Journal of Logistics Management*, vol. 8, no. 2, 1997, p. 2)

Activity-based costing

Activity-based costing (ABC) is a relatively new methodology that assigns costs other than normal conversion costs (labor, factory overhead) directly to products or services by allocation methods other than direct labor or machine hours. The problem with conventional allocation techniques is that they often fail to accurately reflect resource consumption. With activity-based costing, resources are assigned to activities, then activities are assigned to cost objects based on their use.[13] ABC can assist logistics managers by revealing the links between performing particular activities and the demands those activities make on an organization's resources.[14] ABC differs from traditional cost accounting by tracing costs to products according to the activities performed on them.[15] Traditional approaches allocate direct and indirect costs on a proportionate basis using volume-based cost drivers such as direct labor hours, machine hours, or material dollars. Volume-based cost drivers will distort costs whenever products consume resources in disproportionate amounts.[16] As an example, think of a factory manufacturing blue pens and only blue pens. Next door is a factory where 50 percent of production is blue pens and the other half is divided up into short runs of every imaginable ink color. The short runs of course use up more overhead, from processing all the separate orders to time lost in changing ink colors in the production equipment to higher inventory and shipping costs. If overhead is allocated to each plant based on direct labor, and the number of workers is the same in each plant, the total overhead cost is likely to be split evenly between the blue pens division and the multi-color division. Thus, the "cost" of the blue pens goes up, and the "cost" of the specialty colors goes down. In other words, the blue pens made in the second plant appear to be more expensive to make than the identical pens in the first factory. Obviously, that is simply not true.[17]

The assumption of activities causing cost enables ABC to adopt a two-stage assignment procedure for assigning costs to a cost object. The first stage focuses on determining the costs of activities within an organization. The second stage traces activity costs to the products consuming the work performed. As illustrated in figure 14-4, the first step of the assignment process splits apart resources, activities, and products within an organization. Resource drivers trace the consumption of resources by activities that make up the work performed in the company. The second step combines the costs of performing specific activities into cost centers at the activity level. Activity drivers trace the activity costs to the products, or cost objects, consuming the work performed in the organization.[18]

BENEFITS OF ACTIVITY-BASED COSTING *ABC can improve the management and control of overhead by determining the factors that actually result in the requirement for overhead resources.* The ABC approach divides overhead into separate categories supporting the work being performed. These categories might embrace such things as general administration, supervision, supplies, direct labor, or utilities. Resource drivers can then trace costs from these categories to the activities consuming those resources.[19] The costs may reflect actual consumption or may result from an estimate of the effort expended on each activity. The sum of the resource costs becomes the cost of

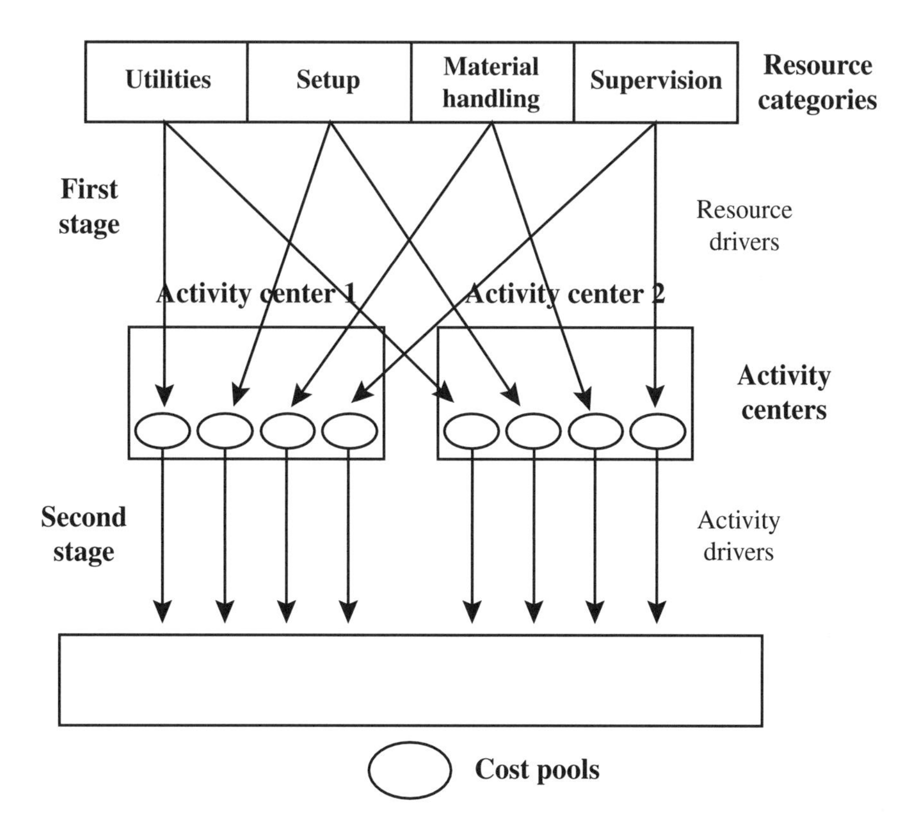

Figure 14-4 Two-stage activity-based cost allocation process
Source: "Understanding the activity costs in an activity-based cost system," *Journal of Cost Management*, Vol. 4, No. 1, as presented in Pohlen, Terrance L. and LaLonde, Bernard J., "Implementing activity-based costing (ABC) in logistics," *Journal of Business Logistics*, vol. 15, no. 2 1994, p. 7

performing an activity. ABC then uses an activity driver to assign the activity costs to specific cost objects such as a product or service. Managers can then look for ways to reduce, eliminate, or reallocate resource consumption to add more value to the customer.[20]

ABC implementation can also provide greater visibility of how different products, customers, or supply channels impact profitability. The organization can more accurately trace costs and determine areas generating the greatest profit or loss. Managers can target high cost products or customers for reduction efforts, and they can use other techniques such as repricing, minimum buy quantities, or charging by service to improve profitability.[21]

ABC achieves greater accuracy than traditional costing techniques by using multiple cost drivers.[22] Traditional techniques typically rely on a few volume-based cost drivers to trace overhead costs to products. ABC uses multiple cost drivers to reflect different relationships occurring between activities and the resources they consume. These cost drivers fall into two broad categories. The first includes cost drivers related to production volume – costs vary in direct proportion to production volume. The second includes cost drivers unrelated to production volume – no direct relationship exists between production volume and the resources consumed.[23]

Performance measures appear as a logical consequence of an ABC system. Activities' descriptions include financial information (which describes the costs or resources necessary for performing the activity) and nonfinancial information (which describe the activity in terms such as the time required, quality, number of transactions, or schedule attainment). Management can use the nonfinancial data to develop performance measures for the activity. The performance measures describe the work done and the results achieved in an activity.[24] The performance measures can then be used to track product returns, damage, claims, or data entry errors. The linkage between the performance measure and the activity provides a relatively direct means for computing the cost of poor or improved performance. Managers can translate how the elimination or reduction of an activity such as handling product returns would impact resource consumption and reduce the firm's costs.[25]

Finally, *ABC supports continuous process improvement* by identifying where incremental improvements at the activity level can improve overall enterprise performance. Functional managers can use the ABC model to reengineer business processes by eliminating redundant or unnecessary tasks and optimizing resource allocations to activities adding the most value to the product or customer.[26]

ABC appears well suited for costing and measuring the performance of logistics processes. Many logistics costs remain buried in overhead, and logistics managers often do not have adequate visibility or control over their costs. Consider, for example, the costing of warehouse operations. Assume that a firm's traditional costing system allocates warehouse costs based upon either the total dollars or weight shipped to each customer and channel. Typically, however, customers, channels and products do not consume warehouse resources (such as labor and machine time) proportionately to their dollar or weight volume, so a traditional cost accounting system will distort the true costs. Suppose a warehouse has a mix of low-valued to high-valued products with a wide range in the dollar value per pound, and it receives, stores, and ships products in everything from individual units (e.g. pharmaceuticals) to pallet quantities (e.g. bulk consumer products). In addition, there are small pick lines (for units), automated conveyor lines (for cases), and forklifts (for bulk pallets) to move product from storage to the shipping dock. Finally, there is a separate pick area to serve the special requirements of the three largest customers, and all modes of transport are used, from truckload to group parcel to next-day air. An ABC view of costs at this facility would differ substantially from that of a traditional volume-based perspective.[27] ABC then more clearly depicts the critical linkage existing between corporate profitability and logistics costs and performance. Logistics confronts many of the same conditions that make

Table 14.1 An example of channel profitability as measured by traditional accounting versus ABC methods

	Mass merchandisers $(MM)	*Wholesalers $(MM)*	*Small retailers $(MM)*	*Total (MM)*
Traditional accounting				
Gross revenue	400	200	100	700
Cost of goods	300	160	70	530
Gross margin	100	40	30	170
Trade promotions	16	2	2	20
Total operating expenses	48	24	12	84
Net Profit	36	14	16	66
Net Profit (%)	9	7	16	9.4
ABC cost-to-serve				
Gross revenue	400	200	100	700
Cost of goods	300	160	70	530
Gross margin	100	40	30	170
Trade promotions	16	2	2	20
ABC assignments				
• Logistics mgmt	8	4	5	17
• Order mgmt	10	5	6	21
• Customer mgmt	10	6	5	21
• Sales force activities	12	5	8	25
Total operating expenses	40	20	24	84
Net profit	44	18	4	66
Net profit (%)	11.0%	9.0%	4.0%	9.4%

(*Source*: Liberatore, Matthew J. and Miller, Tan. "A framework for integrating activity-based costing and the balanced scorecard into the logistics strategy development and monitoring process," *Journal of Business Logistics*, vol. 19, no. 2, 1998, p. 133)

manufacturing enterprises good ABC candidates: diversity of resource consumption, and product and resource consumption not correlated with traditional volume-based allocation measures. Logistics can benefit from the costing and measuring of performance at the activity level. Activity analyses may identify opportunities where process reengineering could reduce operating costs or improve service performance.

Logistics also provides an opportunity to extend ABC across the supply chain. ABC in a supply chain setting could identify opportunities for eliminating redundant activities existing within the supply chain, channel members with excessive resource consumption patterns, or attractive alternatives to the present channel structure. Table 14-1 shows the difference in the net profit generated by three different distribution channels as calculated by traditional, volume-based accounting and then by an ABC approach. While a "volume-driver"-based traditional accounting system may use only sales dollars and/or weight shipped to assign costs, an ABC system employs many more drivers. For example, a warehouse may use a case pick operation to serve small retailers and a bulk pick operation to serve wholesalers and mass merchandisers. An ABC system would accurately calibrate the different costs of serving customers using the two different operations. It would also evaluate the costs of all other major components (such as order management and transportation) involved in serving customers. Thus, in this example, the small retailers actually provide the smallest margin, while the mass merchandise and wholesale channels yield a higher return, a fact traditional accounting methods do not bring out.[28] The seemingly high margin produced by the small retailer channel might falsely lead management to attempt to grow this channel, with the expectation of improving overall net profit. If an ABC system were in place, then the firm would realize that such a strategy would have exactly the opposite effect.[29] In other words, the entire supply chain could use ABC in much the same way to reengineer interorganizational processes to obtain a competitive advantage through cost reduction or service differentiation.[30]

Effecting Meaningful Change

Improved performance can result from addressing three different aspects of logistics output: service quality, productivity, and process effectiveness. Each will be discussed, in turn, below.

Logistics service quality[31]

Service quality can be improved by identifying and eliminating special causes of process variations, by refining the process to reducing remaining variability that results from common causes, and by reengineering the process to achieve breakthrough results. Management must remember that service quality is defined from the customer's point of view; that is, the improvement should occur in an area of importance to the buyer. The passenger airlines, for example, generally measure on-time departure as an indicator of service quality: if the airplane departs the gate within 15 minutes of the scheduled time it is deemed to be "on time." Unfortunately, passengers care less about the departure time than they do the arrival time. It is not unusual for the flight to depart the gate only to be delayed, either at the terminal or on the taxiway, for so long that the scheduled arrival time is compromised. However, from the airline's point of view, they provided quality service.

There are three types of measures necessary to track and improve service quality. **Results** measures provide a look at present performance and answer the question "How are we doing?". **Diagnostic** measures offer a more in-depth look at the reasons and sources of performance below (or above) the goal, while **impact** measures track the direct and indirect costs of performance. An example illustrating each measure is presented in figure 14–5.

Together, these measures allow management to track both results and the processes leading to those results. In other words, measuring service quality can be thought of as assessing the effectiveness with which the logistics process meets customer requirements.

Order accuracy and completeness measures – example

- **Results:** percent of orders delivered "as ordered"
  - Exact product (before substitutions and upgrades)
  - Correct quantity within the agreed-to tolerance
- **Diagnostic:** count and percent of orders incomplete upon delivery with associated reasons; e.g.:
  - Error in order entry
  - Product not produced
  - Product produced short
  - Shipped short/over/incorrect item
  - Could not locate product in storage
  - Not enough space in carrier equipment
  - Received short at customer
  - Mislabeled/miscounted
  - Unauthorized substitution
  - Damage
  - Loss
  - Incorrect product shipped
- **Impact:** "cost" of inaccurate or incomplete orders; e.g.:
  - Value of order refused or cancelled
  - Amount of customer credit allowance
  - Cost of returns handling
  - Excess distribution costs (for premium freight/handling to complete the order)
  - Excess inventory

Figure 14-5 Different types of quality measures
Source: Byrne, Patrick M. and Markham, William J. *Improving Quality and Productivity in Logistics* (Oak Brook, IL, USA: Council of Logistics Management, 1991), p. 152

Productivity[32]

Productivity, on the other hand, measures the efficiency with which the logistics process meets those requirements. Productivity is the ratio of real output divided by real input. There are three ways to improve productivity. First, the process can be reengineered. The implication is that productivity levels are largely designed in when the process is chosen. There may be a certain amount of fine-tuning possible within that design (for example, reallocating space in a manually run warehouse), but typically reengineering involves major expenditures to reconfigure facilities and reallocate or retrain workers. (Consider the implications of moving to a fully automated warehouse from the above mentioned manual one, for instance.) Alternatively, management may try to make better use of existing resources. For example, if a warehouse is capable of storing 200,000 cases but has a peak need to store only 100,000 cases, the unused capacity places a cost penalty on every case passing through the facility. The key to improving utilization is planning so that the actual capacity (of storage space, in this case) matches the true resource need. Once the firm commits to the capacity and its attendant costs, it may be too late to improve utilization. Finally, managers can work to improve performance against goals. For example, if a long-distance truck driver requires 9.5 hours to complete a nine-hour trip, the driver's performance is 94.7 percent (9 hours divided by 9.5 hours). Management can then analyze the reasons for the longer trip and take corrective action as necessary (additional driver training, re-routing, etc.) to improve the operator's productivity.

Process effectiveness[33]

While process analysis tools were discussed in an earlier section, process effectiveness can also be viewed as a measure of internal customer service. Any time physical product or information transfers from one person or department to another, the recipient is an internal customer. This internal supplier–customer relationship is critical because it can have a direct impact on how well the firm services its final customers. The more places an internal service failure can occur, the greater the likelihood the "external" or final customer will see that failure in the form of poor service or product quality. Thus, utilizing process analysis tools can both enhance the effectiveness with which the logistics process meets customer requirements (the service quality aspect of logistics) and improve the efficiency of that process (the productivity aspect of logistics). The end result is that the customer receives more value and the firm is able to utilize logistics as a source of competitive advantage.

Impediments to Improved Logistics Performance

Unfortunately, changing established practices, even for the better, can be very difficult to do. Some of the reasons that business improvement efforts fail are presented below.

Failure to adopt the customer's viewpoint

One of the biggest and most costly mistakes management can make is to focus on improving what *they* believe the customer wants rather than asking buyers what they deem most important. For example, there is little value in measuring the percent of orders that are filled in 24 hours to a retailer, if the retailer is really concerned with

Logistics Profile 14-2
American President Companies

American President Companies (APC) is a broad-based transportation and distribution company, providing services in three markets: the trans-Pacific, the world's largest and fastest growing market for container trade; the intra-Pacific market, which services the rapidly expanding economies of north, south, and west Asia; and the U.S. domestic market. The number one goal and focus at APC is providing customer satisfaction by striving toward a goal of 100% service reliability. Service reliability is defined as keeping promises and has two key criteria: it must meet customer expectations and needs, and it must be free from defects. To APC, service reliability can include many components that, when combined correctly, result in customer satisfaction. These components include such things as on time pick-up and delivery, consistency and frequency of service, rate quotations, billing, tracing, timely and accurate documentation, and claims processing. However, internal research revealed that APC customers rate on time delivery performance as the single most important criterion in evaluating their transportation company's performance. APC then developed performance measures that focused on monitoring those activities based upon how they affected on-time delivery.

The firm relies on their information system to provide relevant information to the logistics manager across four broad categories. First, standard data collection and reporting systems to provide information on what has already happened in terms of costs and time. These are reactive systems and for APC, they facilitate the development of vessel and train scheduling, cost reports, forecasting, and determining equipment requirements. Customer value added support systems, which are proactive systems, are also used. These provide the logistics manager with the ability to perform contingency analysis to determine how the organization should react to future scenarios to maximize the benefit to the customer. Third are employee value added systems that provide employees tools that allow them to better perform their jobs. Finally, the fourth group of systems is used in managing performance and providing operational decision support. These systems allow the logistics manager to anticipate problems and take a proactive approach toward problem resolution. Reports of what has already happened help with analysis, but the ability to react to something at the time it is happening requires much more effort. It is critical that these systems provide the user with the ability to use information to prevent problems and correct them in midstream. In other words, these systems point out problems as they arise and aid the manager in finding the best solution.

Once APC determined their performance measures and designed the systems within which they would operate, they could then analyze deviations from established standards and develop corrective action where required. For example, if a route was booked and the customer was promised twenty-four-day delivery, but the shipment missed the ship to which it was originally committed, an exception report is generated that will explain what happened and why. The exception report will print out and notify the salesman. That salesman will contact the customer, explain the problem, and work out a solution.

For each shipment, a report is generated that details the commitment made to the customer, if it was met, and if not, the reason. Service standards can be in terms of transit time, transit time reliability, or any other service factors that the customer selects. Thus, the customer determines the service standards. To meet these standards, proactive controls have been developed that help people move the cargo through the APC system subject to the standard agreed upon. It is not enough just to have a measure; the tool to accomplish that standard must also be provided. APC shares these measurements with the customer, shows them how APC has done and, if APC has not met expectations, explains why and gives them an action plan as to what APC is doing about it.

(**Source**: Mentzer, John T. and Firman, John. "Logistics control systems in the 21st century," *Journal of Business Logistics*, vol. 15, no. 1, 1994, pp. 215–24)

the percent of time the goods are on the shelf. In this example the manufacturer is focusing on how quickly it can get the order to the retailer while the retailer is more interested in order completeness.[34] The manufacturer may find it is investing time and resources to improve the wrong thing. American President Companies has a successful strategy for improving customer satisfaction that is detailed in logistics profile 14-2.

Lack of requisite cost data

As was mentioned earlier, logistics cost can be grouped under a series of natural accounts rather than by functions. Natural accounts are used to group costs for financial reporting on the firm's income statement and balance sheet. For example, all payments for salaries might be grouped into a salary account. Whether they apply to production, marketing, logistics, or finance, they usually are lumped together and the total shown on the financial statements at the end of the reporting period. Other examples of natural accounts include rent, depreciation, selling expenses, general and administrative expenses, and interest expense.[35]

Obscuring costs in natural accounts makes monitoring specific logistics activities very difficult. The challenge is not so much to create new data, because most of it already exists in one form or another, but to tailor the existing data in the accounting system to meet the needs of the logistics function. Activity-based costing, automated order processing systems, and logistics decision support systems can all be used to remedy this problem of insufficient cost data.[36]

Lack of broad-based management skills

Logistics managers often rise through the ranks of their organizations to assume positions of leadership. That is, they may have originally been hired to work in the warehouse, or perform data-entry functions, without any formal education in logistics, or even business. These employees perform well and are repeatedly promoted, assuming higher levels of responsibility, until they are directing all or part of the logistics function. However, management skills, like any other, must be continually honed and updated to keep up with the latest developments in technology and management thought. In the crush of day-to-day events, the last thing managers may want to do is to learn a new software package or take a course in activity-based costing. As the years go by, those same managers can get farther and farther behind, the result being that they simply cannot utilize the tools at their disposal to keep the logistics activity running at peak effectiveness and efficiency. Given the sophistication, scope, and importance of today's logistics systems, as well as the competitive advantage that the organization can realize from a well-run operation, managers must acquire the skills necessary to enable them to make full use of the latest analytical data and techniques available to them.

Failure to think of logistics as a system

When managers view transportation, warehousing, customer service, etc. as individual functions, they tend to focus on improving only their respective area. For example, the fact that transportation costs will rise as a result of moving to a just-in-time inventory system is of little concern to inventory executives; as long as their costs fall, they are happy. As a result, making changes that benefit the overall system is virtually impossible, because often such alterations mean that one (or more) individual activities are suboptimized even though the total logistics effort is improved. Arguably, this functional focus is as much an organizational problem as it is a philosophical one, but the fact remains that individual activity managers must be able to appreciate how their areas fit and interact with all others to provide value to the customer. Otherwise they will focus on improving their own situation regardless of the ultimate impact on the firm's logistics effort.

Need for cultural change within the organization

For significant improvements to occur within the logistics system, all of the employees must want to make the operation better. To a certain extent, improvement can be mandated through such actions as the imposition of tighter standards, executive fiat, or fear. But significant improvement can only come from a workforce that is enthusiastic and committed to change the old ways of doing business. Several years ago, the management of a passenger airline that had started as a low-price competitor decided to change the entire focus of the company. Executives elected to target business as opposed to leisure fliers and realized that they knew very little about what those customers desired in air travel. A great deal of market research was done and the employees were brought into the process from the beginning. Teams and quality circles were formed and empowered by top executives to identify problems and suggest solutions. But there were a couple of side effects to the whole process that management had not anticipated. First, employee absentee rates dropped by nearly half. Second, turnover of flight attendants and ticket agents was reduced by 25 percent. Essentially, the workers became enthusiastic about the entire project and their part in the improvement process. The company became a better place to work, and people simply enjoyed their jobs more than they had in the past. Clearly, making things better for the airline made things better for the workers as well.

It is worth emphasizing that improving the logistics process does not always mean the implementation of leading-edge philosophies or the latest in computer technology. A survey of logistics executives conducted several years ago found that the most frequent complaints they heard involved basic executional service problems. Nearly two-thirds of the problems cited included product availability, on-time delivery, damaged shipments, lack of information lost shipments – the very "basics" of customer service.[37] Simply put, as increased customer expectations exert upward pressure on service requirements, logistics processes must be improved just to stay abreast of the competition, let alone surpass it.

Creating a World-Class Logistics System

The overall objective, then, should be to strive for world-class excellence. What that term represents is a supply chain or a company whose logistics operation excels in efficiency and serves to differentiate it in the marketplace.[38] A study recently completed by the Council of Logistics Management identified four traits that are necessary to achieve world-class logistics:

- **Positioning** refers to the strategic and structural approaches that guide an organization's logistics operation. Positioning can help a company make its logistics operation a cornerstone of its overall business strategy. For example, an office-supplies company used its logistics capabilities to respond to the emergence of office superstores. By offering overnight delivery of exact quantities direct to customers, the company was able to compete with the superstores on customer service.
- **Integration** is the internal achievement of logistical excellence and the development of supply chain relationships. Integration requires partners in the supply chain to work together across corporate boundaries. The sharing of sales and replenishment data between supplier and manufacturer typifies this competency. A retailer, for example, might share its sales information on a real-time basis with a manufacturer so that the supplier can determine the best time to deliver specific quantities of product to distribution centers or stores.
- **Agility** relates to a firm's ability to respond to its customers' needs and to changing market conditions. An "agile" company can seize unexpected opportunities by

identifying a customer's problems and creating solutions. For instance, a medical-supplies distributor saw a need to improve the way hospitals order and receive supplies. His company created a service that took over storage, inventory control, and delivery of supplies for several area hospitals. Now, the distributor stores products in an off-site warehouse. An electronic link allows the hospital's staff to request delivery of specific items at specified times during the day.

- **Measurement** requires the creation of internal and external monitoring systems to ensure that objectives are met. Not only do world-class companies use internal standards to measure their performance against corporate goals, but they also compare their performance to that of competitors and other excellent companies. They often involve their customers in the process by asking them to rate how well they achieve logistics-related objectives such as on-time delivery and accurate order entry.[39]

The study found that, while none of the companies surveyed had achieved perfection in all four of these areas, logistics excellence is achievable by firms in any industry and in any country.[40]

Chapter Summary

Like managers in other parts of the organization, logisticians must be constantly searching for ways to improve their operations. By adopting some of the tools and practices utilized in manufacturing, logistics professionals can keep close tabs on how the various logistics components are performing while simultaneously positioning themselves to take advantage of improvement opportunities. Process and statistical analysis tools, together with benchmarking and activity-based costing, can give managers the information they need to establish logistics as a source of competitive advantage. Service quality, productivity, and process effectiveness must all be addressed as appropriate if logistics is to consistently add value to the final customer. However, the change process can be difficult, and managers should be aware of, and eliminate, any impediments that might slow or even block their efforts to improve their various logistics activities. The goal must be to elevate the logistics effort to world-class status if the organization is to distinguish itself from the competition in the mind of the customer.

Study Questions

1. Briefly discuss the model known as the Deming wheel and explain its value to the logistics manager.
2. What is the difference between continuous improvement and breakthrough improvement? Give actual examples of each.
3. Briefly discuss process analysis tools and statistical analysis tools. How are they similar? How are they different?

4. What are the possible risks associated with benchmarking?
5. What is activity-based costing? Why is it useful to logistics managers?
6. What are some of the benefits of adopting activity-based costing?
7. How can logistics service quality be improved? What types of measures can be used to effect such improvement?
8. How might a manager attempt to improve the productivity level of a particular process?
9. What are some of the issues that could impede management's attempts to improve logistics performance?
10. How would a manager go about benchmarking his or her order processing system?

Notes

1. Byrne, Patrick M. and Markham, William J. *Improving Quality and Productivity in the Logistics Process* (Oak Brook, IL: Council of Logistics Management, 1991), pp. 109–11.
2. Ibid, pp. 111–12.
3. Ibid, pp. 115–39.
4. Ibid, p. 6.
5. Hanman, Stephen. "Benchmarking your firm's performance with best practice," *The International Journal of Logistics Management*, vol. 8, no. 2, 1997, pp. 1–2.
6. Ibid., p. 1.
7. Blumberg, Donald F. "Strategic benchmarking of service and logistics support operations," *Journal of Business Logistics*, vol. 15, no. 2, 1994, p. 117.
8. Ibid.
9. Byrne and Markham, ibid, p. 140.
10. Ibid, p. 10.
11. Ibid, p. 11.
12. Ibid, pp. 13–14.
13. Raffish, Norm and Turney, Peter B. B. "Glossary of activity-based management," *Journal of Cost Management*, vol. 5, no. 3, 1991, pp. 53–64.
14. Cooper, Robin and Kaplan, Robert S. "Profit priorities from activity-based costing," *Harvard Business Review*, vol. 69, May–June 1991, p. 130.
15. Cooper, Robin. "The rise of activity-based costing – Part Two: When do I need an activity-based cost system?" *Journal of Cost Management*, Summer 1988, p. 45.
16. Pohlen, Terrance L. and LaLonde, Bernard J. "Implementing activity-based costing (ABC) in logistics," *Journal of Business Logistics*, vol. 15, no. 2, 1994, p. 1.
17. Grund, John M. "X-ray accounting," *Oregon Business*, September 1997, vol. 20, no. 10, p.71(2).
18. Beaujon, George and Singhal, Vinod R. "Understanding the activity costs in an activity-based cost system," *Journal of Cost Management*, Spring 1990, p. 52.
19. Turney, Peter B. B. *Common Cents: The ABC Performance Breakthrough* (Hillsboro, OR: Cost Technology, 1991), p. 107.
20. Pohlen and LaLonde, ibid, p. 8.
21. Ibid.
22. Cooper, Robin. "The rise of activity-based costing – Part Three: How many cost drivers do you need and how do you select them?" *Journal of Cost Management*, Winter 1989, p. 34.

23. Cooper, Robin. "The rise of activity-based costing – Part Four: What do activity-based costing systems look like?" *Journal of Cost Management*, Spring 1989, p. 38.
24. Turney, ibid, p. 89.
25. Pohlen and LaLonde, ibid, p. 10.
26. *Corporate Information Management: Process Improvement Methodology for DOD Functional Managers*, 2nd edn (Fairfax, VA: D. Appleton, 1993), p. 56.
27. Liberatore, Matthew J. and Miller, Tan. "A framework for integrating activity-based costing and the balanced scorecard into the logistics strategy development and monitoring process," *Journal of Business Logistics*, vol. 19, no. 2, 1998, p. 132.
28. Ibid, pp. 132–3.
29. Ibid, p. 134.
30. Pohlen and LaLonde, ibid, p. 11.
31. Byrne and Markam, ibid, pp. 147–51.
32. Ibid, pp. 157–62.
33. Ibid, pp. 163–5.
34. Mentzer, John T. and Firman, John. "Logistics control systems in the 21st century," *Journal of Business Logistics*, vol. 15, no. 1, 1994, p. 222.
35. Lambert, Douglas M. and Stock, James R. *Strategic Logistics Management*, 3rd edn (Homewood, IL: Richard D. Irwin, Inc., 1993), pp. 592–3.
36. Ibid.
37. Artman, Les B. and Sabath, Robert E. "Are YOU ready for change?" *American Shipper*, February 1995, p. 43.
38. Cooke, James Aaron. "Are you world class?" *Logistics Management*, vol. 35, no. 9, September 1996, p. 31(2).
39. Ibid.
40. Ibid.

chapter 15

Organizing for Logistics Effectiveness

Introduction	268
Overview of Logistics Organizations	268
Building an Effective Logistics Organization	270
The Role of Logistics in the Firm	273
Variables Influencing Organizational Structure	275
Reconciling Intra- and Inter-Organizational Issues	278
Moving Towards the "Best" Organizational Structure	281
Chapter Summary	281
Study Questions	282

Introduction

In order to provide competitive advantage, superior logistics systems must be organized in a way that supports the firm's customers, objectives, and corporate strategies. There is no single "best" organizational structure for logistics; rather, the approach that advances the long-term goals of a specific firm is the logistics system that should be used. It is very possible that two different companies in the same industry will have radically different approaches to logistics, both of which are successful. The challenge facing corporate executives today is that logistics deals with both internal and external entities, with considerations from both groups influencing the organization structure selected. This chapter examines a number of issues that ultimately interact to influence the nature of the firm's logistics organization.

Overview of Logistics Organizations

Cohesively organizing a company's logistics activities presents a great number of challenges, particularly for managers faced with supporting many diverse global markets. Management must not only struggle with how to achieve the concept of integrated logistics (that is, the internal coordination of logistics with other corporate functions), but with the issue of orchestrating those activities across divisions and/or markets as well.[1]

There are a number of organizational choices available to managers. A **non-integrated** logistics effort is similar to the historical model mentioned earlier. The order-entry manager, warehouse manager, transportation manager, etc. all operate independently of each other within separate corporate departments. There is no consideration given to the benefits of establishing an integrated logistics system.[2] Decisions made in one area can have serious, even detrimental, implications for other parts of the organization, but there is no institutional mechanism for assessing these impacts before action is taken.

A **functionally integrated** approach features close coordination and integration across operating functions. As managers realize the potential for cost/service trade-offs in logistics, they may move to consolidate all of the various activities under a single manager by creating an executive position similar in scope, and on a par with, existing senior managers overseeing production, finance, and personnel matters. Thus, transportation, inventory management, customer service, order processing, etc. which were scattered throughout the corporation are brought together into one department overseen by a single senior logistic leader. However, each division/market operates independently.

Hong Kong Air Cargo Terminals (HACTL) is a firm that continues to be very successful with this type of logistics organization. The company operates under a private franchise incorporating a profit control scheme to provide cargo handling, storage, build-up, breakdown, data and documentation processing services on a 24-hour basis to the more than 60 airlines serving Chek Lap Kok International Airport in Hong Kong. The company now operates two air cargo terminals as an integrated complex, with a total annual throughput capacity of 1,500,000 tons. Service is what the company sells; they perform no functions outside of their buildings.

The entire organization, operating under the Managing Director and the Deputy Managing Director, is made up of just six departments: Finance, Personnel, Planning, Engineering, Information Services, and Operations. Since the bulk of the logistics services provided are based on the handling of information, that department houses almost all the firm's logistics responsibilities. The remainder comes under the purview of Operations.

In a **divisionally integrated** company, the logistics department just described, for example, coordinates across divisions/markets, but remains unintegrated with other corporate functions. With this approach, the logistics manager has responsibility for all phases of the firm's customer support, but must still operate as a separate entity, competing with marketing, production, and other similar corporate departments for resources.

Finally, some organizations are **fully integrated**. That is, there is close logistics coordination and integration across operating functions and across divisions.[3] These firms basically rely on logistics issues to be their primary corporate emphasis. Siemens, the giant German electronics manufacturer, has, for example, experienced competitively enforced price reductions approaching DM 8 billion between 1993 and 1995. The corporation had to compensate for those falling prices through a major program of accelerating and "leaning out" business processes. New post-sales value-added services had to be introduced beyond the construction and delivery of electrical and electronic equipment that was Siemens' traditional business. A rapidly accelerating pace of innovation had to be accommodated as well, and a new "spirit" of more open, informal communications had to be instilled into the staff of more than 300,000 people.

In 1994, Siemens initiated "TOP" (time-optimized processes) as a corporation-wide program to reengineer processes for reduced complexity and speed. Beyond that, TOP aims to change the company culture in ways that encourage holistic entrepreneurial responsibility for supply chain management, innovation, and self-improvement. Indeed, the formal organizational structure of logistics in the corporation is a hybrid of small corporate logistical staff functions and increasingly "diffused" logistics throughout the depth and breadth of the organization.[4] Their experience is discussed in logistics profile 15-1.

Different corporate needs will dictate different approaches to logistics. Businesses that have fairly homogeneous product lines where logistics costs comprise a relatively high percentage of item value tend to find a functional organization most useful because cost control is paramount. On the other hand, firms with very complex, made-to-order production processes where speed and flexibility to meet customer needs are more important favor one of the more integrated organizational structures because service is more important that strict cost control.[5]

Building an Effective Logistics Organization

There are a number of issues that must be considered as managers attempt to develop a value-adding logistics organization. Executives must understand that there is no single "best" logistics structure. Rather, a firm's logistics organization should be consistent with the company's logistics strategy in order to achieve the desired performance. Strategy and structure are developed in light of the internal and external environmental conditions facing the firm.[6]

There are several organizational properties that managers must consider as they put together their logistics activity: centralization versus decentralization, scope of responsibility/span of control, formalization, and integration. Each of these will be discussed in more detail below.

Centralization

The issue of centralization is multi-dimensional. In chapter 14, the centralized versus decentralized performance of logistics activities was addressed in a physical sense. Here, the concept is examined from an organizational point of view. First, managers must consider the issue of concentration, the extent to which the power to make logistics decisions is concentrated in the organization. Management must weigh the ramifications of logistics concentration at the macro or corporate levels and the group or divisional level. The second dimension is the hierarchical distance between logistics decision makers and senior executives who make more strategic decisions on

Logistics Profile 15-1
Rethinking the Business of Technology at Siemens

In preparation for its 150th anniversary next year, Siemens is revitalizing its global structure with TOP, a corporate program that is improving the way it delivers technological solutions to customers. In conventional thinking, competitive problems with the delivery of high-tech products would inevitably lead to an increased scrutiny of one corporate function, R&D. This would then be followed by much wringing of hands over some misleading questions. If national pride is involved, comparisons would be made on which country puts the biggest share of its GNP into basic research; who has the most researchers and technical people; and which firms are outspending competitors on R&D.

In contrast, Siemens AG is taking a holistic approach. It places responsibility on the entire organization – especially on its structure and culture. "Innovation means more than the R&D effort to invent something; innovation means to bring something – a good product – to market and sell it and make a profit with it," explains Walter Kunerth, executive vice president and member of the managing board, Munich, Germany. "Only in that way can Siemens meet the customer's needs for high-tech products – or any product." That thinking forms the basis of a corporate-wide program called TOP that Kunerth is leading to enhance the company's performance in the technology marketplace.

The Siemens' TOP initiative began about three years ago as an outgrowth of productivity-improvement projects in some of the Siemens' companies, explains Kunerth. "Those projects were effective, but it was soon determined that isolated efforts would not be enough to enhance competitiveness in a company of 373,000 people involved in several hundred Siemens divisions, companies, and subsidiaries operating across the globe." Kunerth's description of TOP is amorphous – he asserts it is not a generic term for the application of any specific method. "TOP's meaning is broader. As an acronym it can mean time-optimized processes, indicating the need for processes at Siemens to become faster, but training of people or turn on power are equally appropriate."

Responsibility for the corporate-wide initiative was assigned to the Productivity Center, the part of Kunerth's Corporate Production & Logistics organization in Munich that marshaled the efforts of the productivity-improvement programs. TOP's final form derives from studies of such techniques as time-based management, benchmarking, reengineering, Total Quality Management, and kaizen. In Kunerth's view common principles unite them all: customer and process orientation, cross-functional teams, employee participation, and team-oriented management. Overall goals: to increase per-head productivity by 30 percent and cut the innovation and logistics cycle by 50 percent. In February, at the annual shareholders' meeting, Heinrich von Pieter, president and CEO, noted some progress: "Last year, cost productivity gains averaged 7.9 percent throughout the company, following a 6.3 percent improvement the previous year. In absolute figures this represents cost savings of DM7 billion last year alone. This year we have targeted a further 9 percent improvement."

(**Source**: Teresko, John. "Rethinking the business of technology," *Industry Week*, vol. 245, no. 13, July 1, 1996, p. 42(2))

an organization-wide basis. These two concerns are related, and together address the placement of logistics within the corporate hierarchy. Is logistics a stand-alone entity with a director on the same level as production and marketing, for instance? Or is logistics responsibility pushed down lower in the firm's structure, perhaps with management reporting to, for example, the director of marketing?

Finally, there are customer service issues to consider. For firms serving relatively homogeneous markets or selling similar products, a centralized logistics activity offers economies of scale that can lead to lower costs. When markets and/or products are very different, however, decentralization permits the tailoring of logistics activities to more closely meet different customer needs. American President Companies, for example, uses a decentralized structure to accommodate its international operating arena, serving countries with very different cultural environments and with different telecommunications systems. The need to react quickly to many customers at various locations around the globe also necessitates a more decentralized approach.[7] It is worth noting that a centralized logistics organization may oversee a decentralized logistics operation, and vice versa.

Scope of responsibility/span of control

Scope of responsibility refers to the degree to which logistics activities are grouped together in the same organization or organizational sub-unit. That is, what activities should be included in the logistics department? Scope can be very narrow in the case of a firm with logistics activities scattered throughout existing departments. On the other hand, scope may be broad as illustrated by a company that has grouped all logistics tasks into a single department with its own executive leadership. Span of control is closely related to the idea of scope and refers to the number of subordinates who report to a single superior. The more people responsible to one supervisor, the broader the span of control.

Formalization

Management must consider the degree to which goals, rules, policies, and procedures for logistics activities are precisely and explicitly formulated. This issue reflects in a larger sense the overall role and placement of logistics within the corporation. When logistics is seen as a key element in the attainment of corporate objectives, more formalization tends to be required.

Integration

A central theme of this text is that the concept of integration is central to logistics. However, integration is also a multifaceted term. On one level, integration refers to the coordination of two or more logistics activities within a firm. However, meshing logistics with other corporate activities with the firm (such as finance and marketing, for example), represents another form of integration. Finally, as was mentioned in the introduction to this chapter, managers are becoming increasingly interested in integrating their logistics activities with those of their channel partners. In sum, then, integration represents the degree to which logistics tasks and activities within the firm and across the supply chain are managed in a coordinated fashion.[8]

The Role of Logistics in the Firm

Management's analysis of each of these various properties takes place within a larger framework of corporate policies. That is, management must first assess where logistics fits within the firm overall, before attempting to define the structure of the logistics effort. Firms tend to move through four different stages of development in terms of logistics awareness. Firms at Stage One view logistics as an area of cost minimization only. Management's perception is that the various logistics tasks (transportation, warehousing, inventory management, order processing, etc.) are necessary evils that should be accomplished at the lowest cost possible. Indeed, companies at this stage may not display any formal logistics organization. Stage Two firms, on the other hand, tend to look upon logistics as a profit center. In this case, managers begin to realize the positive impact logistics can have on the company's bottom line. Stage Three companies have advanced farther still, utilizing logistics as both a profit center and a key market segmentation variable. Logistics is seen as providing alternative ways to meet the needs of different customers and different markets. Finally, some organizations are at Stage Four where logistics is seen as a central area of strategic activity within the firm. Essentially, every other part of the organization revolves around logistics. Wal-Mart, for example, owes a great deal to the design of its logistics system, which supports low prices and a broad selection of merchandise.[9] Indeed, with its recent entry into the German market, the firm is hoping to turn its logistics expertise into a competitive advantage in that country as well. Naturally, managers must develop a logistics system that supports corporate goals and objectives. Ideally, every firm would be at Stage Four in terms of how they view logistics; however, the reality is that many companies are still less than committed to logistics as a source of competitive advantage. The challenge is to develop a logistics organization that meets the needs of the firm today, while being flexible enough to assume a more strategic role in the future.

In fact, more and more companies are realizing logistics' potential and are organizing accordingly. A 1995 study conducted by the Graduate School of Management and Technology at the University of Maryland investigated 20 companies identified as following "best practices" in logistics, including Marriott Corp., Union Carbide, and United Parcel Service (UPS). The study confirmed that these firms are moving to consolidate their logistics activities under a centralized headquarters group holding overall management responsibility and authority for corporate logistics.[10] Clearly, these firms have come to see the logistics function as an important way to differentiate themselves, add value, and reduce costs. Thus, in addition to centralizing logistics management, most of the companies surveyed have taken steps to ensure that the logistics function serves the needs of individual business units and contributes measurably to the achievement of strategic goals. The study also noted that logistics departments tend to be treated as profit centers – they bill business units on a usage basis for their services. In addition, the logistics mission is usually integrated into the business units' mission statements. Furthermore, the researchers found increasingly close logistics affiliations between the companies they studied and their respective suppliers and customers, relationships that will be discussed in more detail in a later section.[11] The findings of the 1995 study were reconfirmed in 1997, the follow-up effort noting that the trend to consolidation and centralization of logistics had actually increased since the first study was accomplished.[12] The updated study also identified the beginnings of another trend – albeit in its early stages. Increasing numbers of companies are starting to outsource parts of the logistics function, a decision that places new demands on the firm's logistics organization.[13]

Inter-organizational effectiveness

As noted earlier, the firm's logistics organization must not only be effective internally. It must be structured so as to strengthen the company's position within its channel or supply chain. As discussed in a previous chapter, advances in management information systems and changes in management philosophy have resulted in the reengineering of inter-organizational relationships. As a result, supply chain management has evolved as a powerful concept in logistics. In essence, supply chain management refers to the overall process of smoothing the flow of benefits to the final consumer. Firms that have focused on the elimination of inter-firm conflicts and delays that can lead to customer dissatisfaction have achieved substantial gains. Thus, while addressing the role of logistics within the firm, management must simultaneously consider a number of issues regarding relationships with other channel members. Specifically, there are five structural dimensions that define intra-channel relationships: formalization, intensity, frequency, standardization, and reciprocity.[14]

Formalization is the degree to which norms governing transactions between the various organizations comprising the supply chain are made explicit. For example, many strategic alliances and partnerships are structured around legally binding written agreements detailing the responsibilities of all parties. Other channel arrangements may be informal and largely voluntary. **Intensity** indicates the level of resource investment that an organization has in its relationship with another firm. As the resources committed increase, so does the degree of intensity. Information flows (and hence technological applications such as electronic data interchange and bar coding) are important in determining the degree of intensity because of the investment that may be required to update the firm's computer capability. Supply-chain **frequency** reflects the amount of contact or interaction between organizations. (While the terms intensity and frequency are closely related, the former is a measure of the resources devoted to the relationship, while the latter refers to the number of interactions.) **Standardization** is the degree of similarity in the resources or procedures used by the parties in the relationship. The development of information system links between organizations, for example, requires a high level of resource standardization. As was alluded to earlier, only when the parties agree upon a common set of specifications for conducting the information exchange (e.g. software, hardware, formatting, etc.) does a reliable exchange become possible. Finally, **reciprocity** refers to the degree of symmetry in the relationship, in terms of both contribution and benefit flow. How equal is the flow of benefits between parties? Do different organizations contribute more or less to the relationship than others? Reciprocity can be thought of as a measure of one participant's ability to dominate the other channel members.

Clearly, management's goal is to create a logistics organization that advances the internal efficiency of the firm and its position with the supply chain. As has been discussed, a number of issues must be considered, relating to both intra- and inter-firm concerns. The dynamic nature of the global marketplace, and the firm's competitive positioning, may dictate that the structure of the logistics effort be altered periodically to maintain optimum performance in light of environmental changes.

Variables Influencing Organizational Structure

There are a number of variables that, individually and collectively, can have an impact on the overall effectiveness of the firm's logistics organization. Some of these come from inside the company: the size and structure of the firm itself, the overriding corporate strategy, the importance of logistics to that strategy, and the level of information technology, to name just a few. Others come from outside the firm. These will be discussed under the broader headings of environmental uncertainty and environmental heterogeneity.

Organization size

A study conducted by researchers at Michigan State University showed that size was an extremely important determinant of logistics organization structure. The larger the firm: (1) the greater the span of control and the more layers in the logistics function; (2) the more decentralized the decision making, especially in the area of delivery dates to customers and the number of finished goods field warehouses; (3) the more likely a written logistics mission and strategic plan exist;

(4) the more integrative mechanisms are used and the more likely those efforts focus on logistics strategy; and (5) the more specialists there are. Logistics managers should understand that they need to be adept at managing steady logistics reorganization as the company grows. Indeed, total reorganization of logistics may be necessary if size increases dramatically after a merger, acquisition or strategic alliance.[15]

Corporate structure

The structure imparted to the logistics function must be consistent with that of the organization it supports. If the corporation is highly structured and bureaucratic, the logistics component probably will be as well; conversely, a decentralized firm characterized by a large degree of departmental autonomy will have a logistics activity that reflects those same characteristics. As companies have altered their organizational makeup through reengineering and downsizing, for example, the logistics function has had to adapt to those changes as well.

Corporate strategy

Regardless of the precise way in which corporate strategy is defined, it is important in explaining the relationship between the structure of the logistics organization and performance. For example, if the corporate-level strategy is primarily one of cost leadership, a logistics system built around formalization and centralization may be helpful. Conversely, if the firm uses a "differentiation strategy" (perhaps by providing superior service quality), the cost advantages of formalization and centralization seem more likely to be outweighed by customers (or employees) who feel alienated by autocratic, directive policies handed down from the upper levels of management. In this situation, a decentralized and less formal approach may be most effective. Thus, corporate strategy can have a particular influence on logistics with respect to the inter-corporate relationships that exist within the firm's supply chain.[16]

The importance of logistics

The extent to which logistics activities constitute an important portion of the firm's value-adding activities will also be reflected in how those functions are structured. If logistics costs comprise a large percentage of the firm's total costs, the number of logistics decision elements and the need for sound coordination is high. Positioning the logistics function closer to top management may be an effective way of ensuring that such coordination occurs. Conversely, if logistics constitutes only a trivial portion of the firm's value-adding activities, a manager might find a higher return in designing the logistics organization with other needs (i.e. customer service) in mind.[17]

Corporate information technology

Information technology plays an important role in enabling business processes to be designed and performed well. This characteristic is especially relevant for logistics which, in general, tends to be transactions and information intensive. The recent past has seen exponential improvements in the capability of information technology and substantial reductions in the cost of that capability. The continued development of information systems may favor organizations that do not integrate within a logistics department but that provide a logistics information connection across the corporation. In addition, the growing ability to rapidly exchange more and varied types of information will further the movement toward partnerships and supply chain alliances.[18] Indeed, some firms have found their information systems are actually hindering their ability to take advantage of market opportunities. For example, established European firms with country-specific operations have found themselves with a myriad of business systems and information technologies that are not compatible with the more pan-European approach to business being taken by more visionary companies. It is extremely difficult to integrate disparate local systems together with any degree of efficiency.[19]

Environmental uncertainty

There are two important dimensions that must be captured in measuring environmental uncertainty, which can be defined as the extent to which outcomes are unpredictable. The first is the ability of the decision maker to predict the behavior and expectations of constituent groups such as competitors, suppliers and customers. The other dimension is the range of these behaviors and expectations. Both of these dimensions will impact the structure of the logistics organization and its inter-firm relationships.[20]

Volkswagen, for example, which was formerly a narrow-line manufacturer of cars based in Germany, is currently a maker of 4 million cars per year with revenues of DM 8 billion. The corporation went through crises of efficiency and profitability in the 1970s and 1980s, when overseas competitors invaded traditional markets with highly diversified product offerings that often gave customers a better price-to-performance ratio than Volkswagen's offerings. Today, the corporation has diversified its product range to four brands (Volkswagen, Audi, Seat, and Skoda) and a commercial vehicle division. Plants are located in many countries. Corporate-wide goals have been set to create "customer enthusiasm" on the basis of levels of service, cost, and quality that must be competitive with any other manufacturer. Logistics helps to realize the targets related to the improvement of delivery reliability from slightly more than 50 percent in 1995 to 85 percent in 1997, reduction of order lead times from an average of six weeks to two weeks, and a massive cost reduction.

Management's vision is of a "breathing company," where production is determined by market behavior and breathes with customer demand. It requires an extremely flexible work organization; tightly integrated concurrent planning procedures; and a new real-time ordering process. The formal organization of logistics at Volkswagen currently is a matrix-type structure, where a corporate logistics department, a production process planning department, and a "continuous improvement projects" group interface with logistics functions within the brand divisions and operating units.[21]

Environmental heterogeneity

Environmental heterogeneity is defined as the degree of complexity in the firm's environment (e.g. governments, markets, customers, suppliers, etc.). This complexity may be reflected in the various constituent groups around the organization (customers being the most important). In addition, it may be higher or lower as a consequence of the number of different products/services that the firm sells or the varied global markets within which the company operates. When environmental heterogeneity is low (i.e. more homogeneous), a centralized organization may make it possible to utilize devices such as policies and standard procedures in ways that stimulate performance. Conversely, when environmental heterogeneity is high, it may be necessary to make decisions on a more ad-hoc basis that flows more naturally and easily from a decentralized logistics structure.[22] How some firms have reacted to the growing homogeneity of European markets is illustrated in logistics profile 15-2.

Summary

The linkages between the structure of the logistics organization and its ability to support the corporate mission are multifaceted and complex. There are many factors that act upon and influence logistics system performance. As those variables change, so too must the logistics function. Thus, a logistics organization that is highly efficient today may be hopelessly out of date next year. Management's task is to be aware of changes occurring both within the firm and in the environment so that the logistics effort can be modified as required to continually add value to the final customer.

Reconciling Intra- and Inter-Organizational Issues

As emphasized throughout this chapter, there is no "best" approach to designing the firm's logistics system. Clearly, there is some balance that must be struck between internal and external issues. A recent study conducted by Michigan State University compared the supply chain organizational structures and integrative capabilities of almost 2,000 companies in four major industrialized nations: Australia, Japan, Korea, and the United States. The results provide some interesting insights into what constitutes an effective logistics organization in those countries.[23]

In terms of structural arrangements, Korean firms show the greatest tendency to internal structural integration, which stresses efficient internal relationships between

Logistics Profile 15-2
The Slow Boat to Europe

Five years ago the American sportswear company Nike had an extremely complex European distribution system built around 25 warehouses scattered across the continent. Today it has just one – a huge facility at Laakdal in Belgium that receives clothing and footwear from manufacturing plants in the Far East, America and Europe and ships them out to customers. Nike is a model of pan-European distribution, treating the whole continent as though it was a single country without any borders.

The reconfiguration of European logistics systems is a recent phenomenon. To understand it, one needs to look at European business in an historical perspective. From the Second World War until the late-1980s business in Europe developed along national lines. Companies that wanted to expand within the continent did so on a country-by-country basis. They set up subsidiaries in each country and gave each a large degree of autonomy and local power. The national subsidiaries built up their own sales and marketing operations and established local distribution systems. Each country's distribution network operated more or less independently of the others. The company would have a warehouse in each country that received and distributed its products locally with the national boundaries. Since a country's borders were not just political dividing lines but barriers to trade, the system made sense. Crossing borders, where trucks and products were often held up endless at customs posts, was a time-consuming and expensive business.

All that changed in the 1990s. The arrival of the single European market on 1 January 1993 meant that Europe was no longer a collection of a dozen or more independent national markets but had become a single market without borders, a place where goods, services, capital and people could move freely across national frontiers as though those borders did not exist. An immediate consequence was that companies began to ask themselves whether, if they were facing a single Europe-wide market, they should reorganize themselves as regional entities, approaching their customers wearing a European rather than a national hat and cutting out layers of cost by centralizing functions such as accounting, sales and marketing. They also began to look very critically at their transport and distribution arrangements.

It soon became apparent that distribution systems designed for the old Europe were ill-suited to the new one, particularly if a company's manufacturing, marketing and sales strategies were to be Europeanized. As the late Professor James Cooper, former director of the Centre for Logistics and Transportation at Cranfield School of Management put it shortly after the single market came into being, the new Europe exposed a contradiction. Organizing distribution and warehousing on a country-by-country basis, he said, broke a cardinal rule. This was that storage be located according to patterns of demand. "And patterns of demand don't necessarily relate very closely to where, by an accident of history, a country's borders are."

> Just how powerful the arithmetic of centralization really is can be seen from the case of Becton Dickinson, an American diagnostics manufacturer and supplier which, like Nike, has gained major performance improvements and cost savings from centralizing its transport and distribution system. Becton, which supplies everything from bottles of chemical reagents to analytical instruments, had built up a network of national distribution centres as its European business expanded in the early 1990s. But it soon found that the system was riddled with inefficiencies. It had high inventory costs and stock write-offs due to the shelf life of products expiring. It also suffered from poor stock availability and high distribution costs. As a result, the company redesigned its whole distribution system. It closed national distribution centres in Sweden, France, Germany and Belgium and shifted operations to a single, purpose-built, fully automated facility at Temse in Belgium. The results were astonishing. In less than a year, stock levels were down 45 percent, write-offs were reduced by 65 percent and stock-outs had been reduced by 75 percent.
>
> (**Source**: Brown, Malcolm. "The slow boat to Europe," *Management Today*, June 1997, p. 83(4))

transportation, logistics, sales, purchasing, and manufacturing. Since Korea is a newly industrialized nation, this finding of an internal focus suggests that firms will typically first deal with the integration of their own logistics activities prior to addressing channel relationships.[24] Japan, on the other hand, shows the greatest tendency to external supply chain integration, which stresses the external customers and supply partners of the firm. Specifically, the external structural integration approach used by Japan involves operational planning of physical flows (for example, JIT), the greater use of traditional channel power (e.g. domination of channel members and contractual obligations), and increased organizational loyalty.[25]

Results also showed that both US and Australian firms are similar in using an external relationship integration approach emphasizing external customers and external partners. However, the primary organizational emphasis is on interactive relationships with supply chain members as opposed to channel domination per se. These interactive relationships may include frequent customer and supplier contacts by the firm's logistics personnel; partnership interactions and strategic alliances; and the sharing of both information and performance results. In a similar vein, both US and Australian firms view strategic alliances as more important for supply chain structural integration than do Japanese or Korean firms.[26]

In explaining US firms' emphasis on interactive supply chain structures, comparisons can be made to Japanese Keiretsu structures. Unlike the Keiretsu relationships, US business relationships and strategic alliances are more often voluntary and equal, and roles are mutually agreed upon. Firms must be persuaded to join, and the sharing of risks and rewards is negotiated. All of these practices require interactive relationships among carriers, suppliers, partners, and customers. Given American cultural and business values of autonomy, individualism, and independence, there is much less willingness by firms to put their fate in the hands of central control. Essentially, the American interactive approach to supply chain structure is a partial substitute for the Keiretsu that best fits US antitrust laws and cultural business values.[27]

In sum, the study confirmed what was discussed in a prior section of this chapter, namely that supply chain structures must be adaptive to their business, geographic, and cultural environments. Although successful internal logistics organizations and supply chain structures may be replicated, they must also be viewed within their respective environments. This caution means that intra- and inter-organizational logistics structures cannot be blindly imitated, but must be understood within their present environmental context and, if possible, adapted to fit new situations.[28] This study is particularly valuable in highlighting some of the organizational challenges awaiting firms serving many different global markets.

Moving Towards the "Best" Organizational Structure

There are several overriding issues that must guide the executive in organizing a sound logistics function. First, **corporate objectives and strategies** must be considered as they provide the logistics activity with long-term direction. Since the logistics effort must support the attainment of those goals, management should thoroughly understand where logistics fits in the overall strategic plan and to what extent senior leadership view logistics as a value-adding activity.[29] Second, **corporate size and structure** will be a factor. As was noted earlier, the specific organizational structure of the logistics activity must mesh with that defining the overall firm. For example, in a highly decentralized company, the logistics activity will probably be structured in the same way. The reasons for this consistency stem primarily from the inherent advantages – administrative, financial, personnel – that result from organizational uniformity within a firm.[30] Third, **functional responsibilities** must be determined. Specifically, which activities will fall under the purview of the logistics manager and which will not? It is important to have all or most logistics subfunctions housed under a single division or department. Such an arrangement, with full functional responsibility, allows the firm to implement the concepts of integrated logistics management and total cost/service trade-offs.[31] Finally, **flexibility** must be designed in from the start. Any logistics organization must be able to adapt to changes that inevitably occur. While it may be difficult to anticipate future shifts in the marketplace or the firm, the logistics organization must be receptive to those changes and must respond to them in ways beneficial to the firm.[32]

Chapter Summary

This chapter examined the issues surrounding the design of effective logistics organizations. Today, managers must consider the impact of logistics both within the firm and with respect to the other members of the firm's supply chain. Both intra- and inter-organizational issues were discussed, all of which can have an impact on the type of logistics organization a company adopts. The important thing to note is that different corporations require different types of logistics support. One firm may do very well with a functionally organized logistics activity on a par with, for instance, production and marketing. Another business may rely on logistics to a greater extent, developing a much more integrated organizational structure that spans the entire corporation. Each logistics organization develops to meet the internal and external needs of the firm it supports. As such, there is no single "best" form for that organization.

Study Questions

1. Briefly describe the four major approaches to logistics organizations.
2. Compare and contrast frequency and intensity.
3. Discuss two of the major issues faced when determining the level of centralization of logistics within an organization.
4. Compare and contrast Stages One through Four of logistics development within firms.
5. How does supply chain management impact the structure of a firm's logistics organization.
6. Identify several variables that affect the effectiveness of a firm's logistics organization?
7. Under what circumstances might you find a firm with a centralized logistics organization overseeing a decentralized logistics operation?
8. How do firms in Australia, Korea, Japan, and the United States differ in terms of their approaches to employing logistics functions?
9. Identify two or three factors that have made Volkswagen, Siemens, and HACTL successful logistics models.

Notes

1. Copacino, William C. "Getting organized for the late '90s," *Traffic Management*, Jan. 1994, vol. 33, no. 1, p. 37(2).
2. Tompkins, James A. "Logistics: a challenge for today," *IIE Solutions*, Feb. 1997, vol. 29, no. 2, p. 16(2).
3. Copacino, ibid.
4. Augustin, Siegfried, Klaus, Peter G., Krog, Ernst, W., and Mueller-Steinfahrt, Ulrich. "The evolution of logistics in large industrial organizations in Europe," *Annual Conference Proceedings –1996* (Oak Brook, IL: Council of Logistics Management, 1993), pp. 535–44.
5. Ibid.
6. Chow, Garland, Henriksson, Lennart E, and Heaves, Trevor D. "Strategy, structure and performance: a framework for logistics research," *The Logistics and Transportation Review*, Dec. 1995, vol. 31, no. 4, p. 285(24).
7. Mentzer, John T. and Firman, John. "Logistics control systems in the 21st century,"

Journal of Business Logistics, vol. 15, no. 1, 1994, p. 225.
8. Chow et al., ibid.
9. Stevenson, M. "The store to end all stores," *Canadian Business*, May 1994, pp. 20–9.
10. *Harvard Business Review*, Sept.–Oct. 1995, pp. 11–12.
11. Ibid.
12. *Harvard Business Review*, Sept.–Oct. 1997, pp. 8–9.
13. Ibid.
14. Chow et al., ibid.
15. Droge, Cornelia and Germain, Richard. "The design of logistics organizations," *Transportation Research – E (Logistics and Transportation Review)*, vol. 34, no. 1, 1998, p. 35.
16. Ibid.
17. Ibid.
18. Ibid.
19. Brown, Malcom. "The slow boat to Europe," *Management Today*, June 1997, p. 83(4).
20. Chow et al., ibid.
21. Augustin et al., ibid.
22. Chow et al., ibid.
23. Morash, Edward A. and Clinton, Steven R. "The role of transportation capabilities in international supply chain management," *Transportation Journal*, Spring 1997, vol. 36, no. 3, p. 5(13).
24. Ibid.
25. Ibid.
26. Ibid.
27. Ibid.
28. Ibid.
29. Lambert, Douglas M. and Stock, James R. *Strategic Logistics Management*, 3rd edn (Homewood, Il: Richard D. Irwin, Inc., 1993), p. 646.
30. Ibid.
31. Ibid.
32. Ibid.

Index

3M xiii, 214
80/20 rule 47–8

ABC analysis
  customer service 50
  inventory management 72–4
action planning 213, 247
activity, customer service as 41
activity-based costing (ABC) 254
  benefits 254–8
  data availability 262
act step, PDCA cycle 247, 248
administration
  vendor managed inventory 79
  warehousing function 126
ADtranz 115
aesthetic pollution 117
after-sales parts and service support 6
Agfa-Gevaert NV
  customs brokers 206
  materials handling 144–6
agility, and world-class logistics 264–5
Airbus Industrie 2, 215–16
Air Express International 222–3
Air France 93
air pollution 116–17
air transport 90
  characteristics 86
  congestion 117
  deregulation and liberalization 12, 92–3, 94
  environmental issues 96, 117, 118, 119
  future 225
  intermodal transportation 98–100
  pricing 106, 107, 108
  privatization 93
  service quality 258
Alamshah, Dave 81
Alexander the Great 1
allocations 214–15
Alstrom 204
Amazon.com 132, 145
American President Companies (APC) 261–2, 272
Andersen Consulting
  customer service 42
  warehousing 132
ANSI ASC X12 standard 168
appraisal, cost of 243
Arnott's Biscuits 252
Associated Dairies 252
Association of Southeast Asian Nations (ASEAN) 197
Atlantic Bouquet 26
attributes data 251
Auchan 28
Audi 277
Austin, Terrence A. 42
Australia
  air transport 92
  packaging 152
  strategic alliances 280
  third-party service providers 221
  Toyota 44–5

water transport 94
Australia-New Zealand Direct Line (ANZDL) 241
Australia Post 252
Austria
domestic v. global channels 30
packaging 152
safety laws, transportation 96
traffic congestion 117
automated storage and retrieval systems (AS/RS) 142, 144
Automatic Loading System (ALS) 115
automation
bar code scanners 154
identification, materials handling 147–8
order processing 160–1
warehouses 136, 142–6
automobile makers, channel management 27–8

back-orders 70
Banana Republic 183
bar coding
automated warehouses 144
packaging 154
two-dimensional 172
Barnesandnoble.com 132, 133
barter 23
Bechtel Group 132
Becton Dickinson 280
Belgium
air transport 117
domestic v. global channels 30
ISO 9000 242–3
road transport 225
benchmarking 231–2, 251–2
network 252–3
BILLA 30
bimodal technology 113–14
BMW
corporate strategy 212
EDI 217
JIT 77
Body Shop 212
Boeing 212
Boots Healthcare Company 252
Borders, Lewis 132
Bosch-Siemens 129
BP 252
brainstorming 251
Brazil 112
breakdown facility, warehouse as 127–8
break-even analysis 33–4, 36
breakthrough improvements 248
British Airways 93
British Rail 93
BS5750 241
Bulkeley, Jonathan 132
Bunge 252
Burlington Air Express 222, 223

cabotage 92–3, 94
CalComp 75
Campbells 252
Canada
air transport 92
"domestic" market 10
packaging 152
private trucking 111
Canadian Airlines 231
Cargo Community Network 168
Cargo Interchange Message Procedure (CARGO-IMP) 168
Cargo Sprinter 114
Carlton & United Breweries (CUB) 252
carriers
costs 108–9
price negotiation 110
safety 120
win/win relationship development 103–5
carrying costs 62
cash flow 161
Casino 28
causal forecasting methods 164, 165
cause-and-effect diagrams 249
Celebrity Cruises 16
Central Europe
customs regulations 202
growth of market 10
centralization 220, 270–2
warehousing 128–30
Chanel 150
channels
alternative structures 21–3
designing effective 24
deteriorating relationships with members of 72
development 23
direct 23

domestic v. global 29–30
environmental issues 24–5
flows 23
formal and informal relationships 28–9
future trends in structures 31
integration 216–18
JIT 78
leader/captain 27–8, 217–18
management issues 27–8
supply chain integration 214
checking function, warehousing 126
check sheets 251
check step, PDCA cycle 247, 248
China
air transport 118
customer service 41, 45
domestic v. global channels 30
environmental issues 24
foreign trade zones 203–4
growth of market 10, 30
market opportunities 194, 195–6
packaging 149–50
ports, distribution services upgraded at 37
rail transport 86–7, 119
road transport 89, 118
transportation liberalization 12
China Light & Power Ltd 204
Chrysler 77
CMB Transport 219
Codeca, Renzo 174
commitment of management
to inventory management 72
to quality 238–9
Commonwealth of Independent States (CIS) 10
see also Soviet Union, former
communications
customer service 42
logistics information systems 172, 174–5
wireless 172
Compaq Computer Corporation 60
competition, transportation 95, 105, 106
competitive advantage
automated warehouses 144
benchmarking 252
global organizations 14–15
logistics as source of 8–9
value chain 8
components of logistics systems 3–7
computational efficiency of forecasts 165
computer manufacturers
customer service 42
trade-off analysis 33, 34
conferences 90–1
congestion, traffic 117–19
Conner Peripherals Inc. 184
consolidation function, warehousing 126
consumerism 226
consumer package *see* interior package
Container Industri 100
containers 96–7, 98–100
container ships 98, 99–100
Continental Farms 26–7
continuous environmental scanning 162
continuous improvements 248
ABC analysis 256
quality 240
contracts 28, 29
contract warehousing 133–4, 135–6
control, span of 272
control charts 251
convenience, and customer service 42
Cooper, James 279
cooperation, and quality 231
Cootes Transport Group 252
corporate philosophy, customer service as 41
corporate reconfiguration 25
corporate strategy 276, 281
planning 211–13
cost data, lack of 262
cost-of-service pricing 108, 109
crime 88, 120
Crosby, P. B. 230
cross-docking 126
CSR Readymix 252
culture, national 198
channel management 24
customer service 43, 53
culture, organizational 263–4
customer delivered value 10–11
customer focus 7
customers
alienation 53–6
as barrier to customer service 49
internal 56–7, 60
loss of 70
packaging 150

understanding needs of 50, 239
viewpoint 260–2
customer service 5, 40–1, 57
barriers 47–50
carriers 104
centralization 272
elements 41–3
future 226
global setting 43–6
improving 50–1, 56
inbound logistics 179–80
intermodal transportation 101
internal customer 56–7
inventory management 60, 62, 70
levels 46–7
localization 207
logistics information systems 175
management 207
modern perspective on logistics 2
objectives 25
order processing system 160
poor, consequences 51–6
process effectiveness 260
purchasing 186
service quality model 236
shippers 104
supply chain integration 214
transport infrastructure 112
warehouse location 131–3
customs
brokers 206
documentation 201–2
EDI 169
regulations 202–3
transportation 119–20
cut flowers 26–7
Czech Republic 112

damaged goods 153–4, 155, 156
data availability 232, 262
Dawe, Richard 137
dead inventory 62
decentralization 220, 272
warehouses 128
decision support systems (DSS) 161, 162
data availability 232, 262
demand
forecasting 6
inventory management 61, 72
shipper 107
and supply, balancing 61
Deming, W. Edwards 230, 246
Deming wheel/cycle 246–8
Denmark
logistics information 159
rail system 118
dependability, and customer service 41
deregulation 24
retailing sector, Japan 30
transportation 12, 91–4, 224, 227
DeSantis, Greg 55
descriptive forecasting methods 164
DeSimone, L. D. xiii
Deutsche Bahn 114
Deutsche Post 114
developing high-quality logistics systems 229, 243–4
basic quality concepts 230–3
cost 243
formal quality process 238–40
ISO 9000 241–3
quality process success factors 240–1
service quality model 233–6
total quality management 237
DHL 196
diagnostic measures of service quality 258, 259
direct channels 23
direct selling 45
distribution 25
distribution requirements planning (DRP II) 190
software 74
distribution resource planning (DRP) 75–6, 190
integrated inventory management 80
divisionally integrated logistics organizations 269
Docks de France 28
documentation, international 200–2
Dole Costa Rica 99
domestic channels 29–30
do step, PDCA cycle 247–8
double-stack container trains 97
drive-thru service 45
Dubai 203
duties 202
foreign trade zones 203, 204

ease of use, materials handling

systems 148
Eastern Europe
cargo security 120
changing market opportunities 197
customer delivered value 11
customs regulations 202
domestic v. global channels 30
growth of market 10
ecological issues *see* environmental issues
e-commerce *see* electronic commerce
economic order quantity (EOQ) model 63–4
limitations 64–5
modifications 64
economics and employee outcome 232
economies of scale
global logistics systems 207
inbound logistics 182
inventory management 61, 78
logistics strategies 220
purchasing 189
EDI *see* electronic data interchange
EDIFACT 168, 169, 187
effectiveness *see* logistics effectiveness
Elbe, River 98
Elcint 11
electronic commerce (e-commerce) 14
logistics information systems 170–2
warehousing 132–3, 144, 145–6
electronic data interchange (EDI) 165–9
documentation 201
fully automated logistics systems 13
impediments to global implementation 169–70
purchasing 187–8
vendor managed inventory 79
electronic funds transfer (EFT) 167
Elgas 252
emerging nations, market opportunities 194–6
Emmelhainz, Margaret A. 167
employee outcomes 232
employees
customer service 48, 49, 50–1
training 50–1
English, Welsh and Scottish Railways 93
environmental heterogeneity 278, 279–80
environmental issues 12
future 224, 225
JIT 78
LEGO 149
packaging 152–3
transportation 95–6, 116–19, 225
environmental scanning
corporate strategic planning 212
logistics information systems 162
environmental uncertainty 277–8
eToys Inc. 132, 145
Euromar 169
European Rail Shuttle (ERS) 12
European Union (EU)
air transport 92–3
British "domestic" market 10
changing market opportunities 196–7
channel management 24
documentation 201
homogeneity 279–80
members 197
packaging 152
rail transport 12, 93, 113, 119
road transport 87–9
traffic congestion 117–19
transport infrastructure 225
Eurostar 118
evaluation of performance 247
Evergreen 91
exclusive distribution 25
Exel Logistics 75
exporting 199, 200
export management companies (EMCs) 205
export packers 205–6
export trading companies 205

facilitators, logistics 204–6
facility locations 6
supply chain integration 214
warehouses 128–33
failure, cost of 243
Far East 45
Farr, Anthony Z. 219
FBT Operations 252
Federal Express (FedEx)
competitive advantage 9
corporate strategy 212
customer service 42
e-commerce 145, 171–2
EDI 169
feedback, customer service 50
Fingerhut Companies 145–6

Finland
domestic v. global channels 30
logistics information 159
fishbone diagrams 249
fixed costs, transportation 108
fixed order interval model 66, 67
fixed order point/fixed order quantity model 65–6
fleet operation 111
flexibility 281
materials handling 147
flow charts 249–51
flowers 26–7
Ford Motor Company
foreign trade zones 204
global organization 14
forecasting 163
causal methods 164
centralized warehousing 129
demand 6
logistics needs 165
qualitative methods 163
selecting the right technique 165
time-series methods 163–4
foreign trade zones (FTZs) 203–4
formal channel relationships 28–9
formalization 272–3
intra-organizational effectiveness 274
formal quality process, development 238–40
Fortner, Mitchell 26
forward buying 186
France
air transport 93
channel management issues 28
customer service 42, 43
domestic v. global channels 30
rail transport 86, 93, 117, 119
franchisers 27–8
Francis, Antony 171–2
Franprix 28
fraud 88
free market 226
freight forwarders 204, 205, 220
China 196
frequency, and interorganizational effectiveness 275
Fritz Institute of Global Logistics 137
Fujitsu 212
fulfillment, employee outcome 232
fully integrated logistics organizations 269–70
functionally integrated logistics organizations 269
future
channel structures 31
logistics 223–7
transportation 93–4

Galuska, Dave 55
Gap, The 183
Gap Kids 183
gathering facility, warehouse as 126–7, 128
General Agreement on Tariffs and Trade (GATT) 193
General Agreement on Trade in Services 92
General Motors Corporation (GM)
inbound logistics 180
purchasing 189
third-party service providers 222–3
Germany
air transport 92, 117
culture 198
customer service 43, 45
domestic v. global channels 30
packaging 152
rail transport 93, 112, 114, 119
road transport 112, 225
safety laws, transportation 96
transport infrastructure 112
water transport 90, 112
Glassgen, Gregory 88, 89
global channels 29–30
global distribution strategies 199–200
global logistics environment 193–4, 207–9
alternative global distribution strategies 199–200
changing market opportunities 194–8
control 206–7, 208–9
cultural issues 198
customs 202–3
documentation 200–2
foreign trade zones 203–4
intermediaries and facilitators 204–6
supply chain 194
global organizations
environmental issues 24

logistics in 14–15
global positioning systems (GPS) 14, 174
global setting
customer service 43–6
inventory management 81–2
packaging 153–4
warehousing 136–7
global sourcing 198
global supply chain 194
global trade
future 224
trends 10
government
documentation 201
nationalization 200
regulatory environment 24, 226
retailers owned by 43, 45
government role in transportation 94
direct control and regulation of transport firms 94–5
environmental and safety laws 95–6
infrastructure provision 95
pricing 109
rail 86, 113
Grant, Scott 44
Great Britain
customer service 43
"domestic" market 10
see also United Kingdom
Greece
domestic v. global channels 30
rail transport 93

Habitat 218
Hamburg
documentation 201
dredging project 98
Hamilton Standard 55–6
Hammer, M. 230
handheld bar code scanners 154
Harley-Davidson Motor Company, Inc. 81
Heathrow Airport 112
heuristics models, warehouse location 130–1
Hewlett-Packard Company (HP) 136–7
high-speed sorting/scanning systems 142
hijacking 120
Hilton Hosiery 252
histograms 251
historical forecasting methods *see* time-series forecasting methods
historical perspective on logistics 1–2
Hitler, Adolf 1–2
Hoechst-Celanese 134–5, 136
Hoffman-La Roche 207, 208–9
holding costs 62
honesty 42
Hong Kong
American apparel imports 37
paper-based trade 167
warehousing 141
Hong Kong Air Cargo Terminals (HACTL) 269
horizontal movement systems, automated warehouses 142
Humfeld, Terry 26
Hungary 112
hybrid lift trucks 142

Ikea 29
impact measures of service quality 258, 259
implementation of logistics strategies 218–20
centralized v. decentralized approach 220
corporate performance improvements 223
third-party service providers 220–3
import taxes (duties) 202
foreign trade zones 203, 204
inbound logistics 177, 190–1
activities 178–82
growing importance 177–8
management techniques 190
Inchcape 196
incremental cost, transportation 108
India
air transport 118
cigarettes 29
road transport 118
indifference, point of (break-even analysis) 33–4, 36
Indonesia 203
industrial package 150
informal channel relationships 28, 29
information
logistics *see* logistics information; logistics information systems
packaging 151

information management
  future 227
  inbound logistics 181
  logistics information systems 162
  supply chain integration 215
information technology 6
  continuing advances 13–14
  corporate 277
  logistics information systems 172
  see also electronic data interchange; software
InfoSeek 172
infrastructure, transport 95
  availability and condition 112–16
  future 224, 225
  intermodal transportation 100
integrated carriers 169
integration 273
  inventory management 80–1
  and world-class logistics 264
intensity, and interorganizational effectiveness 274–5
intensive distribution 25
interior package 150
  global markets 153
Intermarch 28
intermediaries, logistics 204–6
intermodal transportation 96–7, 100–1
  air 98–100
  Europe 113–16
  infrastructure issues 100
  ocean 98, 99–100
  rail 97
  road 100
internal customers 56–7
  inventory management 60
international documentation 200–2
International Maritime Organization 99
International Standards Organization (ISO) 241
  ISO 9000 241–3
International Union of Railways (UIC) 115
Internet 170
  see also electronic commerce
inter-organizational effectiveness 274–5
in-transit inventory 62
inventory
  costs 62–3, 129
  purchasing 184, 186
  purposes 61
  square root law 128–9
  supply chain integration 215
  turns 77
  types 61–2
  warehousing 124, 131, 136
inventory management 5, 59, 80–1
  changing view of 13
  classic models 63–70
  customer service 60
  distribution requirements planning *see* distribution requirements planning
  distribution resource planning *see* distribution resource planning
  future 227
  global market 80–1
  Ikea 29
  improving 72–4
  inbound logistics 180
  integrated 80
  just-in-time *see* just-in-time (JIT) systems
  materials requirements planning *see* materials requirements planning
  objectives 62–3
  order processing system 161
  signs of trouble 70–2
  transport infrastructure 112
irregular environmental scanning 162
ISO 9000 241–3
Italy 30
item-picking systems 142
Ivany, Terry 233

Japan
  culture 198
  customer service 45, 53
  deregulation of retail sector 30
  external structural integration 280
  inbound logistics 178
  inventory management 81
  Kobe earthquake 79–80, 165
  rail transport 119
  sogo shosha 205
Jebel Ali Free Zone Authority 203
Johnson, Steve 132
Johnson Controls 77
joint ventures 200
Juran, J. M. 230, 231
just-in-time (JIT) systems 61, 76
  advantages 77–8
  basic tenets 76–7

changing view of inventory 13
disadvantages 78–9
Gap, The 183
Harley-Davidson 81
integrated inventory management 80
JIT II 79
materials management improvements 190
management 31–2
packaging 151–2
purchasing 187
reality 79–80
Saturn 179
transport infrastructure 112

Kalari 252
Kamber, Roman 208
Kareltrans Oy 88–9
Karstadt 28–9
Keiretsu 280, 281
King, Admiral Ernest J. xiii
KLM Royal Dutch Airlines 93
Kobe earthquake 79–80, 165
Kodak 230
Korea 278–80
Kuhne & Nagel 204
Kunerth, Walter 271

Landfill Tax (1997, UK) 152
landscape disfiguration 117
La Rinascente 28
LASH vessels 98
laws *see* legal issues
leadership and quality 230–1
lead times
infrastructure, transport 112
variable 51–3, 54
warehousing 124, 131
Leaphart, Ro 183
learning and quality 231
legal issues
packaging 150, 151
transportation 95–6
LEGO 149
LEP 218
leverage
channel integration strategies 218
purchasing 184, 187
Levi-Strauss 183
Li & Fuang Group 195
liberalization, transportation 11–12
see also deregulation
licensing 199–20
lighter aboard ship (LASH) vessels 98
linear programming 130
local area networks (LANs) 172
location issues 6
supply chain integration 214
warehouses 128–33
logistics 17–18, 20, 37–8
bar coding 154
channels 21–4
competitive advantage 8–9
components 3–7
conceptual model 15, 17
environmental issues 24–5
global environment *see* global logistics environment
global organizations 14–15, 16–17
growing management interest 10–14
high-quality *see* developing high-quality logistics systems
historical perspective 1–2
importance 276
inbound *see* inbound logistics
management 31–2
marketing issues 25–31
marketing/logistics partnership 20–1
modern perspective 2–8
packaging 150, 151–2, 155, 156
profitability enhancement 34–7
quick response 31
role in organization 7–8, 273–5
service quality 258–9
statement of purpose 15
systems perspective 263
trade-off analysis 32–4
warehousing's strategic role 124–5
world-class system, development 264–5
logistics effectiveness 268, 281–2
"best" organizational structure 281
building 270–3
intra- and inter-organizational issues, reconciling 278–81
organizational structure, influence 275–8
overview of logistics organizations 268–70
role of logistics in the firm 273–5
logistics information 159–60, 175

forecasting methods 163–5
linking a global logistics system together 165–70
order processing system 160–1
logistics information systems (LIS) 161
developments 170–5
environmental scanning 162
information management 162
logistics performance, improving 246, 265–6
creating a world-class logistics system 264–5
impediments 260–4
improving organizational performance 246–8
meaningful change 258–60
tools 249–58
logistics strategies 211, 227–8
corporate strategic planning 211–13
formulating 214–16
future issues 223–7
implementing 218–23
integrating the logistics channel 216–18
L'Oreal 187
L. S. Booth 252
Lucky Goldstar 195
Lufthansa 93
Luxembourg 30
Lycos 172

Macy's 145
Maersk Line 98, 99–100
maintainability, materials handling systems 148
maintenance functions 6
inbound logistics 181
management commitment
to inventory management 72
to quality 238–9
management skills, broad-based 263
manual warehouses 141–2, 143–6
manufacturing resource planning (MRP II) 190
marginal cost, transportation 108
marketing
channels 21–5, 27–31
inbound logistics 186
issues 25–31
mix 21, 31–2
packaging 150
partnership with logistics 20–1
purchasing 186
warehouse location issues 128
marketing package *see* interior package
market opportunities
emerging nations 194–6
global sourcing 198
multi-lateral trade organizations 196–7
market structure models, transport pricing 105–6
marking function, warehousing 126
Marks & Spencer
customer service 42
EDI 187
MARNET 169
Marriott Corp. 274
material requirements planning (MRP) 74, 190
integrated inventory management 80
software 74
materials handling 5–6, 140, 155
basic warehouse design 140–1
manual v. automated 141–6
packaging 151
trends 146–9
materials management, logistics defined as 2, 3
Mazda 212
McDonald's
channel management issues 27
customer service 45
joint ventures 200
licensing 199–200
packaging 152, 155
McDonnell Douglas 212
measurement, and world-class logistics 265
Mercedes-Benz
corporate strategy 212
foreign trade zones 204
packaging 151–2, 155
purchasing 184
Mercosur 197
Mexicana/Aeromexico 93
Mexico
air transport 93
transport infrastructure 112
Michelin 217
Ministry of Railways (MoR), China 87
Mitsubishi 195, 196

Mitsui 205
mixed-integer linear programming 130
modern perspective on logistics 2–3, 4
  components of a logistics system 3–7
  role of logistics 7–8
modularity, materials handling 147
monitoring
  customer service 50
  and world-class logistics 265
monopolies, transportation 95, 106, 113
monopolistic competition 106
Motorola 164
MTI Inc. 204
multi-lateral trade organizations 196–7
Murphy's Transport 252
Murray, Mike 145–6

NACO Inc. 115
Napoleon Bonaparte 1–2
narrow-aisle (NA) storage 144
National Association of Warehouse Keepers (UK) 134
nationalization 200
Nestle Confectionery 252
Netherlands, the
  air transport 92, 93, 117
  Customs 202
  domestic v. global channels 30
  packaging 152
  road transport 225
  water transport 225
New Zealand 152
Nies, Vernon 145
Nike 128, 279
NISA Today's 3
noise pollution
  LEGO's control programme 149
  transportation 117
non-integrated logistics organizations 269
non-profit organizations 56
non vessel-owning common carriers (NVOCCs) 205
normal inventory 61
North American Free Trade Association (NAFTA)
  Canadian "domestic" market 10
  changing market opportunities 196–7
  channel management 24
Northern Europe
  domestic v. global channels 30
  inventory management 81
Norway 159
Novack, Robert A. 81

ocean transport *see* water transport
Odense Staalskibsvaerft 99
Old Navy 183
oligopolies 106
Olivetti 187
open-skies agreements 92
open-systems computer networks 172
operational plans 213
optimization models, warehouse location 130
ordering costs 62–3
order processing system 159–61
order selection function, warehousing 126
organization, logistics 215
Orient Overseas Container Line (OOCL) 99, 101
outsourcing *see* third-party service providers
Outspan 219
ownership of a foreign subsidiary 200

packaging 6, 140, 149–50, 157
  bar coding 154
  developments 155
  environmental issues 12, 152–3
  future 227
  for global markets 153–4
  materials 151–2
  organizational influences 150
  reusable 151–2, 153
  role 151
  trade-offs in logistics system 155, 156
  transport infrastructure 112
  types 150
  warehousing 136
packing function, warehousing 126
Panalpina 204
Pareto's Law 47–8
PDCA cycle of improvement 247
performance
  customer service as measure of 41
  improving 246–8
  logistics *see* logistics performance, improving
  logistics strategy 223
  measurement 239
  and quality 232, 239

Philips
  inbound logistics 178
  packaging 155
philosophy, corporate, customer service as 41
physical distribution, logistics defined as 2, 4
Pieter, Heinrich von 271–2
Pioneer 252
pipelines 89
  characteristics 86
  pricing 108
piracy 120
place, marketing mix 21, 31–2
planning, corporate strategy 211–13
plan step, PDCA cycle 247
Poland
  cargo security 120
  customs 119
pollution
  aesthetic 117
  air 116–17
  noise 117, 149
  see also environmental issues
Porter, Michael 7, 10
Portugal 30
positioning, and world-class logistics 264
postponement, inventory management 74, 75
prevention, cost of 243
price
  marketing mix 21
  transportation *see* transportation pricing
private transportation 111
private warehousing 133, 135–6
privatization, transportation 11–12, 93–4
process analysis tools 249–51
process effectiveness 260
process management 231–2
procurement organizations 186, 188–9
Produce Marketing Association (PMA) 26
product
  characteristics 25
  marketing mix 21
production
  inbound logistics 182
  packaging 150
  planning 6
productivity 259–60
  purchasing 188–90
profits
  ABC analysis 255, 257–8
  enhancement with logistics 34–7
promotion, marketing mix 21
protectionism 24
protection of goods 151
public warehouses 134–6
purchasing 6, 177, 182–4, 190–1
  costs 78
  goals 184
  productivity 187–90
  tasks 184–6
pure competition, transportation 105
put-away function, warehousing 126

qualitative forecasts 163
quality 229, 243–4
  cost 243
  external perspective 232–3
  formal quality process 238–40
  inspections 124
  internal perspective 230–2
  ISO 9000 241–3
  JIT 76, 77
  purchasing 184, 185
  service quality model 233–7, 258–9
  success factors 240–1
  total quality management *see* total quality management
quality assurance (QA) 237
quality control (QC) 237
quality of life issues 117–19
Quantum Corporation 186
Queensland Independent Wholesalers 252
quick response logistics 31

radio-controlled devices, automated warehouses 144
radio frequency identification technology (RFID/RFIT) 147, 173–4
rail transport 85–7
  characteristics 86
  congestion 117–19
  environmental issues 117, 118–19
  intermodal transportation 97, 113–16
  liberalization 12
  pricing 106, 108
  privatization 93
receiving function, warehousing 126
reciprocity, and interorganizational

effectiveness 275
recycling 6, 152
reengineering 230, 259–60
Regina Maersk 98, 99–100
regular environmental scanning 162
reliability, materials handling 146
replenishment function, warehousing 126
responsibility, scope of 272
results measures of service quality 258, 259
return goods handling 6
  warehousing 124, 132
reusable packaging 151–2, 153
Rinascente, La 28
RoadRailer 97, 113
road transport 87–9
  cargo security 120
  characteristics 86
  congestion 117–19, 225
  customs 119–20
  environmental issues 96, 117, 118
  future 225
  intermodal transportation 100, 113–15
  liberalization 11–12
  pricing 105, 108
  private 111
robustness of forecasts 165
role of logistics in organization 7–8, 273–5
roll-on, roll-off (RORO) ships 98
Romans 1
Royal Caribbean Cruises Ltd 16–17
Royal Caribbean International 16
run charts 251
Russia
  rail transport 119
  road transport 88–9, 120
Ryder Systems 179

safety issues, transportation 96, 110, 120
safety stock 61–2
  automated order processing 160
  requirements 66–70, 71
  warehousing 131
Safmarine 218, 219
Sainsbury 187
salvage 181
Sandvik Coromant Company 35
Sanyo
  JIT 79–80
  logistics information system 161
Sara Lee 205, 252
Saturn 178, 179, 180
scale economies *see* economies of scale
Scandinavia 159
Schenker/TNT 196
Schiphol airport 202
SCL 219
scope of responsibility 272
scripts 49–50
Seagate Technology Inc. 15
Sea-Land Service Company
  China 196
  container ships 98
  GPS technology 14
seasonal inventory 62
Seat 277
security of cargo 120
segmentation of customers 47–8
selective distribution 25
selling tool, customer service misused as 48
semitrailers 97
service quality model 233–6, 239
services marketing model 235–6
service sector, stock-outs 51
Shell Lubricants 252
Shinkansen technology 119
shippers
  demand 107
  price negotiation 110–11
  win/win relationship development 103–5
  see also water transport
shipping function, warehousing 126
shopping 50
short-term management decisions 48
Siemens AG 269–70, 271–2
simulation models, warehouse location 130
Sinformat SRI 173
Singapore
  air transport 92
  Hamilton Standard 55
  packaging 152
Singapore Airlines (SIA) 2
single sourcing 188
size of organization 275–6, 281
SJ 115
Skoda 277
Smith's Snackfood Company, The 252

Societe Generale de Surveillance 202
software
  automated warehouses 143
  EDI 168
  inventory management 72–4
  warehouse location 131
sogo shosha 205
Sony 212
sourcing
  global 198
  single 188
Southern Europe 30
Southern Star Automobile Company 204
South Korea 278–80
Soviet Union, former
  cargo security 120
  transportation 120–1
  see also Commonwealth of Independent States
  Spain
  customer service 43
  domestic v. global channels 30
  rail transport 86, 93, 119
span of control 272
Spar 28
SPAR 30
Spectrum 168
speculative inventory 62
square root law of inventory 128–9
staging function, warehousing 126
standardization, and interorganizational effectiveness 275
statistical analysis tools 251
statistical forecasting methods 164
statistics usage 232
stock-outs
  consequences 51
  costs 63
  JIT 78, 79
storage 5–6
  inbound logistics 180–1
  space 72, 77
  warehousing 126, 144
  see also inventory; inventory management
Storage Technology Corporation 80
strategic alliances/partnerships 31, 280
strategic planning 213
Streets Ice Cream 252
stress 232
structure, organizational 275–8, 281
Sunicrust Bakeries 252
Sun Tzu Wu 1
suppliers
  and quality 231
  relationship with 188
  selection 185, 198
  see also vendors
supply and demand, balancing 61
supply chain
  ABC analysis 257–8
  global 194
  integration 214–15, 278–81
  management 3, 31, 274–5
swap bodies 97
Sweden
  logistics information 159
  rail transport 93
Switzerland 117
SWOT analysis 212
Syntex Agribusiness, Inc. 73–4
Syntex Corporation 73
systems view, purchasing 184

tactical plans 213
Talgo system 119
TDCC 168
teamwork
  purchasing 188–9
  quality 231
technology
  channel management 25
  future 226
  materials handling 147–8
  see also information technology
Tesco 13
Texas Instruments (TI) 170, 173
TGV 118, 119
third-party service providers 31, 204–6, 220–3
time issues
  customer service 41
  lead times *see* lead times
time-series forecasting methods 163–4, 165
tire manufacturers, trade-off analysis 33, 35
TIRIS Radio Frequency Identification Technology 173–4
TNT 196, 241, 242
total integration, materials handling 147

total quality management (TQM) 230
  channel management 25
  logistics 237
Toyota Motor Corporation
  customer service 44–5
  integrated channel management 217, 218
  inventory management 76
  quality management 185
trade blocs 10
trade-off analysis 32–4
  profitability, enhancing 35, 37
traffic congestion 117–19
trailers 97
Train à Grande Vitesse (TGV) 118, 119
training
  customer service 50–1
  quality logistics systems 241
transportation 5, 84–5, 101
  China 195
  deregulation 12, 91–4, 224, 227
  EDI 117–19
  freight forwarders 204
  future 224, 226–7
  government's role 94–6
  inbound logistics 180
  infrastructure *see* infrastructure, transport
  intermodal 96–101
  liberalization 11–12
  modes 85–91
  non vessel-owning common carriers 205
  private 111
  privatization 11–12, 93–4
  supply chain integration 215
transportation costs
  JIT 78
  packaging 155, 156
Transportation Data Coordinating Committee (TDCC) 168
transportation management issues 103, 120–1
  cargo security 120
  customs 119–20
  environmental and quality of life issues 116–19
  infrastructure availability and condition 112–16
  intermodal transportation 113–16
  pricing 105–11
  private transportation 111
  safety issues 120
  win/win shipper/carrier relationships, developing 103–5
transportation pricing 105
  carrier costs 108–9
  market structure models 105–6
  negotiation 110–11
  in practice 109
  relevant market area 106–7
  shipper demand 107
trigger points 248
two-dimensional bar codes 172

uncertainty, demand 61
UN/EDIFACT 168, 169, 187
Unifruco 219
Unilever
  benchmarking 252
  logistics information systems 173–4
United Kingdom
  domestic v. global channels 30
  environmental concerns 12, 117
  packaging 152
  rail transport 93, 117, 119
  transportation deregulation 11–12
  see also Great Britain
United Parcel Service (UPS)
  "best practice" 274
  competitive advantage 9
  customer service 42
  e-commerce 145, 170–2
  EDI 169
  intermodal transportation 114
  pricing 107
United States of America
  air transport 92–3, 94
  culture 198
  customer service 45, 46, 53
  Customs Service 201–2
  deregulation 12, 24, 91
  e-commerce 170
  imports from Chinese ports, distribution services upgraded 37
  intermodal transportation 97, 113–14
  inventory management 81
  rail transport 86, 97, 115–16, 119
  safety laws, transportation 96
  supply chain structure 280–1
  third-party service providers 221
  water transport 91

Universal Reefers 219
upgradeability, materials handling systems 147

Valeo 129
value
  customer delivered 10–11
  quality 232, 237
value added
  packaging 150
  warehousing 124
value chains 7–8, 186
value-of-service pricing 107, 109
variable costs, transportation 108
variables data 251
vendor managed inventory (VMI) 79
vendors
  co-location with customer
  as partners 76–7
  selection 185, 198
  see also suppliers
very narrow-aisle (VNA) strategy 144
VIA Rail 233
Virgin Group 118
VirtualOrder 171–2
Vogt, Roger 149
Volkswagen 277–8
Volvo 104–5
von Pieter, Heinrich 271–2

Wallenius Lines 8
Wal-Mart
  channel management issues 28
  customer service 46–7
  role of logistics 273
  warehousing 145
Walton, Jim 16, 17
warehousing 123–4, 137–8
  ABC analysis 256
  alternatives 133–5
  basic design 140–1
  concerns in overseas markets 136–7
  functions 125–6
  future 227
  inbound logistics 180–1
  location issues 128–33
  manual v. automated 141–6
  packaging 155, 156
  roles 124–5, 126–8
  strategic role in logistics 124–5
  strategies 135–6
waste
  inbound logistics 181
  packaging 152–3
water transport 90–1
  cargo security 120
  characteristics 86
  congestion 117–19
  future 225
  government control/regulation 95
  intermodal transportation 98, 99
  liberalization 12
  pricing 107, 108, 110–11
Webvan Group Inc. 132
Western Europe
  customer service 46
  road transport 87, 120–1
Whirlpool 129–30
wide area networks (WANs) 172
William Wrigley Jr. Company 41
wireless communication 172
Wisconsin Central 93
working hours, and warehousing 136
World Trade Organization (WTO) 193

Xerox 188

Yahoo 172
Yamatane Corporation 134
Yaohan 30

ZAPP 201